ALL ■ IN ■ ONE

CompTIA
CSA+®
Cybersecurity Analyst
Certification

EXAM GUIDE

(Exam CS0-001)

ALL ∙ IN ∙ ONE

CompTIA
CSA+®
Cybersecurity Analyst
Certification

EXAM GUIDE

(Exam CS0-001)

Fernando J. Maymí
Brent Chapman

New York   Chicago   San Francisco
Athens   London   Madrid   Mexico City
Milan   New Delhi   Singapore   Sydney   Toronto

Cataloging-in-Publication Data is on file with the Library of Congress

McGraw-Hill Education books are available at special quantity discounts to use as premiums and sales promotions, or for use in corporate training programs. To contact a representative, please visit the Contact Us pages at www.mhprofessional.com.

CompTIA CSA+® Cybersecurity Analyst Certification All-in-One Exam Guide (Exam CS0-001)

1 2 3 4 5 6 7 8 9 LCR 21 20 19 18 17

ISBN: Book p/n 978-1-260-01178-4 and CD p/n 978-1-260-01179-1
of set 978-1-260-01181-4

MHID: Book p/n 1-260-01178-X and CD p/n 1-260-01179-8
of set 1-260-01181-X

Sponsoring Editor Lisa McClain	**Technical Editor** Bobby E. Rogers	**Production Supervisor** James Kussow
Editorial Supervisor Jody McKenzie	**Copy Editor** Bart Reed	**Composition** Cenveo® Publisher Services
Project Editor Rachel Gunn	**Proofreader** Paul Tyler	**Illustration** Cenveo Publisher Services
Acquisitions Coordinator Claire Yee	**Indexer** Jack Lewis	**Art Director, Cover** Jeff Weeks

ABOUT THE AUTHORS

Fernando J. Maymí, Ph.D., CISSP, CSA+, is experienced in the research, development, and dissemination of innovative technical solutions, and currently leads Soar Technology's efforts in researching and commercializing cyberspace operations products. Prior to joining the company, Dr. Maymí was the deputy director of the Army Cyber Institute (ACI), a government think tank he helped create for the Secretary of the Army in order to solve future cyberspace operations problems affecting the whole country. While at the ACI, he led significant public-private partnerships involving government, industry, and academia, including the first NYC-wide cyber exercise, which involved 35 major organizations and hundreds of participants. He has served as advisor to congressional leaders, corporate executives, and foreign governments on cyberspace issues. Dr. Maymí taught computer science and cybersecurity at the U.S. Military Academy at West Point for 12 years. He retired from the Army as a lieutenant colonel and is a senior member of the Institute of Electrical and Electronics Engineers. He holds three patents and is the recipient of the Army's Research and Development Achievement Award. Dr. Maymí has written extensively and is the co-author of the seventh edition of the bestselling *CISSP All-in-One Exam Guide*.

Brent Chapman, GCIH, GCFA, CISSP, CSA+, is a cyber operations officer in the United States Army, currently assigned as a project manager at the Secretary of Defense's Defense Innovation Unit Experiment (DIUx) in Silicon Valley. In this role, he works to accelerate the procurement of commercially derived disruptive capabilities to maintain global peace and improve U.S. national security. Prior to DIUx, Brent was researcher at the Army Cyber Institute (ACI), exploring emerging information security and cyber warfare issues with a focus on field-expedient solutions and countermeasures. While at West Point, Brent also served as an instructor in the Department of Electrical Engineering and Computer Science. He is a professional member of the Association of Computing Machinery, FCC Amateur Radio license holder, and contributor to several technical and maker-themed publications.

About the Technical Editor

Bobby E. Rogers is an information security engineer working as a contractor for Department of Defense agencies, helping to secure, certify, and accredit their information systems. His duties include information system security engineering, risk management, and certification and accreditation efforts. He retired after 21 years in the U.S. Air Force, serving as a network security engineer and instructor, and has secured networks all over the world. Bobby has a master's degree in information assurance (IA) and is pursuing a doctoral degree in cybersecurity from Capitol Technology University in Maryland. His many certifications include CISSP-ISSEP, CEH, and MCSE: Security, as well as the CompTIA A+, Network+, Security+, and Mobility+ certifications.

Becoming a CompTIA Certified IT Professional Is Easy

It's also the best way to reach greater professional opportunities and rewards.

Why Get CompTIA Certified?

Growing Demand

Labor estimates predict some technology fields will experience growth of more than 20% by the year 2020. (Source: CompTIA 9th Annual Information Security Trends study: 500 U.S. IT and Business Executives Responsible for Security.) CompTIA certification qualifies the skills required to join this workforce.

Higher Salaries

IT professionals with certifications on their resume command better jobs, earn higher salaries, and have more doors open to new multi-industry opportunities.

Verified Strengths

91% of hiring managers indicate CompTIA certifications are valuable in validating IT expertise, making certification the best way to demonstrate your competency and knowledge to employers. (Source: CompTIA Employer Perceptions of IT Training and Certification.)

Universal Skills

CompTIA certifications are vendor neutral—which means that certified professionals can proficiently work with an extensive variety of hardware and software found in most organizations.

Learn	Certify	Work
Learn more about what the exam covers by reviewing the following:	Purchase a voucher at a Pearson VUE testing center or at CompTIAstore.com.	Congratulations on your CompTIA certification!
• Exam objectives for key study points.	• Register for your exam at a Pearson VUE testing center.	• Make sure to add your certification to your resume.
• Sample questions for a general overview of what to expect on the exam and examples of question format.	• Visit pearsonvue.com/CompTIA to find the closest testing center to you.	• Check out the CompTIA Certification Roadmap to plan your next career move.
• Visit online forums, like LinkedIn, to see what other IT professionals say about CompTIA exams.	• Schedule the exam online. You will be required to enter your voucher number or provide payment information at registration.	
	• Take your certification exam.	

Learn More: Certification.CompTIA.org/certifications/cybersecurity-analyst

CompTIA Disclaimer

CONTENTS AT A GLANCE

Part I   Threat Management

Chapter 1   Applying Reconnaissance Techniques...................................... 3

Chapter 2   Analyzing the Results of Reconnaissance 27

Chapter 3   Responding to Network-Based Threats................................. 51

Chapter 4   Securing a Corporate Network.. 69

Part II   Vulnerability Management

Chapter 5   Implementing Vulnerability Management Processes 95

Chapter 6   Vulnerability Scanning... 119

Part III   Cyber Incident Response

Chapter 7   The Incident Response Process 145

Chapter 8   Determining the Impact of Incidents.................................. 167

Chapter 9   Preparing the Incident Response Toolkit............................. 183

Chapter 10   Selecting the Best Course of Action 203

Part IV   Security Architectures

Chapter 11   Frameworks, Policies, Controls, and Procedures...................... 223

Chapter 12   Identity and Access Management 249

Chapter 13   Putting in Compensating Controls..................................... 269

Chapter 14   Secure Software Development.. 295

Chapter 15   Tool Sets... 315

Part V Appendixes and Glossary

Appendix A Objectives Map 369

Appendix B About the CD-ROM.. 387

Glossary 391

Index.. 399

CONTENTS

Acknowledgments xxi
Introduction xxiii

Part I   Threat Management

Chapter 1   Applying Reconnaissance Techniques 3

Open Source Intelligence 4
    Google 4
    Internet Registries 5
    Job Sites 8
    Social Media 8
Active Reconnaissance 9
    Scanning 9
    Capturing Packets 11
Special Considerations 12
    Wired Network Considerations 12
    Wireless Network Considerations 14
    Virtualization Technologies 15
    Cloud Computing 17
    Defending Against Reconnaissance 18
Tools of the Trade 18
    nmap 19
    Nikto 19
    OWASP Zed Attack Proxy 20
    Nessus 20
    netstat 21
    tcpdump 21
    Wireshark/TShark 22
    Intrusion Detection and Prevention Systems 22
Chapter Review 22
    Questions 23
    Answers 26

Chapter 2   Analyzing the Results of Reconnaissance 27

Data Sources 27
    Firewall Logs 28
    Intrusion Detection/Prevention Systems 28
    Packet Captures 29

System Logs	....	31
nmap Scan Results	....	31
Point-in-Time Analysis	....	32
Packet Analysis	....	32
Protocol Analysis	....	33
Traffic Analysis	....	34
NetFlow Analysis	....	34
Wireless Analysis	....	36
Correlation Analysis	....	36
Anomaly Analysis	....	38
Behavioral Analysis	....	38
Trend Analysis	....	38
Availability Analysis	....	39
Heuristics	....	40
Tools of the Trade	....	40
Security Information and Event Management Systems	.....	40
Packet Analyzers	....	42
Intrusion Detection Systems	....	43
Resource-Monitoring Tools	....	45
NetFlow Analyzers	....	45
Chapter Review	....	46
Questions	....	46
Answers	....	49

Chapter 3 | Responding to Network-Based Threats | .... | 51 |

Network Segmentation	....	52
System Isolation	....	52
Jump Box	....	53
Honeypots and Honeynets	....	54
ACLs	....	54
File System ACLs	....	55
Network ACLs	....	55
Black Hole	....	56
DNS Sinkhole	....	56
Endpoint Security	....	56
Detect and Block	....	57
Sandbox	....	57
Cloud-Connected Protection	....	57
Group Policies	....	58
Device Hardening	....	58
Discretionary Access Control (DAC)	....	59
Mandatory Access Control (MAC)	....	59
Role-Based Access Control (RBAC)	....	60
Compensating Controls	....	60
Blocking Unused Ports/Services	....	60
Patching	....	61

Network Access Control 61
  Time Based 62
  Rule Based 62
  Role Based 62
  Location Based 63
Chapter Review 63
  Questions 64
  Answers 67

Chapter 4   Securing a Corporate Network 69
Penetration Testing 69
  Rules of Engagement 70
Reverse Engineering 73
  Hardware 73
  Software/Malware 76
  Isolation/Sandboxing 80
Training and Exercises 80
  Types of Exercises 81
  Red Team 82
  Blue Team 82
  White Team 83
Risk Evaluation 83
  Impact and Likelihood 84
  Technical Control Review 86
  Operational Control Review 87
Chapter Review 87
  Questions 88
  Answers 91

Part II   Vulnerability Management

Chapter 5   Implementing Vulnerability Management Processes 95
Vulnerability Management Requirements 95
  Regulatory Environments 95
  Corporate Security Policy 97
  Data Classification 97
  Asset Inventory 98
Common Vulnerabilities 99
  Servers 100
  Endpoints 100
  Network Infrastructure 100
  Virtual Infrastructure 101
  Mobile Devices 102
  Interconnected Networks 103
  Virtual Private Networks 103

Industrial Control Systems 104
SCADA Devices 105
Frequency of Vulnerability Scans 106
Risk Appetite 107
Regulatory Requirements 107
Technical Constraints 107
Workflow 108
Tool Configuration 108
Scanning Criteria 108
Tool Updates and Plug-Ins 111
SCAP 112
Permissions and Access 113
Chapter Review 113
Questions 114
Answers 117

Chapter 6   Vulnerability Scanning 119
Execute Scanning 120
Nessus 120
OpenVAS 125
Nikto 126
Generate Reports 128
Automated vs. Manual Distribution 128
Remediation 128
Prioritizing 129
Communication/Change Control 130
Sandboxing/Testing 131
Inhibitors to Remediation 131
Ongoing Scanning and Continuous Monitoring 132
Analyze Reports from a Vulnerability Scan 133
Review and Interpret Scan Results 133
Validate Results and Correlate Other Data Points 134
Compare to Best Practices or Compliance 136
Reconcile Results 136
Review Related Logs and/or Other Data Sources 137
Determine Trends 137
Chapter Review 138
Questions 138
Answers 141

Part III   Cyber Incident Response

Chapter 7   The Incident Response Process 145
A Cast of Characters 145
Key Roles 145
Stakeholders 149

Response Techniques 150
    Containment 151
    Eradication 156
    Validation 158
    Corrective Actions 160
Communication Processes 161
    Internal Communications 162
    External Communications 162
Chapter Review 163
    Questions 163
    Answers 166

Chapter 8   Determining the Impact of Incidents 167

Threat Classification 167
    Known Threats vs. Unknown Threats 167
    Zero Day 168
    Advanced Persistent Threat 169
Factors Contributing to Incident Severity and Prioritization 170
    Scope of Impact 170
    Types of Data 174
Chapter Review 179
    Questions 179
    Answers 181

Chapter 9   Preparing the Incident Response Toolkit 183

Digital Forensics 183
    Phases of an Investigation 184
Forensic Investigation Suite 189
    Acquisition Utilities 189
    Analysis Utilities 191
    OS and Process Analysis 192
    Mobile Device Forensics 194
    Log Viewers 195
Building Your Forensic Kit 195
    Jump Bag 195
Chapter Review 197
    Questions 198
    Answers 201

Chapter 10   Selecting the Best Course of Action 203

Introduction to Diagnosis 203
Network-Related Symptoms 203
    Bandwidth Utilization 204
    Beaconing 204
    Irregular Peer-to-Peer Communication 205
    Rogue Devices on the Network 206
    Scan Sweeps 207

Host-Related Symptoms 208
    Running Processes 208
    Memory Contents 209
    File System 210
    Capacity Consumption 212
    Unauthorized Privileges 213
Application-Related Symptoms 214
    Anomalous Activity 214
    Introduction of New Accounts 215
    Unexpected Output 215
    Unexpected Outbound Communication 215
    Service Interruption 216
    Memory Overflows 216
Chapter Review 217
    Questions 217
    Answers 219

Part IV Security Architectures

Chapter 11 Frameworks, Policies, Controls, and Procedures 223
Security Frameworks 223
    NIST 223
    ISO 225
    COBIT 226
    SABSA 228
    TOGAF 229
    ITIL 230
Policies and Procedures 230
    Security Policies 232
    Procedures 236
Controls 239
    Physical Controls 239
    Logical Controls 239
    Administrative Controls 240
    Control Selection 240
Regulatory Compliance 241
Verification and Quality Control 242
    Audits 242
    Assessments 242
    Certification 243
    Maturity Models 243
Chapter Review 245
    Questions 245
    Answers 247

Chapter 12 Identity and Access Management 249

Security Issues Associated with Context-Based Authentication 250
Time 250
Location 251
Frequency 252
Behavioral 253
Security Issues Associated with Identities 253
Personnel 254
Endpoints 254
Servers 254
Services 256
Roles 257
Applications 258
Security Issues Associated with Identity Repositories 258
Directory Services 258
TACACS+ 259
RADIUS 260
Security Issues Associated with Federation and Single Sign-On 261
Manual vs. Automatic Provisioning/Deprovisioning 262
Self-Service Password Reset 262
Exploits 263
Impersonation 263
Man in the Middle 263
Session Hijack 263
Cross-Site Scripting 264
Privilege Escalation 264
Rootkits 264
Chapter Review 265
Questions 265
Answers 268

Chapter 13 Putting in Compensating Controls 269

Security Data Analytics 269
Data Aggregation and Correlation 269
Trend Analysis 272
Historical Analysis 272
Manual Review 273
Firewall Log 276
Syslog 277
Authentication Logs 278
Event Logs 279
Defense in Depth 280
Personnel 282
Processes 285
Other Security Concepts 290

Chapter Review 290
Questions 290
Answers 294

Chapter 14 Secure Software Development 295

The Software Development Lifecycle 295
Requirements 296
Development 297
Implementation 297
Operation and Maintenance 298
Secure Software Development 298
Secure Coding 299
Security Testing 302
Best Practices 306
Software Engineering Institute 306
OWASP 307
SANS 308
Center for Internet Security 309
Chapter Review 310
Questions 310
Answers 313

Chapter 15 Tool Sets 315

Preventative Tools 315
Firewalls 316
IDS and IPS 318
Host-Based Intrusion Prevention Systems 320
Antimalware 320
Enhanced Mitigation Experience Toolkit 321
Web Proxies 321
Web Application Firewalls 323
Collective Tools 325
Security Information and Event Management 325
Network Scanning 329
Packet Capture 330
Command-line Utilities 333
Analytical Tools 336
Vulnerability Scanning 336
Monitoring Tools 344
Interception Proxy 348
Exploitative Tools 351
Exploitation Frameworks 351
Fuzzers 355
Forensic Tools 356
Forensic Suites 357
Hashing 359

Password Cracking 360
Imaging 363
Chapter Review 363
Questions 363
Answers 366

Part V Appendixes and Glossary

Appendix A Objectives Map 369

Appendix B About the CD-ROM 387
System Requirements 387
Installing and Running Total Tester Premium
  Practice Exam Software 387
Total Tester Premium Practice Exam Software 387
Pre-assessment Test 388
Performance-Based Questions 388
Secured Book PDF 388
Technical Support 389

Glossary 391

Index 399

ACKNOWLEDGMENTS

None of us accomplish anything strictly on our own merits; we all but extend the work of those who precede us. In a way, we are all running a relay race. It would be disingenuous, if not inconsiderate, if we failed to acknowledge those whose efforts contributed to the book you are about to read. Specifically…

- Carol and Gina, for being our better halves and keeping us grounded and balanced.
- Emma and Deborah, for bringing us into this world, shaping our development, and getting us started on what has turned out to be the adventure of our lives.
- Our children, because they will take the batons from us and leave their indelible marks on our world.
- The men and women of our armed forces, who selflessly defend our way of life.

INTRODUCTION

If you are able to join a cybersecurity team and instantly start taking the right steps to improve the security posture of an organization, you will be a very valuable asset. If you can do that, but also engage on-net adversaries in hand-to-hand combat and prevail, then you will be invaluable to your organization. You will not struggle to find and keep jobs that are interesting and pay well. But how do you convey these skills to a prospective employer within the confines of a one- or two-page resume? Using the title CSA+, like a picture, can be worth a thousand words.

Why Become a CSA+?

To be clear, adding four characters to the end of your signature line will not make you the superstar we described in the preceding paragraph. It will, however, elevate employers' expectations. Hiring officials oftentimes screen resumes by looking for certain key terms, such as *CSA+*, before referring them to technical experts for further review. Attaining this certification improves your odds of making it past the first filters, and also sets a baseline for what the experts can expect from you during an interview. It lets them know they can get right to important parts of the conversation without first having to figure out how much you know about the role of a cybersecurity analyst. The certification sets you up for success.

It also sets you up for lifelong self-learning and development. Preparing for and passing this exam will not only elevate your knowledge, but also reveal to you how much you still have to learn. Cybersecurity analysts never reach a point where they know enough. Instead, this is a role that requires continuous learning because both the defenders and attackers are constantly evolving their tools and techniques. The CSA+ domains and objectives provide you a framework of knowledge and skills on which you can plan your own professional development.

The CSA+ Exam

The CSA+ exam is administered at authorized testing centers and will cost you $320. It consists of up to 85 questions, which must be answered in no more than 165 minutes. In order to pass, you must score 750 points out of a maximum possible 900 points. The test is computer-based and adaptive, which means different questions will earn you different numbers of points. The bulk of the exam consists of short, multiple-choice questions with four or five possible responses. In some cases, you will have to select multiple answers in order to receive full credit. Most questions are fairly straightforward, so you should not expect a lot of "trick" questions or ambiguity. Still, you should not be surprised to find yourself debating between two responses that both seem correct at some point.

A unique aspect of the exam is its use of scenario questions. You will only see a few of these (maybe three to five), but they will require a lot of time to complete. In these questions, you will be given a short scenario and a network map. There will be hotspots in the map that you can click to obtain detailed information about a specific node. For example, you might click a host and see log entries or the output of a command-line tool. You will have to come up with multiple actions that explain an observation, mitigate threats, or handle incidents. Deciding which actions are appropriate will require that you look at the whole picture, so be sure to click every hotspot before attempting to answer any of the questions.

Your exam will be scored on the spot, so you will know whether you passed before you leave the test center. You will be given your total score, but not a breakdown by domain. If you fail the exam, you will have to pay the exam fee again, but may retake the test as soon as you'd like. Unlike other exams, there is no waiting period for your second attempt, though you will have to wait 14 days between your second and third attempts if you fail twice.

What Does This Book Cover?

This book covers everything you need to know to become a CompTIA-certified cybersecurity analyst (CSA+). It teaches you how successful organizations manage cyber threats to their systems. These threats will attempt to exploit weaknesses in the systems, so the book also covers the myriad of issues that go into effective vulnerability management. As we all know, no matter how well we manage both threats and vulnerabilities, we will eventually have to deal with a security incident. The book next delves into cyber incident response, including forensic analysis. Finally, it covers security architectures and tools with which every cybersecurity analyst should be familiar.

Though the book gives you all the information you need to pass the test and be a successful CSA+, you will have to supplement this knowledge with hands-on experience on at least some of the more popular tools. It is one thing to read about Wireshark and Snort, but you will need practical experience with these tools in order to know how best to apply them in the real world. The book guides you in this direction, but you will have to get the tools as well as practice the material covered in these pages.

Tips for Taking the CSA+ Exam

Though the CSA+ exam has some unique aspects, it is not entirely unlike any other computer-based test you might have taken. The following is a list of tips in increasing order of specificity. Some may seem like common sense to you, but we still think they're important enough to highlight.

- Get lots of rest the night before.
- Arrive early at the exam site.
- Read all possible responses before making your selection, even if you are "certain" that you've already read the correct option.
- If the question seems like a trick one, you may be overthinking it.

- Don't second-guess yourself after choosing your responses.

- Take notes on the dry-erase sheet (which will be provided by the proctor) whenever you have to track multiple data points.

- If you are unsure about an answer, give it your best shot, mark it for review, and then go on to the next question; you may find a hint in a later question.

- When dealing with a scenario question, read all available information at least once before you attempt to provide any responses.

- Don't stress if you seem to be taking too long on the scenario questions; you will only be given a handful of those.

- Don't expect the exhibits (for example, log files) to look like real ones; they will be missing elements you'd normally expect, but contain all the information you need to respond.

How to Use This Book

Much effort has gone into putting all the necessary information into this book. Now it's up to you to study and understand the material and its various concepts. To best benefit from this book, you might want to use the following study method:

- Study each chapter carefully and make sure you understand each concept presented. Many concepts must be fully understood, and glossing over a couple here and there could be detrimental to you.

- Make sure to study and answer all the questions. If any questions confuse you, go back and study those sections again.

- If you are not familiar with specific topics, such as firewalls, reverse engineering, and protocol functionality, use other sources of information (books, articles, and so on) to attain a more in-depth understanding of those subjects. Don't just rely on what you think you need to know to pass the CSA+ exam.

- If you are not familiar with a specific tool, download the tool (if open source) or a trial version (if commercial) and play with it a bit. Since we cover dozens of tools, you should prioritize them based on how unfamiliar you are with them.

Using the Objectives Map

The Objectives Map included in Appendix A has been constructed to help you cross-reference the official exam objectives from CompTIA with the relevant coverage in the book. A reference has been provided for each exam objective exactly as CompTIA has presented it, the chapter number, and a page reference.

Practice Exams

This book includes practice exams that feature the Total Tester exam software, which allows you to generate a complete practice exam or to generate quizzes by chapter module or by exam domain. For more information about the accompanying software, see Appendix B.

PART I

Threat Management

■ **Chapter 1**   Applying Reconnaissance Techniques
■ **Chapter 2**   Analyzing the Results of Reconnaissance
■ **Chapter 3**   Responding to Network-Based Threats
■ **Chapter 4**   Securing a Corporate Network

Chapter 1
Chapter 2
Chapter 3
Chapter 4

Applying Reconnaissance Techniques

In this chapter you will learn:

- General approaches to conducting reconnaissance
- Specific tasks involved in reconnoitering a target
- Variables that can affect reconnaissance efforts
- Common tools used when reconnoitering

If you know the enemy and know yourself,
you need not fear the result of a hundred battles.

—Sun Tzu

When first learning how to plan and build defensive positions, soldiers are required to walk away from their perimeter and examine the proposed defensive positions as an adversary would. In many cases, a foxhole that initially seemed to make perfect sense is revealed to be obvious and vulnerable, or it turns out that if attackers hide behind a specific tree or rock, the defenders will not be able to fire at them. It is oftentimes an eye-opening, if somewhat embarrassing exercise, as the authors will readily admit from personal experience.

Defending networks has long benefited from the same exercise: if you looked at your network using procedures and tools available to your adversaries, what would you see? Are your firewalls effectively hiding the existence of internal hosts? Did those patches *really* get applied to your web server? Is your DNS server resolving more names than it should, or is it perhaps a bit too chatty? Are your services revealing more about the network topology than you expected? How is your operational security (OPSEC) compromised by careless posts on forums, job sites, or even social media? In this chapter, we cover the process of conducting reconnaissance on your own networks as if you were an attacker looking for a way in. Along the way, we'll cover everything from low-level packet analysis to the always-vulnerable layer 8: the end user.

From an adversary's point of view, the first step to a successful campaign is a thoughtful reconnaissance effort. Getting as much information as possible about the target network not only allows the attacker to get a good feel for your network, but also may make his job much easier when it comes time to commence an attack. Many information sources are completely free of cost. This is especially advantageous for the adversary because it takes nothing more than an investment in time to get a comprehensive profile of the target.

Open Source Intelligence

It is almost always preferable for adversaries to get information about a target without directly touching it. Why? Because the less they touch it, the fewer fingerprints (or log entries) they leave for the defenders and investigators to find. In an ideal case, adversaries gain all the information they need to successfully compromise a target without once visiting it. *Passive reconnaissance* is the process by which an adversary acquires information about a target network without directly interacting with it. A common way to do this is to gather *open source intelligence* (OSINT), or information from third parties that's collected in legitimate ways. OSINT techniques can be focused on individuals as well as companies. Just like individuals, many companies maintain a public face that can give outsiders a glimpse into their internal operations. In the sections that follow, we describe some of the most useful sources of OSINT with which you should be familiar.

 EXAM TIP The terms *passive reconnaissance* and *open source intelligence* have subtly different meanings in certain groups, but they are equivalent for the purposes of the CSA+ exam.

Google

Google's vision statement is to organize all of the data in the world and make it accessible for everyone in a useful way. It should therefore not be surprising that Google can help an attacker gather a remarkable amount of information about any individual, organization, or network. The use of this search engine for target reconnaissance purposes drew much attention in the early 2000s when security researcher Johnny Long started collecting and sharing examples of search queries that revealed vulnerable systems. These queries made use of advanced operators that are meant to allow Google users to refine their searches. Though the list of operators is too long to include in this book, Table 1-1 lists some of

Operator	Restricts Search Results To	Example
site:	The specified domain or site	site:apache.org
inurl:	Having the specified text in the URL	inurl:/administrator/index.php
filetype:	The indicated type of file	filetype:xls
intitle:	Pages with the indicated text in their title	intitle:vitae
link:	Pages that contain a link to the indicated site or URL	link:www.google.com
cache:	Google's latest cached copies of the results	cache:www.eff.org

Table 1-1 Useful Google Search Operators

the ones we've found most useful over the years. Note that many others are available from a variety of sources online, and some of these operators can be combined in a search.

Suppose you have a number of web servers in your organization. A potentially dangerous misconfiguration would be to allow a server to display directory listings to clients. This means that instead of seeing a rendered web page, the visitor could see a list of all the files (HTML, PHP, CSS, and so on) in that directory within the server. Sometimes, for a variety of reasons, it is necessary to enable such listings. More often, however, they are the result of a misconfigured and potentially vulnerable web server. If you wanted to search an organization for such vulnerable server directories, you would type the following into your Google search box, substituting the actual domain or URL in the space delineated by angle brackets:

```
site:<targetdomain or URL> intitle:"index of" "parent directory"
```

This would return all the pages in your target domain that Google has indexed as having directory listings. You might then be tempted to click one of the links returned by Google, but this would directly connect you to the target domain and leave evidence there of your activities. Instead, you can use a page cached by Google as part of its indexing process. To see this page instead of the actual target, look for the downward arrow immediately to the right of the page link. Clicking it will give you the option to select "Cached" rather than connecting to the target (see Figure 1-1).

 EXAM TIP You will not be required to know the specific symbols and words required for advanced Google searches, but it's useful as a security analyst to understand the various methods of refining search engine results, such as Boolean logic, word order, and search operators.

Internet Registries

Another useful source of information about networks is the multiple registries necessary to keep the Internet working. Routable Internet Protocol (IP) addresses as well as domain names need to be globally unique, which means that there must be some mechanism for ensuring that no two entities use the same IP address or domain. The way we,

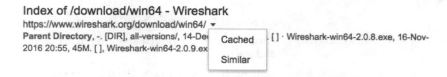

Figure 1-1 Using Google cached pages

as a global community, manage this deconfliction is through the nonprofit corporations described next. They offer some useful details about the footprint of an organization in cyberspace.

Regional Internet Registries

As Table 1-2 shows, five separate corporations control the assignment of IP addresses throughout the world. They are known as the *regional Internet registries* (RIRs), and each has an assigned geographical area of responsibility. Thus, entities wishing to acquire an IP address in Canada, the United States, or most of the Caribbean would deal (directly or through intermediaries) with the American Registry for Internet Numbers (ARIN). The activities of the five registries are coordinated through the Number Resource Organization (NRO), which also provides a detailed listing of each country's assigned RIR.

 EXAM TIP You do not need to know the RIRs, but you do need to understand what information is available through these organizations together with the Internet Corporation for Assigned Names and Numbers (ICANN).

Domain Name System

The Internet could not function the way it does today without the Domain Name System (DNS). Although DNS is a vital component of modern networks, many users are unaware of its existence and importance to the proper functionality of the Web. DNS is the mechanism responsible for associating domain names, such as www.google.com, with their server's IP address(es), and vice versa. Without DNS, you'd be required to memorize and input the full IP address for any website you wanted to visit instead of the easy-to-remember uniform resource locator (URL). Using tools such as nslookup, host, and dig in the command line, administrators troubleshoot DNS and network problems. Using the same tools, an attacker can interrogate the DNS server to derive information about the network. In some cases, attackers can automate this process to reach across many DNS servers in a practice called *DNS harvesting*.

	Registry	Geographic Region
Table 1-2 The Regional Internet Registries	AFRINIC	Africa and portions of the Indian Ocean
	APNIC	Portions of Asia and portions of Oceania
	ARIN	Canada, many Caribbean and North Atlantic islands, and the U.S.
	LACNIC	Latin America and portions of the Caribbean
	RIPE NCC	Europe, the Middle East, and Central Asia

In some cases, it might be necessary to replicate a DNS server's contents across multiple DNS servers through an action called a *zone transfer*. With a zone transfer, it is possible to capture a full snapshot of what the DNS server's records hold about the domain; this includes name servers, mail exchange records, and hostnames. Zone transfers are a potential vulnerable point in a network because the default behavior is to accept any request for a full transfer from any host on the network. Because DNS is like a map of the entire network, it's critical to restrict leakage to prevent DNS poisoning or spoofing.

 NOTE DNS zone transfers are initiated by clients—whether from a secondary DNS server or network host. Because DNS data can be used to map out an entire network, it's critical that only authorized hosts be allowed to request full transfers. This is accomplished by implementing access control lists (ACLs). Zone transfers to unrecognized devices should *never* be allowed.

Whenever a domain is registered, the registrant provides details about the organization for public display. This might include name, telephone, and e-mail contact information, domain name system details, and mailing address. This information can be queried using a tool called WHOIS (pronounced *who is*). Available in both command-line and web-based versions, WHOIS can be an effective tool for incident responders and network engineers, but it's also a useful information-gathering tool for spammers, identity thieves, and any other attacker seeking to get personal and technical information about a target. For example, Figure 1-2 shows a report returned from ICANN's

Figure 1-2 A report returned from ICANN's WHOIS web-based service

WHOIS web-based service. You should be aware that some registrars (the service that you go through to register a website) provide *private* registration services, in which case the registrar's information is returned during a query instead of the registrant's. Although this may seem useful to limit an organization's exposure, the tradeoff is that in the case of an emergency, it may be difficult to reach that organization.

Job Sites

Sites offering employment services are a boon for information gatherers. Think about it: the user voluntarily submits all kinds of personal data, a complete professional history, and even some individual preferences. In addition to providing personally identifying characteristics, these sites often include indications for a member's role in a larger network. Because so many of these accounts are often identified by e-mail address, it's trivial for attackers to automate the collection of these e-mail addresses in a practice called *e-mail harvesting*. An attacker can use this to his benefit, for example, by taking advantage of business contacts to craft a more convincing phishing e-mail.

Beyond the social engineering implications for the users of these sites, the companies themselves can be targets. If a company indicates that it's in the market for an administrator of a particular brand of firewall, then it's likely that the company is using that brand of firewall. This can be a powerful piece on information because it provides clues about the makeup of the company's network and potential weak points.

Social Media

Social media sites are also a highly targeted source for personal information. As with employment sites, an attacker can gain awareness about an individual or company using publicly available information. The online clues captured from personal pages enables an attacker to conduct *social media profiling,* which uses a target's preferences and patterns to determine their likely actions. Profiling is a critical tool for online advertisers hoping to capitalize on highly targeted ads. This information is also useful for an attacker in identifying which users in an organization might be more likely to fall victim to a *social engineering* attack, in which the perpetrator tricks the victim into revealing sensitive information or otherwise compromising the security of a system.

Many attackers know that the best route into a network is through a careless or untrained employee. In a social engineering campaign, an attacker uses deception, often influenced by the profile they've built about the target, to manipulate the target into performing an act that might not be in their best interest. These attacks come in many forms—from advanced phishing e-mails that seem to originate from a legitimate source, to phone calls requesting additional personal information. Phishing attacks continue to be a challenge for network defenders because they are becoming increasing convincing, fooling recipients into divulging sensitive information with regularity. Despite the most advanced technical countermeasures, the human element remains the most vulnerable part of the network.

OSINT in the Real World

One of the authors was asked to teach a class in an allied country to members of its nascent cyberspace workforce. The goal of the one-week course was to expose them to some open domain offensive techniques that they would have to master as a prerequisite to building their own capabilities. The first block of instructions was on reconnaissance, and we (the teachers of this class) were given authorization to be fairly aggressive as long as we didn't actually compromise any systems. In preparation for the class, the author performed a fairly superficial OSINT-gathering exercise and found a remarkable amount of actionable information.

Starting from the regional Internet registry, we were able to identify an individual named Daniel who appeared to be a system administrator for the target organization. We then looked him up on LinkedIn and confirmed his affiliation, but were also able to learn all his experience, skills, and accomplishments. We then looked up the organization in a handful of prominent job sites and were able to confirm (and even refine) the tools the organization was using to manage its networks. We noted that one of the tools was notorious for having vulnerabilities. Finally, we looked up Daniel on Facebook and found a recent public post from his mother wishing him a happy birthday. At this point, we could have sent him an e-mail with a PDF resume attachment or an e-mail with a very convincing message from his "mother" with references to his three siblings and a link to a video of the birthday party. Either way, the probability of Daniel opening a malware-laden attachment or clicking a link would have been fairly high—and all it took was about 15 minutes on the Web.

Active Reconnaissance

Sometimes the information gleaned from OSINT piques enough interest for an attacker to be more interactive with a target network. At this point, an attacker might not have a good sense of the target's network's topology, what other hosts might reside on the network, their various operating systems, or the available services exposed. In this section, we discuss a few methods of how attackers gain a more complete picture of a network by using active techniques.

Scanning

Scanning is a method used to get more detail on the target network or device by poking around and taking note of the responses. Attackers have scanned targets attempting to find openings since the early days of the Internet, starting with a technique called *war dialing*. By using a device to sequentially and automatically dial through a list of phone numbers and listen to the response, an attacker could determine whether it was a human or machine on the other side. Back when many computers connected to the Web via unprotected modems, war dialing was the easiest and most effective method for gaining access to these systems. *Host scanning* remains an effective way to inventory and discover details of a system by sending a message and, based on the response, either classifying that system or taking further exploratory measures. Scanners generally come in three flavors: network mappers, host (or port) scanners, and web app vulnerability scanners.

Network Mapping

The goal of *network mapping* is to understand the topology of the network, including perimeter networks, demilitarized zones, and key network devices. These actions used during network mapping are collectively referred to as *topology discovery*. The first step in creating a network map is to find out what devices exist by performing a "sweep." As with the previous example of war dialing, network sweeping is accomplished by sending a message to each device and recording the response. A popular tool for this is Network Mapper, more commonly referred to as nmap. In executing a network sweep, nmap's default behavior is to send an ICMP Echo Request, a TCP SYN to port 443, a TCP ACK to port 80, and an ICMP Timestamp Request. A successful response to any of these four methods is evidence that the address is in use. Nmap also has a traceroute feature that allows it to map out networks of various complexities using the clever manipulation of the time-to-live values of packets. After mapping a network, an adversary may have an inventory of the network but might want to fill in the details.

Port Scanning

Port scanners are programs designed to probe a host or server to determine what ports are open. They are an important tool for administrators. This method of enumerating the various services a host offers is one means of *service discovery*. It allows an attacker to add details to the broad strokes by getting insight into what services are running on a target. Because network-connected devices often run services on well-known ports such as 80 and 25, port scanning is a reliable source of information on these devices. Depending on the response time, the response type, and other criteria, the scanning software can identify what services are running—and some software can even provide *OS fingerprinting* to identify the device's operating system. However, identifying the OS isn't perfect, because the values that the software relies on for detection can change depending on the network configuration and other settings. With the information provided by the scanner, the attacker is in a better position to choose what kind of attack might be most effective.

 EXAM TIP   OS fingerprinting is not an exact science. You should not conclude that a host is running a given OS simply because the scanner identified it as such.

Web App Vulnerability Scanning

A *web application vulnerability scanner* is an automated tool that scans web applications to determine security vulnerabilities. Included in popular utilities are common tests, such as those for SQL injection, command injection, cross-site scripting, and improper server configuration. As usage of these applications has increased over the years, so have the frequency of attacks by their exploitation. These scanners are extremely useful because they automatically check against many types of vulnerabilities across many systems on a network. The scans are often based on a preexisting database of known exploits, so it's important to consider this when using these types of scanners. Although vulnerability scanners in the strictest definition don't offer anything beyond identification of existing vulnerabilities, some scanners offer additional correlation features or can extend their functionality using plug-ins and APIs.

Capturing Packets

Imagine that you are sitting on a train on your way into the city. You notice that two businessmen are sitting in the same car as you having a conversation. You're sitting just out of earshot, but based on their body language and the dynamics of the conversation, you know that one is pitching an idea to the other, and it's a very sensitive topic. One is clearly the vendor, and the other a demanding client. In this scenario, you could make some strong assumptions about their relationship without actually hearing any of the content of their discussion, and if you move just a few feet closer, you might be able to record the juicy details of their deal.

In networking, the data that moves from source to destination, if not the target itself, might reveal a tremendous amount about the hosts that are communicating. If the traffic is passed in the clear—meaning that no encryption is used between the nodes—then anything that traverses the network can be read in its entirety should it be intercepted. Passwords, images, text, and sounds can all be recovered easily from traffic passed in the clear—thus highlighting the importance of encryption. But just having access to the way that the traffic is moving around can shed some light on what kinds of machines are present.

Capturing the raw traffic on a network requires software designed to intercept and interpret traffic that passes over a monitored interface. Called a *packet sniffer* or *network analyzer,* this software takes note of the packets observed and logs the transactions. Packet sniffers may record the contents of packets, or only a portion called the *header* (or data about the data), to determine the type of traffic that's flowing between source and destination. We'll discuss a popular network protocol analyzer called Wireshark and its command-line version TShark later in this chapter. Wireshark and similar utilities allow the machines they run on to monitor connected networks in *promiscuous mode,* where the network card listens in on all traffic, whether it's meant for that machine or not. Packets will include information about their source and destination in the header, and network cards will ignore any packets not addressed to them. All Internet Protocol version 4 (IPv4) and version 6 (IPv6) packets begin with header information. IPv4 headers are variable in size (between 20 and 60 bytes), and the total size for a standard IPv4 packet maxes out at 65,535 (2^{16}) bytes. Although the maximum packet size for IPv6 is the same as for IPv4 packets, the header size is fixed for IPv4 packets at 40 bytes. In either case, there is a significant size difference between capturing just header information versus capturing the entire packet stream, so greater storage options must be available when setting up for a packet capture. The main advantage with a full capture is that reconstruction of the content of the exchange (text, video, audio, or image) is possible. Of course, if an attacker has direct access to the target machine, he can capture all traffic from the target machine to others on the network by setting the packet sniffer to record all traffic data on a specified host interface. In the situation where there is no direct host access, additional steps must be taken to collect traffic. Setting up to sniff traffic depends on the type of network in play, and we'll discuss the software and hardware requirements in the next section.

Special Considerations

A number of variables must be considered when choosing appropriate methods of conducting active reconnaissance. For instance, it makes a difference whether you are targeting a wired or wireless network, a virtual or physical infrastructure, an internal or external host, and an on-premises setup versus a cloud environment. In the following sections, we discuss some of the salient issues you should keep in mind, particularly as you take the CSA+ exam.

Wired Network Considerations

In a way, wired networks are more secure than their wireless brethren, simply because they require physical proximity or contact in order to glean any information from them. Obviously, some of this advantage is negated by the pervasive connectivity of most hosts to the open Internet, albeit through some sort of protective mechanism.

Taps

Physical access to the network infrastructure should always be highly controlled because the environment provides the best options for full traffic capture and can be damaging for the security posture of the network. With physical access to the network, a common option for packet capture is the network tap. The first type, called a *passive tap,* requires no additional power. In copper medium, this type of tap will form a direct connection to the wires in the cable and split the signal going across the line so that there is power still flowing to the destination, but enough is diverted to the tap to be useful to the sniffer.

Similarly, passive optical taps attempt to split the light beam passing though the fiber and divert a portion to a sensor. While these taps require additional hardware, the original signal is not likely to be impacted greatly, should the device fail. However, there are some disadvantages with this method, particularly on Gigabit speed lines. Gigabit connections are much more sensitive to power and may experience high error rate, distortion, or failure should a passive tap be installed. To tap Gigabit lines, an *active* tap (or active relay) must be used. Active taps completely terminate the signal in the tap device, sending a copy of the signal to a local interface and moving the original signal to a forwarder. That forwarder then amplifies the original signal, if necessary, and passes it to its original destination. This method works well for Gigabit lines, but at the expensive of adding another electrical device in the chain. Should the active tap fail, the entire circuit might remain open, alerting the administrator that something is amiss. It's important to note that tapping a network using these methods has the potential to change the transmission characteristics of the line. As security professionals, we should be prepared to investigate sudden fluctuations in power, impedance, or error rate, as they may be indications of a tapped line.

Hubs

An alternate method of collection is to capture the traffic directly from the intermediary device. If, for some reason, the hosts all connect to a hub, all that's required is for the monitoring machine to connect to the same device via a network cable and start the capture software. Because hubs share traffic coming in and out of all interfaces equally, they're relying on the connected hosts to be honest and only listen in on what's addressed to them. A clever technique is for an attacker to purposefully introduce a hub, placing it at a chokepoint within the networks, and collecting traffic at that point. Hubs are increasingly rare, even in home use, and have been replaced with the more discerning switch.

Switches

In a switched environment, the data units, called *frames,* are only forwarded to destinations they are meant for. As each frame enters the switch, the switch compares the incoming frame's destination Media Access Control (MAC) address with its existing list of addresses and their matching physical ports on the switch. When it finds a match, the switch forwards the data to the appropriate interface and then on to the destination device. The MAC address is an immutable value assigned to the network card during manufacture (although it can be spoofed through the OS), so under normal circumstances, the switch can be sure that the data is going to where it's meant to go. Although some increased scrutiny is given to each parcel of data that flows to a switch, there are still options for data capture with switches.

Before we discuss how capture might be achieved on a switched network, it's important for you to understand how the Address Resolution Protocol (ARP) works. ARP is how networked devices figure out which MAC address a given IP address links to. Every host maintains an *ARP table,* which maps IP and MAC addresses to each other. Therefore, whenever a host needs to send a bit of data out to a IP address, it looks up the corresponding MAC address on its own table and then forwards the data onto the wire. The switch then accepts that data and sends it forward to the right destination interface. If a host does not know what the MAC address is for a given IP address, it will ask the entire network using an ARP request, such as "who has 10.10.10.10?" The machine that recognizes the IP address as its own then replies with its MAC address. The original sender then updates its ARP table and sends the data over to the destination.

ARP Poisoning   There are two methods to sniff traffic in a switched environment using a technique called *ARP poisoning*. The first method of ARP poisoning involves stressing the switch with a stream of ARP replies. Every time the switch receives an update about a MAC address, it adjusts its internal forwarding table to reflect the change.

Do this often enough, and the table will overflow and some switches will fail to forward data correctly and default to hub mode, broadcasting all traffic to all interfaces.

The second method involves tampering with the ARP tables of specific hosts on the network. Suppose the attacker resides on a network with Host A and Host B and is interested in observing the conversation. Normally the switch's MAC-based discretion will not allow this because the attacking machine's MAC address will not be part of the conversation. Taking note of Host A and Host B's IP and MAC addresses, the attacker can take advantage of the inherent trust in ARP. The first step for the attacker is to send a message to Host B with a fake ARP Reply message indicating that Host A's IP address is now associated with the attacker's MAC address. Unfortunately for Host B, this unsolicited piece of information will be accepted at face value, and Host B will update its ARP table. The attacker will then do the same thing to Host A, pretending this time that he is Host B and provide his own MAC address for all future communication associated with Host B's IP address. At this point, both Host A and Host B's ARP tables are poisoned, and when they try to send each other a message, it will end up heading to the attacker. The attacker can do a number of things at this point, such as capturing the data and even modifying and forwarding it over to the original destination. This is known as a *man-in-the-middle* (MITM) attack. In many cases, the attacker's goal with an MITM attack is to collect login and authentication data, encryption keys, or any other secret information by inserting himself into the middle of a communication session and acting as a proxy between the systems.

Mirroring Most enterprise switches support a feature called *port mirroring*, which replicates packet traffic from an individual or selected range of ports and sends these packets to a separate output port on the same device. Port mirroring is used on a network to troubleshooting network problems or facilitate traffic analysis, but it may have serious legal implications if mishandled, even by authorized network administrators. If an attacker had switch access, he could enable port mirroring and collect every bit of data passing through that switch. Note that the destination port to which all replicated packets are passed will receive significantly more activity than all other ports and is therefore much more likely to drop packets—or in the worst case, become inoperable.

 EXAM TIP It is not normally possible to capture all traffic on a switched network unless you do so at a router interface or use ARP poisoning or port mirroring.

Wireless Network Considerations

Wireless networks allow for untethered access to a network using radio frequency (RF) data connections. They work by purposefully blanketing an area with a signal to increase device connectivity and reduce the cost of infrastructure because there are potentially fewer network access points to install. They also introduce new areas to check when designing and securing a network. Because there is no easy way to limit the signal once it goes beyond the limits of an organization's physical presence, it's possible for passersby to observe network traffic using any of the methods previously described. In terms of passive reconnaissance, wireless networks are therefore less secure than their wired equivalents. The quick and easy solution to this is to use a secure encryption algorithm to protect all traffic passing between network devices. This is not costly to employ, and it makes the attacker's job much more difficult because he cannot make sense of any of the captured data.

You also have additional considerations to take when capturing network traffic. Capturing wireless traffic requires understanding the host-to-access-point relationship and what the goals are for the capture. If you are already connected to a wireless network and are only trying to record the traffic between connected devices on the network, Wireshark works well in this situation. Many wireless cards support promiscuous mode, and just as on a wired network, this mode allows the client to see all traffic traversing the network, contingent on the client already being part of the network. If, however, you are sitting outside of the network and are trying to get a sense of which clients are connecting to which access points, you have a few more steps to take. If the client machine is not able to join a wireless network, the wireless network card must be able to operate in *monitor* mode for the capture software to see the 802.11 packets. Monitor mode allows an observer to listen in on all 802.11 activity over multiple channels without being associated with any access point. This is useful in collecting initialization vectors (IVs), for example, when attempting to crack the deprecated Wired Equivalency Protocol (WEP). In many cases, wireless cards can listen in on many channels but only capture on a single channel. Multiple cards would be needed to capture on multiple channels.

Virtualization Technologies

Virtualization is the creation and use of computer and network resources to allow for varied instances of operating systems and applications on an ad-hoc basis. Virtualization technologies have revolutionized IT operations because they have vastly reduced the hardware needed to provide a wide array of service and network functions. Virtualization's continued use has enabled large enterprises to achieve a great deal of agility in their IT operations without adding significant overhead. For the average user, virtualization has proven to be a low-cost way to gain exposure to new software and training. Although virtualization has been around since the early days of the Internet, it didn't gained a foothold in enterprise and home computing until the 2000s.

Hypervisors

As previously described, virtualization is achieved by creating large pools of logical storage, CPUs, memory, networking, and applications that reside on a common physical platform. This is most commonly done using software called a *hypervisor,* which manages the physical hardware and performs the functions necessary to share those resources across multiple virtual instances. In short, one physical box can "host" a range of varied computer systems, or *guests,* thanks to clever hardware and software management. Hypervisors are classified as either Type 1 or Type 2. Type-1 hypervisors are also referred to as *bare-metal* hypervisors because the hypervisor software runs directly on the host computer hardware. Type-1 hypervisors have direct access to all hardware and manage guest operating systems. Today's more popular Type-1 hypervisors include VMware ESX, Microsoft Hyper-V, and Kernel-based Virtual Machine (KVM). Type-2 hypervisors are run from within an already existing operating system. These hypervisors act just like any other piece of software written for an operating system and enable guest operating systems to share the resources that the hypervisor has access to. Popular Type-2 hypervisors include VMware Player, VirtualBox, and Parallels.

Containers

As virtualization software has matured, a new branch called *containers* has emerged. Whereas operating systems sit on top of hypervisors and share the resources provided by the bare metal, containers sit on top of operating systems and share the resources provided by the host OS. Instead of abstracting the hardware for guest operating systems, container software abstracts the kernel of the operating system for the applications running above it. This allows for low overhead in running many applications and improved speed in deploying instances because a whole virtual machine doesn't have to be started for every application. Rather, the application, services, processes, libraries, and any other dependencies can be wrapped up into one unit. Additionally, each container operates in a sandbox, with the only means to interact being through the user interface or application programming interface (API) calls. Containers have enabled rapid development operations because developers can test their code more quickly, changing only the components necessary in the container and then redeploying.

Network Function Virtualization and Software-Defined Networking

So if it makes sense to virtualize hardware for the sake of operating systems and applications, then it may follow that we replace custom hardware for various network functions with virtual clones. Enter network function virtualization (NFV), a critical component of high-volume data centers and cloud computing resources. Key functions such as routing, switching, intrusion prevention, and load balancing can all be provided by the same hardware running virtualized devices. NFV relies heavily on the concept of *orchestration,* or the automatic configuration and management of virtualized resources. Taking it one level up, this management of the network functionality, including traffic analysis and optimization, is the core of software-defined networking (SDN). SDN is best characterized by its separation of the control and data aspects of the network, allowing for the network to evolve independent of the hardware being used. SDN and NFV are complementary and herald a major shift in network architecture and management.

Security

From a security sense, hypervisors add several benefits to an enterprise's operations. Virtualization increases the layers of depth in a system, making it more difficult for an attacker to get an accurate sense of what the real environment is. Add to this the ability to constantly change the network topology using virtual tools, and you have fundamentally changed the cost of performing reconnaissance on a network. This increased investment is often enough to thwart many attackers, since they will often opt to move on to low-hanging fruit.

The rise in popularity of containerization has also allowed the practical use of layer 7 security, or *application-layer* firewalls. A major gripe with traditional practices is that it's laborious if not impossible to define all the rules necessary for a broad range of applications using restrictions imposed on lower-level protocols. For example, a standard firewall can be easily configured to block anything but HTTP traffic. However, attacks that arrive over port 80, such as SQL injection and cross-site scripting (XSS), are still permitted because these firewalls see this malicious code as a valid request. Because there is no easy way to distinguish between malicious and normal application data from layer 3 or 4, traditional firewalls are no longer suitable for our increasingly application-diverse environments. Application-layer firewalls mean that administrators have more granular control and can permit or deny specific web application requests.

Cloud Computing

Cloud computing is a term to describe an extensive range of services enabled by high-performance, distributed computing. Whereas *on-premises* solutions require the hardware and software to be physically located within the organization, cloud solutions generally require only a network connection to the service provider, where much of the computation and storage is held. In describing what the cloud offers, we'll look at three categories: Infrastructure as a Service (IaaS), Platform as a Service (PaaS), and Software as a Service (SaaS).

IaaS

Infrastructure as a Service (IaaS) provides users with complete administrative control over a computing platform hosted by the cloud service provider. An example of this would be spawning an instance of a Windows 2012R2 server that you could then configure in whatever manner you'd like. Cloud computing has been extremely attractive to businesses because it reduces the upfront investment in hardware solutions that will constantly have to be replaced as technology advances. Rather than purchasing hardware in the traditional cycle, companies can now subscribe to IaaS services to perform the same tasks without having to worry about how they're being done. Additionally, companies can scale more easily without waiting to install computing or storage they hadn't planned on needing.

PaaS

In Platform as a Service (PaaS), the user gets access to a computing platform that is typically built on a server operating system. As an example, you could spawn an instance of a Windows Server 2012R2 preconfigured to provide web services rather than building it yourself. The service provider is normally responsible for configuring and securing the platform, however, so the user normally doesn't get administrative privileges over the entire platform. This is how modern development teams collaborate in real time on programming projects. It includes the services required to develop, test, deploy, and maintain applications using a common environment. Facilitated by such technologies as containerization, PaaS allows for development operations from a diverse set of contributors.

SaaS

Software as a Service (SaaS) provides users with access to specific applications hosted by the service provider. Part of the popularity of SaaS is due to the fact that, as users generate and share content on mobile platforms, the need has emerged to move software to the Web. Rather than users working from a local installation of an application, software is run from and managed at a central location. Users are no longer responsible for installation, properly performing patches, and applying updates. Instead, they just use the web interface provided by the software, and everything else happens in the back end.

Security

The cloud enhances usability of applications by improving their availability and speed, making it easier for the average user to take advantage of the benefits of technology. However, because so many resources are decentralized, the challenge of identity management emerges. Verifying identity for access to computer resources, applications, and data, all of which might be mobile, is a challenge.

Defending Against Reconnaissance

Reconnaissance is ubiquitous and can be a low-cost activity for the adversary. Although it's important to engage in responsible network behavior, it may be impractical to try to hide your public footprint completely, particularly if your organization relies heavily on a public face. The best defense, therefore, is to engage in scanning your own networks. Scheduling regular identification of critical points in the network and conducting vulnerability scans against your organization will pay dividends should there be an actual incident. This includes regularly conducting *log reviews* for suspicious traffic as well as inspecting firewall and router access control lists (ACLs) for currency. Keep in mind that modern network devices can generate an enormous amount of data about the activity they're seeing, which may not make manual review a reasonable task. The logs, which come in several flavors, are short notes about something that happened on a system or across a network. The *syslog* is one example of a widely used messaging standard for reporting and storage. Syslogs can be generated on the order of thousands a day, depending of network traffic, so it's important to find a way to manage the messages. The solution to this is to use a *security information and event management (SIEM)* system. By aggregating device logs, SIEMs provide detailed monitoring capability, correlation of events, and dashboard views for analysts and administrators. Many modern SIEMs also include cloud platform integration and advanced modeling capabilities to help organizations makes sense of all their network data.

Tools of the Trade

An abundance of tools is available for conducting environmental reconnaissance. The list in this section is by no means comprehensive, but it does include some notables that you should know as part of your job as an analyst and certainly for the CSA+ exam. This list should simply serve as a starting point for your self-learning.

```
[brent@ubuntu:~$ nmap -A 10.10.10.10

Starting Nmap 7.01 ( https://nmap.org ) at 2017-01-15 11:24 PST
Nmap scan report for 10.10.10.10
Host is up (0.000052s latency).
Not shown: 988 closed ports
PORT       STATE SERVICE          VERSION
135/tcp    open  msrpc            Microsoft Windows RPC
139/tcp    open  netbios-ssn      Microsoft Windows 98 netbios-ssn
445/tcp    open  microsoft-ds     Microsoft Windows Server 2008 R2 microsoft-ds
902/tcp    open  ssl/vmware-auth  VMware Authentication Daemon 1.10 (Uses VNC, SOAP)
912/tcp    open  vmware-auth      VMware Authentication Daemon 1.0 (Uses VNC, SOAP)
3389/tcp   open  ssl/ms-wbt-server?
| ssl-cert: Subject: commonName=W0000
| Not valid before: 2016-09-05T07:34:34
|_Not valid after:  2017-03-07T07:34:34
|_ssl-date: 2017-01-15T14:25:23+00:00; -5h00m33s from scanner time.
49152/tcp open  msrpc            Microsoft Windows RPC
49153/tcp open  msrpc            Microsoft Windows RPC
49154/tcp open  msrpc            Microsoft Windows RPC
49155/tcp open  msrpc            Microsoft Windows RPC
49156/tcp open  msrpc            Microsoft Windows RPC
49157/tcp open  msrpc            Microsoft Windows RPC
Service Info: OSs: Windows, Windows 98, Windows Server 2008 R2; CPE: cpe:/o:microsoft:windows, c
pe:/o:microsoft:windows_98, cpe:/o:microsoft:windows_server_2008:r2

Host script results:
|_nbstat: NetBIOS name: W0000, NetBIOS user: <unknown>, NetBIOS MAC: 00:00:00:00:00:00
| smb-security-mode:
|   account_used: guest
|   authentication_level: user
|   challenge_response: supported
|_  message_signing: disabled (dangerous, but default)
|_smbv2-enabled: Server supports SMBv2 protocol

Service detection performed. Please report any incorrect results at https://nmap.org/submit/ .
Nmap done: 1 IP address (1 host up) scanned in 87.79 seconds
brent@ubuntu:~$
```

Figure 1-3   The nmap command-line output from searching a device for open ports

nmap

Created in 1997 by security researcher Gordon Lyon, nmap is the de facto standard for network scanning. Although originally written for the *nix operating systems, nmap has undergone continuous updates by its user community and is provided under a free software license for Linux, Windows, Mac OS, and various other systems. Nmap's major features include host discovery, port scanning, version detection, and operating system identification. Figure 1-3 show the nmap command-line output from searching a device for open ports.

Nikto

Nikto is another example of a well-supported piece of open source software. Nikto is used primarily as an active reconnaissance tool that performs thousands of tests to determine web server vulnerabilities. After an assessment is performed, Nikto provides the

```
root@kali:~# nikto -host 192.168.192.7
- Nikto v2.1.6
---------------------------------------------------------------------------
+ Target IP:          192.168.192.7
+ Target Hostname:    192.168.192.7
+ Target Port:        80
+ Start Time:         2017-01-18 01:15:06 (GMT-5)
---------------------------------------------------------------------------
+ Server: Apache/2.2.15 (CentOS)
+ Server leaks inodes via ETags, header found with file /, inode: 263125, size: 1861, mtime:
 Thu Jun  5 01:48:01 2014
+ The anti-clickjacking X-Frame-Options header is not present.
+ The X-XSS-Protection header is not defined. This header can hint to the user agent to prot
ect against some forms of XSS
+ The X-Content-Type-Options header is not set. This could allow the user agent to render th
e content of the site in a different fashion to the MIME type
+ Apache/2.2.15 appears to be outdated (current is at least Apache/2.4.12). Apache 2.0.65 (f
inal release) and 2.2.29 are also current.
+ Allowed HTTP Methods: GET, HEAD, POST, OPTIONS, TRACE
+ OSVDB-877: HTTP TRACE method is active, suggesting the host is vulnerable to XST
+ Retrieved x-powered-by header: PHP/5.3.3
+ OSVDB-3268: /icons/: Directory indexing found.
+ OSVDB-3233: /icons/README: Apache default file found.
+ OSVDB-3092: /phpMyAdmin/Documentation.html: phpMyAdmin is for managing MySQL databases, an
d should be protected or limited to authorized hosts.
+ OSVDB-3092: /phpmyadmin/Documentation.html: phpMyAdmin is for managing MySQL databases, an
d should be protected or limited to authorized hosts.
+ 8630 requests: 0 error(s) and 12 item(s) reported on remote host
+ End Time:           2017-01-18 01:15:40 (GMT-5) (34 seconds)
---------------------------------------------------------------------------
+ 1 host(s) tested
root@kali:~# █
```

Figure 1-4   Nikto reporting several potential vulnerabilities on a web server

name of the offending files and a reference to the Open Source Vulnerability Database (OSVDB) entry that explains the vulnerability. Figure 1-4 shows Nikto reporting several potential vulnerabilities on a web server.

OWASP Zed Attack Proxy

Like Nikto, the Open Web Application Security Project's Zed Attack Proxy (ZAP) is an open source web application vulnerability scanner. ZAP can be used to assess existing web servers, but it also has functionality as a web proxy, allowing the user to capture and manipulate web traffic that passes through it. The Open Web Application Security Project (OWASP) is a not-for-profit organization whose goal is to maintain and promote the best practices for web application deployment and usage. As a community-supported organization, OWASP provides a variety of materials via its online site and live events.

Nessus

Nessus is a vulnerability scanner than began its life as a free security scanner. Although Nessus is now proprietary software, its suite of plug-ins is expansive. Nessus is composed of two main components: the software daemon and the Nessus server. Nessus includes basic port scanning functionality, but its real strength lies with its comprehensive configuration checks and reporting. Nessus will check for vulnerabilities, common misconfigurations, default password usage, and compliance level.

netstat

Found in every major operating system, netstat (or network statistics) is a command-line utility tool that displays network connections, interface statistics, listening ports, and process identifiers. Netstat provides a quick way to check who's talking to whom on a given host. For instance, the command **netstat -l** (that's a lowercase *L*) will show all ports that are listening. While we would expect servers to have a variety of such ports, workstations should only have a small handful.

tcpdump

Tcpdump is a command-line tool used to display the raw output of network packets transmitted over the network (see Figure 1-5). While tcpdump has some features beyond simply printing the contents of network packets, it's renowned for its simplicity and ease of use in conducting packet analysis. Note that this program requires administrator privileges to capture traffic promiscuously.

```
root@kali:~# tcpdump
tcpdump: verbose output suppressed, use -v or -vv for full protocol decode
listening on eth0, link-type EN10MB (Ethernet), capture size 262144 bytes
01:32:52.183164 IP 192.168.112.1.17500 > 192.168.112.255.17500: UDP, length 155
01:32:55.784921 IP 192.168.112.1.mdns > 224.0.0.251.mdns: 0 PTR (QM)? _googlecast._tcp.local
. (40)
01:33:22.225017 IP 192.168.112.1.17500 > 192.168.112.255.17500: UDP, length 155
01:33:30.894279 IP kali.52696 > 192.168.192.7.http: Flags [S], seq 1599806789, win 29200, op
tions [mss 1460,sackOK,TS val 1817129 ecr 0,nop,wscale 7], length 0
01:33:30.895020 ARP, Request who-has kali tell 192.168.192.7, length 46
01:33:30.895060 ARP, Reply kali is-at 00:0c:29:5b:6c:86 (oui Unknown), length 28
01:33:30.895208 IP 192.168.192.7.http > kali.52696: Flags [S.], seq 1609934126, ack 15998067
90, win 14480, options [mss 1460,sackOK,TS val 7575809 ecr 1817129,nop,wscale 5], length 0
01:33:30.895339 IP kali.52696 > 192.168.192.7.http: Flags [.], ack 1, win 229, options [nop,
nop,TS val 1817129 ecr 7575809], length 0
01:33:30.895517 IP kali.52696 > 192.168.192.7.http: Flags [P.], seq 1:284, ack 1, win 229, o
ptions [nop,nop,TS val 1817129 ecr 7575809], length 283: HTTP: GET / HTTP/1.1
01:33:30.895853 IP 192.168.192.7.http > kali.52696: Flags [.], ack 284, win 486, options [no
p,nop,TS val 7575810 ecr 1817129], length 0
01:33:30.896280 IP 192.168.192.7.http > kali.52696: Flags [.], seq 1:1449, ack 284, win 486,
 options [nop,nop,TS val 7575811 ecr 1817129], length 1448: HTTP: HTTP/1.1 200 OK
01:33:30.896310 IP kali.52696 > 192.168.192.7.http: Flags [.], ack 1449, win 251, options [n
op,nop,TS val 1817129 ecr 7575811], length 0
01:33:30.896362 IP 192.168.192.7.http > kali.52696: Flags [P.], seq 1449:2132, ack 284, win
486, options [nop,nop,TS val 7575811 ecr 1817129], length 683: HTTP
01:33:30.896368 IP kali.52696 > 192.168.192.7.http: Flags [.], ack 2132, win 274, options [n
op,nop,TS val 1817129 ecr 7575811], length 0
01:33:30.896522 IP 192.168.192.7.http > kali.52696: Flags [F.], seq 284, ack 2132, win 274,
options [nop,nop,TS val 1817129 ecr 7575811], length 0
01:33:30.896697 IP 192.168.192.7.http > kali.52696: Flags [F.], seq 2132, ack 285, win 486,
options [nop,nop,TS val 7575811 ecr 1817129], length 0
01:33:30.896726 IP kali.52696 > 192.168.192.7.http: Flags [.], ack 2133, win 274, options [n
```

Figure 1-5 Tcpdump capturing packets

Wireshark/TShark

Wireshark and its command-line version TShark are two types of network protocol analyzers, or *packet analyzers*. Wireshark is an indispensable tool for network engineers, security analysts, and attackers. Available for Mac OS, Linux, and Windows, this open source software works much like tcpdump but also provides a graphical representation of packet types and advanced filtering. Wireshark can interact directly with some wired and wireless network cards, allowing the user to place the device in promiscuous mode for more complete network capture. For work after the capture is complete, Wireshark provides statistical analysis summary and graphing functionality.

Intrusion Detection and Prevention Systems

A key function of protecting the network is the recognition of suspicious behavior across the network or on the hosts. The purpose of *intrusion detection systems* (IDSs) is to identify suspicious behavior. Available as either a software product or hardware appliance, an IDS works by regularly reviewing network events and analyzing them for signs of intrusion. IDSs aren't just firewalls, which allow or deny traffic based on prescribed rulesets. Rather, IDSs work either by matching to previously identified malicious activity or by analyzing network traffic for indicators. Some IDSs have additional functionality to act on recognition of malicious activity and to stop traffic or quarantine hosts. These IDS devices are called *intrusion prevention systems* (IPSs). If the IDS/IPS is set up to work across a network, it can also be referred to as a *network IDS* (NIDS), whereas a system that operates on an individual host is called a *host IDS* (HIDS).

Chapter Review

Defending against a cyber attacker is much like defending against a physical attacker. Like any good military commander, a sophisticated attacker will spend a great deal of effort setting the stage for the attack by learning all about the target's capabilities. He knows that gaining knowledge of the target's behavior as well as its defensive and offensive competences is critical for a successful campaign. Beginning with harvesting public information about the network's users via public, job site, and social media searches, an attacker can gain a much better sense of the target network via its users. Once a potential way in is found, the attacker may move on to more active exploration by probing with technical tools to get a sense of the system's architecture, the network topology, and network policies. Knowing that a target is using a particular version of a firewall, for example, will help the enemy focus his efforts on developing an exploit against that device. Defending against reconnaissance is tricky because the attacker is relying on the same information that legitimate users use to access services or communicate. The question that remains is, how do you best protect your organization by knowing what its footprint is? It's important to know what your organization looks like from the outside—through the eyes of an attacker.

Questions

1. Which of the following is *not* considered a form of passive or open source intelligence reconnaissance?

   A. Google hacking

   B. nmap

   C. ARIN queries

   D. nslookup

2. Which of the following transmissions are part of nmap's default host-scanning behavior?

   A. ICMP Echo Response

   B. TCP FIN to port 80

   C. TCP ACK to port 80

   D. UDP SYN to port 53

3. Why is operating system (OS) fingerprinting imprecise?

   A. Hosts can run multiple operating systems.

   B. Some hosts run both IPv4 and IPv6.

   C. It is impossible to distinguish major operating systems.

   D. Variants of operating system families (such as Linux) can be hard to differentiate.

4. E-mail harvesting is useful for all of the following reasons except which?

   A. The inbox name is commonly the same as an active user account name.

   B. Publicly visible addresses are likelier to receive phishing e-mails.

   C. E-mail addresses can help yield additional personal information for targeting.

   D. It is difficult to find e-mail addresses for specific individuals or organizations.

5. What is a key consideration when conducting wired versus wireless reconnaissance?

   A. Wireless reconnaissance requires physical access.

   B. Wireless reconnaissance can be performed thousands of feet away.

   C. Wired reconnaissance requires user credentials.

   D. Wired reconnaissance will yield less information than wireless.

Refer to the following illustration for Questions 6–8:

```
root@kali:~# nmap -A 192.168.112.129

Starting Nmap 7.25BETA2 ( https://nmap.org ) at 2017-01-17 23:36 EST
Nmap scan report for 192.168.112.129
Host is up (0.00028s latency).
Not shown: 992 closed ports
PORT      STATE SERVICE      VERSION
135/tcp   open  msrpc        Microsoft Windows RPC
139/tcp   open  netbios-ssn  Microsoft Windows netbios-ssn
445/tcp   open  microsoft-ds Windows 7 Enterprise 7600 microsoft-ds (workgroup: WORKGROUP)
49152/tcp open  msrpc        Microsoft Windows RPC
49153/tcp open  msrpc        Microsoft Windows RPC
49154/tcp open  msrpc        Microsoft Windows RPC
49155/tcp open  msrpc        Microsoft Windows RPC
49156/tcp open  msrpc        Microsoft Windows RPC
MAC Address: 00:0C:29:58:8B:05 (VMware)
Device type: general purpose
Running: Microsoft Windows 7|2008|8.1
OS CPE: cpe:/o:microsoft:windows_7::- cpe:/o:microsoft:windows_7::sp1 cpe:/o:microsoft:windows_se
rver_2008::sp1 cpe:/o:microsoft:windows_8 cpe:/o:microsoft:windows_8.1
OS details: Microsoft Windows 7 SP0 - SP1, Windows Server 2008 SP1, Windows 8, or Windows 8.1 Upd
ate 1
Network Distance: 1 hop
Service Info: Host: WIN-FSV3V67U47I; OS: Windows; CPE: cpe:/o:microsoft:windows

Host script results:
|_clock-skew: mean: -1s, deviation: 0s, median: -1s
|_nbstat: NetBIOS name: WIN-FSV3V67U47I, NetBIOS user: <unknown>, NetBIOS MAC: 00:0c:29:58:8b:05
(VMware)
| smb-os-discovery:
|   OS: Windows 7 Enterprise 7600 (Windows 7 Enterprise 6.1)
|   OS CPE: cpe:/o:microsoft:windows_7::-
```

6. All of the following statements are likely true about the scan *except* which?

    A. There is a firewall between the scanner and the host.

    B. The scan was performed using Kali Linux.

    C. An ICMP Echo Request was part of the scan.

    D. The scanner is attempting to identify the operating system of the target host.

7. Which service is running on the target host?

    A. HTTP

    B. RPC

    C. POP

    D. CPE

8. Which of the following statements is probably not true about the target host?

    A. It is in the same subnet as the scanner.

    B. It is running as a virtual machine.

    C. It is far away from the scanner.

    D. It is running Windows 7 Service Pack 1.

9. Netstat can provide all the following information *except* which?

   A. Listening ports

   B. Remotely connected hosts IP addresses

   C. Name of the program that opened the socket

   D. Name of the user who opened the socket

Use the following scenario to answer Questions 10–12:

Robbie is the security administrator of a company that needs to ensure its employees are practicing good operational security (OPSEC). All employees have received training on social engineering (phishing in particular) and how to control their personal profile on the Internet. Robbie wants to verify externally that his teammates are putting into practice what they have learned.

10. When testing his teammates' online OPSEC, Robbie could do which of the following?

   A. Search employees' Facebook and LinkedIn pages, looking for sensitive personal or work information.

   B. Attempt to guess employees' passwords on Facebook or LinkedIn.

   C. Monitor employees' use of social media sites while at work.

   D. Create fake profiles on Facebook and LinkedIn and attempt to befriend employees.

11. What is the best way to assess his teammates' vulnerability to phishing?

   A. Send simulated phishing e-mail to work addresses and provide additional training to those who fall victim to it.

   B. Monitor inbound phishing e-mails and note which individuals fall victim to them.

   C. Block phishing attempts at the e-mail gateway.

   D. Send simulated phishing e-mail to personal addresses and provide additional training to those who fall victim to it.

12. Robbie could test his teammates' responses to social engineering attempts by all the following *except* which?

   A. Pretexting

   B. Spear-phishing

   C. Footprinting

   D. Tailgating

Answers

1. **B.** Nmap is a scanning tool that requires direct interaction with the system under test. All the other responses allow a degree of anonymity by interrogating intermediary information sources.

2. **C.** Nmap's default behavior is to send an ICMP Echo Request, a TCP SYN to port 443, a TCP ACK to port 80, and an ICMP Timestamp Request.

3. **D.** Although scanning tools such as nmap will likely infer the correct major version of an operating system (such as Windows or Linux), it is difficult to ascertain the specific variant (for example, the service pack for Windows, or CentOS versus Ubuntu for Linux). Furthermore, sophisticated defenders can configure their externally accessible hosts to report the wrong operating system.

4. **D.** A number of techniques and tools can be leveraged to obtain e-mail addresses, either individually or in bulk, so this is not a difficult thing to do.

5. **B.** A key difference between wired and wireless reconnaissance is that the former requires physical connectivity whereas the latter can be done over the airwaves from a distance. In fact, by using a hi-gain directional antenna, it is possible to connect to wireless networks from miles away.

6. **A.** The scan shows that the target host is likely running Windows 7. The default behavior for that system's firewall is to block unsolicited access to all ports. This means that the scan would have not reported any open ports had the firewall been enabled.

7. **B.** You can tell that the Remote Procedure Call (RPC) service is running because TCP port 135 is open, but also because this service is identified by name as running on a number of other ports.

8. **C.** The scan states that the network distance to the host is one hop, which means the target and the scanner are directly connected.

9. **D.** Although it is possible to associate running processes or ports with specific users, this is not a feature offered by netstat.

10. **A.** Searching for openly available information is the only one of the listed approaches that would be permissible for Robbie. All other options, at a minimum, violate terms of service or, at worst, violate the law (for example, guessing passwords).

11. **A.** Conducting internal simulated phishing campaigns is a common way to assess the security posture of an organization with regard to this type of threat. This approach should never be used with personal e-mail addresses without the users' explicit consent.

12. **C.** Footprinting is a reconnaissance and not a social engineering technique.

Analyzing the Results of Reconnaissance

In this chapter you will learn:
- Sources of data to consider in your analysis
- Point-in-time data analysis
- Data correlation and analysis
- Common tools used in security analytics

Experts often possess more data than judgment.

—Colin Powell

Conducting reconnaissance is only the beginning; you must also know what to do with the information you gather. Given a choice, however, an even better approach would be to determine what questions you want to ask, determine what information you need in order to answer them, and then conduct the reconnaissance that will yield that actionable information. Having spent the last chapter looking at common ways to reconnoiter networks, we now turn our attention to how we can focus those efforts to help us identify and characterize network-based threats.

Data Sources

Apart from the means and methods of gathering information about a network externally that we discussed in the previous chapter, there is no shortage of data sources in a well-built information system. It is important that we consider both internal and external data when determining the threats we face. Each source will have its own strengths and limitations, which we can oftentimes balance out by carefully planning our information-gathering activities. In the following sections, we consider some common sources of data that are available on almost any network.

Firewall Logs

It is widely accepted that firewalls alone cannot secure an information system, or even its perimeter. Still, they remain an important part of any security architecture. Fundamentally, a firewall is meant to restrict the flow of data between two or more network interfaces according to some set of rules. This means that it has to examine every packet that arrives at any of the interfaces to ensure compliance with whatever policies are specified in the firewall's configuration files. Whether the packet is accepted, denied, or dropped, the firewall generates a log entry with details that can help us in preventing or recovering from incidents.

NOTE It is important to pay attention to both inbound and outbound traffic. Some incidents will be easier to detect in one versus the other.

The amount of information contained in firewall logs is configurable. Some fairly universal parameters logged by most firewalls are described in Table 2-1. By default, most firewalls provide ample logs for any incident response. Still, it can be frustrating and unhelpful to begin an investigation only to find out that a well-meaning firewall administrator pared down the amount of information that a device would store in its logs. There is no way to recover log data that was never captured.

Intrusion Detection/Prevention Systems

One step up from firewall logs in terms of valuable threat data are the logs and alerts of the intrusion detection system (IDS) and the intrusion prevention system (IPS). The difference between the two is that the former simply generates alerts when it detects

Field	Description
Timestamp	Date and time at which the packet was logged
Source Address	IP address of the source of the packet
Source Port	Port number at the source
Destination Address	IP address of the destination of the packet
Destination Port	Port number at the destination
Protocol	IP protocol of the packet (for example, TCP, UDP, or ICMP)
IN Interface	Firewall interface that received the packet
OUT Interface	Firewall interface on which the packet was forwarded (unless denied or dropped)
Rule Name	Firewall rule that was applied to the packet resulting in whatever action was taken
Action	Action taken by the firewall (for example, accept, deny, or drop)

Table 2-1 Typical Firewall Log Fields

suspected threats and the latter actively blocks them. What oftentimes makes these systems more helpful in finding threats is that their rule language is typically more powerful than a firewall's. Whereas a firewall will allow, drop, or alert on a fairly simple set of rules or heuristics, an IDS/IPS can look for very specific signatures or behaviors. Figure 2-1 shows a Snort alert triggered by a port scan originating in a neighboring node.

 EXAM TIP A Next-Generation Firewall (NGF) incorporates functionality from both traditional firewalls and IPSs. Unless otherwise stated, assume that an IDS/IPS is not an NGF.

Packet Captures

Clearly, there are limits to what information we may glean from examining firewall or IDS/IPS logs. A further step up from there would be to capture all the packets flowing through a network interface. This approach is sometimes called a *full capture,* and although it may seem excessive or even cost-prohibitive, sometimes it makes sense. In fact, many major financial institutions take this approach to ensure they have sufficient data to support any network forensic investigation. The resulting data sets lend themselves to big data analytics, which could in turn provide insights into new tools and techniques that the threat actors may be using without being detected. We'll return to the topic of big data later in this chapter.

Broadly speaking, there are two approaches to capturing packets on a network: header captures and full packet captures. The difference, as the terms imply, is whether we only capture the IP headers or the entire packets, which would include payloads. Although it may be tempting to jump on the full packet bandwagon, it is important to note that this approach comes with significant data management as well as legal issues. Having these very large sets of packet data is only useful if we can gain actionable information from them. One approach would be to keep the data around in case there is a major incident. Still, this doesn't do away with the need to be able to handle this data at that time. There are many solutions for storing and retrieving very large data stores, so the point is not that it shouldn't be done but rather that it should be carefully engineered. The second issue entails potential violations of privacy for those individuals whose every network communication would be monitored. Again, this is not an insurmountable obstacle, but one that must be discussed with legal counsel before implementing.

Figure 2-1
Sample IDS alert

```
[**] [1:469:3] ICMP PING NMAP [**]
[Classification: Attempted Information Leak] [Priority: 2]
01/20-17:30:12.439889 192.168.192.7 -> 192.168.192.8
ICMP TTL:48 TOS:0x0 ID:63971 IpLen:20 DgmLen:28
Type:8 Code:0 ID:56127 Seq:45129 ECHO
[Xref -> http://www.whitehats.com/info/IDS162]

[**] [122:1:0] (portscan) TCP Portscan [**]
01/20-17:30:12.724540 192.168.192.7 -> 192.168.192.8
PROTO255 TTL:0 TOS:0x0 ID:0 IpLen:20 DgmLen:162 DF
```

By way of review, Figure 2-2 shows the header information in IPv4 and IPv6 packets. If you are unfamiliar with any of the fields, we recommend that you review the Internet Engineering Task Force's RFC 791 for version 4 and RFC 5871 (which updates the original RFC 2460) for version 6. You will be expected to be thoroughly familiar with IP packets for the CSA+ exam.

The exam will focus on IPv4, so it is worth reviewing some highlights. The numbers at the top of the headers in Figure 2-2 indicate bits, so this particular header is 160 bits (or 20 bytes) long, which is very typical. You may occasionally see larger (though never smaller) headers. The header length (in 32-bit words) is provided in bits 4 through 7 (labeled IHL or IP Header Length in the figure) and the total length of the packet (including its payload) in bits 16 through 31. Another field of interest is the time to live (TTL), which normally starts off at some value between 64 and 255 and gets decremented each time the packet is received by an interface. If the TTL ever reaches zero, the interface will drop it, typically returning an Internet Control Message Protocol (ICMP) "Time Exceeded" message to the source address. This feature, designed to keep packets from being bounced around forever, is how the ping utility tool works. That tool sends a message to the destination with a TTL of 1, which means that the very first host to receive it will drop it and respond with an ICMP message. This tells us the first host on the path to the destination. The tool then sends the same message, but with a TTL of 2, and so on.

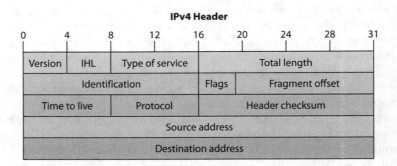

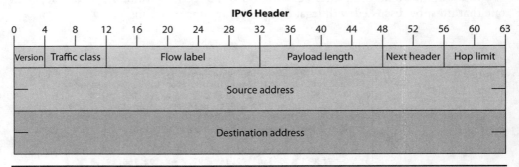

Figure 2-2   IPv4 and IPv6 headers

System Logs

Properly configured, end systems can log a much richer set of data than many network devices. This is partly because network traffic can be encrypted or obfuscated, but the actions on the end system are almost always easier to observe. Another reason why event logs matter tremendously is that there are many threat actors who will acquire domain credentials either before or at an early stage of their attack. Once they impersonate a legitimate user account, the data you capture from the network will be much less insightful to your analysis. It is a very common technique to use real credentials (stolen though they may be) to accomplish lateral movement throughout a targeted network.

System logs come in a variety of formats. The two formats with which you should be familiar as a CSA+ certified professional are the Windows Event Logs and the more generalized syslog. Both are intended to standardize the reporting of events that take place on a computing device. Though they are not the only formats in existence, most applications will generate events in the Windows format if they are running on a Microsoft operating system and in syslog format otherwise. Additionally, various products are available that will take input from one or the other (or any other format for that matter) and aggregate it into one event log.

nmap Scan Results

Nmap scan results are not as rich in diverse content as other data sources, but they offer surgical precision for the information they do yield. Moreover, successive runs of nmap with identical parameters, together with a bit of scripting, allow the user to quickly identify changes to the configuration of a target. Attackers might be interested in new services because they are likelier to have exploitable configuration errors. Defenders, on the other hand, might be interested in new services because they could indicate a compromised host. Nmap is even used by some organizations to inventory assets on a network by periodically doing full scans and comparing hosts and services to an existing baseline.

 NOTE One of the most important defensive measures you can take is to maintain an accurate inventory of all the hardware and software on your network. Nmap can help with this, but various open source and commercial solutions are also available for IT asset management.

Types of Analyses

You need to be familiar with two types of analyses: point-in-time analysis and correlation analysis. As the name implies, the first approach looks at data pertaining to a specific point or window in time. It is perhaps most familiar to incident responders. The second approach looks at multiple collections of data in an attempt to find patterns that may point to an event of interest.

Point-in-Time Analysis

Having discussed the various data outputs that we can leverage for analysis, we now turn our attention to how we might use this data. The first kind of analysis tends to examine one item, whether it be an alert, a packet, or a system event, looking for interesting information. As you may very well know, the amount of data we could analyze on a typical network is immense. For this reason, point-in-time analysis is most helpful when we start off with a clue. For example, if an IDS has generated an alert on a specific session, we may do point-in-time analysis on the packets comprising that session or on system events that were recorded around that time. Either way, we'll be looking at individual items at a point in time in order to discover broader goals or objectives for a threat actor.

Packet Analysis

An analyst can glean a remarkable amount of information from packet capture data. In fact, given enough of it, one can re-create a very precise timeline of events around any network security incident. The ideal case is one in which there are strategically placed sensors throughout the network doing full packet captures. The resulting data files contain a wealth of information but can consume enormous amounts of storage space. This can be a challenge, particularly for security teams with limited resources. Another challenge can be finding the useful data in such a sea of packet captures.

Filters

Filters are commonly used in two ways: for capture and for display. The first approach limits the amount of packets that are captured using some set criteria. For instance, an organization may choose to only capture packets whose source or destination address falls within a specific network range. An application of this could be a file server containing the organization's crown jewels. It may be that limiting packet captures to just those to or from that sensitive server mitigates risks while minimizing undesirable impacts such as cost of storage or potential violations of privacy. The obvious problem with using capture filters is that packets that might be useful for an investigation might never have been captured.

The other approach is to capture everything but to use filters when looking at the data. Extending the previous example, analysts can choose to only look at the packets to or from the sensitive server, but if they discover that other packets might contain useful clues, they can simply change the display filter and gain visibility over those packets as well. It is almost always better to capture too much information than not enough.

 NOTE Performing full packet captures can have legal implications regarding privacy. Ensure that you consult your legal counsel before you start capturing.

TCP Streams

A noteworthy feature of the design of the Internet is that packets may take different routes to their destination and thus arrive at any given time and in any given order.

Although this is normally taken care of by the Transport Control Protocol (TCP) or at the application layer for the User Datagram Protocol (UDP), such mechanisms are not available to an analyst when the packets are captured directly from the network. Packet analysis tools such as Wireshark offer the ability to reconstruct streams of TCP data. This is particularly useful to recover a malicious file that an employee may have inadvertently downloaded, or to see the full contents of web pages visited.

Encryption

One of the biggest problems with packet analysis is that it is of limited utility when dealing with data that has been encrypted. The analyst will still have access to the headers, but the contents may be incomprehensible. Threat actors are known to use encryption to hide their deeds from prying eyes. A way to address this issue is the use of HTTPS (or "SSL") proxies, which are proxy servers that terminate Transport Layer Security (TLS) or Secure Sockets Layer (SSL) connections, effectively acting like a trusted man-in-the-middle that allows the organization to examine or capture the contents of the otherwise encrypted session. If an organization controls the configuration of all clients on its network, it is not difficult to add a Certificate Authority (CA) to its browsers so that the users will not notice anything odd when they connect to an encrypted site through a decrypting proxy.

 NOTE Using HTTPS proxies can have legal implications regarding privacy. Ensure that you consult your legal counsel before leveraging this capability.

Protocol Analysis

Whereas the focal point in packet analysis is the content of the packets under study, protocol analysis deals with the way in which the packets conform to the protocol they are supposed to be implementing. For instance, the Internet Control Message Protocol (ICMP) allows echo request and echo reply packets to have a payload as long as the total packet length is no greater than the network's maximum transmission unit (MTU). This feature was intended to support diagnostic messages, though in practice this is almost never seen. What we do see, however, are threat actors exploiting this protocol to establish ICMP tunnels in which two hosts create a clandestine communications channel using echo requests and replies. Conducting an analysis of ICMP would reveal these channels.

Another application of protocol analysis is in determining the security or, conversely, vulnerabilities of a given protocol. Suppose you purchase or develop an application for deployment in your organization's systems. How would you know the risks it would introduce unless you had a clear understanding of exactly how its protocols were expressed on your networks? Performing protocol analyses can be as simple as sniffing network traffic to ensure that all traffic is encrypted, or as complex as mathematical models and simulations to quantify the probabilities of unintended effects.

EXAM TIP For the purposes of the CSA+ exam, you should focus on the sorts of protocol analyses that look at how well packets conform to established protocols.

Traffic Analysis

Another approach to detecting anomalous behaviors on your networks is to look at where the traffic is originating and terminating. If you are monitoring in real time the communications of your nodes and you suddenly see an odd end point, this could be an indicator of a compromise. Admittedly, you would end up with many false positives every time someone decided to visit a new website. An approach to mitigating these false alarms is to use automation (for example, scripts) to compare the anomalous end points with the IP addresses of known or suspected malicious hosts.

NOTE The website VirusTotal.com can be used to quickly check whether a given URL has been reported as malicious and, if so, by whom.

Traffic analysis can also be done in the aggregate, meaning you keep an eye on the volume of traffic in a given portion of your system. A large increase in traffic coming to or from a given host could indicate a compromise. Like our previous example on monitoring unusual end points, this approach will lead to many false positives absent some mechanism for pruning them. A useful open source tool we've used is called Etherape. As shown on Figure 2-3, it graphically depicts all known end points, both internal and external to your organization, and shows circles around them whose size is proportional to the volume of traffic coming from them at any point in time. A host performing a port scan, for instance, would show up as a very large circle. Then again, so would a server that is streaming high-definition video. The takeaway on traffic analysis is that it is most useful as an early-warning technique that must be backed up or reinforced with additional analysis.

NetFlow Analysis

NetFlow is a system originally developed by Cisco as a packet-switching technology in the late 1990s. Although it didn't serve that role for long, it was repurposed to provide statistics on network traffic, which is why it is important to analysts today. The way it works is by grouping into "flows" all packets that share the following characteristics:

- Arrival interface at the network device (for example, switch or router)
- Source and destination IP addresses
- Source and destination port numbers (or the value zero if not TCP or UDP)
- IP protocol
- IP type of service

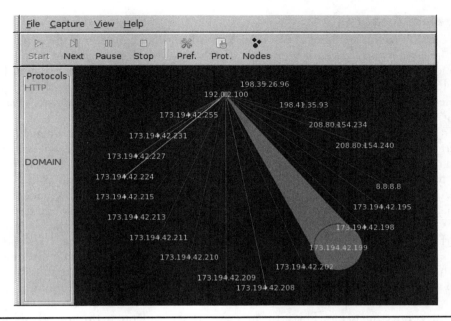

Figure 2-3 Etherape depicting a node transmitting a large amount of HTTP traffic

When a packet arrives at a NetFlow-enabled network device and it does not belong to any known flows, the device will create a new flow for it and start tracking any other related packets. After a preset amount of time elapses with no more packets in a flow, that flow is considered to be finished. The NetFlow-enabled device will aggregate statistics about the flow, such as duration, number of packets, and number of bytes, and then export the record. NetFlow collectors will then receive the data, clean it up a bit if necessary, and store it. The final component of the system is the analysis console, which allows analysts to examine the data and turn it into actionable information.

Notice that the flow data is only available for analysis *after* the flow has ended. This means that this type of analysis is better suited for forensic investigations than for real-time mitigation of attacks. Furthermore, NetFlow captures aggregate statistics and not detailed information about the packets. This type of analysis is helpful in the early stages of an investigation to point the analysts toward the specific packets that should be analyzed in detail (assuming the organization is also doing packet captures).

 EXAM TIP CompTIA separates packet, traffic, and NetFlow as three distinct types of analysis for knowledge organization purposes. In reality, packet and NetFlow analyses are, by definition, types of traffic analysis. Depending on the purpose and approach, protocol and wireless analyses could also be types of traffic analysis. This means traffic analysis is the umbrella term with packet and NetFlow, and sometimes protocol and wireless as subordinate types.

Wireless Analysis

It is difficult to run any kind of corporate network without considering the implications of wireless networks. Even if you don't allow wireless devices at all (not even mobile phones) in your building, how would you know that the policy is being followed by all employees all the time? Admittedly, most organizations will not (and oftentimes cannot) implement such draconian measures, which makes wireless local area network (WLAN) auditing and analysis particularly important.

To conduct a WLAN analysis, you must first capture data. Normally, when a WLAN interface card connects to a wireless access point (WAP), the client device will be in managed mode and the WAP will be in master mode. Master mode (also known as *infrastructure* mode) means that the interface will be responsible for managing all aspects of the WLAN configuration (such as channel and SSID). The client in managed mode is being managed by the master and thus will change channels or other settings when told to do so. Wireless interfaces can also communicate directly in mesh mode, which allows the interface to negotiate directly with another interface in a relationship that does not have master and managed nodes (also known as *ad hoc* mode). In each of these three modes, the interface will be limited to one connection to one network. In order to monitor multiple networks simultaneously, we need a fourth mode of operation. In monitor mode, the wireless interface will be able to see all available WLANs and their characteristics without connecting to any. This is the mode we need in order to perform a WLAN audit. Fortunately, WLAN analyzers, such as Kismet, take care of these details and allow us to simply run the application and see what is out there.

The most important step to a security analysis of your WLANs is to know your devices. Chief among these, of course, are the WAPs, but it is also important to keep track of wireless clients. How would you know that something odd is going on? Quite simply, by keeping track of what "normal" looks like. When analyzing the structure of WLANs, you must start from a known-good list of access points and client devices. Because, presumably, your organization installed (or had someone install) all the WAPs, you should have a record of their settings (for example, protocol, channel, and location) as well as their Media Access Control (MAC) and IP addresses. As you conduct your periodic audits, you will be able to tell if a new WAP shows up in your scan, potentially indicating a rogue access point.

Looking for rogue or unauthorized clients is a bit trickier because it is not hard to change the MAC address on many networked devices. Indeed, all major operating systems have built-in tools that allow you to do just that. Because the main indicator of an end device's identity is so susceptible to forgery, you might not be able to detect unauthorized nodes unless you implement some form of authentication, such as implementing WPA Enterprise and IEEE 802.1x. Absent authentication, you will have a very difficult time identifying all but the most naïve intruders connected to your WLAN.

Correlation Analysis

So, you have reconnoitered your network and gathered a ton of data in the process. At this point, you may have packet captures, NetFlows, and log files from firewalls, IDSs, and system events. Where to start? There are at least two schools of thought on this: you can start with the tool you have in front of you, or you can start with an observation.

When you start your analysis with a tool (or set of tools), you may be following a familiar workflow. The tools you use to capture the data oftentimes include at least some basic tools to analyze it. If nothing else, most of them offer filters that allow you to focus on items of interest. These features, however, will typically be helpful only in a pinch when you don't have access to anything else. For your real analysis work, you will need a comprehensive tool with which to simultaneously look at all the data at your disposal. Broadly speaking, these tools fall into three categories:

- *Security information and event management (SIEM) systems* collect data from a variety of sensors, perform pattern matching and correlation of events, generate alerts, and provide dashboards that allow analysts to see the state of the network. One of the best-known commercial solutions is Splunk, while on the open source side the Elasticsearch-Logstash-Kibana (ELK) stack is very popular.

- *Big data analytics solutions* are designed to deal with massive data sets that are typically beyond the range of SIEMs. The term *big data* refers to data sets that are so big in terms of volume (that is, the number of records), velocity (the rate at which new records are added), and variability (the number of different data formats), that traditional databases cannot handle them. Big data platforms are normally used to complement SIEMs, not to replace them.

- *Locally developed analytics solutions* are typically scripts developed in-house by security analysts. PowerShell and Python are popular languages in which to develop these tools, which are typically built to perform very specific functions in addition to or in lieu of an SIEM.

Another approach to analysis is to start with an observation regardless of the tool that allowed you to make it. Based on that observation, you make a hypothesis that would explain it. The next step is to either prove or disprove that hypothesis through additional observations or experiments. If this sounds familiar, that is because we just described the scientific method, which, as you might imagine, has a lot to do with security analytics. This approach forces us to think beyond the tools at our disposal and ask questions whose answers may not be in the data we already have. This is why we briefly bring this up here. If we limit ourselves and our questions to the tools and information in front of us, we will probably miss novel and potentially crippling attacks.

A Brief Detour on Statistics

A working knowledge of statistics is extremely beneficial to performing rigorous security analytics. Statistics allow us to make descriptive statements about data such as "this is normal" and then state categorically that something is not "normal." Although we all have an intuitive sense of normality based on our experience, we are all subject to a variety of biases that will all too often lead us to the wrong conclusions. If you never learned (or have since forgotten) statistics, we highly recommend that you brush up on them. It is difficult to perform some sorts of analyses, such as anomaly and trend, without some basic statistics.

Anomaly Analysis

Fundamentally, anomaly analysis attempts to answer the question "is this normal?" Obviously, we must have first established what normal means before we can answer the question. The process by which we learn the normal state or flows of a system is called *baselining*. Though we can create baselines for individual systems, it is sometimes more helpful to do so for collections of them. Anomaly analysis focuses on measuring the deviation from this baseline and determining whether that deviation is statistically significant. This last part is particularly important because everything changes constantly. The purpose of anomaly analysis is to determine whether the change could be reasonably expected to be there in a normal situation, or whether it is worth investigating.

An example of an application of anomaly analysis would be a sudden increase in network traffic at a user's workstation. Without a baseline, we would not be able to determine whether or not the traffic spike is normal. Suppose that we have baselined that particular system, and this amount of traffic is significantly higher than any other data point. The event could be classified as an outlier and deemed anomalous. But if we took a step back and looked at the baselines for clusters of workstations, we could find out that the event is consistent with workstations being used by a specific type of user (say, in the media team). Once in a while, one of them sends a large burst (say, to upload a finished film clip), but most of the time they are fairly quiet.

Behavioral Analysis

Behavioral analysis is closely related to anomaly analysis in that it attempts to find anomalous behaviors. In fact, the two terms are oftentimes used interchangeably or in combination with each other, as in *network behavior anomaly analysis*. The difference, to the extent that there is one in practice, is quite small: behavioral analysis looks at multiple correlated data points to define anomalous behavior. For example, it may be normal behavior for a user to upload large files to an Amazon cloud platform during business hours, but it is abnormal for that user to upload large files to a Google cloud platform after hours. So data points relating to size, destination, and time are used together. In a strict interpretation of anomaly analysis, in which data points could be taken in isolation, you might have received two alerts: one for destination and one for time, which you would then have to correlate manually.

 EXAM TIP You should not see questions asking you to differentiate between anomaly analysis and behavioral analysis. You could, however, see questions in which you must recall that they are both examples of data correlation and analytics (as opposed to point-in-time data analysis). You should also remember that they both leverage baselines.

Trend Analysis

Trend analysis is the study of patterns over time in order to determine how, when, and why they change. There are a number of applications for this technique. Most commonly, trend analysis is applied to security by tracking evolving patterns of adversaries' behaviors. Every year, a number of well-known security firms will publish their trend analyses and make projections for the next year based on the patterns they discovered. This approach would, for example, prompt you to prioritize distributed denial of service (DDoS) mitigations if these attacks are trending up and/or in the direction of your specific sector.

Internal Trends

Internal trends can reveal emerging risk areas. For example, there may be a trend in your organization to store increasing amounts of data in cloud resources such as Dropbox. Although this may make perfect sense from a business perspective, it could entail new or increased risk exposure for confidentiality, availability, forensic investigations, or even regulatory compliance. By noting this trend, you will be better equipped to decide the point at which the risk warrants a policy change or the acquisition of a managed solution.

Temporal Trends

Temporal trends show patterns related to time. There are plenty of examples of organizations being breached late on a Friday night in hopes that the incident will not be detected until three days later. Paradoxically, because fewer users will be on the network over the weekend, this should better enable alert defenders to detect the attack since the background traffic would presumably be lower. Another temporal trend could be an uptick in events in the days leading up to the release of a quarterly statement, or an increase in phishing attempts around tax season. These trends can help us better prepare our technical and human assets for likely threats to come.

Spatial Trends

Trends can also exist in specific regions. Though we tend to think of cyberspace as being almost independent of the physical world, in truth every device exists in a very specific place (or series of places for mobile ones). It is a common practice, for instance, to give staff members a "burner" laptop when they travel to certain countries. This device is not allowed to connect to the corporate network, has a limited set of files, and is digitally wiped immediately upon the users' return. This practice is the result of observing a trend of sophisticated compromises of devices traveling to those countries. Another example would be the increasing connection of devices to free Wi-Fi networks at local coffee shops, which could lead to focused security awareness training and the mandated use of virtual private network (VPN) connections.

Availability Analysis

Sometimes, our focus rests on protecting the confidentiality and integrity of our systems at the expense of preventing threats to their availability. Availability analysis is focused on determining the likelihood that our systems will be available to authorized users in a variety of scenarios. Perhaps the most common of these is the mitigation of DDoS attacks, which is in part accomplished by acquiring the services of an anti-DDoS company such as Akamai. These services can be expensive, so an availability analysis could help make the business case for them by determining at which point the local controls would not be able to keep up with a DDoS attack and how much money the organization would lose per unit of time that it was unavailable to its customers.

Another application of availability analysis is in determining the consequences of the loss of a given asset or set of assets. For example, what would be the effects on the business processes of the loss of a web server, or the data server storing the accounting data, or the CEO's computer. Obviously, you cannot realistically analyze every asset in your system, but there are key resources whose unavailability could cripple an organization. Performing an availability analysis over those can shed light on how to mitigate the risk of their loss.

Heuristics

A *heuristic* is a "rule of thumb" or, more precisely, an approach based on experience rather than theory. There are problems in computing that are known to be provably unsolvable, and yet we are able to use heuristics to get results that are close enough to work for us. Heuristic analysis in cybersecurity is the application of heuristics to find threats in practical, if imperfect, ways. This type of analysis is commonly seen in malware detection. We know it is not possible to find malware with 100 percent accuracy, but we also know that the majority of malware samples exhibit certain characteristics or behaviors. These, then, become our heuristics for malware detection.

Next-Generation Firewalls (NGFs) are devices that, in addition to the usual firewall features, include capabilities such as malware detection. This detection is usually accomplished in NGFs through heuristic analysis of the inbound data. The first approach is to take a suspicious payload and open it in a specially instrumented virtual machine (VM) within or under the control of the NGF. The execution of the payload is then observed, looking for telltale malware actions such as replicating itself, adding user accounts, and scanning resources. Obviously, certain malware families might not attempt any of these actions, which is what makes this approach heuristic: it is practical, but not guaranteed.

Tools of the Trade

The number of tools cybersecurity analysts have at their disposal is truly staggering. You probably have experimented with a number of them and use some on a daily basis. Still, CompTIA wants to ensure a baseline of knowledge in certain tool categories. We do not attempt to list all (or even many) of them here, but we will focus on some tools with which you should be familiar for the CSA+ exam.

Security Information and Event Management Systems

The quintessential tool for a cybersecurity analyst is arguably the security information and event management (SIEM) system. We already mentioned Splunk and ELK, but now we dig a bit deeper to ensure you are aware of some of their characteristics. It is worth noting that, technically, both of these systems are data analytics platforms and not simply SIEMs. Their ability to ingest, index, store, and retrieve large volumes of data applies to a variety of purposes—from network provisioning to marketing to enterprise security.

Splunk

As of this book's writing, more organizations used Splunk than any other SIEM, which means that you have either probably already worked with it or will use it sometime in your future. Splunk can ingest data from virtually any source. This data is then indexed and stored. One of the features of Splunk is that it allows you to ingest the raw data straight into the Indexer by using a Universal Forwarder, or you can do the preprocessing and indexing near the source using a Heavy Forwarder and then send to the Indexer a smaller amount of data that is ready to be stored. The second approach is helpful to reduce the amount of data that needs to travel from the individual sources to the indexers. When you think that large corporate environments can generate hundreds of gigabytes of data each day, Heavy Forwarders make a lot of sense. Once at the Indexers, the data is stored redundantly to improve availability and survivability. Apart from Forwarders and Indexers, the other main component of Splunk is the Search Heads, which are the web-based front ends that allow users to search and view the data. Figure 2-4 shows a Splunk interface with a search bar at the top.

ELK

ELK is not a tool as much as it is a system of tools. The name is an acronym for Elasticsearch, Logstash, and Kibana, which are all open source and Java based. These are the three main component tools of ELK. Elasticsearch is one of the most popular search engines. Its main purpose is to index data so that it can quickly search large data sets for specific attributes. Elasticsearch takes care of storing the data, but does not provide

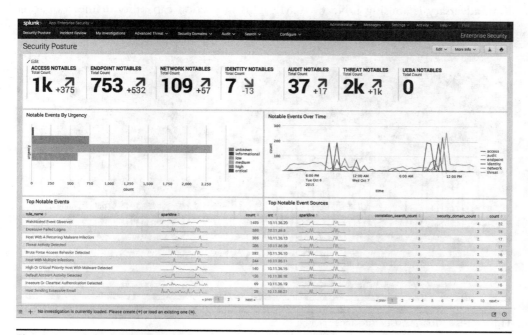

Figure 2-4   Splunk Enterprise Security user interface

a high degree of durability compared to other data management systems. Logstash is a data-processing pipeline that ingests data from a variety of sources (such as firewalls and event logs), performs transformations on it (for example, removing personally identifiable information, or PII, from records), and then forwards it to a data store (or stash). Kibana, shown in Figure 2-5, is a visualization plug-in for Elasticsearch that allows you to develop custom visualizations and reports. It comes with predefined queries and visualizations for common security analytics, but also enables the creation of custom queries. Together, the ELK stack performs many of the same functions that Splunk does, but as one would imagine, the commercial solution has extra features that may or may not be worth the money to your organization.

Packet Analyzers

The venerable Wireshark is probably the most widely used packet analyzer in the world. It allows you to analyze packets in real time as they are being captured, or offline from a variety of capture file formats. It has two features, in particular, that make it extremely powerful in the hands of an analyst: rich filters and deep inspection. The filters allow you to zero in on specific packets based on any combination of header or payload values. Because Wireshark understands hundreds of networking protocols, you can filter captured data based on specific header fields at almost any layer of the protocol stack. It includes both capture and view filters that limit the packets that are captured or displayed on the interface (respectively). The deep inspection feature allows you bit-level visibility on any captured packets, which can be useful when performing protocol analysis to see if an adversary is abusing DNS or ICMP. This inspection capability delineates packet

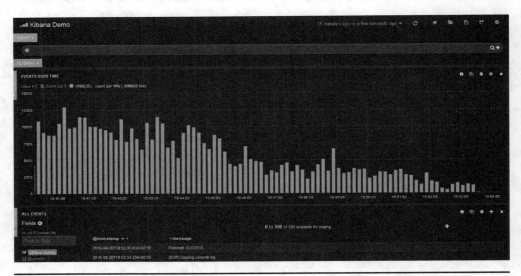

Figure 2-5   Kibana's user interface

headers according to their layer, so it is clear whether you're looking at MAC, IP, or TCP headers. Figure 2-6 shows the details on an Address Resolution Protocol (ARP) request.

Intrusion Detection Systems

Intrusion detection systems (IDSs) can be measured along two dimensions: focus and approach. The focus can be on a host, which makes them host-based IDSs (HIDSs); otherwise, they are network-based IDSs (NIDSs). Their approach can be signature or anomaly based. Finally, they can be standalone or integrated into another platform such as a Next-Generation Firewall.

Snort

Snort is probably the best-known NIDS in the open source community. However, it is more than an NIDS because it can operate as a packet analyzer or as a network intrusion prevention system (NIPS). Snort was originally developed by Martin Roesch in the late 1990s and has been under constant development ever since. Still, it is most known for the richness of its rules language and the abundance of rules that exist for it.

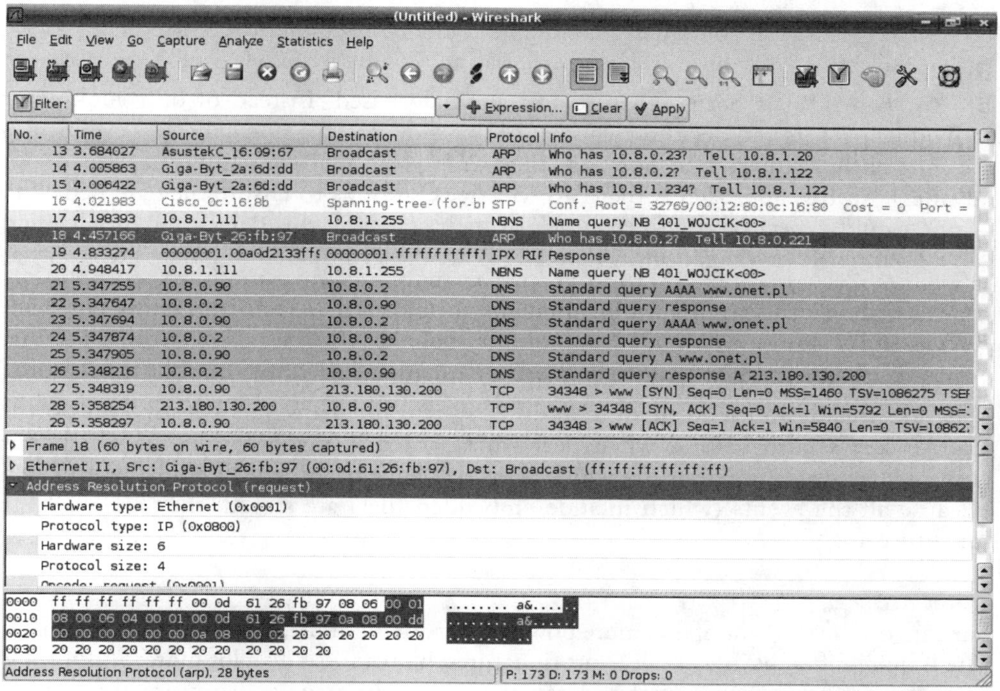

Figure 2-6 Wireshark showing packet details

Snort rules have two parts: the header and options. The header specifies the action Snort will take (for example, alert or drop) as well as the specific protocol, IP addresses, port numbers, and directionality (for example, directional or bidirectional). The real power of the rules, however, is in the options. In this section of a rule, one can specify where exactly to look for signs of trouble as well as what message to display to the user or record in the logs. The following rule shows how to detect a backdoor in the network:

```
alert tcp $EXTERNAL_NET any -> $HOME_NET 7597 (msg:"MALWARE-BACKDOOR QAZ Worm
Client Login access"; content:"qazwsx.hsq";)
```

In this case, we are looking for inbound TCP packets destined for port 7597 containing the text "qazwsx.hsq." If these are found, Snort will raise an alert that says "MALWARE-BACKDOOR QAZ Worm Client Login access." Note that many more options could be written into the rule, such as hashes of known malware.

 NOTE   Threat Intelligence companies will often include Snort signatures for newly discovered threats as part of their subscription services.

Bro

Bro (or Bro-IDS) is both signature and anomaly based. Instead of only looking at individual packets and deciding whether or not they match a rule, it creates events that are inherently neither good nor bad; they simply say that something happened. An advantage in this approach is that Bro will track sessions to ensure they are behaving as one would expect, and it keeps track of their state. All this data is retained, which can help forensic investigations. These events are then compared to policies to see what actions, if any, are warranted. It is here that Bro's power really shines. The policies can do anything from sending an e-mail or text message to updating internal metrics to disabling a user account.

Another powerful feature in Bro is the ability to extract complete executables from network streams and send them to another system for malware analysis. This download feature is also helpful when performing forensic investigations in which, for example, we need to determine which files may have been exfiltrated by an attacker. Because all the events (which include embedded files) are stored, they are available for future analysis.

Suricata

Suricata can be thought of as a more powerful version of Snort, even though its architecture is quite different. It can use Snort signatures, but can also do a lot more. Specifically, it is multithreaded (Snort isn't) and can even take advantage of hardware acceleration (that is, using the graphics accelerator to process packets). Like Bro, it can also extract files from the packet flows for retention or analysis. Like both Bro and Snort, Suricata can be used as an IPS.

Resource-Monitoring Tools

Nagios Core is one of the most popular open source resource-monitoring tools. At a very high level, it allows you to track the status of your network devices, including workstations, servers, switches, routers, and indeed anything that can run a Nagios agent or send data to a plug-in. For each of those devices, it can monitor specific metrics such as processor or disk utilization. When things go wrong, Nagios will log the event and then either send a notification via e-mail or text or take a specific action by running an event handler that can correct the problem. Nagios is remarkably easy to set up initially, but it's also scalable enough to handle complex environments and procedures.

NetFlow Analyzers

NetFlow analyzers are almost essential to leverage the data provided by NetFlow collectors. In a pinch, you can use a packet capture utility with a handful of scripts, but nothing beats having the right tool for the job. A NetFlow analyzer draws data from a collector and allows the analyst to view and query the data in a number of ways. At a minimum, it provides the means to see recent flows and to drill into them for details. Some of the more sophisticated tools will have filters geared toward security analysts that can help identify denial of service, malware command and control, and data exfiltration

Arguably, one of the most popular open source NetFlow analyzers is ntopng. This tool is able to act as both a NetFlow collector (which receives and aggregates data from multiple devices) and an analysis console. It also monitors a variety of other network parameters and data not strictly associated with NetFlow. The tool has a web-based interface, is extensible, and runs on most flavors of Linux as well as Mac OS and Windows. Figure 2-7 shows ntopng in action.

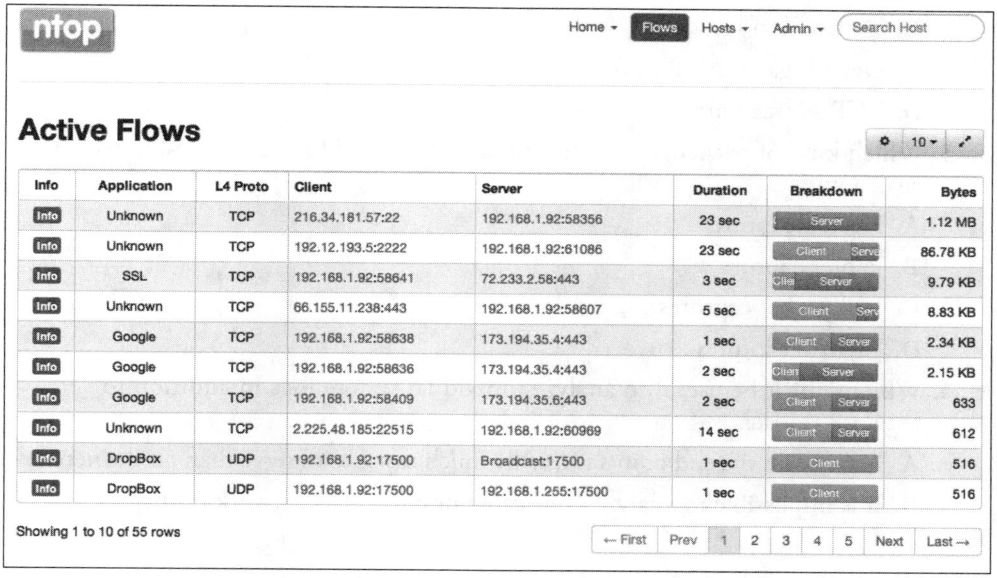

Figure 2-7   The ntopng user interface

Chapter Review

Acquiring data, whether through reconnaissance or routine monitoring, is only the beginning. The real work is in analyzing that data and turning it into information. In this chapter, we covered a multitude of approaches and tools with which to perform security analytics. There is no one-size-fits-all answer for any of this, so it is critical that as cybersecurity analysts, we have enough familiarity with our options to choose the right one for a particular job. The topics brought up in this chapter are by no means exhaustive, but they should serve you well for the CSA+ exam and, perhaps more importantly, as a start point for further lifelong exploration.

Questions

1. What is the key difference between an intrusion detection system (IDS) and an intrusion prevention system (IPS)?

   A. An IPS only relies on a fixed set of rules, or heuristics, when analyzing traffic.

   B. An IDS only analyzes TCP traffic, whereas an IPS analyzes only UDP traffic.

   C. An IDS only detects suspicious traffic, whereas an IPS detects and blocks malicious traffic.

   D. An IPS only detects suspicious traffic, whereas an IDS detects and blocks malicious traffic.

2. Which of the following transmissions is not provided by the NetFlow network protocol?

   A. Source IP address

   B. Destination IP address

   C. Default gateway address

   D. TCP source port

3. Which kind of packet capture technique is preferred for a resource-limited environment?

   A. Header capture

   B. Footer capture

   C. Full packet captures

   D. Payload captures

4. Why might it be useful to analyze individual system logs in addition to network traffic?

   A. Activity on the end points is usually much easier to observe than on the network.

   B. It is impossible to analyze obfuscated or encrypted network traffic.

C. End points are unable to log their system activity.

D. There aren't any useful standards for logging system activity.

5. When performing a capture for wireless analysis, what mode must the wireless card support?

   A. Managed

   B. Ad hoc

   C. Mesh

   D. Monitor

6. The largest unit of data that traverses a network in a single exchange is referred to as what?

   A. ICMP

   B. MTU

   C. TCP

   D. CDMA

Use the following scenario to answer Questions 7–9:

Your company has experienced significant growth over the past few months, and increased traffic has proven too much for the existing set of tools. Your analyst team is looking for a solution to manage the alerts generated by all the enterprise's network devices with minimal interruption to the network's current configuration, and they turn to you as their resident expert for guidance.

7. When searching for a solution, the team comes across the acronym SIEM. What does it stand for?

   A. Simulated incident and environmental management

   B. Security indicators and event monitor

   C. Security information and event management

   D. Simulations, indications, and environmental monitors

8. With the new SIEM tool, the team realizes that they can perform point-in-time analysis much more efficiently. What feature of the SIEM are they likely leveraging for this task?

   A. Query function to investigate past network activity around the time of an alert

   B. Visualization of current network flows

   C. Certificate Authority (CA) verification

   D. A single syslog *warning* message

9. When you're conducting a full packet capture on network traffic, which of the following is *not* a consideration?

   A. Easily identifying the source and destination of the traffic

   B. Legal consequences

   C. Privacy implications

   D. Data storage capacity

Refer to the following illustration for Questions 10–12:

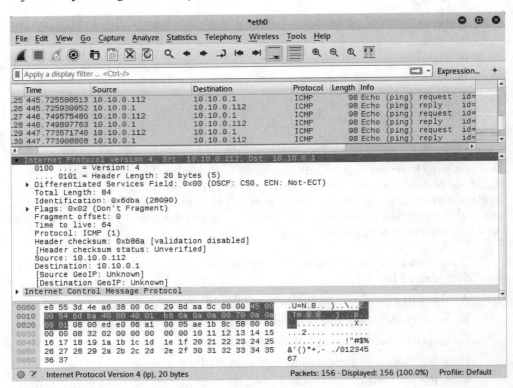

10. What is the total size, in bytes, of the packet's payload?

   A. 84

   B. 64

   C. 44

   D. 24

11. Roughly how much time elapsed between the first ping request and reply?

    A. 35 seconds

    B. 35 milliseconds

    C. 350 milliseconds

    D. .350 milliseconds

12. What is the name of the Windows utility that allows you to easily monitor various program, security, and system activity logs on your computer?

    A. Nmap

    B. Event Viewer

    C. Console

    D. Putty

Answers

1. **C.** Intrusion detection systems (IDSs) simply detect suspected threats, and intrusion prevention systems (IPSs) actively block them.

2. **C.** NetFlow is a traffic-analysis system developed by Cisco that provides information about the arrival interface, source and destination IP addresses and port numbers, and the type of service. The default gateway is a network device that facilitates access for a connected device.

3. **A.** In a header capture, only the IP header data is recorded for analysis, whereas a full capture requires more storage and processing power.

4. **A.** Monitoring local end-point events provides tremendous insight into the computer's process and network activities. Examination of local event logs is an excellent supplement to network analysis and will give a far more accurate picture of the network's state.

5. **D.** To capture wireless traffic, especially when it's not associated with an access point, the network interface card must support monitor mode operation.

6. **B.** The maximum transmission unit (MTU) is the largest single unit of data that traverses the network during an exchange. A larger MTU means that more data moves for every exchange, requiring less processing power over time because fewer units are processed. However, this may result in increased latency because fewer units can occupy a transmission line at a given time.

7. **C.** SIEM, or security information and event management, is a set of security tools that combine security information management (SIM) and security event management (SEM).

8. **A.** Point-in-time analysis is the analysis of various data outputs to determine system events that were recorded around a specified time.

9. **A.** Legal and privacy issues must always be considered before capturing packets. Depending on the duration of the capture, storage capacity can become an issue so one would normally ensure the required space is available before starting. Since there are a number of free and commercial capture and analytic software options that specialize in packet capture and analysis, it is easy to determine the sources and destinations.

10. **B.** The total size of the packet (84 bytes) is the size of the header (20 bytes) plus the size of the payload. The payload size is not provided explicitly, but can be calculated by subtracting the header size from the total size to get 64 bytes.

11. **D.** The time value display in Wireshark is in seconds. The difference between the first and second values listed is about .350 milliseconds.

12. **B.** The Event Viewer is a utility that helps administrators troubleshoot problems on their computers by providing an easy-to-use interface for reviewing system logs, including error, informational, and warning messages.

Responding to Network-Based Threats

In this chapter you will learn:
- Practices for network and host hardening
- Deception techniques for improving security
- Common types of access controls
- Trends in threat detection and endpoint protection

There can never be enough deception in war.

—Sun Tzu

What would you say if I told you that at Fort Knox, the entirety of the gold depository sits in a single large room located at the center of a conspicuous building with a neon sign that reads "Gold Here!"? One guard is posted at each of the 12 entrances, equipped with photographs of all known gold thieves in the area and a radio to communicate with the other guards internally. Sounds absurd, doesn't it? This fictional scenario would be a dream for attackers, but this architecture is how many networks are currently configured: a porous border with sentries that rely on dated data, about only known threats, to make decisions about whom to let in. The only thing better for an attacker would be no security at all.

In reality, the U.S. Bullion Depository is an extremely hardened facility that resides within the boundaries of Fort Knox, an Army installation protected by tanks, armed police, patrolling helicopter gunships, and some of the world's best-trained soldiers. Should an attacker even manage to get past the gates of Fort Knox itself, he would have to make his way through additional layers of security, avoiding razor wire and detection by security cameras, trip sensors, and military working dogs to reach the vault. This design incorporates some of the best practices of physical security that, when governed by strict operating policies, protect some of the nation's most valuable resources. The best protected networks are administered in a similar way, incorporating an efficient use of technology while raising the cost for an attacker.

Network Segmentation

Network segmentation is the practice of separating various parts of the network into subordinate zones. Some of the goals of network segmentation are to thwart the adversary's efforts, improve traffic management, and prevent spillover of sensitive data. Beginning at the physical layer of the network, segmentation can be implemented all the way up to the application layer. One common method of providing separation at the link layer of the network is the use of virtual local area networks (VLANs). Properly configured, a VLAN allows various hosts to be part of the same network even if they are not physically connected to the same network equipment. Alternatively, a single switch could support multiple VLANs, greatly improving design and management of the network. Segmentation can also occur at the application level, preventing applications and services from interacting with others that may run on the same hardware. Keep in mind that segmenting a network at one layer doesn't carry over to the higher layers. In other words, simply implementing VLANs is not enough if you also desire to segment based on the application protocol.

Micro-Segmentation

As cloud usage increases and modern data centers evolve to optimize resource sharing, administrators continue to lose physical control over network resources. Although this may be problematic for certain use cases, such as those in classified environments, it has opened the door for increased use of *micro-segmentation*, or the application of new architectural and deployment models, which include containers, cryptographic restrictions, software-defined networks, and virtualized infrastructures.

System Isolation

Even within the same subnetwork or VLAN, there might be systems that should only be communicating with certain other systems, and it becomes apparent that something is amiss should you see loads of traffic outside of the expect norms. One way to ensure that hosts in your network are only talking to the machines they're supposed to is to enforce system isolation. This can be achieved by implementing additional policies on network devices in addition to your segmentation plan. System isolation can begin with physically separating special machines or groups of machines with an *air gap,* which is a physical separation of these systems from outside connections. There are clearly tradeoffs in that these machines will not be able to communicate with the rest of the world. However, if they only have one specific job that doesn't require external connectivity, then it may make sense to separate them entirely. If a connection is required, it's possible to use access control lists (ACLs) to enforce policy. Like a firewall, an ACL allows or denies certain access, and does so depending on a set of rules applicable to the layer it is operating on, usually at the network or file system level. Although the practice of system isolation takes a bit of forethought, the return on investment for the time spent to set it up is huge.

Jump Box

To facilitate outside connections to segmented parts of the network, administrators sometimes designate a specially configured machine called a *jump box* or *jump server.* As the name suggests, these computers serve as jumping-off points for external users to access protected parts of a network. The idea is to keep special users from logging into a particularly important host using the same workstation they use for everything else. If that daily-use workstation were to become compromised, it could be used by an attacker to reach the sensitive nodes. If, on the other hand, these users are required to use a specially hardened jump box for these remote connections, it would be much more difficult for the attacker to reach the crown jewels.

A great benefit of jump boxes is that they serve as a chokepoint for outside users wishing to gain access to a protected network. Accordingly, jump boxes often have high levels of activity logging enabled for auditing or forensic purposes. Figure 3-1 shows a very simple configuration of a jump box in a network environment. Note the placement of the jump box in relation to the firewall device on the network. Although it may improve overall security to designate a sole point of access to the network, it's critical that the jump box is carefully monitored because a compromise of this server may allow access to the rest of the network. This means disabling any services or applications that are not necessary, using strict ACLs, keeping up to date with software patches, and using multifactor authentication where possible.

 EXAM TIP You will likely see jump boxes on the exam in the context of privileged account users (for example, system admins) using them to remotely log into sensitive hosts.

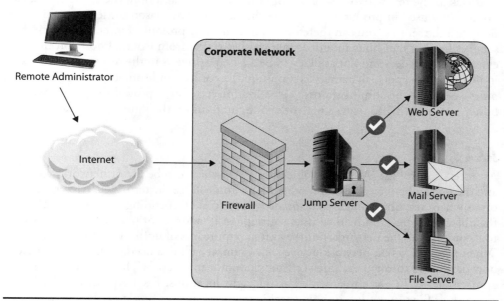

Figure 3-1 Network diagram of a simple jump box arrangement

Honeypots and Honeynets

Believe it or not, sometimes admins will design systems to attract attackers. Honeypots are a favorite tool for admins to learn more about the adversary's goals by intentionally exposing a machine that appears to be a highly valuable, and sometimes unprotected, target. Although the honeypot may seem legitimate to the attacker, it is actually isolated from the normal network and has all its activity monitored and logged. This has several benefits from a defensive point of view. By convincing an attacker to focus his efforts against the honeypot machine, an administrator can gain insight in the attacker's tactics, techniques, and procedures (TTPs). This can be used to predict behavior or aid in identifying the attacker via historical data. Furthermore, honeypots may delay an attacker or force him to exhaust his resources in fruitless tasks.

Honeypots have been in use for several decades, but they have been difficult or costly to deploy because this often meant dedicating actual hardware to face attackers, thus reducing what could be used for production purposes. Furthermore, in order to engage an attacker for any significant amount of time, the honeypot needs to look like a real (and ideally valuable) network node, which means putting some thought into what software and data to put on it. This all takes lots of time and isn't practical for very large deployments. Virtualization has come to the rescue and addressed many of the challenges associated with administering these machines because the technology scales easily and rapidly.

With a honeynet, the idea is that if some is good, then more is better. A *honeynet* is an entire network designed to attract attackers. The benefits of its use are the same as with honeypots, but these networks are designed to look like real network environments, complete with real operating systems, applications, services, and associated network traffic. You can think of honeynets as a highly interactive set of honeypots, providing realistic feedback as the real network would. For both honeypots and honeynets, the services are not actually used in production, so there shouldn't be any reason for legitimate interaction with the servers. You can therefore assume that any prolonged interaction with these services implies malicious intent. It follows that traffic from external hosts on the honeynet is the real deal and not as likely to be a false positive as in the real network. As with individual honeypots, all activity is monitored, recorded, and sometimes adjusted based on the desire of the administrators. Virtualization has also improved the performance of honeynets, allowing for varied network configurations on the same bare metal.

ACLs

An access control list (ACL) is a table of objects, which can be file or network resources, and the users who may access or modify them. You will see the term *ACL* referenced most often when describing file system or network access. Depending on the type of ACL, the object may be an individual user, a group, an IP address, or port. ACLs are powerful tools in securing the network, but they often require lots of upfront investment in setup. When using ACLs on network devices, for example, admins need to understand exactly how data flows through each device from endpoint to gateway. This will ensure that the appropriate ACLs are implemented at the right locations. Each type of ACL, whether network or file system, has its own specific requirements for best use.

File System ACLs

In early computing environments, files and directories had *owners* who had complete control to read, write, or modify them. The owners could belong to *groups,* and they could all be granted the necessary permissions with respect to the file or directory. Anyone else would fall into an *other* category and could be assigned the appropriate permissions as well. These permissions provided a basic way to control access, but there was no way to assign different levels of access for different individual users. ACLs were developed to provide granular control over a file or directory. Note the difference in access to the bar.txt file in Figure 3-2. As the owner of the file, "root" has read and write access and has given read access to the user "nobody."

Network ACLs

Like file system ACLs, network ACLs provide the ability to selectively permit or deny access, usually for both inbound and outbound traffic. The access conditions depend on the type of device used. Switches, for example, may use the IP or MAC address of the source and destination to decide on whether to allow traffic because they are layer 2 devices. Routers, as layer 3 and 4 devices, may use IP, network protocol, port, or another feature to decide. In virtual and cloud environments, ACLs can be implemented to filter traffic in a similar way.

 EXAM TIP   The order of the ACL rules is very important. Traffic is checked against the list of rules sequentially, and if a packet matches multiple rules, the first rule takes precedence.

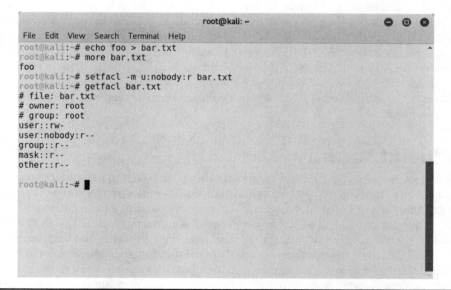

```
                           root@kali: ~                        ⊖ ▣ ⊗
  File  Edit  View  Search  Terminal  Help
  root@kali:~# echo foo > bar.txt
  root@kali:~# more bar.txt
  foo
  root@kali:~# setfacl -m u:nobody:r bar.txt
  root@kali:~# getfacl bar.txt
  # file: bar.txt
  # owner: root
  # group: root
  user::rw-
  user:nobody:r--
  group::r--
  mask::r--
  other::r--

  root@kali:~# █
```

Figure 3-2   Listing of a directory ACL in Linux

Black Hole

When probing a network, an adversary relies a great deal on feedback provided by other hosts to get his bearings. It's a bit like a submarine using sonar to find out where it is relative to the sea floor, obstacles, and perhaps an enemy craft. If a submarine receives no echo from the pings it sends out, it can assume that there are no obstacles present in that direction. Now imagine that it never receives a response to any of the pings it sends out because everything around it somehow has absorbed every bit of acoustic energy; it would have no way to determine where it is relative to anything else and would be floating blindly.

A *black hole* is a device that is configured to receive any and all packets with a specific source or destination address and not respond to them at all. Usually network protocols will indicate that there is a failure, but with black holes there's no response at all because the packets are silently logged and dropped. The sender isn't even aware of the delivery failure.

DNS Sinkhole

The *DNS sinkhole* is a technique like DNS spoofing in that it provides a response to a DNS query that does not resolve to the actual IP address. The difference, however, is that DNS sinkholes target the addresses for known malicious domains, such as those associated with a botnet, and return an IP address that does not resolve correctly or that is defined by the administrator. Here's a scenario of how this helps with securing a network: Suppose you receive a notice that a website, www.malware.evil, is serving malicious content and you confirm that several machines in your network are attempting to contact that server. You have no way to determine which computers are infected until they attempt to resolve that hostname, but if they are able to resolve it they may be able to connect to the malicious site and download additional tools that will make remediation harder. If you create a DNS sinkhole to resolve www.malware.evil to your special server at address 10.10.10.50, you can easily check your logs to determine which machines are infected. Any host that attempts to contact 10.10.10.50 is likely to be infected because there would otherwise be no reason to connect there. All the while, the attackers will not be able to further the compromise because they won't receive feedback from the affected hosts.

Endpoint Security

Focusing on security at the network level isn't always sufficient to prepare for an attacker. While we aim to mitigate the great majority of threats at the network level, the tradeoff between usability and security emerges. We want network-based protection to be able to inspect traffic thoroughly, but not at the expense of network speed. Though keeping an eye on the network is important, it's impossible to see everything and respond quickly. Additionally, the target of malicious code is often the data that resides on the hosts. It doesn't make sense to only strengthen the foundation of the network if the rest is left without a similar level of protection. It's therefore just as important to ensure that the hosts are fortified to withstand attacks and provide an easy way to give insight into what processes are running.

Detect and Block

Two general types of malware detection for endpoint solutions appear in this category. The first, signature-based detection, compares hashes of files on the local machine to a list of known malicious files. Should there be a match, the endpoint software can quarantine the file and alert the administrator of its presence. Modern signature-based detection software is also capable of identifying families of malicious code.

But what happens when the malicious file is new to the environment and therefore doesn't have a signature? This might be where behavior-based malware detection can help. It monitors system processes for telltale signs of malware, which it then compares to known behaviors to generate a decision on the file. Behavior-based detection has become important because malware writers often use polymorphic (constantly changing) code, which makes it very difficult to detect using signature methods only.

There are limitations with both methods. False positives, files incorrectly identified as malware, can cause a range of problems. At best, they can be a nuisance, but if the detection software quarantines critical system files, the operating system may be rendered unusable. Scale this up several hundred or thousand endpoints, and it becomes catastrophic for productivity.

Sandbox

Creating malware takes a lot of effort, so writers will frequently test their code against the most popular detection software to make sure that it can't be seen before releasing it to the wild. Endpoint solutions have had to evolve their functionality to cover the blind spots of traditional detection by using a technique called *sandboxing*. Endpoint sandboxes can take the form of virtual machines that run on the host to provide a realistic but restricted operating system environment. As the file is executed, the sandbox is monitored for unusual behavior or system changes, and only until the file is verified as being safe might it be allowed to run on the host machine. Historically, sandboxes were used by researchers to understand how malware was executing and evolving, but given the increase in local computing power and the advances in virtualization, sandboxes have become mainstream. Some malware writers have taken note of these trends and have started producing malware that can detect whether its operating in a sandbox using built-in logic. In these cases, if the malware detects the sandbox, it will remain dormant to evade detection and become active at some later point. This highlights the unending battle between malware creators and the professionals who defend our networks.

Cloud-Connected Protection

Like virtualization, the widespread use of cloud computing has allowed for significant advancements in malware detection. Many modern endpoint solutions use cloud computing to enhance protection by providing the foundation for rapid file reputation determination and behavioral analysis. Cloud-based security platforms use automatic sharing of threat detail across the network to minimize the overall risk of infection from known and unknown threats. Were this to be done manually, it would take much more time for analysts to prepare, share, and update each zone separately.

> **Trust**
> The concept of inherent trust in networks presents many challenges for administrators. Humans make mistakes—they lose devices or unwittingly create entry points into the network for attackers. Thus, the practice of a zero-trust environment is emerging as the standard for enterprise networks, in which the network's design and administration consider that threats may come from external *and* internal sources.

Group Policies

The majority of enterprise devices rely on a *directory service*, such as Active Directory, to give them access to shared resources such as storage volumes, printers, and contact lists. In a Windows-based environment, Active Directory is implemented through the domain controller, which provides authentication and authorization services in addition to resource provision for all connected users. Additionally, the Active Directory service allows for remote administration using policies. Using group policies, administrators can force user machines to a baseline of settings. Features such as password complexity, account lockout, registry keys, and file access can all be prescribed though the group policy mechanism. Security settings for both machines and user accounts can be set at the local, domain, or network level using group policies.

Device Hardening

The application of the practices in this chapter is part of an effort to make the adversary work harder to discover what our network looks like, or to make it more likely for his efforts to be discovered. This practice of *hardening* the network is not static and requires constant monitoring of network and local resources. It's critical that we take a close look at what we can do at the endpoint to prevent only relying on detection of an attack. Hardening the endpoint requires careful thought about the balance of security and usability. We cannot make the system so unusable so that no work can get done. Thankfully, there are some simple rules to follow. The first is that resources should only be accessed by those who need them to perform their duties. Administrators also need to have measures in place to address the risk associated with a requirement if they are not able to address the requirement directly. Next is that hosts should be configured with only the necessary applications and services necessary for the role. Does the machine need to be running a web server, for example? Using policies, these settings can be standardized and pushed to all hosts on a domain. And finally, updates should be applied early and often. In addition to proving functional improvements, many updates come with patches for recently discovered flaws.

Usability vs. Security

Sometimes, the more secure we try to make a system, the less secure it becomes in practice. Think about it: if you make password requirements so difficult to remember for users, they'll start writing their passwords down on sticky notes and storing them under keyboards and on monitors for easy access. Does this make for a more secure system? It might be hard to imagine a world without passwords. No complex string of letters and number to remember and almost instant access to systems often means an immensely usable but woefully insecure system. However, usability and security are not mutually exclusive concepts. There is an entire field of information security dedicated to improving the usability of systems while keeping a high level of confidentiality, integrity, and availability. As we work toward improving usability while maintaining high security, it's important that we understand the tradeoffs in our current systems so that we can make smart decisions about our security policy.

Discretionary Access Control (DAC)

Looking back on our discussion of file system ACLs, we saw that simple permissions were the predominant form of access control for many years. This schema is called *discretionary access control,* or DAC. It's discretionary in the sense that the content owner or administrator can pass privileges on to anyone else at their discretion. Those recipients could then access the media based on their identity or group membership. The validation of access occurs at the resource, meaning that when the user attempts to access the file, the operating system will consult with the file's list of privileges and verify that the user can perform the operation. You can see this in action in all major operating systems today: Windows, Linux, and Mac OS.

Mandatory Access Control (MAC)

For environments that require additional levels of scrutiny for data access, such as those in military or intelligence organizations, the *mandatory access control* (MAC) model is a better option than DAC. As the name implies, MAC *requires* explicit authorization for a given user on a given object. The MAC model has additional labels for multilevel security—Unclassified, Confidential, Secret, and Top Secret—that are applied to both the subject and object. When a user attempts to access a file, a comparison is made between the security labels on the file, called the *classification level,* and the security level of the subject, called the *clearance level.* Only users who have these labels in their own profiles can access files at the equivalent level, and verifying this "need to know" is the main strength of MAC. Additionally, the administrator can restrict further propagation of the resource, even from the content creator.

Role-Based Access Control (RBAC)

What if you have a tremendous number of files that you don't want to manage on a case-by-case basis? Role-based access control (RBAC) allows you to grant permissions based on a user's role, or group. The focus for RBAC is at the role level, where the administrators define what the role can do. Users are only able to do what their roles allow them to do, so there isn't the need for an explicit denial to a resource for a given role. Ideally, there are a small number of roles in a system, regardless of total number of users, so the management becomes much easier. You may wonder what the difference is between groups in the DAC model and RBAC. The difference is slight in that permissions in DAC can be given to both a user and group, so there exists the possibility that a user can be denied, but the group to whom he belongs may have access. With RBAC, every permission is applied to the role, or group, and never directly to the user, so it removes the possibility of the loophole previously described.

Compensating Controls

Compensating controls are any means for organizations to achieve the goals of a security requirement even if they were unable to meet the goals explicitly due to some legitimate external constraint or internal conflict. An example would be a small business that processes credit card payments on its online store and is therefore subject to the Payment Card Industry Digital Security Standard (PCI DSS). This company uses the same network for both sensitive financial operations and external web access. Although best practices would dictate that physically separate infrastructures be used, with perhaps an air gap between the two, this may not be feasible because of cost. A compensating control would be to introduce a switch capable of VLAN management and to enforce ACLs at the switch and router level. This alternative solution would "meet the intent and rigor of the original stated requirement," as described in the PCI DSS standard.

Blocking Unused Ports/Services

I'm always amazed at how many consumer products designed to be connected to a network leave unnecessary services running, sometimes with default credentials. Some of these services are shown in Figure 3-3. If you do not require a service, it should be disabled. Running unnecessary services not only means more avenues of approach for an adversary, it's also more work to administer. Services that aren't used are essentially wasted energy because the computers will still run the software, waiting for a connection that is not likely to happen by a legitimate user.

 EXAM TIP The UDP and TCP ports between 0 and 1023 are known as the *well-known ports* because they are used for commonly used services. Some notable well-known ports are 20 (FTP), 22 (SSH), 25 (SMTP), and 80 (HTTP). Ports 1024 to 49151 are *registered* ports, and ports above 49151 are *ephemeral* or *dynamic* ports.

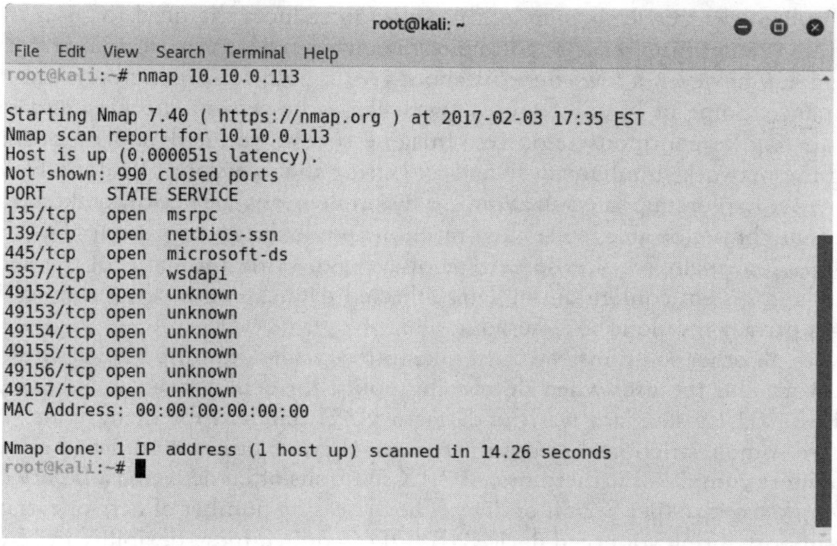

```
                              root@kali: ~                          ⊖ ⊙ ⊗
 File  Edit  View  Search  Terminal  Help
 root@kali:~# nmap 10.10.0.113

 Starting Nmap 7.40 ( https://nmap.org ) at 2017-02-03 17:35 EST
 Nmap scan report for 10.10.0.113
 Host is up (0.000051s latency).
 Not shown: 990 closed ports
 PORT      STATE SERVICE
 135/tcp   open  msrpc
 139/tcp   open  netbios-ssn
 445/tcp   open  microsoft-ds
 5357/tcp  open  wsdapi
 49152/tcp open  unknown
 49153/tcp open  unknown
 49154/tcp open  unknown
 49155/tcp open  unknown
 49156/tcp open  unknown
 49157/tcp open  unknown
 MAC Address: 00:00:00:00:00:00

 Nmap done: 1 IP address (1 host up) scanned in 14.26 seconds
 root@kali:~#
```

Figure 3-3   Listing of open ports on an unprotected Windows 8 machine

Patching

Patching is a necessary evil for administrators. You don't want to risk network outages due to newly introduced incompatibilities, but you also don't need old software being exploited because of your reservations about patching. For many years, vendors tried to ease the stress of patching by regularly releasing their updates in fixed intervals. Major vendors such as Microsoft and Adobe got into a rhythm with issuing updates for their products. Admins could therefore make plans to test and push updates with some degree of certainty. Microsoft recently ended its practice of "Patch Tuesday," however, in part due to this predictability. A downside of the practice emerged as attackers began reverse engineering the fixes as soon as they were released to determine the previously unknown vulnerabilities. Attackers knew that many administrators wouldn't be able to patch all their machines before they figured out the vulnerability, and thus the moniker "Exploit Wednesday" emerged. Although humorous, it was a major drawback that convinced the company to instead focus on improving its automatic update features.

Network Access Control

In an effort to enforce security standards for endpoints beyond baselining and group policies, engineers developed the concept of Network Access Control (NAC). NAC provides deeper visibility into endpoints and allows policy enforcement checks before the device is allowed to connect to the network. NAC ties in features such as RBAC, verification of endpoint malware protection, and version checks to address a wide swath of security requirements. Some NAC solutions offer transparent remediation for noncompliant devices. In principle, this solution reduces the need for user intervention while streamlining security and management operations for administrators.

There are, however, a few concerns about NAC: both for user privacy and network performance. Some of NAC's features, particularly the version checking and remediation, can require enormous resources. Imagine several hundred noncompliant nodes joining the network simultaneously and all getting their versions of Adobe Flash, Java, and Internet Explorer updated all at once. This often means the network takes a hit; plus, the users might not be able to use their machines while the updates are applied. Furthermore, NAC normally requires some type of agent to verify the status of the endpoint's software and system configuration. This collected data can have major implications on user data privacy should it be misused.

As with all other solutions, we must take into consideration the implications to both the network and the user when developing policy for deployment of NAC solutions. The IEEE 802.1X standard was the de facto NAC standard for many years. While it supported some restrictions based on network policy, its utility diminished as networks became more complex. Furthermore, 802.1X solutions often delivered a binary decision on network access: either permit or deny. The increasing number of networks transitioning to support "bring your own device" (BYOD) required more flexibility in NAC solutions. Modern NAC solutions support several frameworks, each with its own restrictions, to ensure endpoint compliance when attempting to join the enterprise network. Administrators may choose from a variety of responses that modern NAC solutions provide in the case of a violation. Based on the severity of the incident, they may completely block the device's access, quarantine it, generate an alert, or attempt to remediate the endpoint. We'll look of the most commonly used solutions next.

Time Based

Does your guest network need to be active at 3 A.M.? If not, then a time-based network solution might be for you. Time-based solutions can provide network access for fixed intervals or recurring timeframes, and enforce time limits for guest access. Some more advanced devices can even assign different time policies for different groups.

Rule Based

NAC solutions will query the host to verify operating system version, the version of security software, the presence of prohibited data or applications, or any other criteria as defined by the list of rules. These rules may also include hardware configurations, such as the presence of unauthorized storage devices. Often they can share this information back into the network to inform changes to other devices. Additionally, many NAC solutions are also capable of operating in a passive mode, running only as a monitor functionality and reporting violations when they occur.

Role Based

In smaller networks, limiting the interaction between nodes manually is a manageable exercise, but as the network size increases, this become exponentially more difficult due in part to the variety of endpoint configurations that may exist. Using RBAC, NAC solutions can assist in limiting the interaction between nodes to prevent unauthorized data disclosure, either accidental or intentional. As discussed, RBAC provides users with a set of authorized actions necessary to fulfill their role in the organization. NAC may reference the existing RBAC policies using whatever directory services are in use across the network and enforce them accordingly. This helps with data loss prevention (DLP) because the process of locating sensitive information across various parts of the network becomes much faster. NAC therefore can serve as a DLP solution, even when data has left the network, because it can either verify the presence of host-based DLP tools or conduct the verification itself using RBAC integration.

Location Based

Along with the surge in BYOD in networks, an increasing number of employees are working away from the network infrastructure, relying on virtual private network (VPN) software or cloud services to gain access to company resources. NAC can consider device location when making its decision on access, providing the two main benefits of identity verification and more accurate asset tracking.

Chapter Review

Proactively preparing against intrusion is a critical step in ensuring that your network is ready to respond to the unlikely event of a successful attack. By appropriately identifying critical assets on the network and segmenting them into subordinate zones, you can limit damage by using sensible network architecture. By smartly managing permissions and access control, you can be sure that only those parties who need to access data, even from within, can do so. Your policy should be so comprehensive as to include complementary or even redundant controls. In cases where certain technical means are not possible due to budget or other restrictions, these alternate controls should be put into place to address the affected areas. While you put attention into making sure the whole network is healthy and resilient, it's also important to include endpoint and server hardening into the calculation. Turning off unnecessary services and keeping systems and software up to date are vital tasks in improving their security baseline.

What's more, prevention is not enough as a part of your security strategy. Your security team must assess the network and understand where deception tools can add value. As a strategy used for years in war, deception was employed to make an adversary spend time and resources in ultimately futile efforts, thus providing an advantage to the deceiver. Modern deception techniques for cybersecurity supplement the tools actively monitoring for known attack patterns. They aim to lure attackers away from production resources using network decoys and to observe them to gain insight into their latest techniques, tactics, and procedures.

Enterprises are increasingly using mobile, cloud, and virtualization technologies to improve products and offer employees increases in speed and access to their resources; therefore, the definition of the perimeter changes daily. As the perimeter becomes more porous and blurred, adversaries have taken advantage and used the same access to gain illegal entry into systems. We must take steps to adjust to this new paradigm and prepare our systems to address these and future changes. The solutions discussed in the chapter provide the technical means to prepare for and respond to network-based threats.

Our discipline of information security requires a strong understanding of the benefits and limitations of technology, but it also relies on the skillful balance between security and usability. The more we understand the goals of our information systems and the risk associated with each piece of technology, the better off we will be pursuing that balance.

Questions

1. Which of the following is the correct term for a network device designed to deflect attempts to compromise the security of an information system?

   A. ACL

   B. VLAN

   C. Jump box

   D. Honeypot

2. Network Access Control (NAC) can be implemented using all of the following parameters *except* which one?

   A. Domain

   B. Time

   C. Role

   D. Location

3. You are reviewing the access control list (ACL) rules on your edge router. Which of the following ports should normally *not* be allowed outbound through the device?

   A. UDP 53

   B. TCP 23

   C. TCP 80

   D. TCP 25

4. What is the likeliest use for a sinkhole?

   A. To protect legitimate traffic from eavesdropping

   B. To preventing malware from contacting command-and-control systems

   C. To provide ICMP messages to the traffic source

   D. Directing suspicious traffic toward production systems

5. Which of the following is *not* a technique normally used to segregate network traffic in order to thwart the efforts of threat actors?

    A. Micro-segmentation

    B. Virtual LANs

    C. Jump server

    D. NetFlow

6. Which of the following terms is used for an access control mechanism whose employment is deliberately optional?

    A. DAC

    B. MAC

    C. RBAC

    D. EBAC

Refer to the following illustration for Questions 7–9:

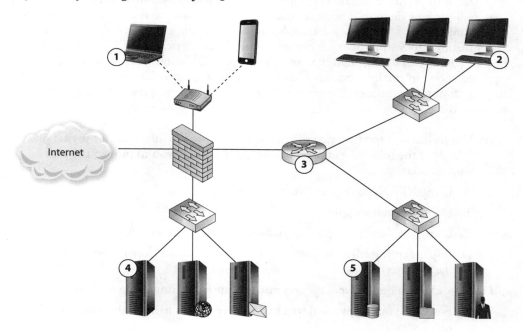

7. Where would be the best location for a honeypot?

    A. Circle 2

    B. Circle 4

    C. Either circle 2 or 5

    D. None of the above

8. Which would be the best location at which to use a sandbox?

    A. Any of the five circled locations

    B. Circle 3

    C. Circles 4 and 5

    D. Circles 1 and 2

9. Where would you expect to find access control lists being used?

    A. Circles 1 and 2

    B. Circle 3

    C. All the above

    D. None of the above

Use the following scenario to answer Questions 10–11:

Your industry sector is facing a wave of intrusions by an overseas crime syndicate. Their approach is to persuade end users to click a link that will exploit their browsers or, failing that, will prompt them to download and install an "update" to their Flash Player. Once they compromise a host, they establish contact with the command-and-control (C2) system using DNS to resolve the ever-changing IP addresses of the C2 nodes. You are part of your sector's Information Sharing and Analysis Center (ISAC), which gives you updated access to the list of domain names. Your company's culture is very progressive, so you cannot take draconian measures to secure your systems, lest you incur the wrath of your young CEO.

10. You realize that the first step should be preventing the infection in the first place. Which of the following approaches would best allow you to protect the user workstations?

    A. Using VLANs to segment your network

    B. Deploying a honeypot

    C. Using sandboxing to provide transparent endpoint security

    D. Implementing MAC so users cannot install software downloaded from the Internet

11. How can you best prevent compromised hosts from connecting to their C2 nodes?

    A. Force all your network devices to resolve names using only your own DNS server.

    B. Deploy a honeypot to attract traffic from the C2 nodes.

    C. Implement a DNS sinkhole using the domain names provided by the ISAC.

    D. Resolve the domain names provided by the ISAC and implement an ACL on your firewall that prevents connections to those IP addresses.

12. You start getting reports of successful intrusions in your network. Which technique lets you contain the damage until you can remediate the infected hosts?

   A. Instruct the users to refrain from using their web browser.

   B. Add the infected host to its own isolated VLAN.

   C. Deploy a jump box.

   D. Install a sandbox on the affected host.

Answers

1. D. Honeypots are fake systems developed to lure threat actors to them, effectively deflecting their attacks. Once the actors start interacting with the honeypot, it may slow them down and allow defenders to either study their techniques or otherwise prevent them from attacking real systems.

2. A. Network Access Control (NAC) uses time, rules, roles, or location to determine whether a device should be allowed on the network. The domain to which the device claims to belong is not used as a parameter to make the access decision.

3. B. TCP port 23 is assigned to telnet, which is an inherently insecure protocol for logging onto remote devices. Even if you allow telnet within your organization, you would almost certainly want to encapsulate it in a secure connection. The other three ports are almost always allowed to travel outbound through a firewall, because DNS (UDP 53), HTTP (TCP 80), and SMTP (TCP 25) are typically required by every organization.

4. B. Sinkholes are most commonly used to divert traffic away from production systems without notifying the source (that is, without sending ICMP messages to it). They do not provide protection from eavesdropping and, quite the opposite, would facilitate analysis of the packets by network defenders. A very common application of sinkholes is to prevent malware from using DNS to resolve the names of command-and-control nodes.

5. D. NetFlow is a system designed to provide statistics on network traffic. Micro-segmentation, virtual LANs, and jump servers (or jump boxes) all provide ways to isolate or segregate network traffic.

6. A. The discretionary access control (DAC) model requires no enforcement by design. The other listed approaches are either mandatory (MAC) or agnostic to enforcement (RBAC and EBAC).

7. B. Honeypots, sinkholes, and black holes should all be deployed as far from production systems as possible. Therefore, the unlabeled server on the DMZ would be the best option.

8. D. Sandboxes are typically used at endpoints when executing code that is not known to be benign. Circles 1 and 2 are end-user workstations, which is where we would normally deploy sandboxes because the users are prone to run code from unknown sources. Because anything running on a router or server should be carefully vetted and approved beforehand, circles 3 and 5 are not where we would normally expect to deploy sandboxes. Circle 4 might be a possible location if it were designated solely for that purpose, but it was bundled with the data server at circle 5, which makes it less than ideal.

9. **C.** Access control lists (ACLs) can be found almost anywhere on a network. Endpoints use them to control which users can read, modify, or execute files, while routers can also use them to control the flow of packets across their interfaces.

10. **C.** Using sandboxes helps protect the endpoints with minimal impact to the users. It would be ideal to prevent them from installing malware, but the organizational culture in the scenario makes that infeasible (for now).

11. **C.** More often than not, malware comes loaded with hostnames and not IP addresses for their C2 nodes. The reason is that a hostname can be mapped to multiple IP addresses over time, making the job of blocking them harder. The DNS sinkhole will resolve all hostnames in a given list of domains to a dead end that simply logs the attempts and alerts the cybersecurity analyst to the infected host. Blocking IPs will not work as well, because those addresses will probably change often.

12. **B.** An extreme form of network segmentation can be used to keep infected hosts connected to the network but unable to communicate with anyone but forensic or remediation devices.

Securing a Corporate Network

In this chapter you will learn:

- Penetration testing
- Reverse engineering
- Training and exercises
- Risk evaluation

Trust, but verify.

—Russian proverb

The title of this chapter might seem a bit misleading because we won't address the entirety of the effort of securing a corporate network. It would take a very long book to do so. In this chapter, we focus on the specific aspects of this effort that would fall in the purview of a cybersecurity analyst. Apart from your daily job in the trenches looking for the telltale signs of nefarious actors in your systems, you will likely be involved in risk evaluations, penetration tests, training, and exercises. You should also be at least familiar with reverse engineering, because it is usually required in the more sophisticated incidents with which you will be involved. Let's start with our favorite: penetration testing.

Penetration Testing

Penetration testing, also known as *pen testing,* is the process of simulating attacks on a network and its systems at the request of the owner, senior management. It uses a set of procedures and tools designed to test and possibly bypass the security controls of a system. Its goal is to measure an organization's level of resistance to an attack and to uncover any weaknesses within the environment. A penetration test emulates the same methods attackers would use, so penetration attacks should align with the hacking tactics, techniques, and procedures (TTPs) of likely adversaries.

The type of penetration test that should be used depends on the organization, its security objectives, and the leadership's goals. Some corporations perform periodic penetration tests on themselves using different types of tools, or they use scanning devices that continually examine the environment for new vulnerabilities in an automated fashion.

Other corporations ask a third party to perform the vulnerability and penetration tests to provide a more objective view.

Penetration tests can evaluate web servers, Domain Name System (DNS) servers, router configurations, workstation vulnerabilities, access to sensitive information, remote dial-in access, open ports, and the properties of available services that a real attacker might use to compromise the company's overall security. Some tests can be quite intrusive and disruptive. The timeframe for the tests should be agreed upon so productivity is not affected and personnel can bring systems back online if necessary.

NOTE Penetration tests are not necessarily restricted to information technology, but may include physical security as well as personnel security. Ultimately, the purpose is to compromise one or more controls, and these could be technical, physical, or operational.

The result of a penetration test is a report given to management that describes the vulnerabilities identified and the severity of those vulnerabilities, along with suggestions on how to deal with them properly. From there, it is up to management to determine how the vulnerabilities are actually dealt with and what countermeasures are implemented.

When performing a penetration test, the team goes through a four-step process called the kill chain:

1. **Reconnaissance** Footprinting and gathering information about the target
2. **Exploitation** Compromising a security control or otherwise gaining illicit access
3. **Lateral movement** Compromising additional systems from the breached one
4. **Report to management** Delivering to management documentation of test findings along with suggested countermeasures

The penetration testing team can have varying degrees of knowledge about the penetration target before the tests are actually carried out:

- **Zero knowledge** The team does not have any knowledge of the target and must start from ground zero. This is also known as *black-box pen testing*.
- **Partial knowledge** The team has some information about the target. This is also known as *gray-box pen testing*.
- **Full knowledge** The team has intimate knowledge of the target. This is also known as *white-box pen testing*.

Rules of Engagement

Robert Frost is famously quoted as saying "good fences make good neighbors." This could not be truer in penetration testing. Many of the tasks involved in this activity are illegal in most countries, absent the consent of the system owner. Even if all legal precautions are in place, the risk of costly disruptions to critical business processes requires careful consideration. Finally, if the penetration testers focus their attention on the wrong targets, the value to the organization may be lessened. For all these reasons, it is absolutely critical to carefully define the timing, scope, authorizations, exploitation techniques, and communication mechanisms before the first cyber shot is fired.

Timing

Penetration tests can be expensive and risky, so it is important to consider timing issues. First of all, the scope of the exercise typically dictates the minimum required duration. Testing the software development subnet on a regional bank can be done a lot quicker than testing a multinational corporation. Part of the responsibility of the project champion is to balance the number of risk areas being tested against the number of days (and concomitant cost) that would be required to thoroughly assess them.

Another timing consideration is during which hours the pen testers will be active. If the test takes place during normal business hours, extra care must be taken to ensure no production systems are adversely affected in a way that could jeopardize real business. This schedule also allows defenders to better react to any detected attacks. Conversely, conducting the test after work hours mitigates the risk against business processes, but may lessen the training value for the defenders. When deciding which approach to use, it may be helpful to consider the time zone in which likely attackers would be operating. If attacks typically come at night or on weekends, then it may be best to allow the pen testing team to operate during those hours as well.

Scope

There is a common misconception that the penetration testers should try to be as realistic as possible and should therefore choose the networks and systems they target. There are many problems with this approach, not the least of which is that the testers must receive assurances that their targets are actually owned by whomever is telling them to attack them. It is not uncommon for organizations to outsource portions of their information infrastructure. Absent a very specific scope for the test, the evaluators run the risk of targeting systems owned by other parties that have not consented to the event.

Typically, a penetration test is scoped in at least two ways: what is definitely in scope and what is surely out of scope. For instance, the organization may provide the testers with specific IP subnets within which any and all nodes are fair game, except for those on a specific list. Apart from business reasons for excluding systems, it is possible that there are regulatory considerations that would forbid probing them. Protected personal healthcare information (PHI) is a notable example of this. If the pen testers successfully compromised a host and extracted PHI, this could be in violation of federal law in the United States.

Having been given a list of "go" and "no-go" systems, the test team will sometimes come across nodes that are not on either list. It is important to define beforehand how these situations will be handled. If an ambiguous node needs to be manually verified, it could consume valuable test time. Some organizations, therefore, either whitelist or blacklist systems for the penetration testers, with whitelisting being the preferred approach.

Authorization

It is critical that senior management be aware of any risks involved in performing a penetration test before it gives the authorization for one. In rare instances, a system or application may be taken down inadvertently using the tools and techniques employed during the test. As expected, the goal of penetration testing is to identify vulnerabilities, estimate the true protection the security mechanisms within the environment are providing, and see how suspicious activity is reported. However, accidents can and do happen.

Security professionals should obtain an authorization letter that includes the extent of the testing authorized, and this letter or memo should be available to members of the team during the testing activity. This type of letter is commonly referred to as a "Get Out of Jail Free Card." Contact information for key personnel should also be available, along with a call tree in the event something does not go as planned and a system must be recovered.

 NOTE A "Get Out of Jail Free Card" is a document you can present to someone who thinks you are up to something malicious, when in fact you are carrying out an approved test. There have been many situations in which an individual (or a team) was carrying out a penetration test and was approached by a security guard or someone who thought this person was in the wrong place at the wrong time.

Exploitation

Exploitation is the act of using a vulnerability in a computer system in order to cause an unintended, unanticipated, or unauthorized behavior to occur in that system. Typically, exploitation involves a compromise to the confidentiality, integrity, or availability of the target. It is the very purpose of conducting a penetration test: to demonstrate that vulnerabilities are actually exploitable and to show how.

Exploitation often involves the use of specially crafted software, data, or commands called *exploits* that trigger the vulnerability and cause the desired behavior. These exploits are not all created equal; some are innocuous while others can cause temporary or even permanent damage to the target. It is because of the latter possibility that the methods of exploitation must be carefully discussed as part of the rules of engagement. It may be acceptable to cause the occasional blue screen of death on a workstation, but the same is typically not true of a production server.

Communication

When things go wrong in a penetration test (which is not all that unusual), the test team must have a clear communication mechanism that has been pre-coordinated. You don't want to wait until you knock over a production server on a Friday evening to start figuring out whom you should call. Along the same lines, how bad do things have to get before the CEO gets a call in the middle of the night? We all hope it never gets to that, but many of us have found ourselves in crisis situations before. It is best to have thought about all possibilities (particularly the really bad ones).

There is another communication consideration during a penetration test: who knows what and when? There are some tests in which the defenders (apart from key leaders) are not aware that a pen testing team is attacking them. This is called a *double-blind test* when neither the penetration testers nor the defenders are given information about each other. The attackers are probing the network (initially) blindly, while the defenders are unaware that the attack is not a real one. Carefully planned communications processes become indispensable when this is the approach to testing.

Reporting

Once the penetration test is over and the interpretation and prioritization are done, the team will provide a detailed report showing many of the ways the company could be successfully attacked. This report usually provides a step-by-step methodology that was shown to be successful as well as recommended ways to mitigate the risk of real attackers doing the same thing. This is the input to the next cycle in what should be a continuous risk management process. All organizations have limited resources, so only a portion of the total risk can be mitigated. Balancing the risks and risk appetite of the company against the costs of possible mitigations and the value gained from each is part of what a cybersecurity analyst must be able to do. An oversight program is required to ensure that the mitigations work as expected and that the estimated cost of each mitigation action is closely tracked by the actual cost of implementation.

Reverse Engineering

Reverse engineering is the process of deconstructing something in order to discover its features and constituents. The features tell us what the system is capable of doing. They tell us *what* a thing can do. The constituents or parts tell us *how* it was put together to do what it does. Reverse engineering is necessary whenever we don't have full documentation for a system but still have to ensure we understand what it does and how.

Hardware

There is a belief that hardware is immutable. That may have once been true, but we are increasingly seeing a move towards software-defined "things" such as radios and networks that used to be implemented almost exclusively in hardware. Increasingly, the use of custom electronics is yielding to an approach by which more generalized hardware platforms are running custom software. This makes both business and technical sense, because it is easier, faster, and cheaper to update software than it is to replace hardware. Still, at some point, we need hardware to run the software, and that software has to be trusted.

Source Authenticity

In 2012, there were multiple reports in the media of counterfeit networking products finding their way into critical networks in both industry and government. By one account, some of these fakes were even found in sensitive military networks. Source authenticity, or the assurance that a product was sourced from an authentic manufacturer, is important for all of us, but particularly so if we handle sensitive information.

Two particular problems with fake products affect a cybersecurity analyst: malicious features and lower quality.

It is not hard to imagine organizations or governments that would want to insert their own fake or modified version of a popular router into a variety of networks. Apart from a source of intelligence or data theft, it could also provide them with remote "kill" switches that could be leveraged for blackmail or in case of hostilities. The problem, of course, is that detecting these hidden features in hardware is often well beyond the means of most organizations. Ensuring your devices are legitimate and came directly from the vendor can greatly decrease this risk.

Another problem with counterfeit hardware is that, even if there is no malicious design, it is probably not built to the same standard as the genuine hardware. It makes no sense for a counterfeiter to invest the same amount of resources into quality assurance and quality control as the genuine manufacturer. Doing so would increase their footprint (and chance of detection) as well as drive their costs up and profit margins down. For most of us, the greatest risk in using counterfeits is that they will fail at a higher rate and in more unexpected ways than the originals. And when they do fail, you won't be able to get support from the legitimate manufacturer.

Counterfeit Products: What Can You Do?

Counterfeits are a very real and growing problem. Fortunately, there are some very basic steps you can take to significantly reduce your exposure to this threat. Here are our top three principles for dealing with counterfeit products.

- **You get what you pay for**   If the price of a device seems too good to be true, it probably is. Much of the appeal of counterfeits is that they can lure customers looking for bargains.
- **Buy from authorized retailers**   Most major manufacturers of networking and security equipment will have a network of retailers authorized to sell their products. Purchasing from these retailers will both decrease your chances of buying a counterfeit and improve your odds of remediation.
- **Check the serial number**   Most manufacturers will have a mechanism for you to verify that a serial number maps to a legitimate product. If the serial number is copied, they will alert you to the duplicate as well.

Trusted Foundry

In their novel *Ghost Fleet,* authors P.W. Singer and August Cole describe a string of battles that go terribly wrong for the U.S. The cause, unbeknownst to the hapless Americans, is a sophisticated program to insert undetectable backdoors into the computer chips that run everything from missiles to ships. Although their account is fictional, there have been multiple reports in the open media about counterfeit products introducing vulnerabilities into networks, including some in the military.

The threat is real. In 2004, the U.S. Department of Defense (DoD) instituted the Trusted Foundry Program. The goal is to ensure that mission-critical military and government systems can be developed and fielded using a supply chain that is hardened against external threats. A *trusted foundry* is an organization capable of developing prototype or production-grade microelectronics in a manner that ensures the integrity of their products. The trust is ensured by the National Security Agency through a special review process. At the time of this writing, 77 vendors were rated as trusted foundries and available to U.S. DoD customers.

OEM Documentation

Original equipment manufacturers (OEMs) almost always provide detailed documentation on the features of their products. They also sometimes provide detailed performance parameters and characteristics that can be used to verify that the product you have is performing as intended. Though OEM documentation is of limited use in reverse engineering hardware, it can be helpful in some cases if you are trying to ensure that your products are genuine.

Reversing Hardware

In the previous sections, we discussed a variety of reasons why you should be suspicious of some hardware devices. If you really want to discover what a device does, and perhaps how, you will need to break it apart to find out. Although the topic of reversing hardware is worthy of its own book, there are some general approaches that can help point you in the right direction for future research.

 NOTE The hardware reverse engineering techniques we discuss in this section will likely void your warranty and could even violate laws in some jurisdictions. Be sure to read your end user license and any legal warnings that apply to your product. If in doubt, check with your legal team before proceeding.

The easiest approach is to simply open the enclosure and take a peek inside. The chips on the boards and their very layout will give you a good starting point. You may be able to search online for photos that others have taken of the product, which would alert you to any suspicious components. Apart from that, you will be able to inventory many of the component chips, because these are almost always distinctly labeled. Chip manufacturers publish technical datasheets with detailed information about their products. These not only tell you what the chip does, but they also provide very specific information about every input and output pin on the chip. Figure 4-1 shows the block diagram for an Analog Devices analog-to-digital (A/D) converter, with detailed pin information.

Firmware is software that is permanently (or semi-permanently) programmed into read-only memory (ROM) on a hardware component. If you really want to know what a device does, you will probably have to extract the firmware and analyze it. You will likely need a general-purpose ROM programmer because these have the ability to read the

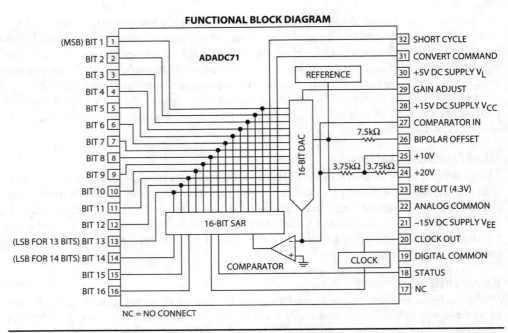

FUNCTIONAL BLOCK DIAGRAM

Figure 4-1 Functional block diagram from a technical datasheet

software (for the purpose of verifying the write operation). You may need a chip-specific tool you could obtain from the manufacturer. Either way, you will end up with binary code, which you will have to reverse engineer too. We'll get to software reversing in the next section.

Another approach to reverse engineering hardware is to capture the signals at its interfaces and analyze them. This can be done at the device level using a packet analyzer, which will give you a high-level view of the communications patterns. You can also look at the raw voltage level fluctuations using an oscilloscope or logic analyzer. These tools tend to be expensive, but they tell you exactly what is happening at the physical layer. With these tools, you can also monitor individual chip component behaviors and even inject your own inputs to see if there are any hidden features.

Software/Malware

As interesting and important as hardware reverse engineering is, most of us are likelier to be involved in efforts to reverse software and, in particular, malware. The process requires in-depth understanding of the architecture of the processors on which the software is intended to run. Reversing binaries is significantly different for ARM processors compared to x86 processors. The principles are the same, but the devil, as they say, is in the details.

Fingerprinting/Hashing

Sometimes we can save ourselves a lot of trouble by simply fingerprinting or hashing known-good or known-bad binary executable files. Just like fingerprints have an astronomically small probability of not being unique among humans, the result of running a file through a secure hashing function is extremely unlikely to be the same for any two files. The net result is that, when you compute the SHA-256 value of a known-good file like a Windows Dynamically Linked Library (DLL), the probability of an adversary modifying that file in any way (even by changing a single bit) and having it produce the same hash value is remote. But we are getting ahead of ourselves here.

A *hashing function* is a one-way function that takes a variable-length sequence of data such as a file and produces a fixed-length result called a "hash value." For example, if you want to ensure a given file does not get altered in an unauthorized fashion, you would calculate a hash value for the file and store it in a secure location. When you want to ensure the integrity of that file, you would perform the same hashing function and then compare the new result with the hash value you previously stored. If the two values are the same, you can be sure the file was not altered. If the two values are different, you would know the file was modified, either maliciously or otherwise, so you would then investigate the event.

We can also apply hashes to malware detection. We discussed full packet captures in Chapter 2, and one of the benefits of doing this is that you can assemble binaries that are transported across the network. Having those, you can take a hash of the suspicious file and compare it to a knowledge base of known-bad hashes. One of the indispensable tools in any analyst's toolkit is VirusTotal.com, a website owned and operated by Google that allows you to upload the hashes (or entire files) and see if anyone else has reported them as malicious or suspicious before. Figure 4-2 shows the results of submitting a hash for a suspicious file that has been reported as malicious by 40 out of 40 respondents.

 NOTE Uploading binaries to VirusTotal will allow the entire worldwide community, potentially including the malware authors, to see that someone is suspicious about these files. There are many documented cases of threat actors modifying their code as soon as it shows up on VirusTotal.

Decomposition

We can tell you from personal experience that not every suspicious file is tracked by VirusTotal. Sometimes, you have to dig into the code yourself to see what it does. In these situations, it is important to consider that computers and people understand completely different languages. The language of a computer, which is dictated by the architecture of its hardware, consists of patterns of ones and zeroes. People, on the other hand, use words that are put together according to syntactical rules. In order for people to tell computers what to do, which is what we call "programming," there must be some mechanism that translates the words that humans use into the binary digits that computers use. This is the job of the compiler and the assembler. As Figure 4-3 shows, a human programmer writes code in a high-level language like C, which is compiled to assembly language, which is in turn assembled into a binary executable.

Figure 4-2 VirusTotal showing the given hash corresponds to a malicious file

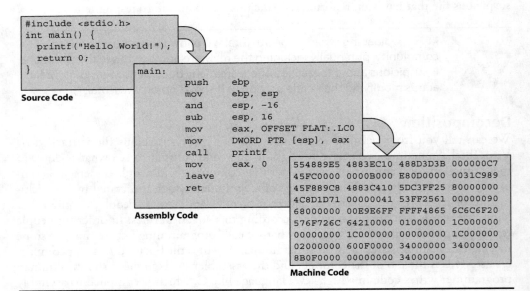

Figure 4-3 Source code being compiled and then assembled

Binary executables are specific to an operating system and processor family, which means that you cannot run a Linux program on a Windows machine. Windows programs are packaged in what is known as the Portable Executable (PE) format, in which every file starts with the 2-byte sequence 5A 4D (or 4D 5A, depending on which operating system you are using to inspect the file). By contrast, Linux executables are in what is known as the Executable and Linkable Format (ELF), in which every file starts with the 4-byte sequence 7F 45 4C 46. These starting sequences, or "magic numbers," allow you to quickly determine which operating system is targeted by a given malware sample.

Generations of Computer Languages

In many aspects of our lives, successive generations are better than their predecessors and render the latter obsolescent. Not so when describing computer languages. These generations coexist in modern computing systems and will likely continue to do so for the foreseeable future.

- **First generation** When computers were first invented, the only way to program them was to do so in *machine language,* which is a sequence of operators and arguments represented as sequences of ones and zeros, sometimes represented in hexadecimal. This language is very specific to a particular family of processors (for example, Intel x86) and very difficult for most programmers to understand.

- **Second generation** Programming in machine language is absolutely no fun, and it is very prone to errors. It is not surprising that it didn't take us long to come up with a more human-friendly way to program. Assembly language represents machine language operators and arguments using easier-to-remember operation codes (opcodes) and symbolic variables. Because we still have to somehow get to machine language, we invented the assemblers, which turn second-generation assembly language into machine code.

- **Third generation** Assembly language was a huge step in the right direction, but it still required significant expertise about a particular computer architecture. Some very smart people decided it would be nice to be able to program in a more human-like language without having to know about the underlying architecture. This epiphany led to the invention of languages such as BASIC, Pascal, C/C++, Java, and Python. We still had to get down to machine language, but this time we got to leverage the assemblers we already created. The missing part is the compiler, which translates third-generation programming languages into assembly language, which is then turned by the assembler into machine code.

When we are analyzing malware, it is a rare thing to have access to the source code. Instead, all we usually get is a machine language binary file. In order to reverse engineer this program, we need a disassembler, such as IDA Pro. The disassembler converts the machine language back into assembly language, which can then be analyzed by a reverse engineer. Some decompilers also exist, but those are more "hit or miss" because there are many possible programs that would compile to a given assembly language file. This means that, on average, decompilers are not worth the effort.

Isolation/Sandboxing

We already touched on isolation techniques and sandboxing in Chapter 3 in the context of endpoint protection. Now we return to it for the purpose of more deliberate assessments of what hardware and software are actually doing. Sometimes we are unable or unwilling to invest the effort into reverse engineering a binary executable, but still want to find out what it does. This is where an isolation environment or sandbox comes in handy. Unlike endpoint protection sandboxes, this variety of tools is usually instrumented to assist the security analyst in understanding what a running executable is doing.

Cuckoo Sandbox is a popular open source isolation environment for malware analysis. It uses either VirtualBox or VMware Workstation to create a virtual computer on which to safely run the suspicious binary. Unlike other environments, Cuckoo is just as capable in Windows, Linux, Mac OS, or Android virtual devices. Another tool with which you may want to experiment is REMnux, which is a Linux distribution loaded with malware reverse engineering tools.

Training and Exercises

General George Patton is famously quoted as having said "you fight like you train," but this idea, in various forms, has spread to a multitude of groups beyond the Army. It speaks to the fact that each of us has two mental systems: the first is a fast and reflexive one, and the second is slow and analytical. Periodic, realistic training develops and maintains the "muscle memory" of the first system, ensuring that reflexive actions are good ones. In the thick of a fight, bombarded by environmental information in the form of sights, sounds, smells, and pain, soldiers don't have the luxury of processing it all, and must almost instantly make the right calls. So do we when we are responding to security incidents on our networks.

Admittedly, the decision times in combat and incident response are orders of magnitude apart, but you cannot afford to learn or rediscover the standard operating procedures when you are faced with a real incident. We have worked with organizations in which seconds can literally mean the loss of millions of dollars. The goal of your programs for training and exercises should then be to ensure that all team members have the muscle memory to quickly handle the predictable issues and, in so doing, create the time to be deliberate and analytical about the others.

The general purpose of a training event is to develop or maintain a specific set of skills, knowledge, or attributes that allow individuals or groups to do their jobs effectively or better. An *exercise* is an event in which individuals or groups apply relevant skills, knowledge, or attributes in a particular scenario. Although it could seem that training is a prerequisite for exercises (and, indeed, many organizations take this approach), it is also possible for exercises to be training events in their own right.

All training events and exercises should start with a set of goals or outcomes, as well as a way to assess whether or not those were achieved. This makes sense on at least two levels: at an operational level, it tells you whether you were successful in your endeavor or need to do it again (perhaps in a different way), and at a managerial level it tells decision makers whether or not the investment of resources is worth the results. Training and exercises tend to be resource intensive and should be applied with prudence.

Types of Exercises

Though cybersecurity exercises can have a large number of potential goals, they tend to be focused on testing tactics, techniques, and procedures (TTPs) for dealing with incidents and/or assessing the effectiveness of defensive teams in dealing with incidents. Either way, a key to success is to choose scenarios that facilitate the assessment process. The two major types of cybersecurity exercises are tabletop and live-fire.

Tabletop Exercises

Tabletop exercises (TTXs) may or may not happen at a tabletop, but they do not involve a technical control infrastructure. TTXs can happen at the executive level (for example, CEO, CIO, or CFO), at the team level (for example, security operations center or SOC), or anywhere in between. The idea is usually to test out procedures and ensure they actually do what they're intended to and that everyone knows their role in responding to an event. TTXs require relatively few resources apart from deliberate planning by qualified individuals and the undisturbed time and attention of the participants.

After determining the goals of the exercise and vetting them with the senior leadership of the organization, the planning team develops a scenario that touches on the important aspects of the response plan. The idea is normally not to cover every contingency, but to ensure the team is able to respond to the likeliest and/or most dangerous scenarios. As they develop the exercise, the planning team will consider branches and sequels at every point in the scenario. A *branch* is a point at which the participants may choose one of multiple approaches to the response. If the branches are not carefully managed and controlled, the TTX could wander into uncharted and unproductive directions. Conversely, a *sequel* is a follow-on to a given action in the response. For instance, as part of the response, the strategic communications team may issue statements to the news media. A sequel to that could involve a media outlet challenging the statement, which in turn would require a response by the team. Like branches, sequels must be carefully used in order to keep the exercise on course. Senior leadership support and good scenario development are critical ingredients to attract and engage the right participants. Like any contest, a TTX is only as good as the folks who show up to play.

Live-Fire Exercises

A *live-fire exercise* (LFX) is one in which the participants are defending real or simulated information systems against real (though friendly) attackers. There are many challenges in organizing one of these events, but the major ones are developing an infrastructure that is representative of the real systems, getting a good red (adversary) team, and getting the right blue (defending) team members in the room for the duration of the exercise. Any one of these, by itself, is a costly proposition. However, you need all three for a successful event.

On the surface, getting a good cyber range does not seem like a major challenge. After all, many or our systems are virtualized to begin with, so cloning several boxes should be easy. The main problem is that you cannot use production boxes for a cyber exercise because you would compromise the confidentiality, integrity, and perhaps availability of real-world information and systems. Manually creating a replica of even one of your subnets takes time and resources, but is doable given the right level of support. Still, you won't have any pattern-of-life (POL) traffic on the network. POL is what makes networks realistic. It's the usual chatter of users visiting myriads of websites, exchanging e-mail messages, and interacting with data stores. Absent POL traffic, every packet on the network can be assumed to come from the red team.

A possible solution would be to have a separate team of individuals who simply provide this by simulating real-world work for the duration of the event. Unless you have a bunch of interns with nothing better to do, this gets cost-prohibitive really fast. A reasonable compromise is to have a limited number of individuals logged into many accounts, thus multiplying the effect. Another approach is to invest in a traffic generator that automatically injects packets. Your mileage will vary, but these solutions are not very realistic and will be revealed as fake by even a cursory examination. A promising area of research is in the creation of autonomous agents that interact with the various nodes on the network and simulate real users. Through the use of artificial intelligence, the state of the art is improving, but we are not there just yet.

Red Team

A red team is a group that acts as adversaries during an exercise. The red team need not be "hands on keyboard" because red-teaming extends to TTXs as well as LFXs. These individuals need to be very skilled at whatever area they are trying to disrupt. If they are part of a TTX and trying to commit fraud, they need to know fraud and anti-fraud activities at least as well as the exercise participants. If the defenders (or blue team members) as a group are more skilled than the red team, the exercise will not be effective or well-received.

This requirement for a highly skilled red team is problematic for a number of reasons. First of all, skills and pay tend to go hand-in-hand, which means these individuals will be expensive. Because their skills are so sought after, they may not even be available for the event. Additionally, some organizations may not be willing or able to bring in external personnel to exploit flaws in their systems even if they have signed a nondisclosure agreement (NDA). These challenges sometimes cause organizations to use their own staff for the red team. If your organization has people whose full-time job is to red team or pen test, then this is probably fine. However, few organizations have such individuals on their staff, which means that using internal assets may be less expensive but will probably reduce the value of the event. In the end, you get what you pay for.

Blue Team

The blue team is the group of participants who are the focus of an exercise. They perform the same tasks during a notional event as they would perform in their real jobs if the scenario was real. Though others will probably also benefit from the exercise, it is the blue team that is tested and/or trained the most. The team's composition depends on the scope of the event. However, because responding to events and incidents typically requires coordinated actions by multiple groups within an organization, it is important to ensure that each of these groups is represented in the blue team.

The biggest challenge in assembling the blue team is that they will not be available to perform their daily duties for the duration of the exercise as well as for any pre- or post-event activities. For some organizations, this is too high of a cost and they end up sending the people they can afford to be without, rather than those who really should be participating. If this happens, the exercise might be of great training value for these participants, but may not allow the organization as a whole to assess its level of readiness. Senior or executive leadership involvement and support will be critical to keep this from happening.

White Team

The white team consists of anyone who will plan, document, assess, or moderate the exercise. Although it is tempting to think of the members of the white team as the referees, they do a lot more than that. These are the individuals who come up with the scenario, working in concert with business unit leads and other key advisors. They structure the schedule so that the goals of the exercise are accomplished and every participant is gainfully employed. During the conduct of the event, the white team documents the actions of the participants and interferes as necessary to ensure they don't stray from the flow of the exercise. They may also delay some participants' actions to maintain synchronization. Finally, the white team is normally in charge of conducting an after-action review by documenting and sharing their observations (and, potentially, assessments) with key personnel.

Risk Evaluation

Risk is the possibility of damage to or loss of any information system asset, as well as the ramifications should this occur. It is common to think of risk as the product of its impact on the organization and the likelihood of this risk materializing. For example, if you are considering the risk of a ransomware infection, the value of the assets could be measured by either the expected ransom (assuming you decide to pay it) or the cost to restore all the systems from backup (assuming you have those backups in the first place) or the cost to your business of never getting that information back.

Clearly, not all risks are equal. If you use the formula of value times probability, the result could give you an idea of the risks you ought to address first. Presumably, you would focus on the greatest risks first, since they have a higher value or probability (or both) than other risks on your list. There is another advantage to using this quantitative approach: it helps you determine whether the cost of mitigating the risk is appropriate. Suppose that a given risk has a value of $10,000 and can be mitigated by a control that costs only $1,000. Implementing that control would make perfect sense and would probably not be difficult for you to get support from your leadership.

Risk evaluation is the process of ranking risks, categorizing them, and determining which controls can mitigate them to an acceptable business value. There is no such thing as a 100 percent secure environment, which means that the risks will always have a value greater than zero. The main purpose of a risk evaluation is to help us balance the value of a risk with the cost of a control that mitigates it.

Impact and Likelihood

The two approaches to quantifying impacts and likelihood are quantitative and qualitative. A *quantitative analysis* is used to assign numeric (for example, monetary) values to all assets that could be impacted by a given risk. Each element within the analysis (for example, asset value, threat frequency, severity of vulnerability, impact damage, safeguard costs, safeguard effectiveness, uncertainty, and probability items) is quantified and entered into equations to determine total and residual risks. It is more of a scientific or mathematical approach to risk evaluation compared to qualitative. A *qualitative analysis* uses a "softer" approach to the data elements of a risk evaluation. It does not quantify that data, which means that it does not assign numeric values to the data so that they can be used in equations. As an example, the results of a quantitative risk analysis could be that the organization is at risk of losing $100,000 if a buffer overflow is exploited on a web server, $25,000 if a database is compromised, and $10,000 if a file server is compromised. A qualitative analysis would not present these findings in monetary values, but would assign ratings to the risks such as high, medium, and low. A common technique for doing qualitative analysis that yields numeric values is to replace the "high" category with the number 3, "medium" would be 2, and "low" would be 1. We will focus on the qualitative analysis in this book.

Examples of qualitative techniques to gather data are brainstorming, storyboarding, focus groups, surveys, questionnaires, checklists, one-on-one meetings, and interviews. The team that is performing the risk evaluation gathers personnel who have experience and education on the threats being evaluated. When this group is presented with a scenario that describes risks and loss potential, each member responds with their gut feeling and experience on the likelihood of the threat and the extent of damage that may result.

The expert in the group who is most familiar with this type of risk should review the scenario to ensure it reflects how the risk would materialize. Safeguards that would diminish the damage of this risk are then evaluated, and the scenario is played out for each safeguard. The exposure possibility and loss possibility can be ranked as high, medium, or low on a scale of 1 to 5, or 1 to 10. A common qualitative risk matrix is shown in Figure 4-4. Keep in mind that this matrix is just an example. Your organization may prioritize risks differently.

 EXAM TIP You should be able to categorize impacts and likelihoods as being high, medium, or low for the exam. With those categories, you should then be able to evaluate the fitness of technical and operational controls.

Once the selected personnel rank the possibility of a threat happening, the loss potential, and the advantages of each safeguard, this information is compiled into a report and presented to management to help it make better decisions on how best to implement safeguards into the environment. The benefits of this type of analysis are that communication must happen among team members to rank the risks, safeguard strengths, and

Likelihood	Impact				
	Insignificant	Minor	Moderate	Major	Severe
Very Likely	Medium	Medium	High	High	High
Likely	Medium	Medium	Medium	High	High
Possible	Low	Low	Medium	High	High
Unlikely	Low	Low	Medium	Medium	Medium
Rare	Low	Low	Medium	Medium	Medium

Figure 4-4 Qualitative analysis of likelihood versus impact

identify weaknesses, and the people who know these subjects the best provide their opinions to management.

Let's look at a simple example of a qualitative risk analysis. The risk analysis team presents a scenario explaining the threat of a hacker accessing confidential information held on the five file servers within the company. The risk analysis team then distributes the scenario in a written format to a team of five people (the cybersecurity analyst, database administrator, application programmer, system operator, and operational manager), who are also given a sheet to rank the threat's severity, loss potential, and each safeguard's effectiveness, with a rating of 1 to 5, 1 being the least severe, effective, or probable. Table 4-1 shows the results.

Risk: Ransomware	Likelihood of Risk Taking Place	Potential Loss to the Company	Effectiveness of Network Backups	Effectiveness of Intrusion Prevention System	Effectiveness of Security Awareness
Cybersecurity analyst	2	4	4	3	1
Database administrator	4	4	3	4	1
Application programmer	3	3	4	2	1
System operator	4	3	4	2	2
Operational manager	4	4	4	4	2
Results	3.4	3.6	3.8	3	1.4

Table 4-1 Example of a Qualitative Analysis

This data is compiled and inserted into a report and presented to management. When management is presented with this information, it will see that its staff (or a chosen set) feels that purchasing a network-based managed backup system will protect the company from this threat more than purchasing an intrusion prevention system or implementing user security awareness training. This is the result of looking at only one threat, and management will view the severity, probability, and loss potential of each risk so it knows which should be addressed first.

Avoiding Group Biases

It is ideal to perform risk evaluations as a group, but this could also introduce the problem of group biases. These biases, sometimes called groupthink, can cause the group members to arrive at similar results when evaluating issues such as likelihood, impact, and effectiveness. The following are tips for ensuring everyone presents their own opinions untarnished by those of others:

- Keep the group small (no more than 12).
- Have participants quietly write down opinions before sharing them.
- Encourage respectful disagreements.
- Include plenty of time for discussion, but also put a time limit.

Technical Control Review

Technical controls (also called logical controls) are security controls implemented mainly through software or hardware components, as in firewalls, IDS, encryption, identification, and authentication mechanisms. A *technical control review* is a deliberate assessment of technical control choices and how they are implemented and managed. You may have decided during your risk evaluation that a firewall might be the best control against a particular risk, but several months later how do you know it is working as you intended it to? Apart from ensuring that it is still the best choice against a given risk, the review considers issues like the ones listed here:

- Is the control version up to date?
- Is it configured properly to handle the risk?
- Do the right people (and no others) have access to manage the control?
- Are licenses and/or support contracts current?

Even in organizations that practice strict configuration management, it is common to find hardware or software that were forgotten or that still have account access for individuals who are no longer in the organization. Additionally, the effectiveness of a technical control can be degraded or even annulled if the threat actor changes procedures. These are just some of the reasons why it makes sense to periodically review technical controls.

Operational Control Review

Operational controls (also called policy or administrative controls) are security controls implemented through business processes and codified in documents such as policy letters or standing operating procedures (SOPs). Examples of administrative controls are security documentation, risk management, personnel security, and training. Unlike technical controls, operational controls typically require no purchases.

Like technical controls, our policies can become outdated, Furthermore, it is possible that people are just not following them, or attempting to do so in the wrong way. An *operational control review* is a deliberate assessment of operational control choices and how they are implemented and managed. The review first validates that the controls are still the best choice against a given risk, and then considers issues like the ones listed here:

- Is the control consistent with all applicable laws, regulations, policies, and directives?
- Are all affected members of the organization aware of the control?
- Is the control part of newcomer or periodic refresher training for the affected personnel?
- Is the control being followed?

Operational controls, like technical ones, can become ineffective with time. Taking the time to review their effectiveness and completeness is an important part of any security program.

Chapter Review

This chapter was all about proactive steps you can take to ensure the security of your corporate environment. The implication of this discussion is that security is not something you architect once and then walk away from. It is a set of challenges and opportunities that needs to be revisited periodically and even frequently. You may have done a very through risk analysis and implemented appropriate controls, but six months later many of those may be moot. You wouldn't know this to be the case unless you periodically (and formally) review your controls for continued effectiveness. It is also wise to conduct periodic penetration tests to ensure that the more analytical exercise of managing risks actually translates to practical results on the real systems. Control reviews and pen tests will validate that your security architecture is robust.

There are also issues that go beyond the architecture. Regardless of how well you secure your environment, sooner or later you will face a suspicious hardware device or executable file that needs to be analyzed. Though having the in-house skills to reverse engineer hardware or software is not within the reach of every organization, as an analyst you need to be aware of what the issues are and where to find those who can help.

Finally, the human component of your information systems must also be considered. Training is absolutely essential both to maintain skills and to update awareness to current issues of concern. However, simply putting the right information into the heads of your colleagues is not necessarily enough. It is best to test their performance under conditions that are as realistic as possible in either table-top or live-fire exercises. This is where you will best be able to tell whether the people are as prepared as the devices and software to combat the ever-changing threats to your organization.

Questions

1. The practice of moving, or pivoting, from a compromised machine to another machine on the network is referred to as what?

    A. Exploitation

    B. Trusted foundry

    C. Decomposition

    D. Lateral movement

2. Which is not a consideration to take during a penetration test?

    A. None, the goal is to be as realistic as possible.

    B. Personal healthcare information.

    C. Time limitations.

    D. Effects on production services.

3. Who is the ultimate giver of consent for a penetration test?

    A. The penetration tester or analyst

    B. The security company

    C. The system owner

    D. The FBI

4. In an exercise, which type of team is the focus of the exercise, performing their duties as they would normally in day-to-day operations?

    A. Blue team

    B. Red team

    C. Gray team

    D. White team

5. Which of the following addresses the vulnerabilities associated with component supply chains?

    A. Exploitation bank

    B. Partial knowledge

    C. Reporting chain

    D. Trusted foundry

Refer to the following illustration for Questions 6 and 7:

0	4D5A9000	03000000	04000000	FFFF0000	B8000000	MZê ¨¨ ∏
20	00000000	40000000	00000000	00000000	00000000	@
40	00000000	00000000	00000000	00000000	00000000	
60	80000000	0E1FBA0E	00B409CD	21B8014C	CD215468	Ä ∫ ¥ Õ!∏ LÕ!Th
80	69732070	726F6772	616D2063	616E6E6F	74206265	is program cannot be
100	2072756E	20696E20	444F5320	6D6F6465	2E0D0D0A	run in DOS mode.
120	24000000	00000000	50450000	4C010700	8C753853	$ PE L âu8S
140	00000000	00000000	E0000F03	0B010217	00320000	‡ 2
160	00340000	00020000	00100000	00100000	00500000	4 P
180	00004000	00100000	00020000	04000000	01000000	@
200	04000000	00000000	00C00000	00040000	0C940000	¿ î
220	03004001	00002000	00100000	00001000	00100000	@
240	00000000	10000000	00000000	00000000	00900000	ê

6. You are analyzing a suspicious executable you suspect to be malware. In what language is this file being viewed?

   A. Natural language

   B. High-level language

   C. Assembly language

   D. Machine language

7. Which operating system is this program designed for?

   A. Linux

   B. Windows

   C. Mac OS

   D. iOS

8. What two factors are considered in making a quantitative assessment on risk?

   A. Expected value and probability of occurrence

   B. Expected value and probability of vulnerability

   C. Potential loss and probability of occurrence

   D. Potential loss and expected value

Use the following scenario to answer Questions 9–12:

Your company was hired to perform a penetration test on a small financial services company. The company has no in-house expertise in security assessments and is relying on your team to help them addresses their challenges. The Chief Information Officer invites you to review the network with his network engineer. Since they are a small company, the engineer tells you that they haven't been targeted for many attacks. Additionally, most of the production systems see the most traffic during local business hours of 9 A.M. to 5 P.M., and they cannot, under any circumstances, be disrupted.

9. Based on the meeting with the CIO, what kind of penetration test will you be conducting?

    A. Partial knowledge

    B. Red box

    C. Total recall

    D. Zero knowledge

10. Before leaving the office, you ask the CIO to provide which formal document authorizing you to perform certain activities on the network?

    A. Syslogs

    B. Network flows

    C. Certificate Authority

    D. Authorization memo

11. Considering the scope of this test, what is your recommendation for the best times to conduct the test?

    A. Any time during normal business hours

    B. Beginning at 7 P.M.

    C. Over lunchtime

    D. Exactly at 9 A.M.

12. You complete the pen test and are preparing the final report. Which areas should you normally *not* include in the deliverables?

    A. Information that could be gleaned about the company from open sources

    B. Specific exploitable technical features of the network

    C. Audit of the existing physical infrastructure

    D. Full packet captures

Answers

1. **D.** Lateral movement is the act of compromising additional systems from the initially breached one.

2. **A.** A successful penetration requires lots of preparation, which includes defining the scope, objectives, off-limit areas, timing, and duration of the test.

3. **C.** Consent of the system owner is critical for a penetration test because many of the tasks involved in this activity are illegal in most countries.

4. **A.** The blue team is the group of participants who are the focus of an exercise and will be tested the most while performing the same tasks in a notional event as they would perform in their real jobs.

5. **D.** A trusted foundry is an organization capable of developing prototype or production-grade microelectronics in a manner that ensures the integrity of their products.

6. **D.** Machine language is represented as a series of ones and zeroes, or sometimes (as in the illustration) in hexadecimal.

7. **B.** Windows executables always start with the byte sequence 5A4D or 4D5A, depending on which operating system you are using to inspect the file. They also typically include the string "This program cannot be run in DOS mode" for backward compatibility.

8. **C.** Quantitative risk assessment is calculated using the amount of the potential loss and the probability that the loss will occur.

9. **A.** Because the CIO and network engineer provided you with upfront information about the target, you have partial knowledge about this system.

10. **D.** An authorization memo includes the extent of the testing authorized, and should be made available to team members during the testing period.

11. **B.** Because the CIO prioritizes uptime of critical production systems, it's best to avoid performing the pen test during those hours.

12. **D.** Penetration testing isn't restricted to technology only. The report should cover all discovered vulnerabilities in physical and information security, including the successful use of social engineering. You would normally not want to include full packet captures because, absent specific authorizations, this could lead to privacy or regulatory problems.

PART II

Vulnerability Management

- **Chapter 5** Implementing Vulnerability Management Processes
- **Chapter 6** Vulnerability Scanning

Implementing Vulnerability Management Processes

In this chapter you will learn:

- The requirements for a vulnerability management process
- How to determine the frequency of vulnerability scans you need
- The types of vulnerabilities found in various systems
- Considerations when configuring tools for scanning

Of old, the expert in battle would first make himself invincible and then wait for his enemy to expose his vulnerability.

—Sun Tzu

Vulnerability Management Requirements

Like many other areas in life, vulnerability management involves a combination of things we want to do, things we should do, and things we have to do. Assuming you don't need help with the first, we'll focus our attention for this chapter on the latter two. First of all, we have to identify the requirements that we absolutely have to satisfy. Broadly speaking, these come from external authorities (for example, laws and regulations), internal authorities (for example, organizational policies and executive directives) and best practices. This last source may be a bit surprising to some, but keep in mind that we are required to display due diligence in our application of security principles to protecting our information systems. To do otherwise risks liability issues and even our very jobs.

Regulatory Environments

A *regulatory environment* is an environment in which an organization exists or operates that is controlled to a significant degree by laws, rules, or regulations put in place by government (federal, state, or local), industry groups, or other organizations. In a nutshell, it is what happens when you have to play by someone else's rules, or else risk serious consequences. A common feature of regulatory environments is that they have enforcement groups and procedures to deal with noncompliance.

You, as a cybersecurity analyst, might have to take action in a number of ways to ensure compliance with one or more regulatory requirements. A sometimes-overlooked example is the type of contract that requires one of the parties to ensure certain conditions are met with regard to information systems security. It is not uncommon, particularly when dealing with the government, to be required to follow certain rules, such as preventing access by foreign nationals to certain information or ensuring everyone working on the contract is trained on proper information-handling procedures.

In this section, we discuss some of the most important regulatory requirements with which you should be familiar in the context of vulnerability management. The following three standards cover the range from those that are completely optional to those that are required by law.

ISO/IEC 27001 Standard

The International Organization for Standardization (ISO, despite the apparent discrepancy in the order of the initials) and the International Electrotechnical Commission (IEC) jointly maintain a number of standards, including 27001, which covers Information Security Management Systems (ISMS). ISO/IEC 27001 is arguably the most popular voluntary security standard in the world and covers every important aspect of developing and maintaining good information security. One of its provisions, covered in control number A.12.6.1, deals with vulnerability management.

This control, whose implementation is required for certification, essentially states that the organization has a documented process in place for timely identification and mitigation of known vulnerabilities. ISO/IEC 27001 certification, which is provided by an independent certification body, is performed in three stages. First, a desk-side audit verifies that the organization has documented a reasonable process for managing its vulnerabilities. The second stage is an implementation audit aimed at ensuring that the documented process is actually being carried out. Finally, surveillance audits confirm that the process continues to be followed and improved upon.

Payment Card Industry Data Security Standard

The Payment Card Industry Data Security Standard (PCI DSS) applies to any organization involved in processing credit card payments using cards branded by the five major issuers (Visa, MasterCard, American Express, Discover, and JCB). Each of these organizations had its own vendor security requirements, so in 2006 they joined efforts and standardized these requirements across the industry. The PCI DSS is periodically updated and, as of this writing, is in version 3.2.

Requirement 11 of the PCI DSS deals with the obligation to "regularly test security systems and processes," and Section 2 describes the requirements for vulnerability scanning. Specifically, it states that the organization must perform two types of vulnerability scans every quarter: internal and external. The difference is that internal scans use qualified members of the organization, whereas external scans must be performed by approved scanning vendors (ASVs). It is important to know that the organization must be able to show that the personnel involved in the scanning have the required expertise to do so. Requirement 11 also states that both internal and external vulnerability scans must be performed whenever there are significant changes to the systems or processes.

Finally, PCI DSS requires that any "high-risk" vulnerabilities uncovered by either type of scan be resolved. After resolution, another scan is required to demonstrate that the risks have been properly mitigated.

Health Insurance Portability and Accountability Act

The Health Insurance Portability and Accountability Act (HIPAA) establishes penalties (ranging from $100 to $1.5 million) for covered entities that fail to safeguard protected health information (PHI). Though HIPAA does not explicitly call out a requirement to conduct vulnerability assessments, Section 164.308(a)(1)(i) requires organizations to conduct accurate and thorough vulnerability assessments and to implement security measures that are sufficient to reduce the risks presented by those assessed vulnerabilities to a reasonable level. Any organization that violates the provisions of this act, whether willfully or through negligence or even ignorance, faces steep civil penalties.

 EXAM TIP You do not have to memorize the provisions of ISO/IEC 27001, PCI DSS, or HIPAA, but you need to know there are regulatory environments that require vulnerability management. Although these examples are intended to be illustrative of the exam requirement, being somewhat familiar with them will be helpful.

Corporate Security Policy

A *corporate security policy* is an overall general statement produced by senior management (or a selected policy board or committee) that dictates what role security plays within the organization. Security policies can be organizational, issue specific, or system specific. In an organizational security policy, management establishes how a security program will be set up, lays out the program's goals, assigns responsibilities, shows the strategic and tactical value of security, and outlines how enforcement should be carried out. An issue-specific policy, also called a *functional policy*, addresses specific security issues that management feels need more detailed explanation and attention to make sure a comprehensive structure is built and all employees understand how they are to comply with these security issues. A system-specific policy presents the management's decisions that are specific to the actual computers, networks, and applications.

Typically, organizations will have an issue-specific policy covering vulnerability management, but it is important to note that this policy is nested within the broader corporate security policy and may also be associated with system-specific policies. The point is that it is not enough to understand the vulnerability management policy (or develop one if it doesn't exist) in a vacuum. We must understand the organizational security context within which this process takes place.

Data Classification

An important item of metadata that should be attached to all data is a classification level. This classification tag is important in determining the protective controls we apply to the information. The rationale behind assigning values to different types of data is that it

PART II

enables a company to gauge the resources that should go toward protecting each type of data because not all of it has the same value to the company. There are no hard-and-fast rules on the classification levels an organization should use. Typical classification levels include the following:

- **Private**   Information whose improper disclosure could raise personal privacy issues
- **Confidential**   Data that could cause grave damage to the organization
- **Proprietary (or sensitive)**   Data that could cause some damage, such as loss of competitiveness to the organization
- **Public**   Data whose release would have no adverse effect on the organization

Each classification should be unique and separate from the others and not have any overlapping effects. The classification process should also outline how information is controlled and handled throughout its life cycle (from creation to termination). The following list shows some criteria parameters an organization might use to determine the sensitivity of data:

- The level of damage that could be caused if the data were disclosed
- The level of damage that could be caused if the data were modified or corrupted
- Lost opportunity costs that could be incurred if the data is not available or is corrupted
- Legal, regulatory, or contractual responsibility to protect the data
- Effects the data has on security
- The age of data

Asset Inventory

You cannot protect what you don't know you have. Though inventorying assets is not what most of us would consider glamorous, it is nevertheless a critical aspect of managing vulnerabilities in your information systems. In fact, this aspect of security is so important that it is prominently featured at the top of the Center for Internet Security's (CIS's) Critical Security Controls (CSC). CSC #1 is the inventory of authorized and unauthorized devices, and CSC #2 deals with the software running on those devices.

Keep in mind, however, that an asset is anything of worth to an organization. Apart from hardware and software, this includes people, partners, equipment, facilities, reputation, and information. For the purposes of the CSA+ exam, we focus on hardware, software, and information. You should note that determining the value of an asset can be difficult and is oftentimes subjective. In the context of vulnerability management, the CSA+ exam will only require you to decide how you would deal with critical and noncritical assets.

Critical

A *critical asset* is anything that is absolutely essential to performing the primary functions of your organization. If you work at an online retailer, this set would include your web platforms, data servers, and financial systems, among others. It probably wouldn't include the workstations used by your web developers or your printers. Critical assets, clearly, require a higher degree of attention when it comes to managing vulnerabilities. This attention can be expressed in a number of different ways, but you should focus on at least two: the thoroughness of each vulnerability scan and the frequency of each scan.

Noncritical

A *noncritical asset,* though valuable, is not required for the accomplishment of your main mission as an organization. You still need to include these assets in your vulnerability management plan, but given the limited resources with which we all have to deal, you would prioritize them lower than you would critical ones.

 EXAM TIP   Every security decision—including how, when, and where to conduct vulnerability assessments—must consider the implications of these controls and activities on the core business of the organization.

Common Vulnerabilities

Most threat actors don't want to work any harder than they absolutely have to. Unless they are specifically targeting your organization, cutting off the usual means of exploitation is oftentimes sufficient for them to move on to lower-hanging fruit elsewhere. Fortunately, we know a lot about the mistakes that many organizations make in securing their systems because, sadly, we see the same issues time and again. Before we delve into common flaws on specific types of platforms, here are some that are applicable to most if not all systems:

- **Missing patches/updates**   A system could be missing patches or updates for numerous reasons. If the reason is legitimate (for example, an industrial control system that cannot be taken offline), then this vulnerability should be noted, tracked, and mitigated using an alternate control.

- **Misconfigured firewall rules**   Whether or not a device has its own firewall, the ability to reach it across the network, which should be restricted by firewalls or other means of segmentation, is oftentimes lacking.

- **Weak passwords**   Our personal favorite was an edge firewall that was deployed for an exercise by a highly skilled team of security operators. The team, however, failed to follow its own checklist and was so focused on hardening other devices that it forgot to change the default password on the edge firewall. Even when default passwords are changed, it is not uncommon for users to choose weak ones if they are allowed to.

Servers

Perhaps the most common vulnerability seen on servers stems from losing track of a server's purpose on the network and allowing it to run unnecessary services and open ports. The default installation of many servers includes hundreds if not thousands of applications and services, most of which are not really needed for a server's main purpose. If this extra software is not removed, disabled, or at the very least hardened and documented, it may be difficult to secure the server.

Another common vulnerability is the misconfiguration of services. Most products offer many more features than what are actually needed, but many of us simply ignore the "bonus" features and focus on configuring the critical ones. This can come back to haunt us if these bonus features allow attackers to easily gain a foothold by exploiting legitimate system features that we were not even aware of. The cure to this problem is to ensure we know the full capability set of anything we put on our networks, and disable anything we don't need.

 NOTE Network appliances are computers that are specifically designed to perform one or more functions such as proxying network traffic or serving files. They will normally exhibit the same vulnerabilities as other servers, though it may be easier for IT staff to overlook the need to secure or patch them.

Endpoints

Endpoints are almost always end-user devices (mobile or otherwise). They are the most common entry point for attackers into our networks, and the most common vectors are e-mail attachments and web links. In addition to the common vulnerabilities discussed before (especially updates/patches), the most common problem with endpoints is lack of up-to-date malware protection. This, of course, is the minimum standard. We should really strive to have more advanced, centrally managed, host-based security systems.

Another common vulnerability at the endpoint is system misconfiguration or default configurations. Though most modern operating systems pay attention to security, they oftentimes err on the side of functionality. The pursuit of a great user experience can sometimes come at a high cost. To counter this vulnerability, you should have baseline configurations that can be verified periodically by your scanning tools. These configurations, in turn, are driven by your organizational risk management processes as well as any applicable regulatory requirements.

Network Infrastructure

Perhaps the most commonly vulnerable network infrastructure components are the wireless access points (WAPs). Particularly in environments where employees can bring (and connect) their own devices, it is challenging to strike the right balance between security and functionality. It bears pointing out that the Wired Equivalent Privacy (WEP) protocol has been known to be insecure since at least 2004 and has no place in our networks. (Believe it or not, we still see them in smaller organizations.) For best results, use the Wi-Fi Protected Access 2 (WPA2) protocol.

Even if your WAPs are secured (both electronically and physically), anybody can connect a rogue WAP or any other device to your network unless you take steps to prevent this from happening. The IEEE 802.1X standard provides port-based Network Access Control (NAC) for both wired and wireless devices. With 802.1X, any client wishing to connect to the network must first authenticate itself. With that authentication, you can provide very granular access controls and even require the endpoint to satisfy requirements for patches/upgrades.

Virtual Infrastructure

Increasingly, virtualization is becoming pervasive in our systems. One of the biggest advantages of virtual computing is its efficiency. Many of our physical network devices spend a good part of their time sitting idle and thus underutilized, as shown for a Mac OS workstation in Figure 5-1. This is true even if other devices are over-utilized and becoming performance bottlenecks. By virtualizing the devices and placing them on the same shared hardware, we can balance loads and improve performance at a reduced cost.

Apart from cost savings and improved responsiveness to provisioning requirements, this technology promises enhanced levels of security—assuming, of course, that we do things right. The catch is that by putting what used to be separate physical devices on the same host and controlling the system in software, we allow software flaws in the hypervisors to potentially permit attackers to jump from one virtual machine to the next.

Virtual Hosts

Common vulnerabilities in virtual hosts are no different from those we would expect to find in servers and endpoints, which were discussed in previous sections. The virtualization of hosts, however, brings some potential vulnerabilities of its own. Chief among these is the sprawl of virtual machines (VMs). Unlike their physical counterparts, VMs can easily multiply. We have seen plenty of organizations with hundreds or thousands of VMs in various states of use and/or disrepair that dot their landscape. This typically happens when requirements change and it is a lot easier to simply copy an existing VM than to start from scratch. Eventually, one or both VMs are forgotten, but not properly disposed of. While most of these are suspended or shut down, it is not uncommon to see poorly secured VMs running with nobody tracking them.

VMs are supposed to be completely isolated from the operating system of the host in which they are running. One of the reasons this is important is that if a process in the VM was able to breach this isolation and interact directly with the host, that process would have access to any other VMs running on that host, likely with elevated privileges. The virtualization environment, or *hypervisor,* is responsible for enforcing this property but, like any other software, it is possible that exploitable flaws exist in it. In fact, the Common Vulnerabilities and Exposures (CVE) list includes several such vulnerabilities.

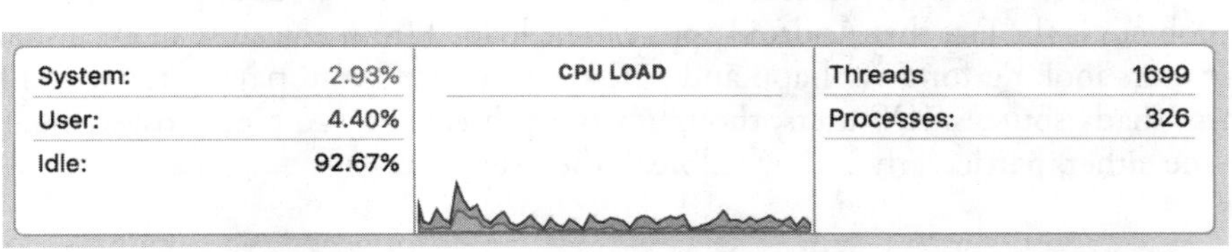

System:	2.93%	CPU LOAD	Threads	1699
User:	4.40%		Processes:	326
Idle:	92.67%			

Figure 5-1 Mac OS Performance Monitor application showing CPU usage

Virtual Networks

Virtual networks are commonly implemented in two ways: internally to a host using network virtualization software within a hypervisor, and externally through the use of protocols such as the Layer 2 Tunneling Protocol (L2TP). In this section, we address the common vulnerabilities found in internal virtual networks and defer discussion of the external virtual networks until a later section.

As mentioned before, a vulnerability in the hypervisor would allow an attacker to escape a VM. Once outside of the machine, the attacker could have access to the virtual networks implemented by the hypervisor. This could lead to eavesdropping, modification of network traffic, or denial of service. Still, at the time of this writing there are very few known actual threats to virtual networks apart from those already mentioned when we discussed common vulnerabilities in VMs.

Management Interface

Because virtual devices have no physical manifestation, there must be some mechanism by which we can do the virtual equivalent of plugging an Ethernet cable into the back of a server or adding memory to it. These, among many other functions, are performed by the virtualization tools' management interfaces, which frequently allow remote access by administrators. The most common vulnerability in these interfaces is their misconfiguration. Even competent technical personnel can forget to harden or properly configure this critical control device if they do not strictly follow a security technical implementation guide.

Mobile Devices

There is a well-known adage that says that if I can gain physical access to your device, there is little you can do to secure it from me. This highlights the most common vulnerability of all mobile devices: theft. We have to assume that every mobile device will at some point be taken (permanently or temporarily) by someone who shouldn't have access to it. What happens then?

Although weak passwords are common vulnerabilities to all parts of our information systems, the problem is even worse for mobile devices because these frequently use short numeric codes instead of passwords. Even if the device is configured to wipe itself after a set number of incorrect attempts (a practice that is far from universal), there are various documented ways of exhaustively trying all possible combinations until the right one is found.

Another common vulnerability of mobile devices is the app stores from which they load new software. Despite efforts by Google to reduce the risk by leveraging their Google Bouncer technology, its store is still a source of numerous malicious apps. Compounding this problem is the fact that Android apps can be loaded from any store or even websites. Many users looking for a cool app and perhaps trying to avoid paying for it will resort to these shady sources. iOS users, though better protected by Apple's ecosystem, are not immune either, particularly if they jailbreak their devices.

Finally, though lack of patches/updates is a common vulnerability to all devices, mobile ones (other than iOS) suffer from limitations on how and when they can be upgraded. These limitations are imposed by carriers. We have seen smartphones that are running three-year-old versions of Android and cannot be upgraded at all.

Interconnected Networks

In late 2013, the consumer retail giant Target educated the entire world on the dangers of interconnected networks. One of the largest data breaches in recent history was accomplished, not by attacking the retailer directly, but by using a heating, ventilation, and air conditioning (HVAC) vendor's network as an entry point. The vendor had access to the networks at Target stores to monitor and manage HVAC systems, but the vulnerability induced by the interconnection was not fully considered by security personnel. In a world that grows increasingly interconnected and interdependent, we should all take stock of which of our partners might present our adversaries with a quick way into our systems.

Virtual Private Networks

Virtual private networks (VPNs) connect two or more devices that are physically part of separate networks, and allow them to exchange data as if they were connected to the same LAN. These virtual networks are encapsulated within the other networks in a manner that segregates the traffic in the VPN from that in the underlying network. This is accomplished using a variety of protocols, including the Internet Protocol Security's (IPSec) Layer 2 Tunneling Protocol (L2TP), Transport Layer Security (TLS), and the Datagram Transport Layer Security (DTLS) used by many Cisco devices. These protocols and their implementations are, for the most part, fairly secure.

 NOTE In considering VPN vulnerabilities, we focus exclusively on the use of VPNs to connect remote hosts to corporate networks. We do not address the use of VPNs to protect mobile devices connecting to untrusted networks (for example, coffee shop WLANs) or to ensure the personal privacy of network traffic in general.

The main vulnerability in VPNs lies in what they potentially allow us to do: connect untrusted, unpatched, and perhaps even infected hosts to our networks. The first risk comes from which devices are allowed to connect. Some organizations require that VPN client software be installed only on organizationally owned, managed devices. If this is not the case and any user can connect any device, provided they have access credentials, then the risk of exposure increases significantly.

Another problem, which may be mitigated for official devices but not so much for personal ones, is the patch/update state of the device. If we do a great job at developing secure architectures but then let unpatched devices connect to them, we are providing adversaries a convenient way to render many of our controls moot. The best practice for mitigating this risk is to implement a Network Access Control (NAC) solution that actively checks the device for patches, updates, and any required other parameter *before* allowing it to join the network. Many NAC solutions allow administrators to place noncompliant devices in a "guest" network so they can download the necessary patches/updates and eventually be allowed in.

Finally, with devices that have been "away" for a while and show back up on our networks via VPN, we have no way of knowing whether they are compromised. Even if they don't spread malware or get used as pivot points for deeper penetration into our systems, any data these devices acquire would be subject to monitoring by unauthorized third parties. Similarly, any data originating in such a compromised host is inherently untrustworthy.

Industrial Control Systems

Industrial control systems (ICSs) are cyber-physical systems that allow specialized software to control the physical behaviors of some system. For example, ICSs are used in automated automobile assembly lines, building elevators, and even HVAC systems. A typical ICS architecture is shown in Figure 5-2. At the bottom layer (level 0), we find the actual physical devices such as sensors and actuators that control physical processes. These are connected to remote terminal units (RTUs) or programmable logic controllers (PLCs), which translate physical effects to binary data, and vice versa. These RTUs and PLCs at level 1 are, in turn, connected to database servers and Human-Machine Interaction (HMI) controllers and terminals at level 2. These three lower levels of the architecture are known as the operational technology (OT) network. The OT network was traditionally isolated from the IT network that now comprises levels 3 and 4 of the architecture. For a variety of functional and business reasons, this gap between OT (levels 0 through 2) and IT (levels 3 and 4) is now frequently bridged, providing access to physical processes from anywhere on the Internet.

Much of the software that runs an ICS is burned into the firmware of devices such as programmable logic controllers (PLC), like the ones that run the uranium enrichment centrifuges targeted by Stuxnet. This is a source of vulnerabilities because updating this software cannot normally be done automatically or even centrally. The patching and updating, which is pretty infrequent to begin with, typically requires that the device be brought offline and manually updated by a qualified technician. Between the cost and effort involved and the effects of interrupting business processes, it should not come as a surprise to learn that many ICS components are never updated or patched. To make matters worse, vendors are notorious for not providing patches at all, even when vulnerabilities are discovered and made public. In its 2016 report on ICS security, FireEye described how 516 of the 1552 known ICS vulnerabilities had no patch available.

Another common vulnerability in ICSs is passwords. Unlike previous mentions of this issue in this chapter, here the issue is not the users choosing weak passwords, but the manufacturer of the ICS device setting a trivial password in the firmware, documenting it so all users (and perhaps abusers) know what it is, and sometimes making it difficult if not impossible to change. In many documented cases, these passwords are stored in plain text. Manufacturers are getting better at this, but there are still many devices with unchangeable passwords controlling critical physical systems around the world.

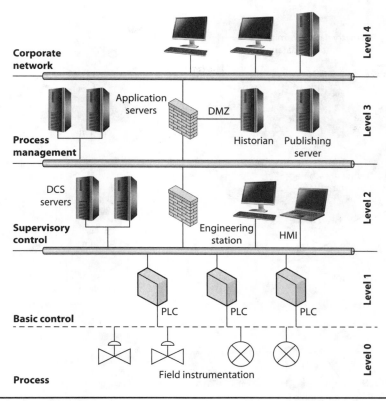

Figure 5-2   Simple industrial control system (ICS)

SCADA Devices

Supervisory Control and Data Acquisition (SCADA) systems are a specific type of ICS that is characterized by covering large geographic regions. Whereas an ICS typically controls physical processes and devices in one building or a small campus, a SCADA system is used for pipelines and transmission lines covering hundreds or thousands of miles. SCADA is most commonly associated with energy (for example, petroleum or power) and utility (for example, water or sewer) applications. The general architecture of a SCADA system is depicted in Figure 5-3.

SCADA systems introduce two more types of common vulnerabilities in addition to those found in ICS. The first of these is induced by the long-distance communications links. For many years, most organizations using SCADA systems relied on the relative obscurity of the communications protocols and radio frequencies involved to provide a degree (or at least an illusion) of security. In what is one of the first cases of cyber attack against SCADA systems, an Australian man apparently seeking revenge in 2001 connected a rogue radio transceiver to an RTU and intentionally caused millions of gallons of sewage to spill into local parks and rivers. Though the wireless systems have mostly been modernized and hardened, they still present potential vulnerabilities.

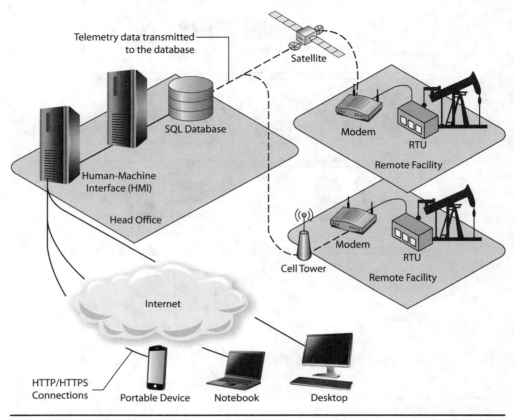

Figure 5-3   Typical architecture of a SCADA system

The second weakness, particular to a SCADA system, is its reliance on isolated and unattended facilities. These remote stations provide attackers with an opportunity to gain physical access to system components. Though many of these stations are now protected by cameras and alarm systems, their remoteness makes responding significantly slower compared to most other information systems.

Frequency of Vulnerability Scans

With all these very particular vulnerabilities floating around, how often should we be checking for them? As you might have guessed, there is no one-size-fits-all answer to that question. The important issue to keep in mind is that the *process* is what matters. If you haphazardly do vulnerability scans at random intervals, you will have a much harder time answering the question of whether or not your vulnerability management is being effective. If, on the other hand, you do the math up front and determine the frequencies and scopes of the various scans given your list of assumptions and requirements, you will have much more control over your security posture.

Risk Appetite

The *risk appetite* of an organization is the amount of risk that its senior executives are willing to assume. You will never be able to drive risk down to zero because there will always be a possibility that someone or something causes losses to your organization. What's more, as you try to mitigate risks, you will rapidly approach a point of diminishing returns. When you start mitigating risks, you will go through a stage in which a great many risks can be reduced with some commonsense and inexpensive controls. After you start running out of such low-hanging fruit, the costs (for example, financial and opportunity) will start rapidly increasing. You will then reach a point where further mitigation is fairly expensive. How expensive is "too expensive" is dictated by your organization's risk appetite.

When it comes to the frequency of vulnerability scans, it's not as simple as doing more if your risk appetite is low, and vice versa. Risk is a deliberate process that quantifies the likelihood of a threat being realized and the net effect it would have in the organization. Some threats, such as hurricanes and earthquakes, cannot be mitigated with vulnerability scans. Neither can the threat of social engineering attacks or insider threats. So the connection between risk appetite and the frequency of vulnerability scans requires that we dig into the risk management plan and see which specific risks require scans and then how often they should be done in order to reduce the residual risks to the agreed-upon levels.

Regulatory Requirements

If you thought the approach to determining the frequency of scans based on risk appetite was not very definitive, the opposite is true of regulatory requirements. Assuming you've identified all the applicable regulations, then the frequencies of the various scans will be given to you. For instance, requirement 11.2 of the PCI DSS requires vulnerability scans (at least) quarterly as well as after any significant change in the network. HIPAA, on the other hand, imposes no such frequency requirements. Still, in order to avoid potential problems, most experts agree that covered organizations should run vulnerability scans at least semiannually.

Technical Constraints

Vulnerability assessments require resources such as personnel, time, bandwidth, hardware, and software, many of which are likely limited in your organization. Of these, the top technical constraints on your ability to perform these tests are qualified personnel and technical capacity. Here, the term *capacity* is used to denote computational resources expressed in cycles of CPU time, bytes of primary and secondary memory, and bits per second (bps) of network connectivity. Because any scanning tool you choose to use will require a minimum amount of such capacity, you may be constrained in both the frequency and scope of your vulnerability scans.

If you have no idea how much capacity your favorite scans require, quantifying it should be one of your first next steps. It is possible that in well-resourced organizations such requirements are negligible compared to the available capacity. In such an environment, it is possible to increase the frequency of scans to daily or even hourly for high-risk assets. It is likelier, however, that your scanning takes a noticeable toll on assets that are also required for your principal mission. In such cases, you want to carefully balance the mission and security requirements so that one doesn't unduly detract from the other.

Workflow

Another consideration when determining how often you conduct vulnerability scanning is established workflows of security and network operations within your organization. As mentioned in the preceding section, qualified personnel constitute a limited resource. Whenever you run a vulnerability scan, someone will have to review and perhaps analyze the results in order to determine what actions, if any, are required. This process is best incorporated into the workflows of your security and/or network operations centers personnel.

A recurring theme in this chapter has been the need to standardize and enforce repeatable vulnerability management processes. Apart from well-written policies, the next best way to ensure this happens is by writing it into the daily workflows of security and IT personnel. If I work in a security operations center (SOC) and know that every Tuesday morning my duties include reviewing the vulnerability scans from the night before and creating tickets for any required remediation, then I'm much more likely to do this routinely. The organization, in turn, benefits from consistent vulnerability scans with well-documented outcomes, which, in turn, become enablers of effective risk management across the entire system.

Tool Configuration

Just as you must weigh a host of considerations when determining how often to conduct vulnerability scans, you also need to think about different but related issues when configuring your tools to perform these scans. Today's tools typically have more power and options than most of us will sometimes need. Our information systems might also impose limitations or requirements on which of these features can or should be brought to bear.

Scanning Criteria

When configuring scanning tools, you have a host of different considerations, but here we focus on the main ones you will be expected to know for the CSA+ exam. The list is not exhaustive, however, and you should probably grow it with issues that are specific to your organization or sector.

Sensitivity Levels

Earlier in this chapter, we discussed the different classifications we should assign to our data and information, as well as the criticality levels of our other assets. We return now to these concepts as we think about configuring our tools to do their jobs while appropriately protecting our assets. When it comes to the information in our systems, we must take great care to ensure that the required protections remain in place at all times. For instance, if we are scanning an organization covered by HIPAA, we should ensure that nothing we do as part of our assessment in any way compromises protected health information (PHI). We have seen vulnerability assessments that include proofs such as sample documents obtained by exercising a security flaw. Obviously, this is not advisable in the scenario we've discussed.

Besides protecting the information, we also need to protect the systems on which it resides. Earlier we discussed critical and noncritical assets in the context of focusing attention on the critical ones. Now we'll qualify that idea by saying that we should scan them in a way that ensures they remain available to the business or other processes that made them critical in the first place. If an organization processes thousands of dollars each second and our scanning slows that down by an order of magnitude, even for a few minutes, the effect could be a significant loss of revenue that might be difficult to explain to the board. Understanding the nature and sensitivity of these assets can help us identify tool configurations that minimize the risks to them, such as scheduling the scan during a specific window of time in which there is no trading.

Vulnerability Feed

Unless you work in a governmental intelligence organization, odds are that your knowledge of vulnerabilities mostly comes from commercial or community feeds. These services have update cycles that range from hours to weeks and, though they tend to eventually converge on the vast majority of known vulnerabilities, one feed may publish a threat significantly before another. If you are running hourly scans, then you would obviously benefit from the faster services and may be able to justify a higher cost. If, on the other hand, your scans are weekly, monthly, or even quarterly, the difference may not be as significant. As a rule of thumb, you want a vulnerability feed that is about as frequent as your own scanning cycle.

If your vulnerability feed is not one with a fast update cycle, or if you want to ensure you are absolutely abreast of the latest discovered vulnerabilities, you can (and perhaps should) subscribe to alerts besides those of your provider. The National Vulnerability Database (NVD) maintained by the National Institute of Standards and Technologies (NIST) provides two Rich Site Summary (RSS) feeds, one of which will alert you to any new vulnerability reported, and the other provides only those that have been analyzed. The advantage of the first feed is that you are on the bleeding edge of notifications. The advantage of the second is that it provides you with specific products that are affected as well as additional analysis. A number of other organizations provide similar feeds that you should probably explore as well.

Assuming you have subscribed to one or more feeds (in addition to your scanning product's feed), you will likely learn of vulnerabilities in between programmed scans. When this happens, you will have to consider whether to run an out-of-cycle scan that looks for that particular vulnerability or to wait until the next scheduled event to run the test. If the flaw is critical enough to warrant immediate action, you may have to pull from your service provider or, failing that, write your own plug-in to test the vulnerability. Obviously, this would require significant resources, so you should have a process by which to make decisions like these as part of your vulnerability management program.

PART II

Scope

Whether you are running a scheduled or special scan, you have to carefully define its scope and configure your tools appropriately. Though it would be simpler to scan everything at once at set intervals, the reality is that this is oftentimes not possible simply because of the load this places on critical nodes, if not the entire system. What may work better is to have a series of scans, each of which having a different scope and parameters.

Whether you are doing a global or targeted scan, your tools must know which nodes to test and which ones to leave alone. The set of devices that will be assessed constitutes the scope of the vulnerability scan. Deliberately scoping these events is important for a variety of reasons, but one of the most important ones is the need for credentials, which we discuss next.

Credentialed vs. Noncredentialed

A noncredentialed vulnerability scan evaluates the system from the perspective of an outsider, such as an attacker just beginning to interact with a target. This is a sort of black-box test in which the scanning tool doesn't get any special information or access into the target. The advantage of this approach is that it tends to be quicker while still being fairly realistic. It may also be a bit more secure because there is no need for additional credentials on all tested devices. The disadvantage, of course, is that you will most likely not get full coverage of the target.

 EXAM TIP Noncredentialed scans look at systems from the perspective of the attacker but are not as thorough as credentialed scans.

In order to really know all that is vulnerable in a host, you typically need to provide the tool with credentials so it can log in remotely and examine the inside as well as the outside. Credentialed scans will always be more thorough than noncredentialed ones, simply because of the additional information that login provides the tool. Whether or not this additional thoroughness is important to you is for you and your team to decide. An added benefit of credentialed scans is that they tend to reduce the amount of network traffic required to complete the assessment.

 NOTE It is very rare to need full domain admin credentials to perform a vulnerability scan. If you are doing credentialed scans, you should avoid using privileged accounts unless you are certain you cannot otherwise meet your requirements.

Server Based vs. Agent Based

Vulnerability scanners tend to fall into two classes of architectures: those that require a running process (agent) on every scanned device, and those that do not. The difference is illustrated in Figure 5-4. A server-based (or agentless) scanner consolidates all data and processes on one or a small number of scanning hosts, which depend on a fair amount

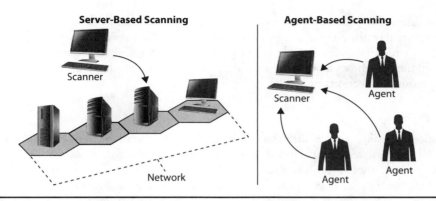

Figure 5-4 Server-based and agent-based vulnerability scanner architectures

of network bandwidth in order to run their scans. It has fewer components, which could make maintenance tasks easier and help with reliability. Additionally, it can detect and scan devices that are connected to the network, but do not have agents running on them (for example, new or rogue hosts).

Agent-based scanners have agents that run on each protected host and report their results back to the central scanner. Because only the results are transmitted, the bandwidth required by this architectural approach is considerably less than a server-based solution. Also, because the agents run continuously on each host, mobile devices can still be scanned even when they are not connected to the corporate network.

EXAM TIP   Agent-based (or serverless) vulnerability scanners are typically better for scanning mobile devices.

Types of Data
Finally, as you configure your scanning tool, you must consider the information that should or must be included in the report, particularly when dealing with regulatory compliance scans. This information will drive the data that your scan must collect, which in turn affects the tool configuration. Keep in mind that each report (and there may multiple ones as outputs of one scan) is intended for a specific audience. This affects both the information in it as well as the manner in which it is presented.

Tool Updates and Plug-Ins
Vulnerability scanning tools work by testing systems against lists of known vulnerabilities. These flaws are frequently being discovered by vendors and security researchers. It stands to reason that if you don't keep your lists up to date, whatever tool you use will eventually fail to detect vulnerabilities that are known by others, especially your adversaries. This is why it is critical to keep your tool up to date.

A vulnerability scanner plug-in is a simple program that looks for the presence of one specific flaw. In Nessus, plug-ins are coded in the Nessus Attack Scripting Language (NASL), which is a very flexible language able to perform virtually any check imaginable. Figure 5-5 shows a portion of a NASL plug-in that tests for FTP servers that allow anonymous connections.

SCAP

Question: how do you ensure that your vulnerability management process complies with all relevant regulatory and policy requirements *regardless of which scanning tools you use?* Each tool, after all, may use whatever standards (for example, rules) and reporting formats its developers desire. This lack of standardization led the National Institute of Standards and Technologies (NIST) to team up with industry partners to develop the Security Content Automation Protocol (SCAP). SCAP is a protocol that

```
#
# The script code starts here :
#

include("ftp_func.inc");

port = get_kb_item("Services/ftp");
if(!port)port = 21;

if (get_kb_item('ftp/'+port+'/backdoor')) exit(0);

state = get_port_state(port);
if(!state)exit(0);
soc = open_sock_tcp(port);
if(soc)
{
 domain = get_kb_item("Settings/third_party_domain");
 r = ftp_log_in(socket:soc, user:"anonymous", pass:string("nessus@", domain));
 if(r)
 {
  port2 = ftp_get_pasv_port(socket:soc);
  if(port2)
  {
   soc2 = open_sock_tcp(port2, transport:get_port_transport(port));
   if (soc2)
   {
    send(socket:soc, data:'LIST /\r\n');
    listing = ftp_recv_listing(socket:soc2);
    close(soc2);
    }
  }
 }

 data = "
This FTP service allows anonymous logins. If you do not want to share data
with anyone you do not know, then you should deactivate the anonymous account,
since it may only cause troubles.
```

Figure 5-5 NASL script that tests for anonymous FTP logins

uses specific standards for the assessment and reporting of vulnerabilities in the information systems of an organization. Currently in version 1.2, it incorporates about a dozen different components that standardize everything from an asset reporting format (ARF) to Common Vulnerabilities and Exposures (CVE) to the Common Vulnerability Scoring System (CVSS).

At its core, SCAP leverages baselines developed by the NIST and its partners that define minimum standards for vulnerability management. If, for instance, you want to ensure that your Windows 10 workstations are complying with the requirements of the Federal Information Security Management Act (FISMA), you would use the appropriate SCAP module that captures these requirements. You would then provide that module to a certified SCAP scanner (such as Nessus), and it would be able to report this compliance in a standard language. As you should be able to see, SCAP enables full automation of the vulnerability management process, particularly in regulatory environments.

Permissions and Access

Apart from the considerations in a credentialed scan discussed already, the scanning tool must have the correct permissions on whichever hosts it is running, as well as the necessary access across the network infrastructure. It is generally best to have a dedicated account for the scanning tool or, alternatively, to execute it within the context of the user responsible for running the scan. In either case, minimally privileged accounts should be used to minimize risks (that is, do not run the scanner as root unless you have no choice).

Network access is also an important configuration, not so much of the tool as of the infrastructure. Because the vulnerability scans are carefully planned beforehand, it should be possible to examine the network and determine what access control lists (ACLs), if any, need to be modified to allow the scanner to work. Similarly, network IDS and IPS may trigger on the scanning activity unless they have been configured to recognize it as legitimate. This may also be true for host-based security systems (HBSSs), which might attempt to mitigate the effects of the scan.

Finally, the tool is likely to include a reporting module for which the right permissions must be set. It is ironic that some organizations deploy vulnerability scanners but fail to properly secure the reporting interfaces. This allows users who should be unauthorized to access the reports at will. Although this may seem like a small risk, consider the consequences of adversaries being able to read your vulnerability reports. This ability would save them significant effort because they would then be able to focus on the targets you have already listed as vulnerable. As an added bonus, they would know exactly how to attack the hosts.

Chapter Review

This chapter has focused on developing deliberate, repeatable vulnerability management processes that satisfy all the internal and external requirements. The goal is that you, as a cybersecurity analyst, will be able to ask the right questions and develop appropriate approaches to managing the vulnerabilities in your information systems.

Vulnerabilities, of course, are not all created equal, so you have to consider the sensitivity of your information and the criticality of the systems on which it resides and is used. As mentioned repeatedly, you will never be able to eliminate every vulnerability and drive your risk to zero. What you can and should do is assess your risks and mitigate them to a degree that is compliant with applicable regulatory and legal requirements, and is consistent with the risk appetite of your executive leaders.

You can't do this unless you take a holistic view of your organization's operating environment and tailor your processes, actions, and tools to your particular requirements. Part of this involves understanding the common types of vulnerabilities associated with the various components of your infrastructure. You also need to understand the internal and external requirements to mitigating the risks of flaws. Finally, you need to consider the impact on your organization's critical business processes—that is, the impact of both the vulnerabilities and the process of identifying and correcting them. After all, no organization exists for the purpose of running vulnerability scans on its systems. Rather, these assessments are required in order to support the real reasons for the existence of the organization.

Questions

1. The popular framework that aims to standardize automated vulnerability assessment, management, and compliance level is known as what?
   A. CVSS
   B. SCAP
   C. CVE
   D. PCAP

2. An information system that might require restricted access to, or special handling of, certain data as defined by a governing body is referred to as a what?
   A. Compensating control
   B. International Organization for Standardization (ISO)
   C. Regulatory environment
   D. Production system

3. Which of the following are parameters that organizations should *not* use to determine the classification of data?
   A. The level of damage that could be caused if the data were disclosed
   B. Legal, regulatory, or contractual responsibility to protect the data
   C. The age of data
   D. The types of controls that have been assigned to safeguard it

4. What is the term for the amount of risk an organization is willing to accept in pursuit of its business goals?

   A. Risk appetite

   B. Innovation threshold

   C. Risk hunger

   D. Risk ceiling

5. Insufficient storage, computing, or bandwidth required to remediate a vulnerability is considered what kind of constraint?

   A. Organizational

   B. Knowledge

   C. Technical

   D. Risk

6. Early systems of which type used *security through obscurity*, or the flawed reliance on unfamiliar communications protocols as a security practice?

   A. PCI DSS

   B. SCADA

   C. SOC

   D. PHI

7. What is a reason that patching and updating occur so infrequently with ICS and SCADA devices?

   A. These devices control critical and costly systems that require constant uptime.

   B. These devices are not connected to networks, so they do not need to be updated.

   C. These devices do not use common operating systems, so they cannot be updated.

   D. These devices control systems, such as HVAC, that do not need security updates.

8. All of the following are important considerations when deciding the frequency of vulnerability scans *except* which?

   A. Security engineers' willingness to assume risk

   B. Senior executives' willingness to assume risk

   C. HIPAA compliance

   D. Tool impact on business processes

Use the following scenario to answer Questions 9–12:

A local hospital has reached out to your security consulting company because it is worried about recent reports of ransomware on hospital networks across the country. The hospital wants to get a sense of what weaknesses exist on the network and get your guidance on the best security practices for its environment. The hospital has asked you to assist with its vulnerability management policy and provided you with some information about its network. The hospital provides a laptop to its staff and each device can be configured using a standard baseline. However, the hospital is not able to provide a smartphone to everyone and allows user-owned devices to connect to the network. Additionally, its staff is very mobile and relies on a VPN to reach back to the hospital network.

9. When reviewing the VPN logs, you confirm that about half of the devices that connect are user-owned devices. You suggest which of the following changes to policy?

   A. None, the use of IPSec in VPNs provides strong encryption that prevents the spread of malware

   B. Ask all staff members to upgrade the web browser on their mobile devices

   C. Prohibit all UDP traffic on personal devices

   D. Prohibit noncompany laptops and mobile devices from connecting to the VPN

10. What kind of vulnerability scanner architecture do you recommend be used in this environment?

    A. Zero agent

    B. Server based

    C. Agent based

    D. Network based

11. Which vulnerabilities would you expect to find mostly on the hospital's laptops?

    A. Misconfigurations in IEEE 802.1X

    B. Fixed passwords stored in plaintext in the PLCs

    C. Lack of VPN clients

    D. Outdated malware signatures

12. Which of the following is *not* a reason you might prohibit user-owned devices from the network?

    A. The regulatory environment might explicitly prohibit these kinds of devices.

    B. Concerns about staff recruiting and retention.

    C. There is no way to enforce who can have access to the device.

    D. The organization has no control over what else is installed on the personal device.

Answers

1. **B.** The Security Content Automation Protocol (SCAP) is a method of using open standards, called *components*, to identify software flaws and configuration issues.

2. **C.** A regulatory environment is one in which the way an organization exists or operates is controlled by laws, rules, or regulations put in place by a formal body.

3. **D.** Although there are no fixed rules on the classification levels that an organization uses, some common criteria parameters used to determine the sensitivity of data include the level of damage that could be caused if the data were disclosed; legal, regulatory, or contractual responsibility to protect the data; and the age of data. The classification should determine the controls used and not the other way around.

4. **A.** Risk appetite is a core consideration when determining your organization's risk management policy and guidance, and will vary based on factors such as criticality of production systems, impact to public safety, and financial concerns.

5. **C.** Any limitation on the ability to perform a task on a system due to limitations of technology is a technical constraint and must have acceptable compensating controls in place.

6. **B.** Early Supervisory Control and Data Acquisition (SCADA) systems had the common vulnerability of relying heavily on obscure communications protocols for security. This practice only provides the illusion of security and may place the organization in worse danger.

7. **A.** The cost involved and potential negative effects of interrupting business and industrial processes often dissuade these device managers from updating and patching these systems.

8. **A.** An organization's risk appetite, or amount of risk it is willing to take, is a legitimate consideration when determining the frequency of scans. However, only executive leadership can make that determination.

9. **D.** Allowing potentially untrusted, unpatched, and perhaps even infected hosts onto a network via a VPN is not ideal. Best practices dictate that VPN client software be installed only on organizationally owned and managed devices.

10. **C.** Because every laptop has the same software baseline, an agent-based vulnerability scanner is a sensible choice. Agent-based scanners have agents that run on each protected host and report their results back to the central scanner. The agents can also scan continuously on each host, even when not connected to the hospital network.

11. **D.** Malware signatures are notoriously problematic on endpoints, particularly when they are portable and not carefully managed. Although VPN client problems might be an issue, they would not be as significant a vulnerability as outdated malware signatures. IEEE 802.1X problems would be localized at the network access points and not on the endpoints. PLCs are found in ICS and SCADA systems and not normally in laptops.

12. **B.** Staff recruiting and retention are frequently quoted by business leaders as reasons to allow personal mobile devices on their corporate networks. Therefore, staffing concerns would typically not be a good rationale for prohibiting these devices.

Vulnerability Scanning

In this chapter you will learn:

- Best practices for executing vulnerability scans
- Remediation techniques for uncovered vulnerabilities
- How to review and interpret results of vulnerability scan reports
- Trend analysis techniques for vulnerability management

To kill an error is as good a service as, and sometimes even better than,
the establishing of a new truth or fact.

—Charles Darwin

Vulnerability scanning is a key part of securing a network. In short, it's the practice of automating security checks against your systems. These checks help focus our efforts on protecting the network by pointing out the weak parts of the system. In many cases, these tools even suggest options for remediation. Although we promote the regular use of vulnerability scanners, there are some important limitations of this practice you must consider before beginning use. Many vulnerability scanners do a tremendous job of identifying weaknesses, but they are often single-purpose tools. Specifically, they often lack the functionality of capitalizing on a weakness and elevating to the exploit stage automatically. As a defender, you must understand that a real attacker will combine the result from his own vulnerability scan, along with other intelligence about the network, to formulate a smart plan on how to get into the network. What's more, these tools will usually not be able to perform any type of advanced correlation on their own. You'll likely require additional tools and processes to determine the overall risk of operating the network. This is due not only to the large variety of network configurations, but also to other nontechnical factors such as business requirements, operational requirements, and organizational policy.

A simple example might be in the case of the discovery of several low-risk vulnerabilities across the network. Although the vulnerability scanner might classify each of these occurrences as "low risk," without the context of the security posture in other areas of the network, it's impossible to truly understand the cumulative effect that each of these low-risk vulnerabilities might have. It might even turn out that the cumulative effect is beyond what the additive effect might be. A weak password for both an administrator and a normal user are both problematic, but the potential effect of a compromise of an administrator's account can have far great impact on the organization. No single tool is going to be able to provide such a depth of insight automatically, so it's just as important to understand the limitations of your tools as their capabilities.

Execute Scanning

Modern scanners cannot find weaknesses they're not aware of or do not understand. Although they can only identify weaknesses they're aware of, the most popular vulnerability scanners have amassed enormous libraries of vulnerabilities. We'll discuss three popular vulnerability scanners on the market: Tenable Network Security's Nessus, Greenbone Network's OpenVAS, and the Nikto Web Scanner. These tools can scan your network from the perspective of an outsider, as well as from the perspective of a legitimate user. In the latter case, the scanner will perform what's called an *authenticated scan*. There are two primary ways to conduct an authenticated scan. The first is to install local agents on the endpoints to synchronize with the vulnerability scan server and provide analysis on the endpoint during the course of the scan. The second method is to provide administrative credentials directly to the scanner, which it will invoke as necessary during the scan. It's good practice to use both authenticated and unauthenticated scans during an assessment because the use of one might uncover vulnerabilities that would not be seen by the other.

Nessus

Nessus, a popular and powerful scanner, began its life as an open source and free utility in the late 1990s and has since become a top choice for conducting vulnerability scans. With over 80,000 plug-ins, Nessus allows users the ability to schedule and conduct scans across multiple networks based on custom policies. You may recall in our discussion of port-scanning tools that Nessus includes basic port-scanning functionality. Its real power, however, lies with its multitude of features for vulnerability identification, misconfiguration detection, default password usage, and compliance determination. The standard installation includes the Nessus server, which will coordinate the vulnerability scan, generate reports, and facilitate the vulnerability management feature. It can reside on the same machine as the Nessus web client or can be located elsewhere on the network. The client is designed to be run from the web interface, which allows the administrator to manipulate scan settings using any browser that supports HTML5. Figure 6-1 shows the Nessus architecture as used against several targets on the network. Located on the Nessus server are the various plug-ins used in conducting assessments against the targets. With registration, Tenable updates these plug-ins and the server software often, usually once a day.

Figure 6-1
Nessus
client/server
architecture
shown against
several network
targets

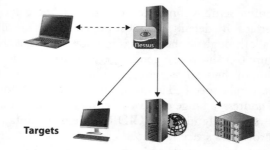

Targets

Assuming the server is running on the same local machine as the client, as is often the case, you can access the Nessus web interface by pointing your browser to http:// localhost:8834, as shown in Figure 6-2. When you start Nessus for the first time, there is a bit of a delay for initial configuration, registration, and updating. Be patient, and you'll soon be ready to conduct your first scan.

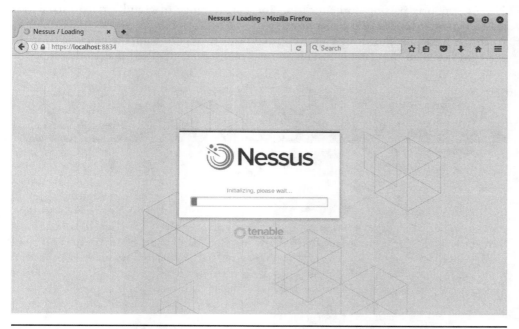

Figure 6-2   View of the initial Nessus loading from a standard web browser

Once the initial setup is complete, you can specify the details for any type of scan from the same interface. By default, the most popular scans are already enabled, but it's good practice to walk through all the settings to know what exactly will be happening on your network. Figure 6-3 shows the general settings page, which provides space for a name and description of the scan. Scans created here can be used for immediate or scheduled action. Targets can be specified in one of several ways, including via a single IPv4 address, a single IPv6 address, a range of IPv4 or IPv6 addresses, or a hostname. In addition, the server will also correctly interpret CIDR or netmask notation to specify IPv4 subnets. Nessus also provides a space to upload groups of specific target machines in ASCII text format, making it easy to reuse pre-populated lists. In this setting screen, you can also set schedules for scans, adjust notification preferences, and define certain technical limits for the scan. Nessus classifies some plug-ins as dangerous, meaning that their use may cause damage to some systems in certain conditions. When you're preparing to execute a scan, it might be useful to use the Nessus "safe checks" option to avoid launching potentially destructive attacks. We'll step through setting up for a basic scan over the next few pages.

Nessus allows for great flexibility and depth in the scanning process. You can configure Nessus to pass along any credentials that might be useful. In the configuration screen example shown in Figure 6-4, there is space to configure credentials for Windows hosts. Nessus supports passing authentication for a wide range of cloud services, databases, hosts, network devices, and hypervisors.

In the next tab, shown in Figure 6-5, you can configure compliance checks for the scan. Included in the default installation are many preconfigured checks developed in

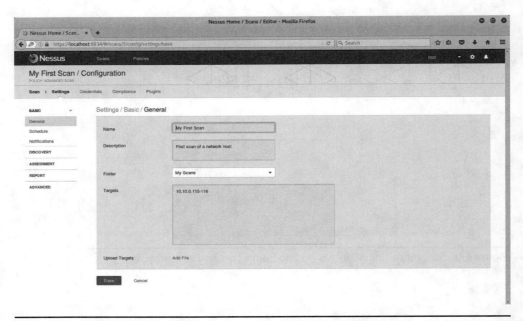

Figure 6-3   Nessus configuration screen before conducting a vulnerability scan

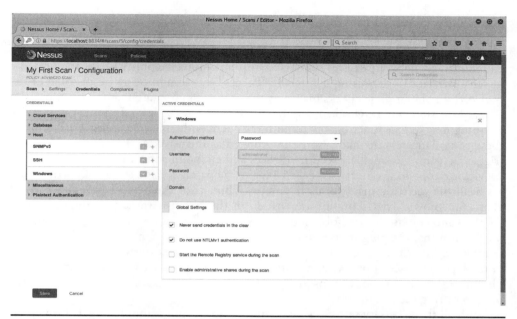

Figure 6-4   Nessus credentials screen

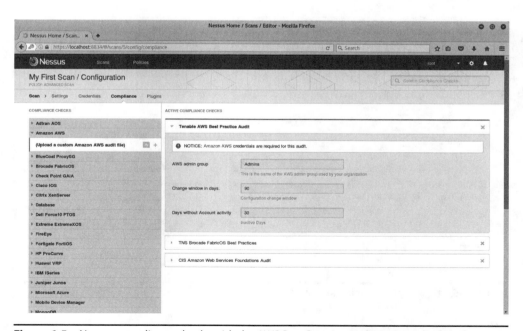

Figure 6-5   Nessus compliance checks with the AWS Best Practice Audit options displayed

house, or based on industry best practices and benchmarks. As an admin, you can also develop and upload your own custom configuration, called an *audit file,* for use in the compliance check. The audit file gives instructions used to assess the configuration of endpoints and network devices systems against a compliance policy or for the presence of sensitive data. When using compliance checks, you should be aware of some of the tradeoffs. Enabling these checks may slow down the scan because many more aspects of the target system will be checked, and potentially at a deeper level. In some cases, active scanning may reduce functionality of both the client and target machines. Furthermore, these compliance checks may also be interpreted as intrusive by the target, which may trigger alerts on intermediate security devices and endpoint software.

Moving over to the next tab, called Plugins, you can see the status of all the plug-ins available for scanning. Nessus maintains a library of these small programs, which check for known flaws. Plug-ins are written in the Nessus Attack Scripting Language (NASL) and contain information about the vulnerability, its remediation steps, and the mechanism that the plug-in uses to determine the existence of the vulnerability. Usually released within 24 hours of a public disclosure, plug-ins are constantly updated as part of the Nessus subscription. As shown in Figure 6-6, you can activate (or deactivate) any plug-ins required for the scan, or just get details into what exactly is performed by the plug-in during the assessment.

With all the necessary settings saved, you can now begin scanning targets for vulnerabilities.

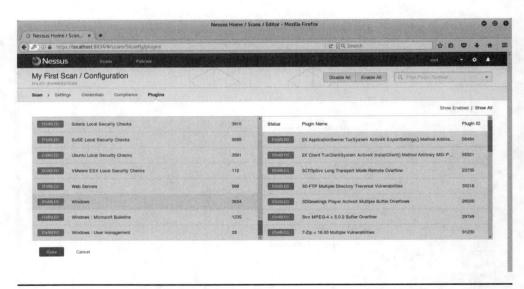

Figure 6-6   Nessus plug-in selection interface

OpenVAS

The Open Vulnerability Assessment System, or OpenVAS, is a free framework that consists of several analysis tools for both vulnerability identification and management. OpenVAS is a fork of the original Nessus project that began shortly after Tenable closed development of the Nessus framework. OpenVAS is similar to Nessus in that it supports browser-based access to its OpenVAS *Manager,* which uses the OpenVAS *Scanner* to conduct assessments based on a collection of over 47,000 network vulnerability tests (NVTs). Results of these NVTs are then sent back to the Manager for storage. You can access OpenVAS's interface by using a standard browser to access http://localhost:9392. Figure 6-7 shows the welcome screen from which an admin can access all settings for both the OpenVAS Manager and OpenVAS Scanner. There is also an empty field on the right side of the screen that can be used to launch quick scans.

OpenVAS also provides details on active NVTs used in the scan, as shown in Figure 6-8. You can see the status of each of the tests and, as with Nessus, get details on the test itself. In addition to the summary of the NVT, a vulnerability score is given, plus a level of confidence assigned to the detection method.

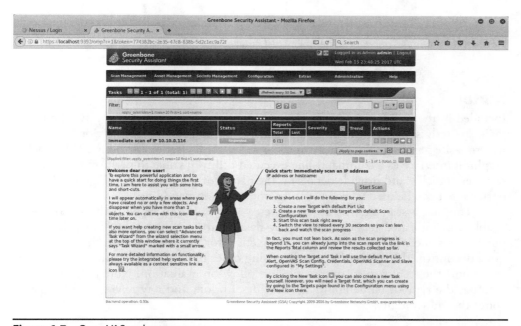

Figure 6-7 OpenVAS welcome screen

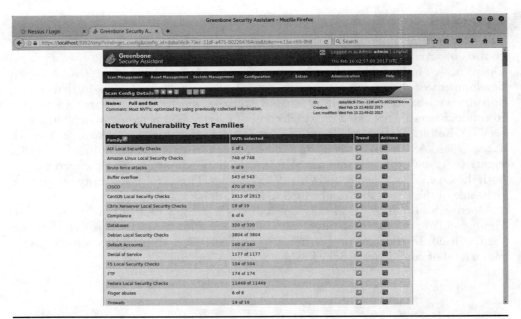

Figure 6-8   OpenVAS network vulnerability test families

Nikto

Included in the Kali Linux distribution, Nikto is a web server vulnerability scanner. Its main strength is finding vulnerabilities such as SQL and command injection susceptibility, cross-site scripting (XSS), and improper server configuration. Although Nikto lacks a graphical interface as a command-line executed utility, it's able to perform thousands of tests very quickly and provide details on the nature of the weaknesses. Figure 6-9 shows options that can be used when executing from the command line.

To conduct a scan against a web server, you specify the IP with the **-host** option enabled, as indicated in Figure 6-10. By default, the results of the scan will be output to the same window. Although not practical for detailed analysis, this is useful to quickly confirm the status of a host. By using other options in the command line, you can export the results to an output file for follow-on evaluation. Note that the output includes the type of vulnerability, a short description, and any reference information about the vulnerability.

EXAM TIP   Although we focus on specific vulnerability scanners in this chapter, the workflow of vulnerability scanning execution, report generation, and report distribution is similar with nearly all other types of vulnerability scanners on the market.

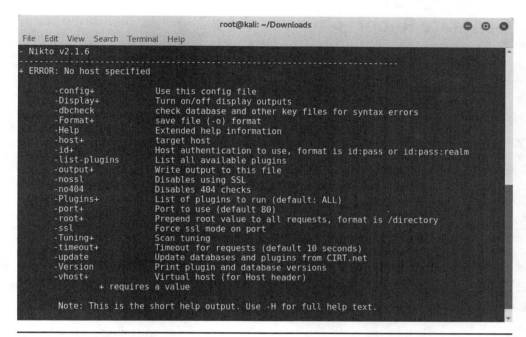

Figure 6-9   Nikto command-line options

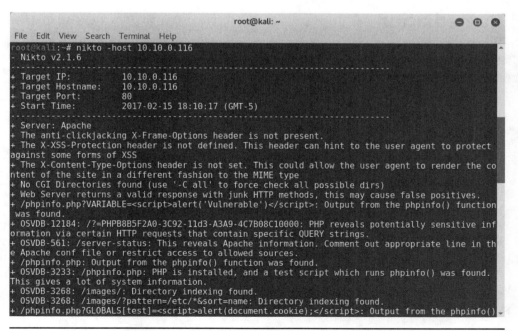

Figure 6-10   Result of Nikto scan in terminal window

Generate Reports

Report generation is an important part of the incident response process and is particularly critical for vulnerability management. All vulnerability scanners perform reporting functions of some kind, but they don't all come with customization options. Nessus provides its reports in common formats such as PDF, HTML, and CSV. Additionally, you can also use Nessus's own formats.

As an administrator, it's important that you consider what kinds of reporting your utility is capable of and how you might automate the reporting process. Getting the pertinent information to the right people in a timely fashion is the key to successfully capitalizing on vulnerability scans.

Automated vs. Manual Distribution

Creating reporting templates allows you to rapidly prepare customized reports based on vulnerability scan results, which can then be forwarded to the necessary points of contact. For example, you can have all the web server vulnerabilities automatically collected and sent to the web server administrator. Similarly, you can have occurrences of data storage violations sent to your spillage team for faster action. Unless there is only one administrator, it might make sense to automate the report delivery process to alleviate the primary administrator from having to manually manage every report. The service administrators can be more efficient because they are getting the reports that are most relevant to their role.

Remediation

When the scanner uncovers a vulnerability, it provides as much information about it as possible. Figure 6-11 shows the detail screen provide by OpenVAS on an uncovered vulnerability. This screen shows a summary of the vulnerability, the location of the resource of concern, the vulnerability's impact, how it was discovered, and any solutions or workarounds.

Remediation of network vulnerabilities should be done as quickly as possible after discovery, but not so haphazardly as to make the situation worse. Effective remediation requires a continuous examination for vulnerabilities combined with a thoughtful process to remedy problems to keep the organization's resources confidential and accessible. The simplest mechanism for verifying remediation is to compare consecutive vulnerability scans to determine that vulnerabilities were addressed via software patch or upgrade. Many vendors offer solutions to manage the whole process of patching in a separate practice called patch management. Should a compensating control be used, you can provide feedback into the vulnerability management system by adding a note to the report or you can override the alert. This helps document the actions you took to address the problem in the event that you are unable to apply an update.

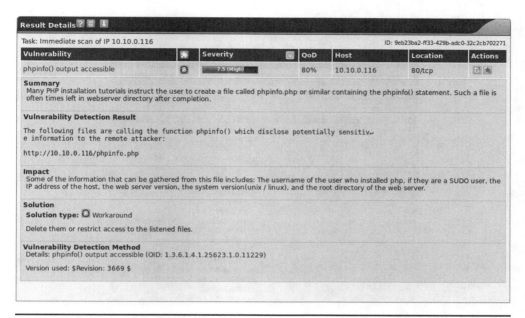

Figure 6-11   OpenVAS vulnerability detail screenshot

Prioritizing

Systems administrators can easily be overwhelmed with the sheer volume of results. This is where prioritization of the vulnerabilities and the associated remediation steps can help. Ideally, the discussion on how to prioritize the response includes the capabilities of the technical staff as well as the overall business goals of the organization. Including key stakeholders in the discussion, or at the very least making them aware of your methodology, will ensure buy-in for future policy changes.

Criticality

The decision on how to respond to the results of a scan is driven by economics; we either have limited time, money, or personnel that can be used to remediate an issue, so we must be judicious in our response. To help with this, both Nessus and OpenVAS provide quick visual references for the overall severity of a discovered vulnerability on its result pages, as shown in Figure 6-12. Color-coding the results and making them sortable will help decision-makers quickly focus on the most critical issues and make the best use of limited resources.

A well-known standard for quantifying severity is the Common Vulnerability Scoring System (CVSS). As a framework designed to standardize the severity ratings for vulnerabilities, its model ensures accurate quantitative measurement so that users can better understand the impact of these weaknesses. With the CVSS scoring standard, members of industries, academia, and governments can communicate clearly across their communities.

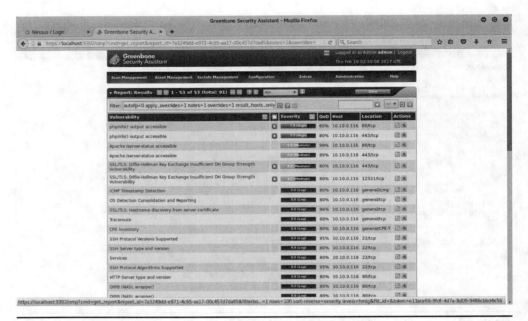

Figure 6-12   Results of an OpenVAS vulnerability scan, sorted by severity

EXAM TIP   The Common Vulnerability Scoring System (CVSS) is the de facto standard for assessing the severity of vulnerabilities. Therefore, you should be familiar with CVSS and its metric groups: base, temporal, and environmental.

Difficulty of Implementation

You may encounter challenges in remediation due to the difficulty in implementing a solution. In cases where there is a significant delay in implementation due to technical reasons or cost, you should still work to achieve the goals of a security requirement using some compensating control. Including members of the nontechnical team will help in adoption of whatever alternate plan is developed while working toward implementation of the primary solution.

Communication/Change Control

You can see that a tremendous amount of effort goes into managing the actions after getting the results of a vulnerability scan. Although implementing every recommendation may seem like a good idea on the surface, we cannot go about it all at once. Without a systematic approach to managing all the necessary security changes, we risk putting ourselves in a worse place than when we began. The purpose of establishing formal communication and change management procedures is to ensure that the right changes are made the first time, that services remain available, and that resources are used efficiently throughout the changes.

Change Advisory Board

Many organizations use a change advisory board (CAB) to approve major changes to a company's policies and to assist change management in the monitoring and assessment of changes. Members of the CAB often include any entity that could be adversely affected by the proposed changes. These include customers, managers, technical staff, and company leadership. When convening, members of the board ensure that all proposed changes address the issue and make sense from both a business and a technical perspective.

Sandboxing/Testing

In September of 2016, the OpenSSL Project, which maintains an open source implementation of the widely used SSL and TLS protocols, released what it thought was a routine security patch as part of its periodic updates. The included advisory indicated that under certain conditions the unsafe code could lead to a denial of service and was given a severity rating of "low." The patch, however, was found to have introduced another much more serious vulnerability that could allow an attacker to execute arbitrary code. Now imagine deploying the first patch across a very large network without testing it first on a subset of devices or in a sandbox. Not only would you have dramatically increased the attack surface of your organization but also the downtime because you would have to patch multiple times. This illustrates the importance of testing patches in a safe environment before deploying across the whole enterprise.

Inhibitors to Remediation

Even a solid plan for remediation that has stakeholder buy-in sometimes faces obstacles. Many of the challenges arise from processes that have major dependencies on the IT systems or from a stale policy that fails to adequately address the changing technological landscape. In this section, we cover some common obstacles to remediation and how we might avoid them.

Memorandum of Understanding

The memorandum of understanding (MOU) outlines the duties and expectations of all concerned parties. As with a penetration test, a vulnerability scan should have a clearly defined scope, along with formal rules of engagement (ROE) that dictate above all else what can be done during the assessment and in the event of a vulnerability discovery. For example, conducting a scan on production systems during times of high usage would not be suitable. There might also be a situation that, without a formal MOU in place, would leave too much ambiguity. It wouldn't be hard to imagine that the discovery of a vulnerability on your network might have implications on an adjacent network not controlled by you. Also, a misconfiguration of an adjacent network might have a direct impact on your organization's services. In either case, an MOU that covers such conditions will clarify how to proceed in a way that's satisfactory for everyone involved.

Service Level Agreement

Many IT service providers perform their services based on an existing service level agreement (SLA) between them and the service recipient. An SLA is a contract that can exist within a company (say, between a business unit and the IT staff) or with the organization and an outside provider. SLAs exist to outline what the roles and responsibilities are for the service providers, including the limit of the services they can perform. Unless remediation is explicitly part of an SLA, providers cannot be compelled to perform those steps.

Organizational Governance

The system of processes and rules an organization uses to direct and control its operations is call its *corporate governance*. Corporate governance aims to strike a sensible balance between the priorities of company stakeholders. In some cases, governance may interrupt the application of remedial steps because those actions might negatively affect other business areas. This highlights the importance of communicating your actions with corporate leadership so that they can factor the effects of remedial action in with other issues to make a decision. Strong communication enables timely decision-making in the best interest of the company.

Business Process Interruption

There's never a good time to apply a patch or take other remedial actions. Highly efficient business and industrial processes such as just-in-time manufacturing have allowed businesses to reduce process time and increase overall efficiency. Underpinning these systems are production IT systems that themselves are optimized to the business. A major drawback, however, is that some systems might be more susceptible to disruption due to their optimized states. This fear of unpredictably or instability in the overall process is often enough for company leadership to delay major changes to production systems, or to avoid them altogether.

Degrading Functionality

Although there's no equivalent to the Hippocratic Oath in network administration, we must always try to "do no harm" to our production systems. Sometimes the recommended treatment, such as quarantining key systems due to critical vulnerabilities, might be deemed unacceptable to leadership. How much risk you and your leadership are willing to underwrite is a decision for your organization, but you should aim to have the most accurate information about the state of the vulnerabilities as possible. If you discover that an important remedial action breaks critical applications in a test environment, then the alternative isn't to avoid patching. Rather, you must devise other mitigating controls to address the vulnerabilities until a suitable patch can be developed.

Ongoing Scanning and Continuous Monitoring

Where feasible, you should schedule automated vulnerability scanning to occur daily. Depending on the types of networks you operate and your security policies, you might opt to perform these more often, always using the most updated version of the scanning tool. You should pay extra attention to critical vulnerabilities and aim to remediate them within 48 hours. Recognizing that maintaining software, libraries, and reports might be tedious for administrators, some companies have begun to offer web-based scanning solutions. Qualys and Tenable, for example, both provide cloud-enabled web application security scanners that can be run from any number of cloud service providers. Promising increased scalability and speed across networks of various sizes, these companies provide several related services based on subscription tier.

Analyze Reports from a Vulnerability Scan

Given the diversity and scale of the modern network, making sense of the output of a vulnerability scan might be a daunting task. Fortunately, tools such as Nessus deliver their comprehensive reports with visual tools and technical details behind the vulnerabilities they uncover. Understanding why vulnerabilities exist and how they can be exploited will assist you in analyzing the final scan report. Figure 6-13 show the screen generated by Nessus after a vulnerability scan. The tool assigns certain colors to different levels of severity and produces simple graphs to indicate the distribution of vulnerabilities.

Review and Interpret Scan Results

No automated vulnerability report is ever perfectly accurate. It is up to the analyst to review and make sense of it before passing it on to others in the organization. The two most important outcomes of the review process are to identify false positives and exceptions to policies. Once entries in these categories are removed from consideration, one must then prioritize response actions.

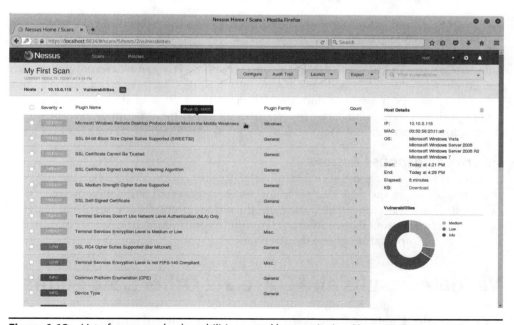

Figure 6-13   List of uncovered vulnerabilities sorted by severity in a Nessus report

Identify False Positives

Reporting a problem when no such issue exists is a challenge when dealing with any type of scanner. False positives with vulnerability scanners are particularly frustrating because the effort required to remediate a suspected issue might be resource intensive. A 2 percent false positive rate may not be a problem for smaller organizations, but the same rate on a large network with thousands of endpoints will cause significant problems for the security staff. Although it's important to quickly produce a solution to an uncovered vulnerability, you should take a moment to consider the reasons why a scanner might cry wolf. Sometimes the logic that a check, NVT, or plug-in uses might be flawed, resulting in a report of a vulnerability that might not exist. Understand that these tests are authored with certain assumptions about a system and that it may be impossible to write logic in such a way that it applies perfectly to every system.

NOTE Although vulnerability scanners have improved over the years, OS and software detection in vulnerability scanners isn't perfect. This makes detection in environments with custom operating systems and devices particularly challenging. Many devices use lightweight versions of Linux and Apache web server that are burned directly onto the device's read-only memory. You should expect to get a higher number of alerts in these cases because the vulnerability scanner might not be able to tell exactly what kind of system it is. However, you should also take care not to immediately dismiss alerts on these systems either. Sometimes a well-known vulnerability may exist in unexpected places because of how the vulnerable software packages were ported over to the new system.

Identify Exceptions

There are always exceptions, even on networks. There is no way for the authors of a vulnerability test to know the details of your network, so they must create rules that are sometimes less granular, which may lead to false positives. In this case, it might be useful to customize your own test once that false positive is discovered. Another reason for a false positive could be that you've already determined the appropriate compensating control for an issue but have not correctly disposed of the alert.

Prioritize Response Actions

The aim is to have the most accurate information about your network because it means more confidence in the decisions made by your technical staff and company leadership. With vulnerability accurately identified and the most appropriate courses of action developed and refined through open lines of communication, you can prioritize responses that have minimal impact throughout the company.

Validate Results and Correlate Other Data Points

Armed with the feedback from the vulnerability scan reports, it can straightforward to verify its results. Figure 6-14 shows the output for an uncovered vulnerability on a Windows host located at 10.10.0.115 that's related to the Remote Desktop functionality.

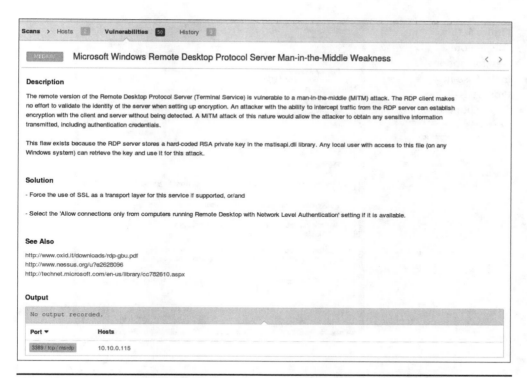

Figure 6-14 Details on a vulnerability in the Remote Desktop Protocol on a Windows host

The protocol was found to have a weakness in its implementation of the cryptographic exchange during identity verification. As a solution, Nessus suggests that we either force the use of SSL for the service or enable Network Level Authentication. When we move over to the Windows host shown in Figure 6-15, we can see that the option for the use of Network Level Authentication is available for us to select.

We see that the vulnerability scanner successfully identified the less-secure state of the Windows host. Fortunately for us, we don't have to manually verify and adjust for every occurrence; this can all be automated by enforcing a new group policy or by using any number of automated remediation solutions.

NOTE The goal of major databases such as the Open Source Vulnerability Database (OSVDB) and National Vulnerability Database (U.S.) is to publish Common Vulnerabilities and Exposures (CVE) for public awareness. These databases are incredibly useful but do not always have complete information on vulnerabilities because many are still being researched. Therefore, you should use supplemental sources in your research, such as the Bugtraq, OWASP, and CERT.

Figure 6-15
The Remote
Desktop options
in the System
Properties dialog
for a Windows 7
host

Compare to Best Practices or Compliance

Several benchmarks across industry, academia, and government are available for you to improve your network's security. On military networks, the most widely used set of standards is developed by the Defense Information Systems Agency (DISA). Its Security Technical Implementation Guides (STIGs), combined with the National Security Agency (NSA) guides, are the configuration standards used on DoD information systems. Figure 6-16 shows the DISA STIG port, with a small sample of the latest guides.

STIGs provide the technical steps required to harden network devices, endpoints, and software. Note that although many STIG benchmarks are available to the public, some require a Department of Defense PKI certificate, such as those found in Common Access Cards (CACs), for access. Using the Security Content Automation Protocol (SCAP) specification, you can apply these standards or monitor for compliance across your network.

Reconcile Results

If there's one thing that's certain in incident response and forensic analysis, it's that taking thorough notes will make your job much easier in the end. These include the steps you take to configure a device, validate its configuration, verify its operation, and of course test vulnerabilities. Taking notes on how you uncovered and dealt with a vulnerability will aid in continuity, and it might be required based on the industry in which you operate. Both Nessus and OpenVAS provide ways to track how the corrective action performs on network devices. Should your network activity be examined by an investigation, it's

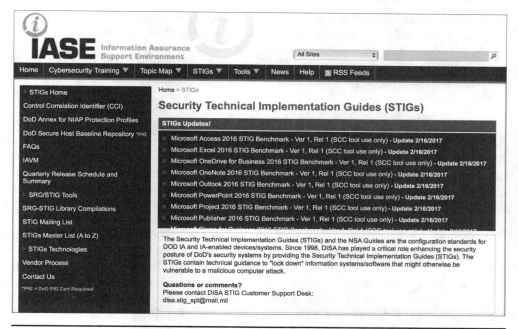

Figure 6-16   The Security Technical Implementation Guides portal

also good to know you've taken thorough notes about every action you performed to make the network safer.

Review Related Logs and/or Other Data Sources

When reviewing the report, you should also review event logs and network data. You can compare running services, listening ports, and open connections against a list of authorized services to identify any abnormal behavior. Correlating the vulnerability scan output with historical network and service data serves several functions. First, it verifies that your logging mechanism is capturing the activities related to the vulnerability scans, because these scans will often trigger logging. Second, you should be able to see changes in the network based on the patches or changes you've made because of compensating controls. Finally, the logs may give insight into whether any of the uncovered vulnerabilities have been acted upon already. Security information and event management (SIEM) tools can assist tremendously with validation because they will likely be able to visualize all the scanning activity, and because you are likely already ingesting other log data, these tools provide a useful place to begin correlation.

Determine Trends

Using either the built-in trending functionality or with help from other software, you can track how vulnerabilities in the network have changed over time. Trending improves context and allows your security response team to tailor its threat mitigation strategies to its efforts more efficiently. Additionally, you can also determine if any of your solutions are taking hold and are effective. Linking the vulnerability scanners with existing SIEM platforms isn't the only option; you can also track progress on fixing problems using existing trouble ticket software. This helps with the internal tracking of the issues, and allows for visibility from leadership, in the case that outside assistance is required to enforce a policy change.

Chapter Review

Vulnerability scanning is a key responsibility of any security team. Taking the steps to understand and track the vulnerabilities a network faces is important in determining the best mitigation strategies. Keeping key stakeholders involved in the effort will also enable you to make decisions that are in the best interests of the organization. When you increase the visibility of the vulnerability status of your network, you ensure that your security team can focus its efforts in the right place and that leadership can devote the right resources to keeping the network safe. We covered several tools, including Nessus, OpenVAS, and Nikto, all of which provide vulnerability scan information using continuously updated libraries of vulnerability information. Some of these tools also offer the ability to automate the process and output in formats for ingestion in other IT systems. Vulnerability scanning is a continuous process, requiring your security team to monitor the network regularly to determine changes in detected vulnerabilities, gauge the efficacy of the patches and compensating controls, and adjust its efforts accordingly to stay ahead of threats.

Questions

1. Which of the following is an open source vulnerability scanner that lacks a graphical user interface?
   A. OpenVAS
   B. NASL
   C. Nessus
   D. Nikto

2. When prioritizing the remediation of newly discovered vulnerabilities, you should consider all the following *except* which?
   A. Criticality
   B. SCAP score
   C. Difficulty of implementation
   D. CVSS

3. All of the following might be inhibitors to the remediation of vulnerabilities *except* which?

   A. SLAs

   B. TLAs

   C. Governance

   D. Business processes interruption

4. Which of the following statements is true about false positives?

   A. False positives are not generally a problem, but true negatives might be.

   B. False positives are indicative of human error in an automated scanning process.

   C. False positives are more problematic for smaller organizations than larger ones.

   D. False positives waste organizational resources.

Refer to the following illustration for Questions 5–8:

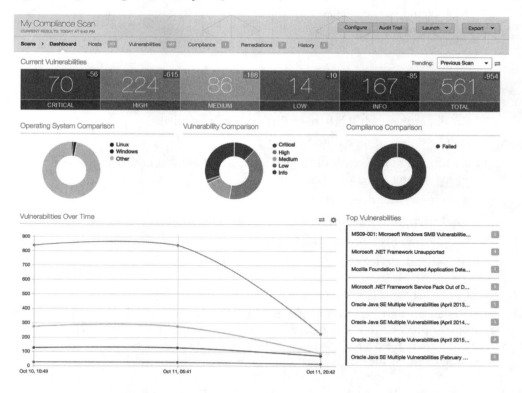

PART II

5. All of the following might account for the sudden drop in vulnerabilities on October 11 *except* which?

   A. The team decided to prioritize remediation by difficulty of implementation.

   B. The tool was tuned to reduce the number of false positives.

   C. A malfunctioning software update server was repaired on the morning of October 11.

   D. The team decided to prioritize remediation by criticality.

6. If your performance was measured strictly in terms of the total number of vulnerabilities, what might you do on October 12?

   A. Prioritize remediation by criticality.

   B. Focus on "high" vulnerabilities.

   C. Prioritize remediation by difficulty of implementation.

   D. Suspend change management protocols.

7. What would be the likeliest impediment to correcting the 70 remaining "critical" vulnerabilities?

   A. The organization lacks governance processes related to vulnerability management.

   B. The vulnerabilities exist in servers that are needed for mission-critical business processes.

   C. All pertinent MOUs have expired or been rescinded.

   D. The organization has no SLAs in place.

8. What could most likely lead to an increase in the number of vulnerabilities detected during a scan on October 12?

   A. Software security patches

   B. Further tuning of the vulnerability scanner

   C. Vulnerability scanner updates/plug-ins

   D. Network device configuration improvements

Use the following scenario to answer Questions 9–12:

You are asked to start performing vulnerability scans as part of a broader vulnerability management process. You have been running scans every 48 hours for the last couple of weeks and have noticed a high rate of false positives on your end-user workstations. More concerning to you is the fact that several critical vulnerabilities exist in both the primary and backup database servers used by the accounting department. With the end of the fiscal year approaching, you are pretty sure that the business impact will be considered too high to allow for remediation.

9. How might you best be able to reduce the high rate of false positive results?

   A. Validating the logic of the checks against your IT environment

   B. Using a different vendor's scanner to double-check your results

   C. Limiting your vulnerability scans to the critical hosts on your network

   D. Prioritizing your response actions

10. Apart from reducing the rate of false positives, how else might you deal with them?

    A. Correlate them to other data points.

    B. Compare them to best practices.

    C. Prioritize your response actions.

    D. Review related logs.

11. Which of the following actions is *least* likely to help you get permission to remediate the critical vulnerabilities found on the database servers?

    A. Scheduling the remediation on a weekend

    B. Implementing an SLA for your organization

    C. Using a sandbox to test the remediation process

    D. Presenting a rollback plan in case the remediation fails

12. What should you do with your growing library of vulnerability scan reports?

    A. Ensure you keep the last two sets of results.

    B. Present them to your change advisory board.

    C. Keep them for regulatory compliance.

    D. Track how vulnerabilities in the network have changed over time.

Answers

1. **D.** Nikto is a web server vulnerability scanner with only a command-line interface. NASL is not a vulnerability scanner but rather the Nessus Attack Scripting Language.

2. **B.** The Security Content Automation Protocol (SCAP) defines the manner in which security software (such as a vulnerability scanner) communicates information about flaws and security configurations. It plays no role in the prioritization of remediation. The Common Vulnerability Scoring System (CVSS), on the other hand, can be used to determine the criticality of vulnerabilities.

3. **B.** Memorandums of understanding (MOUs), service level agreements (SLAs), organizational governance, business process interruptions, and degradation of functionality are all important factors that could delay remediation.

4. **D.** False positives typically result in wasted resources because they have to be manually investigated to ensure they are not real issues.

5. **D.** The drop in critical vulnerabilities between the last two scans was only 56 (for a 44 percent improvement), compared to a drop of 615 (or 73 percent) in high vulnerabilities and 188 (or 67 percent) in medium vulnerabilities. The greater drops in less-critical vulnerabilities make it less likely that focus was on criticality.

6. **C.** The fastest way to reduce the total count of vulnerabilities is to go after the easier ones to fix first. It is important to note, however, that this may not be the most effective way to reduce the overall risk to the organization, because the easier fixes might not be the ones that mitigate the greatest risks.

7. **B.** Mission-critical business processes often pose challenges to remediation because the fixes need to take place after business hours and typically require extensive testing and rollback planning. The lack of governance, MOUs, or SLAs would likely expedite rather than hinder remediation.

8. **C.** Vulnerability scanners are periodically updated to respond to newly discovered vulnerabilities. These tools can also be calibrated or tuned to change the rate of false positives, though this process can sometimes blind the scanner to real vulnerabilities.

9. **A.** Sometimes the logic that a check or plug-in uses is flawed, or makes bad assumptions about your environment. It is sometimes helpful to examine the checks that yield the highest false-positive rates and look for opportunities to tune them. Adding a second scanner will probably increase the total number of false positives, while the last two responses do nothing to reduce that number.

10. **C.** If you are unable to reduce false-positive rates, one option is simply to prioritize other results higher in terms of taking action. Over time, analysts become adept at identifying the likely false positives and could just move them to the bottom of the queue. The risk in doing this is that, unless you are certain that the result is unimportant, you risk deferring a real issue indefinitely.

11. **B.** Service level agreements (SLAs) almost always exist between an organization and an external service provider, so one wouldn't help you get permission. The other three actions, particularly if they are taken together, can present a compelling case to senior management.

12. **D.** Trend analysis improves context and allows your security response team to tailor its threat mitigation strategies to its efforts more efficiently. Depending on your specific organization's regulatory environment, you may be required to keep some of these reports. However, because this is not universally true, keeping the reports for regulatory compliance is not the best answer.

PART III

Cyber Incident Response

■ **Chapter 7**   The Incident Response Process
■ **Chapter 8**   Determining the Impact of Incidents
■ **Chapter 9**   Preparing the Incident Response Toolkit
■ **Chapter 10**   Selecting the Best Course of Action

The Incident Response Process

In this chapter you will learn:

- The stakeholders during incident response
- Containment techniques
- Eradication techniques
- Response validation
- Corrective actions
- The purpose of communications processes

I am prepared for the worst, but hope for the best.

—Benjamin Disraeli

A Cast of Characters

Before we dive into the myriad technical issues to consider as part of incident response, we should start at the same topic with which we will wrap up this chapter: people. In the midst of incident responses, it is all too easy to get so focused on the technical challenges that we forget the human element, which is arguably at least as important. We focus our discussion on the various roles involved and the manner in which we must ensure these roles are communicating effectively with each other and with those outside the organization.

Key Roles

Broadly speaking, the key roles required in incident responses can be determined beforehand based on established escalation thresholds. The in-house technical team will always be involved, of course, but when and how are others brought in? This depends on the analysis that your organization performed as part of developing the incident response (IR) plan. Figure 7-1 shows a typical escalation model followed by most organizations.

The technical team is unlikely to involve management in routine responses such as when an e-mail with a malicious link or attachment somehow gets to a user's inbox but is not clicked on. You still have to respond to this and will probably notify others

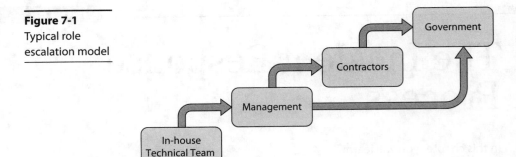

Figure 7-1
Typical role
escalation model

(for example, the user, supervisor, and threat intelligence team) of the attempt, but management will not be "in the loop" at every step of the response. The situation is different when the incident or response has a direct impact on the business, such as when you have to reboot a production server in order to eradicate malware on it. Management needs to be closely involved in decision-making in this scenario. At some point, the skills and abilities of the in-house team will probably be insufficient to effectively deal with an incident, which is when the response is escalated and you bring in contractors to augment your team or even take over aspects of the response. Obviously, this is an expensive move, so you want to carefully consider when to do this, and management will almost certainly be involved in that decision. Finally, there are incidents that require government involvement. Typically, though not always, this comes in the form of notifying and perhaps bringing in a law enforcement agency such as the FBI or Secret Service. This may happen with or without your organization calling in external contractors, but will always involve senior leadership. Let's take a look at some of the issues involved with each of the roles in this model.

Technical Staff

The composition of the technical team that responds to an incident is usually going to depend on the incident itself. Some responses will involve a single analyst, while others may involve dozens of technical personnel from many different departments. Clearly, there is no one-size-fits-all team, so we need to pull in the right people to deal with the right problem. The part of this that should be prescribed ahead of time is the manner in which we assemble the team and, most importantly, who is calling the shots during the various stages of incident response. If you don't build this into your plan, and then periodically test it, you will likely lose precious hours (or even days) in the food fight that will likely ensue during a major incident.

A best practice is to leverage your risk management plan to identify likely threats to your systems. Then, for every threat (or at least the major ones), you can "wargame" the response to a handful of ways in which it might become manifest. At each major decision point in the process, you should ask the question, who decides? Whatever the answer is, the next question should be, does that person have the required authority? If the person does, you just check it off and move to the next one. If the authority is lacking, you have to decide whether someone else should make the decision or whether that authority should be delegated in writing to the first person you came up with. Either way, you don't want to be in the midst of an IR only to find you have to sit on your hands for a few hours while the decision is vetted up and down the corporate chain.

Tales from the Trenches: Pulling the Plug

We recently ran a large, multisector cyber-exercise for a major U.S. city. At one point, the attackers compromised the domain controller for a financial institution and created a new domain admin account with which they were expanding their footprint. An astute analyst in the security operations center (SOC) detected this and sent a change request to have the host taken offline. They watched the box and could tell the attacker was not active, but it was a tense wait. At the first sign of a remote login to that account and having received no response from the change approval authority, the SOC Director pulled the plug himself. When the exercise referees challenged him on his "unauthorized" move, he was able to produce a response plan that explicitly delegated the authority to take systems offline if they appeared to have been compromised and posed an immediate risk to the security of the network. He was able to quickly stop an attack because his organization had anticipated this scenario and granted the appropriate authorities to the technical staff. The red team was not happy.

Contractors

No matter how skilled or well-resourced an internal technical team is, there may come a point when you have to bring in hired guns. Very few organizations, for example, are capable of responding to incidents involving nation-state offensive operators. Calling in the cavalry, however, requires a significant degree of prior coordination and communication. Apart from the obvious service contract with the incident response firm, you have to plan and test exactly how they would come into your facility, what they would have access to, who would be watching and supporting them, and what (if any) parts of your system are off-limits to them. These companies are very experienced in doing this sort of thing and can usually provide a step-by-step guide as well as templates for nondisclosure agreements (NDA) and contracts. What they cannot do for you is to train your staff (technical or otherwise) on how to deal with them once they descend upon your networks. This is where rehearsals and tests come in handy: in communicating to every stakeholder in your organization what a contractor response would look like and what their roles would be.

It is possible to go too far in embedding these IR contractors. Some organizations outsource all IR as a perceived cost-saving measure. The rationale is that you'd pay only for what you need because, let's face it, qualified personnel are hard to find, slow to develop in-house, and expensive. The truth of the matter, however, is that this approach is fundamentally flawed in at least two ways. The first is that incident response is inextricably linked with critical business processes whose nuances are difficult for third parties to grasp. This is why you will always need at least one qualified, hands-on incident responder who is part of the organization and can at least translate technical actions into business impacts. The second reason is that IR can be at least as much about interpersonal communications and trust as it is about technical controls. External parties will have a much more difficult time dealing with the many individuals involved. One way or another, you are better off having some internal IR capability and augmenting it to a lesser or greater degree with external contractors.

Management

Incident response almost always has some level of direct impact (sometimes catastrophic) on an organization's business processes. For this reason, the IR team should include key senior leaders from every affected business unit. Their involvement is more than just to provide support, but to shape the response process to minimize disruptions, address regulatory issues, and provide an interface into the affected personnel in their units as well as to higher-level leaders within the organization. Effective incident response efforts almost always have the direct and active involvement of management as part of a multi-disciplinary response team.

Integrating these business leaders into the team is not a trivial effort. Even if they are as knowledgeable and passionate about cybersecurity as you are (which is exceptionally rare in the wild), their priorities will oftentimes be at odds with yours. Consider a compromise of a server that is responsible for interfacing with your internal accounting systems as well as your external payment processing gateway. You know that every second you keep that box on the network you risk further compromises or massive exfiltration of customer data. Still, every second that box is off the network will cause the company significantly in terms of lost sales and revenue. If you approach the appropriate business managers for the first time when you are faced with this situation, things will not go well for anybody. If, on the other hand, there is a process in place with which they're both familiar and supportive, then the outcome will be better, faster, and less risky.

Law Enforcement

A number of incidents will require you to involve a law enforcement agency (LEA). Sometimes, the laws that establish these requirements also have very specific timelines, lest you incur civil or even criminal penalties. In other cases, there may not be a requirement to involve an LEA, but it may be a very good idea to do so all the same. The scenario we just described involving the payment processor is just one example of a situation in which you probably want to involve an LEA. If you (or the rest of your team) don't know which incidents fall into these two categories of required or recommended reporting, you may want to put that pretty high on your priority list for conversations to be had with your leadership and legal counsel.

When an LEA is involved, they will bring their own perspective on the response process. Whereas you are focused on mitigation and recovery, and management is keen on business continuity, law enforcement will be driven by the need to preserve evidence (which should be, but is not always, an element of your IR plan anyway). These three sets of goals can be at odds with each other, particularly if you don't have a thorough, realistic, and rehearsed plan in place. If your first meeting with representatives from an LEA occurs during an actual incident response, you will likely struggle with it more than you would if you rehearse this part of the plan.

Stakeholders

The term *stakeholder* is broad and could include a very large set of people. For the purposes of the CSA+ exam, what we call IR stakeholders are those individuals and teams who are part of your organization and have a role in helping with some aspects of some incident response. They each have a critical role to play in some (maybe even most) but not all responses. This presents a challenge for the IR team because the supporting stakeholders will not normally be as accustomed to executing response operations as the direct players are. Extra efforts must be taken to ensure they know what to do and how to do it when bad things happen.

Human Resources

The likeliest involvement of human resources (HR) staff in a response is when the team determines that a member of the organization probably had a role in the incident. The role need not be malicious, mind you, because it could be a failure to comply with policies (for example, connecting a thumb drive into a computer when that is not allowed) or repeated failures to apply security awareness training (for example, clicking a link in an e-mail even after a few rounds of remedial training). Malicious, careless, or otherwise, the actions of our teammates can and do lead to serious incidents. Disciplinary action in those cases all but requires HR involvement.

There are other situations in which you may need a human resources employee as part of the response, such as when overtime is required for the response, or when key people need to be called in from time off or vacation. The safe bet is to involve HR in your IR planning process and especially in your drills, and let them tell you what, if any, involvement they should have in the various scenarios.

Legal

Whenever an incident response escalates to the point of involving government agencies such as law enforcement, you will almost certainly be coordinating with legal counsel. Apart from reporting criminal or state-sponsored attacks on your systems, there are regulatory considerations such as those we discussed in Chapter 5. For instance, if you work in an organization covered by HIPAA and you are responding to an incident that compromised the protected health information (PHI) of 500 or more people, your organization will have some very specific reporting requirements that will have to be reviewed by your legal and/or compliance team(s).

The law is a remarkably complicated field, so even actions that would seem innocuous to many of us may have some onerous legal implications. Though some lawyers are very knowledgeable in complex technological and cybersecurity issues, most have only a cursory familiarity with them. In our experience, starting a dialogue early with the legal team and then maintaining a regular, ongoing conversation are critical to staying out of career-ending trouble.

Marketing

Managing communications with your customers and investors is critical to successfully recovering from an incident. What, when, and how you say things is of strategic importance, so you're better off leaving it to the professionals who, most likely, reside in your marketing department. If your organization has a dedicated strategic communications, public relations, media, or public affairs team, it should also be involved in the response process.

Like every other aspect of IR, planning and practice are the keys to success. When it comes to the marketing team, however, this may be truer than with most others. The reason is that these individuals, who are probably only vaguely aware of the intricate technical details of a compromise and incident response, will be the public face of the incident to a much broader community. Their main goal is to mitigate the damage to the trust that customers and investors have in the organization. To do this, they need to have just the right amount of technical information and present it in a manner that is approachable to broad audiences and can be dissected into effective sound bites (or tweets). For this, they will rely heavily on those members of the technical team who are able to translate techno-speak into something the average person can understand.

 EXAM TIP When you see references on the exam to the marketing team, think of it as whatever part of the organization communicates directly with the general public. Don't overthink the question if your organization calls this team something else.

Management

We already mentioned management when we discussed the roles of incident response. We return to this group now to address its involvement in incident response for managers who are not directly participating in it. This can happen in a variety of ways, but consider the members of senior management in your organization. They are unlikely to be involved in any but the most serious of incidents, but you still need their buy-in and support to ensure you get the right resources from other business areas. Keeping them informed in situations in which you may need their support is a balancing act; you don't want to take too much of their time (or bring them into an active role), but you need to have enough awareness so all it takes is a short call for help and they'll make things happen.

Another way in which members of management are stakeholders for incident response is not so much in what they do, but in what they don't do. Consider an incident that takes priority over some routine upgrades you were supposed to do for one of your business units. If that unit's leadership is not aware of what IR is in general, or of the importance of the ongoing response in particular, it could create unnecessary distractions at a time when you can least afford them. Effective communications with leadership can build trust and provide you a buffer in times of need.

Response Techniques

Although we commonly use the terms interchangeably, there are subtle differences between an *event*, which is any occurrence that can be observed, verified, and documented, and an *incident*, which is one or more related events that compromise the

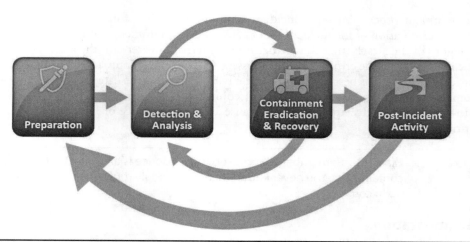

Figure 7-2 The incident response lifecycle

organization's security posture. *Incident response* is the process of negating the effects of an incident on an information system.

There are many incident response models, but all share some basic characteristics. They all require us to take some preparatory actions before anything bad happens, to identify and analyze the event in order to determine the appropriate counter-actions, to correct the problem(s), and finally to keep this incident from happening again. Clearly, efforts to prevent future occurrences tie back to our preparatory actions, which creates a cycle. Figure 7-2 shows the entire process, which is described in NIST Special Publication 800-61 (Revision 2). In this chapter, we focus on correcting the problems caused by an incident. We'll assume that someone has already detected and analyzed the incident for us, and we take it from there.

NOTE Though we are following the CSA+ exam objectives here and focusing on containment and eradication, it is important to note that these are just part of a holistic incident management process that should include procedures for detecting, analyzing, and recovering from incidents. Recovery is the part that restores the functionality of an information system to its pre-incident state.

Containment

Once you know that a threat agent has compromised the security of your information system, your first order of business is to keep things from getting worse. Containment is a set of actions that attempts to deny the threat agent the ability or means to cause further damage. The goal is to prevent or reduce the spread of this incident while you strive to eradicate it. This is akin to confining highly contagious patients in an isolation room of a hospital until they can be cured to keep others from getting infected. A proper containment process buys the incident response team time for a proper investigation and determination of the incident's root cause. The containment should be based on the category of the attack (that is, whether it was internal or external), the assets affected by the incident, and the criticality of those assets. Containment approaches can be proactive or reactive. Which is best depends on the environment and the category of the attack. In some cases, the best action might be to disconnect the affected system from the network. However, this reactive approach could cause a denial of service or limit functionality of critical systems.

EXAM TIP Remember that preserving evidence is an important part of containment. You never know when a seemingly routine response will end up in court.

Segmentation

A well-designed security architecture (we get to this in Part IV of this book) will segment our information systems by some set of criteria such as function (for example, finance or HR) or sensitivity (for example, unclassified or secret). *Segmentation* is the breaking apart of a network into subnetworks (or segments) so that hosts in different segments are not able to directly communicate with each other. This can be done by either physically wiring separate networks or by logically assigning devices to separate virtual local area networks (VLANs). In either case, traffic between network segments must go through some sort of gateway device, which is oftentimes a router with the appropriate access control lists (ACLs). For example, the accounting division may have its own VLAN that prevents users in the research and development (R&D) division from directly accessing the financial data servers. If certain R&D users had legitimate needs for such access, they would have to be added to the gateway device's ACL, which could place restrictions based on source/destination addresses, time of day, or even specific applications and data to be accessed.

The advantages of network segmentation during incident response should be pretty obvious: compromises can be constrained to the network segment in which they started. To be clear, it is still possible to go from one segment to another, like in the case in the R&D users example. Some VLANs may also have vulnerabilities that could allow an attacker to jump from one to another without going through the gateway. Still, segmentation provides an important layer of defense that can help contain an incident. Without it, the resulting "flat" network will make it more difficult to contain an incident.

Isolation

Although it is certainly helpful to segment the network as part of its architectural design, we already saw that this can still allow an attacker to easily move between hosts on the same subnet. As part of your preparations for IR, it is helpful to establish an isolation VLAN, much like hospitals prepare isolation rooms before any patients actually need them. The IR team would then have the ability to quickly move any compromised or suspicious hosts to this VLAN until they can be further analyzed. The isolation VLAN would have no connectivity to the rest of the network, which would prevent the spread of any malware. This isolation would also prevent compromised hosts from communicating with external hosts such as command-and-control (C2) nodes. About the only downside to using isolation VLANs is that some advanced malware can detect this situation and then take steps to eradicate itself from the infected hosts. Although this may sound wonderful from an IR perspective, it does hinder our ability to understand what happened and how the compromise was executed so that we can keep it from happening in the future.

While a host is in isolation, the response team is able to safely observe its behaviors to gain information about the nature of the incident. By monitoring its network traffic, we can discover external hosts (for example, C2 nodes and tool repositories) that may be part of the compromise. This allows us to contact other organizations and get their help in shutting down whatever infrastructure the attackers are using. We can also monitor the compromised host's running processes and file system to see where the malware resides and what it is trying to do on the live system. This all allows us to better understand the incident and how to best eradicate it. It also allows us to create indicators of compromise (IOCs) that we can then share with others such as the Computer Emergency Readiness Team (CERT) or an Information Sharing and Analysis Center (ISAC).

Removal

At some point in the response process, you may have to remove compromised hosts from the network altogether. This can happen after isolation or immediately upon noticing the compromise, depending on the situation. Isolation is ideal if you have the means to study the behaviors and gain actionable intelligence, or if you're overwhelmed by a large number of potentially compromised hosts that need to be triaged. Still, one way or another, some of the compromised hosts will come off the network permanently.

When you remove a host from the network, you need to decide whether you will keep it powered on, shut it down and preserve it, or simply rebuild it. Ideally, the criteria for making this decision is already spelled out in the IR plan. Here are some of the factors to consider in this situation:

- **Threat intelligence value**   A compromised computer can be a treasure trove of information about the tactics, techniques, procedures (TTPs), and tools of an adversary—particularly a sophisticated or unique one. If you have a threat intelligence capability in your organization and can gain new or valuable information from a compromised host, you may want to keep it running until its analysis is completed.

- **Crime scene evidence**   Almost every intentional compromise of a computer system is a criminal act in many countries, including the U.S. Even if you don't plan to pursue a criminal or civil case against the perpetrators, it is possible that future IR activities change your mind and would benefit from the evidentiary value of a removed host. If you have the resources, it may be worth your effort to make forensic images of the primary storage (for example, RAM) before you shut it down and of secondary storage (for example, the file system) before or after you power it off.

- **Ability to restore**   It is not a happy moment for anybody in our line of work when we discover that, though we did everything by the book, we removed and disposed of a compromised computer that had critical business information that was not replicated or backed up anywhere else. If we took and retained a forensic image of the drive, then we could mitigate this risk, but otherwise, someone is going to have a bad day. This is yet another reason why you should, to the extent that your resources allow, keep as much of a removed host as possible.

The removal process should be well documented in the IR plan so that the right issues are considered by the right people at the right time. We address chain-of-custody and related issues in Chapter 9, but for now suffice it so say that what you do with a removed computer can come back and haunt you if you don't do it properly.

Reverse Engineering

Though not technically a containment technique, reverse engineering (RE) can help contain an incident if the information gleaned from it helps identify other compromised hosts. *Reverse engineering* is the detailed examination of a product to learn what it does and how it works. In the context of incident response, RE relates exclusively to malware. The idea is to analyze the binary code to find, for example, the IP addresses or host/domain names it uses for C2 or the techniques it employs to achieve permanence in an infected host, or to identify a unique characteristic that could be used as a signature for the malware.

Generally speaking, there are two approaches to reverse engineering malware. The first doesn't really care about what the binary *is*, but rather with what the binary *does*. This approach, sometimes called *dynamic analysis,* requires a sandbox in which to execute the malware. This sandbox creates an environment that looks like a real operating system to the malware and provides such things as access to a file system, network interface, memory, and anything else the malware asks for. Each request is carefully documented to establish a timeline of behavior that allows us to understand what it does. The main advantage of dynamic malware analysis is that it tends to be significantly faster and require less expertise than the alternative (described next). It can be particularly helpful for code that has been heavily obfuscated by its authors. The biggest disadvantage is that it doesn't reveal all that the malware does, but rather simply all that it did during its execution in the sandbox. Some malware will actually check to see if it is being run in a sandbox before doing anything interesting. Additionally, some malware doesn't immediately do anything nefarious, waiting instead for a certain condition to be met (for example, a time bomb that only activates at a particular date and time).

The alternative to dynamic code analysis is, unsurprisingly, static code analysis. In this approach to malware RE, a highly skilled analyst will either disassemble or decompile the binary code to translate its ones and zeroes into either assembly language or whichever higher-level language it was created in. This allows a reverse engineer to see all possible functions of the malware, not just the ones that it exhibited during a limited run in a sandbox. It is then possible, for example, to see all the domains the malware would reach out to given the right conditions, as well as the various ways in which it would permanently insert itself into its host. This last insight allows the incident response team to look for evidence that any of the other persistence mechanisms exist in other hosts that were not considered infected up to that point.

Engineering and Reversing Software

Computers can only understand sequences of ones and zeroes (sometimes represented in hexadecimal form for our convenience), which is why we call this representation of software *machine language*. It would be tedious and error prone to write complex programs in machine language, which is why we invented assembly language many decades ago. In this language, the programmer uses operators (for example, push and add) and operands (for example, memory addresses, CPU registers, and constants) to implement an algorithm. The software that translates assembly language to machine language is called an *assembler*. Though this was a significant improvement, we soon realized that it was still rather ineffective, which is why we invented higher-level programming languages (such as C/C++). This higher-level source code is translated into assembly language by a compiler before being assembled into binary format, as shown here.

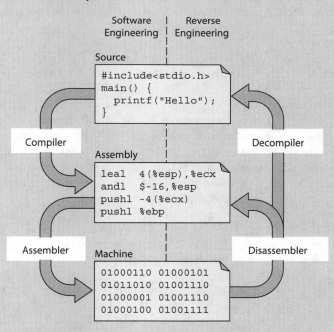

When reverse engineering binary code, we can translate it into assembly language using a tool called a *disassembler*. This is the most common way of reversing a binary. In some cases, we can also go straight from machine language to a representation of source code using a decompiler. The problem with using decompilers is that there are infinitely many ways to write source code that will result in a given binary. The decompiler makes educated guesses as to what the original source code looked like, but it's unable to exactly replicate it.

Eradication

Once the incident is contained, we turn our attention to the eradication process, in which we return all systems to a known-good state. It is important to gather evidence before we recover systems because in many cases we won't know that we need legally admissible evidence until days, weeks, or even months after an incident. It pays, then, to treat each incident as if it will eventually end up in a court of justice.

Once all relevant evidence is captured, we fix all that was broken. The aim is to restore full, trustworthy functionality to the organization. For hosts that were compromised, the best practice is to simply reinstall the system from a gold master image and then restore data from the most recent backup that occurred prior to the attack.

 NOTE An attacked or infected system should never be trusted because you do not necessarily know all the changes that have taken place and the true extent of the damage. Some malicious code could still be hiding somewhere. Systems should be rebuilt to ensure they are trustworthy again.

Sanitization

According to NIST Special Publication 800-88 Revision 1 (Guidelines for Media Sanitization), *sanitization* refers to the process by which access to data on a given medium is made infeasible for a given level of effort. These levels of effort, in the context of incident response, can be cursory and sophisticated. What we call cursory sanitization can be accomplished by simply reformatting a drive. It may be sufficient against run-of-the-mill attackers who look for large groups of easy victims and don't put too much effort into digging their hooks deeply into any one victim. On the other hand, there are sophisticated attackers who may have deliberately targeted your organization and will go to great lengths to persist in your systems or, if repelled, compromise them again. This class of threat actor requires more advanced approaches to sanitization.

The challenge, of course, is that you don't always know which kind of attacker is responsible for the incident. For this reason, simply reformatting a drive is a risky approach. Instead, we recommend one of the following techniques, listed in increasing level of effectiveness at ensuring the adversary is definitely removed from the medium:

- **Overwriting** Overwriting data entails replacing the ones and zeroes that represent it on storage media with random or fixed patterns of ones and zeroes in order to render the original data unrecoverable. This should be done at least once (for example, overwriting the medium with ones, zeroes, or a pattern of these), but may have to be done more than that.

- **Encryption** Many mobile devices take this approach to quickly and securely render data unusable. The premise is that the data is stored on the medium in encrypted format using a strong key. In order to render the data unrecoverable, all the system needs to do is to securely delete the encryption key, which is many times faster than deleting the encrypted data. Recovering the data in this scenario is typically computationally infeasible.

- **Degaussing** This is the process of removing or reducing the magnetic field patterns on conventional disk drives or tapes. In essence, a powerful magnetic force is applied to the media, which results in the wiping of the data and sometimes the destruction of the motors that drive the platters. Note that degaussing typically renders the drive unusable.

- **Physical destruction** Perhaps the best way to combat data remanence is to simply destroy the physical media. The two most commonly used approaches to destroying media are to shred them or expose them to caustic or corrosive chemicals. Another approach is incineration.

Reconstruction

Once a compromised host's media is sanitized, the next step is to rebuild the host to its pristine state. The best approach to doing this is to ensure you have created known-good, hardened images of the various standard configurations for hosts on your network. These images are sometimes called *gold masters* and facilitate the process of rebuilding a compromised host. This reconstruction is significantly harder if you have to manually reinstall the operating system, configure it so it is hardened, and then install the various applications and/or services that were in the original host. We don't know anybody who, having gone through this dreadful process once, doesn't invest the time to build and maintain gold images thereafter.

Another aspect of reconstruction is the restoration of data to the host. Again, there is one best practice here, which is to ensure you have up-to-date backups of the system data files. This is also key for quickly and inexpensively dealing with ransomware incidents. Sadly, in too many organizations, backups are the responsibility of individual users. If your organization does not enforce centrally managed backups of all systems, then your only other hope is to ensure that data is maintained in a managed data store such as a file server.

Secure Disposal

When you're disposing of media or devices as a result of an incident response, any of the four techniques covered earlier (overwriting, encryption, degaussing, or physical destruction) may work, depending on the device. Overwriting is usually feasible only with regard to hard disk drives and might not be available on some solid-state drives. Encryption-based purging can be found in multiple workstation, server, and mobile operating systems, but not in all. Degaussing only works on magnetic media, but some of the most advanced magnetic drives use stronger fields to store data and may render older degaussers inadequate. Note that we have not mentioned network devices such as switches and routers, which typically don't offer any of these alternatives. In the end, the only way to securely dispose of these devices is by physically destroying them using an accredited process or service provider. This physical destruction involves the shredding, pulverizing, disintegration, or incineration of the device. Although this may seem extreme, it is sometimes the only secure alternative left.

Validation

The validation process in an incident response is focused on ensuring that we have identified the corresponding attack vectors and implemented effective countermeasures against them. This stage presumes that we have analyzed the incident and verified the manner in which it was conducted. This analysis can be a separate post-mortem activity or can take place in parallel with the response.

Patching

Many of the most damaging incidents are the result of an unpatched software flaw. This vulnerability can exist for a variety of reasons, including failure to update a known vulnerability or the existence of a heretofore unknown vulnerability, also known as a "zero day." As part of the incident response, the team must determine which cause is the case. The first would indicate an internal failure to keep patches updated, whereas the second would all but require notification to the vendor of the product that was exploited so a patch can be developed.

Many organizations rely on endpoint protection that is not centrally managed, particularly in a "bring your own device" (BYOD) environment. This makes it possible that a user or device fails to download and install an available patch, and this causes an incident. If this is the case in your organization, and you are unable to change the policy to required centralized patching, then you should also assume that some number of endpoints will fail to be patched and you should develop compensatory controls elsewhere in your security architecture. For example, by implementing Network Access Control (NAC), you can test any device attempting to connect to the network for patching, updates, anti-malware, and any other policies you want to enforce. If the endpoint fails any of the checks, it is placed in a quarantine network that may allow Internet access (particularly for downloading patches) but keeps the device from joining the organizational network and potentially spreading malware.

If, on the other hand, your organization uses centralized patches and updates, the vulnerability was known, and still it was successfully exploited, this points to a failure within whatever system or processes you are using for patching. Part of the response would then be to identify the failure, correct it, and then validate that the fix is effective at preventing a repeated incident in the future.

Permissions

There are two principal reasons for validating permissions before you wrap up your IR activities. The first is that inappropriately elevated permissions may have been a cause of the incident in the first place. It is not uncommon for organizations to allow excessive privileges for their users. One of the most common reasons we've heard is that if the users don't have administrative privileges on their devices, they won't be able to install whatever applications they'd like to try out in the name of improving their efficiency. Of course, we know better, but this may still be an organizational culture issue that is beyond your power to change. Still, documenting the incidents (and their severity) that are the direct result of excessive privileges may, over time, move the needle in the direction of common sense.

Not all permissions issues can be blamed on the end users. We've seen time and again system or domain admins who do all their work (including surfing the Web) on their admin account. Furthermore, most of us have heard of (or had to deal with) the discovery that a system admin who left the organization months or even years ago still has a valid account. The aftermath of an incident response provides a great opportunity to double-check on issues like these.

Finally, it is very common for interactive attackers to create or hijack administrative accounts so that they can do their nefarious deeds undetected. Although it may be odd to see an anonymous user in Russia accessing sensitive resources on your network, you probably wouldn't get too suspicious if you saw one of your fellow admin staff members moving those files around. If there is any evidence that the incident leveraged an administrative account, it would be a good idea to delete that account and, if necessary, issue a new one to the victimized administrator. While you're at it, you may want to validate that all other accounts are needed and protected.

Scanning

By definition, every incident occurs because a threat actor exploits a vulnerability and compromises the security of an information system. It stands to reason, then, that after recovering from an incident you would want to scan your systems for other instances of that same (or a related) vulnerability. Although it is true that we will never be able to protect against every vulnerability, it is also true that we have a responsibility to mitigate those that have been successfully exploited, whether or not we thought they posed a high risk before the incident. The reason is that we now know that the probability of a threat actor exploiting it is 100 percent because it already happened. And if it happened once, it is likelier to happen again absent a change in your controls. The inescapable conclusion is that after an incident you need to implement a control that will prevent a recurrence of the exploitation, and develop a plug-in for your favorite scanner that will test all systems for any residual vulnerabilities.

Monitoring

So you have successfully responded to the incident, implemented new controls, and ran updated vulnerability scans to ensure everything is on the up and up. These are all important preventive measures, but you still need to ensure you improve your ability to react to a return by the same (or a similar) actor. Armed with all the information on the adversary's TTPs, you now need to update your monitoring plan to better detect similar attacks.

We already mentioned the creation of IOCs as part of isolation efforts in the containment phase of the response. Now you can leverage those IOCs by incorporating them into your network monitoring plan. Most organizations would add these indicators to rules in their intrusion detection or prevention system (IDS/IPS). You can also cast a wider net by providing the IOCs to business partners or even competitors in your sector. This is where organizations such as the US-CERT and the ISACs can be helpful in keeping large groups of organizations protected against known attacks.

Corrective Actions

No effective business process would be complete without some sort of introspection or opportunity to learn from and adapt to our experiences. This is the role of the corrective actions phase of an incident response. It is here that we apply the lessons learned and information gained from the process in order to improve our posture in the future.

Lessons-Learned Report

In our time in the Army, it was virtually unheard of to conduct any sort of operation (training or real world), or run any event of any size, without having a hotwash (a quick huddle immediately after the event to discuss the good, the bad, and the ugly) and/or an after action review (AAR) to document issues and recommendations formally. It has been very heartening to see the same diligence in most non-governmental organizations in the aftermath of incidents. Although there is no single best way to capture lessons learned, we'll present one that has served us well in a variety of situations and sectors.

The general approach is that every participant in the operation is encouraged or required to provide his observations in the following format:

- **Issue** A brief (usually single-sentenced) label for an important (from the participant's perspective) issue that arose during the operation.
- **Discussion** A (usually paragraph-long) description of what was observed and why it is important to remember or learn from it for the future.
- **Recommendation** Usually starts with a "sustain" or "improve" label if the contributor felt the team's response was effective or ineffective (respectively).

Every participant's input is collected and organized before the AAR. Usually all inputs are discussed during the review session, but occasionally the facilitator will choose to disregard some if he feels they are repetitive (of others' inputs) or would be detrimental to the session. As the issues are discussed, they are refined and updated with other team members' inputs. At the conclusion of the AAR, the group (or the person in charge) decides which issues deserve to be captured as lessons learned, and those find their way into a final report. Depending on your organization, these lessons-learned reports may be sent to management, kept locally, and/or sent to a higher-echelon clearinghouse.

Change Control Process

During the lessons learned or after action review process, the team will discuss and document important recommendations for changes. Although these changes may make perfect sense to the IR team, we must be careful about assuming that they should automatically be made. Every organization should have some sort of change control process. Oftentimes, this mechanism takes the form of a change control board (CCB), which consists of representatives of the various business units as well as other relevant stakeholders. Whether or not there is a board, the process is designed to ensure that no significant changes are made to any critical systems without careful consideration by all who might be affected.

Going back to an earlier example about an incident that was triggered by a BYOD policy in which every user could control software patching on their own devices, it is possible that the incident response team will determine that this is an unacceptable state of affairs and recommend that all devices on the network be centrally managed. This decision makes perfect sense from an information security perspective, but would probably face some challenges in the legal and human resources departments. The change control process is the appropriate way to consider all perspectives and arrive at sensible and effective changes to the systems.

Updates to Response Plan

Regardless of whether the change control process implements any of the recommendations from the IR team, the response plan should be reviewed and, if appropriate, updated. Whereas the change control process implements organization-wide changes, the response team has much more control over the response plan. Absent sweeping changes, some compensation can happen at the IR team level.

As shown in earlier Figure 7-2, incident management is a process. In the aftermath of an event, we take actions that allow us to better prepare for future incidents, which starts the process all over again. Any changes to this lifecycle should be considered from the perspectives of the stakeholders with which we started this chapter. This will ensure that the IR team is making changes that make sense in the broader organizational context. In order to get these stakeholders' perspectives, establishing and maintaining positive communications is paramount.

Summary Report

The post-incident report can be a very short one-pager or a lengthy treatise; it all depends on the severity and impact of the incident. Whatever the case, we must consider who will read the report and what interests and concerns will shape the manner in which they interpret it. Before we even begin to write it, we should consider one question: what is the purpose of this report? If the goal is to ensure the IR team remembers some of the technical details of the response that worked (or didn't), then we may want to write it in a way that persuades future responders to consider these lessons. This writing would be very different than if our goal was to persuade senior management to modify a popular BYOD policy to enhance our security even if some are unhappy as a result. In the first case, the report would likely be technologically focused, whereas in the latter case it would focus on the business's bottom line.

Communication Processes

We know return to the topic with which we started this chapter: the variety of team members and stakeholders involved in incident responses and the importance of maintaining effective communications among all. This is true of the internal stakeholders we already mentioned, but it is equally true of external communications. You may have a textbook-perfect response to an incident that ends up endangering your entire organization simply because of ineffective communication processes.

Internal Communications

One of the key parts of any incident response plan is the process by which the trusted internal parties will be kept abreast of and consulted about the response to an incident. It is not uncommon, at least for the more significant incidents, to designate a war room in which the key decision-makers and stakeholders will meet to get periodic updates and make decisions. In between these meetings, the room serves as a clearinghouse for information about the response activities. This means that at least one knowledgeable member of the IR team will be stationed there for the duration of the response in order to address these drop-ins. It is ideal when the war room is a physical space, but a virtual one might work as well, depending on your organization.

Apart from meetings (formal or otherwise) in the war room, it may be necessary to establish a secure communications channel with which to keep key personnel up to date on the progress of the response. This could be a group text, e-mail, or chat room, but it must include all the key personnel who might have a role or stake in the issue. When it comes to internal communications, there is no such thing as too much information.

External Communications

Communications outside of the organization, on the other hand, must be carefully controlled. Sensible reports have a way of getting turned into misleading and potentially damaging sound bites, so it is best to designate a trained professional for the role of handling external communications. Some of these, after all, may be regimented by regulatory or statutory requirements.

The first and most important sector for external communications is made up of government entities. Whether it's the Securities Exchange Commission or the FBI or some other government entity, if there is a requirement to communicate with them in the course of an incident response, then the legal team must be part of the crafting of any and all messages. This is one area that few organizations get to mess up and emerge unscathed. This is not to say that the government stakeholders are adversarial, but that when the process is regulated by laws or regulations, the stakes are much higher.

Next on the list of importance are customers. Though there may be some regulatory requirements with regard to compromised customer data, our focus here is on keeping the public informed so that it perceives transparency and trustworthiness from the organization. This is particularly important when the situation is interesting enough to make headlines or go viral on social media. Just as the lawyers were critical to government communications, the media relations (or equivalent) team will carry the day when it comes to communicating with the masses. The goal here is to assuage fears and concerns as well as to control the narrative to keep it factually correct. To this end, press releases and social media posts should be templated even before the event so that all that is needed is to fill in some blanks before an effective communiqué can be quickly pushed out.

Still another group with which we may have to communicate deliberately and effectively is the key partners, such as business collaborators, select shareholders, and investors. The goal of this communications thrust is to convey the impact on the business's bottom line. If the event risks driving down the price of the company's stock, then the conversation has to include ways in which the company will mitigate such losses. If the event could spread to the systems of partner organizations, then the focus should be on how to mitigate that risk. In any event, the business leaders should carry on these conversations, albeit with substantial support from the senior response team leaders.

We cannot be exhaustive in our treatment of how to communicate during incident responses in this chapter, but we hope to have conveyed the preeminence of the interpersonal and interorganizational communications in these few pages. Even the best-handled technical incident response can be overshadowed very quickly by an inability to communicate effectively, both internally and externally.

Chapter Review

This chapter sets the stage for the rest of our discussion on incident responses. It started and ended with a focus on the interpersonal element of IR. Even before we discussed the technical process itself, we discussed the various roles and stakeholders that you, as a team member, must be tracking and with whom you must develop an effective rapport before an incident has even occurred—and you must maintain this relationship during and after response activities. Many an incident has turned into an RGE (resume generating event) for highly skilled responders who did not understand the importance of the various characters in the play.

The technical part, by comparison, is a lot more straightforward. The incident recovery and post-incident response process consists of five discrete phases: containment, eradication, validation, corrective actions, and final reporting. Your effectiveness in this process is largely dictated by the amount of preparation you and your teammates put into it. If you have a good grasp on the risks facing your organization, develop a sensible plan, and rehearse it with all the key players periodically, you will likely do very well when your adversaries breach your defenses. In the next few chapters, we get into the details of the key areas of technical response.

Questions

1. When decisions are made that involve significant funding requests or reaching out to law enforcement organizations, which of the following parties will be notified?

   A. Contractors

   B. Public relations staff

   C. Senior leaders

   D. Technical staff

2. The process of dissecting a sample of malicious software to determine its purpose is referred to as what?

   A. Segmentation

   B. Frequency analysis

   C. Traffic analysis

   D. Reverse engineering

3. When would you consult your legal department in the conduct of an incident response?

   A. Immediately after the discovery of the incident

   B. When business processes are at risk because of a failed recovery operation

   C. In cases of compromise of sensitive information such as PHI

   D. In the case of a loss of more than 1 terabyte of data

4. During the IR process, when is a good time to perform a vulnerability scan to determine the effectiveness of corrective actions?

   A. Change control process

   B. Reverse engineering

   C. Removal

   D. Validation

5. What is the term for members of your organization who have a role in helping with some aspects of some incident response?

   A. Shareholders

   B. Stakeholders

   C. Insiders

   D. Public relations

6. What process during an IR is as important in terms of expectation management and reporting as the application of technical controls?

   A. Management process

   B. Change control process

   C. Communications process

   D. Monitoring process

Refer to the following scenario for Questions 7-12:

You receive an alert about a compromised device on your network. Users are reporting that they are receiving strange messages in their inboxes and having problems sending e-mails. Your technical team reports unusual network traffic from the mail server. The team has analyzed the associated logs and confirmed that a mail server has been infected with malware.

7. You immediately remove the server from the network and route all traffic to a backup server. What stage are you currently operating in?

   A. Preparation

   B. Containment

   C. Eradication

   D. Validation

8. Now that the device is no longer on the production network, you want to restore services. Before you rebuild the original server to a known-good condition, you want to preserve the current condition of the server for later inspection. What is the first step you want to take?

   A. Format the hard drive.

   B. Reinstall the latest operating systems and patches.

   C. Make a forensic image of all connected media.

   D. Update the antivirus definitions on the server and save all configurations.

9. What is the most appropriate course of action regarding communication with organizational leadership?

   A. Provide updates on progress and estimated time of service restoration.

   B. Forward the full technical details on the affected server(s).

   C. Provide details until after law enforcement is notified.

   D. Provide details only if unable to restore services.

10. Your team has identified the strain of malware that took advantage of a bug in your mail server version to gain elevated privileges. Because you cannot be sure what else was affected on that server, what is your best course of action?

    A. Immediately update the mail server software.

    B. Reimage the server's hard drive.

    C. Write additional firewall rules to allow only e-mail-related traffic to reach the server.

    D. Submit a request for next-generation antivirus for the mail server.

11. Your team believes it has eradicated the malware from the primary server. You attempt to bring affected systems back into the production environment in a responsible manner. Which of the following tasks will *not* be a part of this phase?

    A. Applying the latest patches to server software

    B. Monitoring network traffic on the server for signs of compromise

    C. Determining the best time to phase in the primary server into operations

    D. Using a newer operating system with different server software

12. Your team has successfully restored services on the original server and verified that it is free from malware. What activity should be performed as soon as practical?

    A. Preparing the lessons-learned report

    B. Notifying law enforcement to press charges

    C. Notifying industry partners about the incident

    D. Notifying the press about the incident

Answers

1. **C.** Decisions to reach out to external law enforcement bodies or employ changes that will incur significant cost will likely require organizational leadership involvement. They will provide guidance to company priorities, assist in addressing regulatory issues, and provide the support necessary to get through the IR process.

2. **D.** Reverse engineering malware is the process of decomposing malware to understand what it does and how it works.

3. **C.** There are regulatory reporting requirements when dealing with compromises of sensitive data such as protected health information. Since these can lead to civil penalties or even criminal charges, it is important to consult legal counsel.

4. **D.** Additional scanning should be performed during validation to ensure that no additional vulnerabilities exist after remediation.

5. **B.** Stakeholders are those individuals and teams who are part of your organization and have a role in helping with some aspects of some incident response.

6. **C.** The communications process is a vital part of the IR process and will allow for an efficient recovery from an incident.

7. **B.** Containment is the set of actions that attempts to deny the threat agent the ability or means to cause further damage.

8. **C.** Since unauthorized access of computer systems is a criminal act in many areas, it may be useful to take a snapshot of the device in its current state using forensic tools to preserve evidence.

9. **A.** Organizational leadership should be given enough information to provide guidance and support. Management needs to be closely involved in critical decision-making points.

10. **B.** Generally, the most effective means of disposing of an infected system is a complete reimaging of a system's storage to ensure that any malicious content was removed and to prevent reinfection.

11. **D.** The goal of the IR process is to get services back to normal operation as quickly and safely as possible. Introducing completely new and untested software may introduce significant challenges to this goal.

12. **A.** Preparing the lessons-learned report is a vital stage in the process after recovery. It should be performed as soon as possible after the incident to record as much information and complete any documentation that might be useful for the prosecution of the incident and to prevent future incidents from occurring.

Determining the Impact of Incidents

In this chapter you will learn:
- Criteria for classifying threats to the network
- How to determine the severity level of an incident
- Best practices for prioritizing security incident response
- The most common types of sensitive and protected data

Predicting rain doesn't count. Building arks does.

—Warren Buffett

Threat Classification

Before going too deeply into the technical details on threats you may encounter while preparing or responding to an incident, it's important to define the term *incident*. We use the term to describe any action that results in direct harm to your system, or increases the likelihood for unauthorized exposure of your sensitive data. The first step in knowing that something is harmful and out of place is to understand what normal looks like. Establishing a baseline of your systems is the first step in preparation for an incident. Without knowing what normal is, it becomes incredibly difficult to see the warning signs of an attack. In this case, you will likely only know that you've been breached when your systems go offline. Making a plan for incident response isn't just a good idea—it might be compulsory, depending on your operating environment. As your organization's security expert, you will be entrusted to put into place the technical measures and recommend policy that keeps your personal data safe while keeping your organization out of court.

Known Threats vs. Unknown Threats

In previous chapters, we covered the concepts of signature-based and anomaly-based methods of detection for intrusion detection systems. Antivirus software works in a similar way. You may recall that signature-based systems rely on prior knowledge of a threat and that these systems are only as good as the historical data companies have collected. Although this is useful for identifying threats that already exist, it doesn't do much for threats that constantly change their form, or have not been previously observed. These will slip by the systems undetected. The alternative is to use a solution that looks at what the file is doing, rather than what it looks like. This kind of system relies on *heuristic analysis* to observe the commands the executable invokes, the files it writes, and any attempts to conceal itself. Often, these heuristic systems will sandbox a file in a virtual operating system and allow it to perform what it was designed to do. With the way that malware is evolving, security practices are shifting to reduce the number of assumptions made when developing policy. A report that indicates that no threat is present just means that the scanning engine couldn't find a match. A clean report isn't worth much if the methods of detection aren't able to detect the newest types of threats. In other words, the absence of evidence is not evidence of absence. Vulnerabilities and threats are being discovered at a rate that outpaces what traditional detection technology can spot. Because threats still exist even if we cannot detect them, we must either evolve our detection techniques or treat the entire network as an untrusted environment. There is nothing inherently wrong about the latter; it just requires a major shift in thinking about how we design our networks.

Zero Day

The term *zero day*, once used exclusively among security professionals, is quickly becoming part of the public dialect. It refers to either a vulnerability or exploit never before seen in public. A *zero-day vulnerability* is a flaw in a piece of software that the vendor is unaware of and thus has not issued patch or advisory for. The code written to take advantage of this flaw is called the *zero-day exploit*. When writing software, vendors often focus on providing usability and getting the most functional product out to the market as quickly as possible. This often results in products that require numerous updates as more users interact with the software. Ideally, the number of vulnerabilities decreases as time progresses, as adoption increases, and as patches are issued. However, this doesn't mean that you should let your guard down because of some sense of increased security. Rather, you should be more vigilant; an environment that has complete adoption of software means that it's defenseless should a zero-day exploit be used against it.

Zero-day exploits were once extremely rare, but the security community has observed a significant uptick in their usage and discovery. As security companies improve their software, malware writers have worked to evolve their products to evade these systems, creating a malware arms race of sorts. Modern zero-day vulnerabilities are extremely valuable, and as with anything else of perceived value, markets have formed. Black markets for zero-day exploits exist with ample participation from criminal groups. On the opposite end of the spectrum, vendors have used *bug bounty* programs to supplement internal vulnerability discovery, inviting researchers and hackers to actively probe their software for bugs in exchange for money and prizes. Even the Pentagon, a traditionally bureaucratic and risk-averse organization, saw the value in crowdsourcing security in this way. In March of 2016, it launched the "Hack the Pentagon" challenge, a pilot program designed to identify security vulnerabilities on public-facing Defense Department sites.

Preparation

Preparing to face unknown and advanced threats like zero-day exploits requires a sound methodology that includes technical and operational best practices. The protection of critical business assets and sensitive data should never be trusted to a single solution. You should be wary of solutions that suggest they are one-stop-shops for dealing with these threats because you are essentially placing the entire organization's fate in a single point of failure. Although the word "response" is part of the IR plan, your team should develop a methodology that includes proactive efforts as well. This approach should involve active efforts to discover new threats that have not yet impacted the organization. Sources for this information include research organizations and threat intelligence providers. The SANS Internet Storm Center and the CERT Coordination Center at Carnegie Mellon University are two great resources for discovering the latest software bugs. Armed with this new knowledge about attacker trends and techniques, you may be able to detect malicious traffic before it has a chance to do any harm. Additionally, you will give your security team time to develop controls to mitigate security incidents, should a counter-measure or patch not be available.

Advanced Persistent Threat

In 2003, analysts discovered a series of coordinated attacks against Department of Defense, Department of Energy, NASA, and the Department of Justice. Found to have been in progress for at least three years at that point, the actors appeared be on a mission and took extraordinary steps to hide evidence of their existence. These events, known later as "Titan Rain," would be classified as the work of an advanced persistent threat (APT), which is the name given to any number of stealthy and continuous computer hacking efforts, often coordinated and executed by an organization or government with significant resources. The goal for an APT is to gain and maintain persistent access to target systems while remaining undetected. Attack vectors often include spam messages, infected media, social engineering, and supply-chain compromise. The support infra-structure behind their operations; their techniques, tactics, and procedures (TTPs) dur-ing operations; and the types of targets they choose are all part of what makes APTs stand out. It's useful to analyze each word in the acronym to identify the key discriminators between APT and other actors.

Advanced

The operators behind these campaigns are often well equipped, using techniques that indicate formal training and significant funding. Their attacks indicate a high degree of coordination between technical and nontechnical information sources. These threats are often backed with a full spectrum of intelligence support, from digital surveillance methods to traditional techniques focused on human targets.

Persistent

Because these campaigns are often coordinated by government and military organiza-tions, it shouldn't be surprising that each operator is focused on a specific task rather than rooting around without direction. Operators will often ignore opportunistic targets and remain focused on their piece of the campaign. This behavior implies strict rules of engagement and an emphasis on consistency and persistence above all else.

Threat

APTs do not exist in a bubble. Their campaigns show capability and intent, aspects which highlight their use as the technical implementation of a political plan. Like a military operation, APT campaigns often serve as an extension of political will. Although their code might be executed by machines, the APT framework is designed and coordinated by humans with a specific goal in mind. Due to the complex nature of APTs, it may be difficult to handle them alone. The concept of automatic threat intelligence sharing is a recent development in the security community. Because speed is often the discriminator between a successful and unsuccessful campaign, many vendors provide solutions that automatically share threat data and orchestrate technical countermeasures for them.

 EXAM TIP Advanced persistent threats, regardless of affiliation, are characterized by resourcing, consistency, and a military-like efficiency during their actions to compromise systems, steal data, and cover their tracks.

Factors Contributing to Incident Severity and Prioritization

Preparation is key for the smooth operation of any team, and it's particularly important for dealing with unexpected challenges. Whether it's an outage due to a failed component or the result of a malware infection, having a comprehensive response strategy will reduce the damage done in these situations.

Scope of Impact

It's important to have a reference point to know the true scope of impact during a suspected incident. Simply noting that the network seems slow will not be enough to make a good determination on what to do next. *Scope of impact* is the formal determination of whether an event is enough of a deviation from normal operations to be called an incident, and the degree to which services were affected. Keep in mind that some actions you perform in the course of your duties as a systems administrator might trigger security devices and appear to be an attack. Documenting these types of legitimate anomalies will reduce the number of false positives and allow you to have more confidence in your alerting system. In the case of a legitimate attack, you must collect as much data as possible from sources throughout your network, such as log files from network devices. Having as much information as possible in this step will help when deciding on the next steps for your incident responders.

Once an event is confirmed to have been legitimate, you should quickly communicate with your team to identify who needs to be contacted outside of your security group and key leadership. Whom you must contact may be dictated by your local policy—and in some cases, law or regulation. Opening communication channels early will also ensure that you get the appropriate support for any major changes to the organization's resources. We already covered the communications process in detail in Chapter 7.

For some organizations, the mere mention of a successful breach can be damaging, regardless of what was compromised. In 2011, security company RSA was the victim of a major breach. RSA's SecureID, a line of two-factor authentication token-based products, was used by over 40 million businesses at the time for the purposes of securing their own network. These tokens, which were the cornerstone of their authentication service, were revealed to have been compromised after a thorough investigation of the incident, prompting the company to replace all 40 million tokens. Almost as damaging as the financial cost of replacing the tokens was the damage done to RSA's reputation because the story made headlines throughout the world. How could a security company be the victim of a hack? In cases like this, it's critical that only those playing a role in the incident response and decision-makers be informed. The first reason is to reduce confusion across the organization as a clear path forward is determined. Second, you might not want an attacker to be tipped off that he has been discovered. As an incident responder, you must be prepared to inform leadership with your technical assessment for them to make decisions in the best interest of the organization.

Downtime

Networks exist to provide resources to those who need them, when they need them. Without a network and services that are available when they need to be, nothing can be accomplished. Every other metric in determining network performance such as stability, throughput, scalability, and storage all require the network to be up. The decision on whether to take a network completely offline to handle a breach is not a small one by any measure. Understanding that a complete shutdown of the network might not be possible, you should move to isolate infected systems to prevent additional damage. The priority here is to prevent additional losses and minimize impact on the organization. This is not dissimilar to operations in an emergency room: your team must work to quickly perform triage on your network to determine the extent of the damage and prevent additional harm, all while keeping the organization running.

The key is to determine which of the organization's critical systems are needed for survival and estimate the outage time that can be tolerated by the company as a result of an incident. The outage time that can be endured by an organization is referred to as the *maximum tolerable downtime (MTD)*, which is illustrated in Figure 8-1.

The following are some MTD estimates that an organization might use. Note that these are sample estimates that will vary from organization to organization and from business unit to business unit:

- **Nonessential** 30 days
- **Normal** 7 days
- **Important** 72 hours
- **Urgent** 24 hours
- **Critical** Minutes to hours

Figure 8-1
Maximum
tolerable
downtime (MTD)

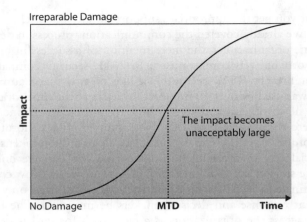

Each business function and asset should be placed in one of these categories, depending on how long the organization can survive without it. These estimates will help determine how to prioritize response team efforts to restore these assets. The shorter the MTD, the higher the priority of the function in question. Thus, the items classified as Urgent should be addressed before those classified as Normal.

Recovery Time

Time is money, and the faster you can restore your network to a safe operating condition, the better it is for the organization's bottom line. Although there may be serious financial implications for every second a network asset is offline, you should not sacrifice speed for completeness. You should keep lines of communication open with organization management to determine acceptable limits to downtime. Having a sense of what the key performance indicators (KPIs) are for detection and remediation will clear up confusion, manage expectations, and potentially allow you to demonstrate how prepared your team is should you exceed these guidelines. This may also be useful in the long run for the reputation of the team and may be useful in securing additional budgets for training and tools.

The recovery time objective (RTO) is oftentimes used, particularly in the context of disaster recovery, to denote the earliest time within which a business process must be restored after an incident to avoid unacceptable consequences associated with a break in business processes. The RTO value is smaller than the MTD value, because the MTD value represents the time after which an inability to recover significant operations will mean severe and perhaps irreparable damage to the organization's reputation or bottom line. The RTO assumes that there is a period of acceptable downtime. This means that an organization can be out of production for a certain period of time (RTO) and still get back on its feet. But if it cannot get production up and running within the MTD window, the organization may be sinking too fast to properly recover.

Data Integrity

Taking a network down isn't always the goal of a network intrusion. For malicious actors, tampering with data may do enough to disrupt operations and provide them with the outcome they were looking for. Financial transaction records, personal data, and professional correspondence are types of data that are especially susceptible to this type of attack. There are cases when attacks on data are obvious, such as those involving ransomware. In these situations, malware will encrypt data files on a system so the users cannot access them without submitting payment for the decryption keys. However, it may not always be apparent that an attack on data integrity has taken place. It might be only after a detailed inspection that you discover the unauthorized insertion, modification, or deletion of data. This illustrates why it's critical to back up data and system configurations, and keep them sufficiently segregated from the network so that they are not themselves affected by the attack. Having an easily deployable backup solution will allow for very rapid restoration of services. The authors will caution, however, that much like Schrödinger's cat, the condition of any backup is unknown until a restore is attempted. In other words, having a backup alone isn't enough. It must be verified over time to ensure that it's free from corruption and malware.

Ransomware

Organized crime groups frequently set up malicious sites that serve malware convincingly disguised as games or other files. The malware contained in these files is often installed silently without user knowledge and encrypts a portion of the host's system, requiring payment for the decryption keys. For these groups, this is a source of significant and reliable income because so many users and organizations have poor backup habits. Ironically, these groups rarely renege on an exchange because it would be very damaging to the business model. If you knew that you'd never see your data again, what would be the point of submitting payment?

Economic

It's difficult to predict the second- and third-order effects of network intrusions. Even if some costs are straightforward to calculate, the complete economic impact of network breaches is difficult to quantify. A fine levied against an organization that had not adequately secured its workers' personal information is an immediate and obvious cost, but how does one accurately calculate the future losses due to identity theft, or the damage to the reputation of the organization due to the lack of confidence? It's critical to include questions like these in your discussion with stakeholders when determining courses of action for dealing with an incident.

Another consideration in calculating the economic scope of an incident is the value of the assets involved. The value placed on information is relative to the parties involved, what work was required to develop it, how much it costs to maintain, what damage would result if it were lost or destroyed, what enemies would pay for it, and what liability penalties could be endured. If an organization does not know the value of the information and the other assets it is trying to protect, it does not know how much money and time it should spend on protecting or restoring them. If the calculated value of a company's trade secret is x, then the total cost of protecting or restoring it should be some value less than x.

The previous examples refer to assessing the value of information and protecting it, but this logic applies toward an organization's facilities, systems, and resources. The value of facilities must be assessed, along with all printers, workstations, servers, peripheral devices, supplies, and employees. You do not know how much is in danger of being lost if you don't know what you have and what it is worth in the first place.

System Process Criticality

As part of your preparation, you must determine what processes are considered essential for the business's operation. These processes are associated with tasks that must be accomplished with a certain level of consistency for the business to remain competitive. Each business's list of critical processes will be different, but it's important to identify those early so that they can be the first to come back up during a recovery. The critical process lists aren't restricted to only technical assets; they should include the essential staff required to get these critical systems back online and keep them operational. It's important to educate members across the organization as to what these core processes are, how their work directly supports the goals of the processes, and how they benefit from successful operations. This is effective in getting the appropriate level of buy-in required for successfully responding to incidents and recovering from any resulting damage.

EXAM TIP Criticality and probability are the primary components of risk analysis. Whereas *probability* describes the chance of a future event occurring, *criticality* is the impact of that future event. Criticality is often expressed by degree, such as high, moderate, or low. Low criticality indicates little impact to business operations, moderate indicates impaired or degraded performance, and high indicates a significant impairment of business functions.

Types of Data

While we take measures to protect all kinds of data on our network, there are some types that need special consideration for their storage and transmission. The following examples of data are all kinds whose unauthorized disclosure may have serious adverse effects on the associated business, government, or individual.

Personally Identifiable Information (PII)

Personally identifiable information (PII) is information that can be used to distinguish an individual's identity. This information can be unique, such as a Social Security number or biometric profile, or it may be used with other data to trace back to an individual, as is the case with name and date of birth. This information is often used by criminals to conduct identity theft, fraud, or any other crime that targets an individual. Depending on the regulatory environment your organization operates it, you may have additional requirements to meet with respect to the handling of PII, in addition to federal and state laws. A United States federal law called the Privacy Act of 1974 established strict rules regarding the collection, storage, use, and sharing of PII when it is provided to federal entities. In the Department of Defense, documents that contain PII are required to have appropriate markings or a cover sheet with them, as show in Figure 8-2.

Privacy Act Data Cover Sheet

To be used on
all documents
containing personal
information

DOCUMENTS ENCLOSED ARE SUBJECT TO THE PRIVACY ACT OF 1974

Contents shall not be disclosed, discussed, or shared with individuals unless they have a direct need-to-know in the performance of their official duties. Deliver this/these document(s) directly to the intended recipient. **DO NOT** drop off with a third-party.

The enclosed document(s) may contain personal or privileged information and should be treated as "For Official Use Only." Unauthorized disclosure of this information may result in **CIVIL** and **CRIMINAL** penalties. If you are not the intended recipient or believe that you have received this document(s) in error, do not copy, disseminate or otherwise use the information and contact the owner/creator or your Privacy Act officer regarding the document(s).

Privacy Act Data Cover Sheet

DD FORM 2923, SEP 2010

Figure 8-2 Department of Defense Form 2923, Privacy Act data cover sheet

PART III

Personal Health Information (PHI)

The Health Insurance Portability and Accountability Act of 1996 (HIPAA) is a law that established standards to protect individuals' personal health information (PHI). PHI is any data that relates to an individual's past, present, or future physical or mental health condition. Usually, this information is handled by a healthcare provider, employer, public health authority, or school. HIPAA requires appropriate safeguards to protect the privacy of personal health information, and it regulates what can be shared and with whom without patient authorization. HIPAA prescribes specific reporting requirements for violations. There are significant penalties for violations of HIPAA and the unauthorized disclosure of PHI, including fines and jail sentences for criminally liable parties.

Payment Card Information

In previous chapters, we discussed the importance of having technical controls in place to remain compliant with standards such as the Payment Card Industry Data Security Standard (PCI DSS). PCI DSS was created to reduce credit card fraud and protect cardholder information. As a global standard for protecting stored, processed, or transmitted data, it prescribes general guidelines based on industry best practices, as shown in Figure 8-3.

Goals	PCI DSS Requirements
Build and Maintain a Secure Network and Systems	1. Install and maintain a firewall configuration to protect cardholder data 2. Do not use vendor-supplied defaults for system passwords and other security parameters
Protect Cardholder Data	3. Protect stored cardholder data 4. Encrypt transmission of cardholder data across open, public networks
Maintain a Vulnerability Management Program	5. Protect all systems aginst malware and regularly update anti-virus software or programs 6. Develop and maintain secure system and applications
Implement Strong Access Control Measures	7. Restrict access to cardholder data by business need to know 8. Identify and authenticate access to system components 9. Restrict physical access to cardholder data
Regularly Monitor and Test Networks	10. Track and monitor all access to network resources and cardholder data 11. Regularly test security systems and processes
Maintain an Information Security Policy	12. Maintain a policy that addresses information security for all personnel

Figure 8-3 PCI DSS goals and requirements for merchants and other entities involved in payment card processing

As you can see, PCI DSS does not specifically identify what technologies should be used to achieve the associated goals. Rather, it offers broad requirements that may have multiple options for compliance. Though used globally, PCI DSS is not a federal standard in the United States. While more states enact laws to prevent unauthorized disclosure and abuse of payment card information, PCI DSS remains the de facto standard for payment card information protection.

Intellectual Property

Intellectual property is the lifeblood of a business. It's the special knowledge on how to make something, or a unique creation that allows an organization to distinguish itself from the competition. Like tangible property, there are laws that govern the rights of the property owner. As a security professional, you should be aware of intellectual property that resides on the network so that you can put into place appropriate measures to prevent its unauthorized disclosure. Even with the best technical measures for protecting intellectual property, companies are still vulnerable to exposure of their intellectual property. Your policy must incorporate the latest legal guidance to ensure that employees understand the importance of protecting this information as well as the consequences of unauthorized disclosure for both the company and themselves.

Intellectual Property Types

Intellectual property falls under four categories: patent, copyright, trademark, and trade secrets. When an inventor develops a new and useful process or thing and patents it, a patent will provide the holder the exclusive privilege to make, use, market, and sell that process or thing. Copyright is the tangible manifestation of an original creative expression, whether it's a book, musical piece, painting, or even architectural design. Copyright protection extends to works that are published and unpublished. It's important to note that under the "fair use" doctrine, any criticism, commentary, or teaching based on the copyrighted work may be used to justify a violation of the copyright. A trademark is also known as a brand name. It's the unique term or name that a business uses to differentiate it or its products from others. Unlike trademarks, which companies want the public to be aware of, trade secrets are specially protected data about how a company produces something. Trade secrets are different from the other forms of intellectual property in that their details are usually not disclosed to any registration party or otherwise.

 NOTE Intellectual property laws vary by country. The protections granted by patents issued by the United States Patent Office, for example, are only enforceable in U.S. territories. It's therefore important to understand the local laws that govern intellectual property where you operate to know what is protected under law.

Operation Aurora

In 2010, Google disclosed that it was the victim of a sophisticated attack that appeared to have two distinct goals: monitor the e-mail communications of human rights activists and gain control of sensitive source code. The campaign, determined to be part of a larger campaign called "Operation Aurora," was linked to several other breaches and intellectual property theft at high-profile companies such as Adobe, Juniper Networks, Northrop Grumman, and Morgan Stanley. The attackers used a zero-day exploit for Internet Explorer, encrypted tunneling, and clever obfuscation methods, indicative of an APT actor. The exploit allowed malware to load onto corporate computers, at which point intellectual property could be funneled out of the network. Though details are limited on the attack, Google claimed that this operation was the responsibility of the Chinese government. As a direct result, Google shut down its search engine service in the country, despite China having over twice as many Internet users as in the United States.

Corporate Confidential

Information about the internal operations of a company is called *corporate confidential information*. This may include correspondence about upcoming changes to the company hierarchy, details about a marketing campaign, or any other information that may not be suitable for public consumption. Corporate confidential information is often referred to as *proprietary information*. You will often see the markings on corporate documents to indicate that dissemination should be tightly controlled.

Accounting Data   Financial data about a company requires special handling and protection in a similar way to other sensitive data, even if it may not reveal health or personal data. In a way, financial data gives insight into the health of an organization, and should be treated as such. Corporate policies and legal guidance may dictate the general procedures for handling and storing the information, but you should take extra steps to segment accounting data from those within the company who do not have the need-to-know.

Mergers and Acquisitions   Data about upcoming mergers and acquisitions of a company is a type of sensitive corporate information whose misuse is most often associated with fraud and conspiracy. If information about an upcoming acquisition were to be prematurely disclosed because of a malicious actor, it could have grave consequences on the finances of both companies. Companies about to be acquired might be vulnerable to manipulation or loss of their competitive advantage. If an employee trades a public company's stock because of privileged knowledge about a company's finance or a pending acquisition that is not yet public knowledge, he has committed a serious crime called *insider trading,* which has both civil and criminal penalties. The Securities and Exchange Commission's Fair Disclosure regulation mandates that if special knowledge about a company is disclosed to one shareholder, then it must be disclosed to the public.

Chapter Review

Regardless of the size of your organization, you will be a target of an attacker. The nature of how attackers conduct their campaigns is constantly evolving. Individual actors, activist groups, and nation-states have far easier access to malicious software than ever before. The question becomes less *if* you will have an incident and more *when*. Ignoring this fact will place you and your organization in a precarious position. Proper planning for an incident will indicate to your customers, stakeholders, and key leadership that you take security seriously and will instill confidence in their business systems. Should an incident occur, your preparation will allow you to quickly identify the scope of damage because you will have identified the data that requires special handling and protection, including PII, PHI, intellectual property, corporate confidential information, and financial information about your organization. However, preparation isn't just an effort for your security team. It means that you assist organizational leadership in communicating the goals of the security policy and the importance of the employees' roles in supporting it. Aside from the benefit of having a smoother recovery, having a comprehensive incident-handling process regarding special data may protect you from civil or criminal procedures should your organization be brought to court for failing to protect sensitive data. Once you've gotten buy-in from organization leadership for your incident response plan, you need to continue to refine and improve it as threats evolve. Should the day come that you need to put the plan into play, you will have the confidence and support to get through the challenge.

Questions

1. Which of the following statements is true about a zero-day exploit?
   A. It is a flaw in a piece of software of which the vendor is unaware.
   B. It is code written to take advantage of a software flaw unknown to its vendor.
   C. It is the day on which a vendor is notified of a flaw in its software.
   D. It is a cyber weapon developed exclusively by a nation-state adversary.

2. Advanced persistent threats (APTs) are best exemplified by which of the following?
   A. Nation-state adversaries
   B. Cybercrime syndicates
   C. Hacktivist collectives
   D. Script kiddies

3. All of the following are factors contributing to a determination of the scope of impact of an incident *except* which?
   A. Recovery time
   B. Downtime
   C. Uptime
   D. Data integrity

4. Of the following types of data, which is likeliest to require notification of government entities if it is compromised, lest your organization incur fines or jail sentences?

   A. Personally identifiable information (PII)

   B. Personal health information (PHI)

   C. Intellectual property

   D. Accounting data

5. All of the following are types of protected intellectual property *except* which?

   A. Trade secrets

   B. Patents

   C. Copyrights

   D. Items covered by the "fair use" doctrine

6. What makes information about mergers and acquisitions so sensitive?

   A. It can give an unfair advantage to the company being acquired.

   B. It is regulated by the PCI DSS.

   C. If it is disclosed to the public, it could lead to charges of insider trading.

   D. Its disclosure might violate Securities and Exchange Commission's regulations.

Use the following scenario to answer Questions 7–10:

You work for a large private hospital that specializes in a rare form of cancer treatment. Its reputation is such that its patients include some of the most prominent people from all over the world. Just last month, a multinational health services conglomerate quietly started an effort to acquire your hospital. Before the deal is finalized or made public, you are called in to respond to a particularly sophisticated incident after a three-letter government agency alerted your boss to a likely compromise. The threat actors appear to be targeting your accounting systems, but no data appears to have been modified or deleted. The initial attack vector appears to have been a previously unknown vulnerability in your perimeter firewall. It appears that the actors have been exfiltrating information from your systems for several months, but this is the first you hear of it.

7. Who is the likeliest threat actor?

   A. An APT

   B. A cybercrime syndicate

   C. A disgruntled insider

   D. Script kiddies

8. Your team has confirmed that the initial attack vector targeted a zero-day vulnerability in your firewall. What should you do next?

   A. Notify the firewall vendor.

   B. Scan the firewall for vulnerabilities.

   C. Apply the latest patches to the firewall.

   D. Implement ACLs that mitigate the vulnerability.

9. Which of the following factors is most important in determining the impact of the incident?

   A. System process criticality

   B. Economic considerations

   C. Data integrity

   D. Recovery time

10. In which of the following types of data is the attacker most likely interested?

    A. Payment card information

    B. Intellectual property

    C. PII or PHI

    D. Merger and acquisition

Answers

1. **B.** The code written to take advantage of a flaw that is unknown to its vendor or users is called a zero-day exploit.

2. **A.** Advanced persistent threat (APT) is the name given to any number of stealthy and continuous computer-hacking efforts, often coordinated and executed by an organization or government with significant resources. Although the term can refer to certain powerful criminal organizations, nation-state adversaries is a better answer.

3. **C.** The key factors to consider when determining the scope of impact of an incident are downtime, recovery time, data integrity, economic considerations, and system process criticality.

4. **B.** Personal health information (PHI) is strictly regulated in the U.S., and its disclosure could result in civil or criminal penalties. None of the other types of information listed are normally afforded this level of sensitivity.

5. **D.** Intellectual property falls under four categories: patent, copyright, trademark, and trade secrets.

6. **D.** The Securities and Exchange Commission's Fair Disclosure regulation mandates that if special knowledge about a company is disclosed to one shareholder, then it must be disclosed to the public, so this information must be carefully controlled.

7. **A.** The combination of using a zero-day exploit and being on the network for months without making any demands, selling any information, or breaking anything strongly points to an advanced persistent threat (APT), which is further supported by the hospital's distinguished clientele.

8. **A.** A zero-day vulnerability is a flaw in a piece of software that the vendor is unaware of and thus has not issued a patch or advisory for. It is unlikely that you can mitigate the damage yourself, apart from switching to a different firewall. The best course of action is to notify the vendor immediately so it can develop a patch.

9. **D.** The attacker has been very stealthy and does not appear to have publicly released any of the harvested information. This points to an operation that is focused on surveillance rather than financial profit. Furthermore, the attacker does not appear to have modified or destroyed data or to have interfered with any critical processes. This means the best factor based on the information available is the amount of time it will take you to recover from this incident.

10. **C.** The attacker does not appear to be motivated by monetary profits, so credit card information is unlikely to be the goal. Similarly, the fact the attack appears to have started before the acquisition makes it less likely that the merger and acquisition information was targeted. Though it is possible that the attacker is after intellectual property regarding the cancer treatments, it is more likely that an APT would be interested in PII and/or PHI about prominent world figures.

Preparing the Incident Response Toolkit

In this chapter you will learn:

- How digital forensics is related to incident response
- Basic techniques for conducting forensic analyses
- Familiarity with a variety of forensic utilities
- How to assemble a forensics toolkit

Condemnation without investigation is the height of ignorance.

—Albert Einstein

Digital Forensics

Digital forensics is the process of collecting and analyzing data in order to determine whether and how an incident occurred. The word *forensics* can be defined as an argumentative exercise, so it makes sense that a digital forensic analyst's job is to build compelling, facts-based arguments that explain an incident. The digital forensic analyst answers the questions *what, where, when,* and *how,* but not *who* or *why.* These last two questions are answered by the rest of the investigative process of which digital forensics is only a part.

The investigation of a security incident need not end up in a courtroom, but it is almost impossible to predict whether it will. This means that we should treat every digital forensic investigation as if it will ultimately be held to the level of scrutiny of a criminal case. We all know that this is not always possible when trying to bring critical business processes back online or simply based on the required workload. Still, the closer we stay to the principles of legal admissibility in court, the better off we'll be in the end. The National Institute of Justice identifies the following three principles that should guide every investigation:

- Actions taken to secure and collect digital evidence should not affect the integrity of that evidence.

- Persons conducting an examination of digital evidence should be trained for that purpose.

- Activity relating to the seizure, examination, storage, or transfer of digital evidence should be documented, preserved, and available for review.

Phases of an Investigation

Forensic investigations, like many other standardized processes, can be broken down into phases. In this case, we normally recognize four: seizure, acquisition, analysis, and reporting. Seizure is the process of controlling the crime scene and the state of potential evidentiary items. Acquisition is the preservation of evidence in a legally admissible manner. The analysis takes place in a controlled environment and without unduly tainting the evidence. Finally, the goal is to produce a report that is complete, accurate, and unbiased.

NOTE We break down digital forensics into four phases—seizure, acquisition, analysis, and reporting—though many organizations have reduced this to three phases by combining seizure and acquisition.

Seizure

The goal of seizure is to ensure that neither the perpetrators nor the investigators make any changes to the evidence. An overly simplistic, but illustrative, example is to put yellow "Crime Scene" tape and guards around the area wherein a murder took place so murderers can't come back and pick up shell casings with their fingerprints on them. Obviously, the digital crime scene is different in that the perpetrator may continue to invisibly be in the scene making changes even as the investigators are trying to gather evidence.

Controlling the Crime Scene

Whether the crime scene is physical or digital, it is important to control who comes in contact with the evidence of the crime to ensure its integrity. The following are just some of the steps that should take place to protect the crime scene:

- Only allow authorized individuals access to the scene.
- Ensure everyone involved in technical tasks is trained and certified for his or her role.
- Document who is at the crime scene.
- Document who were the last individuals to interact with the systems.
- If the crime scene does become contaminated, document it. The contamination may not negate the derived evidence, but it will make investigating the crime more challenging.

One of the most important steps you can take is to *not* power off anything you don't have to. The one universal exception to this rule is if you are pretty sure that there is a running process that is deliberately destroying evidence. There are many reasons for keeping the devices running, but a key one is that memory forensics (that is, digital forensics on the primary storage units of computing devices) has dramatically evolved over the past few years. Although it is possible for a threat actor to install rootkits that hide processes, connections, or files, it is almost impossible to hide tracks in running memory. Furthermore, an increasing number of malware never touches the file system directly and lives entirely in memory. Shutting down a device without first acquiring the contents of memory could make it impossible to piece together the incident accurately.

> **NOTE** In order to acquire volatile memory, you will likely have to make some changes to the computer, which typically include connecting an external device and executing a program. As long as you document everything you do, this should not render the evidence inadmissible in court.

Another important, if seemingly mundane, step is to document the entire physical environment around a device. An easy way to do this is to take lots of photos of the scene. Specific shots you typically want to take are listed here. Regardless of whether you take pictures, you should certainly take notes describing not only the environment but also each action your team takes to seize the evidence.

- Computer desktop showing running programs (if the device is unlocked)
- Peripherals connected to the device (for example, thumb drives and external drives)
- Immediate surroundings of the device (for example, physical desktop)
- Proximate surroundings of the device (for example, the room or cubicle)

Tales from the Trenches: A Picture Is Worth...

We were once chatting with a federal law enforcement agent about best practices for photographing crime scenes. He described a case in which he raided a suspect's home and seized a large amount of evidence, including a stack of dozens of CDs. When they attempted to acquire the contents of the hard drive, they found out it was protected by strong full-disk encryption. They asked the suspect for the passphrase, but he happily informed them that he didn't know it. Incredulous, our friend asked him how that was possible. The suspect responded that he never memorized the passphrase because it was simply the first character in each CD's title. To his horror, our friend realized that he didn't take any photos that showed the stack of CDs in order and the disks had been shuffled during handling.

After you have documented the environment, it is time to start unplugging things and taking them away. It is important to properly tag, label, and inventory everything you seize so there are no questions about what was where later. You also need disassembly and removal tools such as antistatic bands, pliers, and screwdrivers. Finally, you need appropriate packaging such as antistatic bags and evidence bags. You should keep in mind that weather conditions (for example, extreme temperatures, snow, or rain) may also impose additional requirements on your packaging and transportation arrangements.

Chain of Custody   A *chain of custody* is a history that shows how evidence was collected, transported, and preserved at every stage of the process. Because digital evidence can be easily modified, a clearly defined chain of custody demonstrates that the evidence is trustworthy. It is important to follow very strict and organized procedures when collecting and tagging evidence in every single case. Furthermore, the chain of custody should follow evidence through its entire life cycle, beginning with identification and ending with its destruction, permanent archiving, or return to the owner. Figure 9-1 shows a sample form that could be used for this purpose.

Servers   Conducting a forensic analysis of a server requires addressing additional issues compared to workstations. For starters, it may not be possible to take the server offline and remove it to a safe analysis room. Instead, you may have no choice but to conduct an abbreviated analysis onsite. *Live forensics* (or live response) is the conduct of digital forensics on a device that remains operational throughout the investigation. We already touched on a related issue earlier when we described the importance of capturing the contents of volatile memory before shutting off a device. If you cannot remove the server from a production environment, then the next-best thing is to capture its memory contents and files of interest (for example, log files).

Figure 9-1
Evidence
container data

EVIDENCE

Station/Section/Unit/Dept_____

Case number_____ Item#_____

Type of offense_____

Description of evidence_____

_____

_____

Suspect_____

Victim_____

Date and time of recovery_____

Location of recovery_____

Recovered by_____

CHAIN OF CUSTODY

Received from_____ By_____

Date_____Time_____A.M./P.M.

Received from_____ By_____

Date_____Time_____A.M./P.M.

Received from_____ By_____

Date_____Time_____A.M./P.M.

Received from_____ By_____

Date_____Time_____A.M./P.M.

WARNING: THIS IS A TAMPER EVIDENT SECURITY PACKAGE. ONCE SEALED, ANY
ATTEMPT TO OPEN WILL RESULT IN OBVIOUS SIGNS OF TAMPERING.

Another consideration when dealing with servers is that they typically have significantly more storage (both primary and secondary) than workstations. This is guaranteed to make the process longer, but may also require special tools. For example, if your server uses a redundant array of inexpensive disks (RAID), you will likely need specialized tools to deal with those disks. Apart from the hardware differences, you will also have to consider the particular architectures of the software running on servers. Microsoft Exchange Server has a large number of features that help a forensic investigator, but that person will have to know his or her way around Exchange's complex architecture. This point also holds for database management systems (DBMS) and in-house web applications.

Mobile Devices   It is uncommon for criminal investigations these days not to include mobile device forensics. Though this is somewhat lesser of a case in the corporate world, you should be aware of the unique challenges that mobile devices present. Chief among these is that the device will continue to communicate with the network unless you power it off (which we already said might not be a good idea). This means that a perpetrator can remotely wipe the device or otherwise tamper with it. A solution to this problem is to place the device into a Faraday container that prevents it from communicating over radio waves. Faraday bags have special properties that absorb radio frequency (RF) energy and redistribute it, preventing communication between devices in the container and those outside. Obviously, you will also need a larger Faraday facility in which to analyze the device after you seize it.

Acquisition

Forensic acquisition is the process of extracting the digital contents from seized evidence so that they may be analyzed. This is commonly known as taking a forensic image of a hard drive, but it actually involves more than just that. The main reason you want to extract the contents is that you want to conduct your analysis on a copy of the evidence and not on the original. Throughout the process, preserving the integrity of the original evidence is paramount. To acquire the original digital evidence in a manner that protects and preserves the evidence, the following steps are generally considered best practices:

1. *Prepare the destination media.* You will need a place to store the digital contents of your seized evidence. This destination may be a removable hard drive or a storage area network (SAN). You must ensure that the destination is free of any content that may taint the evidence. The best way to do this is to securely wipe the media by overwriting it with a fixed pattern of ones and/or zeroes.

2. *Prevent changes to the original.* The simple act of attaching a device to a computer or duplicator will normally cause its contents to change in small but potentially significant ways. To prevent any changes at all, you must use write-protection mechanisms such as hardware write blockers (described later in this chapter). There are also forensic acquisition software products that enable software-based write protection, but it is almost always better to use physical ones.

3. *Hash the original evidence.* Before you copy anything, you should take a cryptographic hash of the original evidence. Most products support MD5 and SHA-1 hashes. Though these protocols have been shown to be susceptible to collisions and are no longer recommended for general use, we have seen no pushback from the courts on their admissibility in criminal trials.

4. *Copy the evidence.* A variety of applications will let you do a forensic copy of digital media, including the venerable dd utility in Linux systems. What these applications all have in common is that they perform complete binary copies of the entire source medium. Copying the files is not enough because you might not acquire relevant data in deleted or unallocated spaces.

5. *Verify the acquisition.* After the copy is complete, you take a cryptographic hash of the copy and compare it to the original. As long as they match, you will be able to perform analyses of the copy and be assured that it is perfectly identical to the original.

6. *Safeguard the original evidence.* Because you now have a perfect copy of the evidence, you store the original in a safe place and ensure nobody gains access to it.

Analysis

Analysis is the process of interpreting the extracted data to determine its significance to the case. Some examples of the types of analysis that may be performed include time-frame (that is, what happened when), data hiding (that is, things that have been intentionally concealed), application and file (that is, which applications accessed which files), and ownership and possession (that is, which user accounts accessed which applications and files). Though the specific applications and commands you would use may vary depending on the operating or file systems involved, the key issues are the same.

One of the most important tools to a forensic analyst is the timeline. It establishes a framework for comparing the state of the system at different points in time. For example, you may suspect that a user might have stolen files by copying them to a thumb drive last Friday, but you don't see that drive registered on the system until Monday. Absent evidence of tampering with the data and time on the system, you can conclude that the exfiltration mechanism was not that particular thumb drive. The timeline is simply an ordered list of actions taken on the system. These actions can be categorized as read, write, modify, and delete operations on an item of interest. Many investigators we know simply keep track of their timelines in a spreadsheet with columns like the ones listed here:

- Data and time
- Time zone
- Source (for example, Windows Registry or syslog)
- Item name (for example, Registry key name or filename)
- Item location (full path)
- Description

EXAM TIP You should always regard system timestamps with a healthy dose of skepticism. Threat actors are known to sometimes modify the system clock to hide the true sequence of their actions. This practice is known as *timestomping*.

At every step of the process, you should be keeping copious notes on each specific action you take, down to the command and parameters you use. If you use a forensic analysis suite such as EnCase or FTK (the Forensic Toolkit), the tool will record your actions for you. Even so, it is a best practice to keep notes on your own throughout the investigation.

Reporting

If you have been taking notes, you have been writing parts of the report as you conducted the investigation. Once you arrive at sound conclusions based on the evidence available, you simply have to put together narrative statements that present your arguments and conclusions in a readable fashion. Like any form of communication, knowing your audience is crucial. If the report is geared toward executive leaders, the document would be different than if you were presenting it in a court of law. All major commercial suites also have a feature that will generate a draft report you can then customize for your own purposes.

Forensic Investigation Suite

Forensic investigations are extremely time-consuming by their very nature. Fortunately, a number of software developers have created suites of tools to facilitate many aspects of the process.

Acquisition Utilities

The acquisition phase of a forensic investigation is perhaps the most critical point in terms of ensuring the admissibility of evidence, analysis, and conclusions. This is where you want to slow down, use a checklist, and ensure you make no mistakes at all because doing so would possibly invalidate all the work that follows.

Forensic Duplicators

Forensic duplicators are systems that copy data from a source to a destination while ensuring that not even a single bit gets altered in the process. What sets them apart from any copying utility is that they do not rely on file system operations, which means they can recover file system artifacts such as the Master File Table (MFT) in Windows systems and the inode table in Linux ones.

dd The venerable workhorse in Linux is the dd utility that comes by default with most systems. Because almost everything in the extended file system (ext) used in Linux is a "file" (even network connections and peripheral devices), dd can duplicate data across files, devices, partitions, and volumes. The following command will do a bit-for-bit copy

PART III

of hard drive "hda" to a file called case123.img using a block size of 4096 bytes, and it will fill the rest of a block with null symbols if it encounters an error:

```
dd if=/dev/hda of=case123.img bs=4k conv=noerror,sync
```

Note that this command does not generate a hash of the output file, which we need for verification. The solution is to simply use the **sha1sum** command separately.

FTK Imager   FTK Imager is a free data preview and imaging tool developed by Access Data. Unlike the dd utility, this imager is a full-featured product that allows you to perform a forensically sound acquisition, verify it by generating MD5 and/or SHA-1 hashes, and even preview the files and folders in a read-only fashion. FTK Imager will also read registry keys from Windows and let you preview them and their values. It also supports compression, encryption, and multiple output formats, including EnCase Evidence File format (E01) and the raw format generated by dd (001).

Password Crackers

It is increasingly common to find encrypted files or drives in everything from mobile devices to back-end servers. If the suspect is unable or unwilling to provide the password, or if there is no suspect to interrogate in the first place, you may have to resort to specialized software that is designed to guess passwords and decrypt the protected resources. A popular commercial solution in this space is called Passware Kit Forensic. It can operate on its own or be integrated with EnCase. Passware Kit Forensic can decrypt over 280 different types of protected files, including BitLocker, FileVault, iCloud, and Dropbox. Additionally, because password cracking can take a very long time, this tool can take advantage of graphics processing units (GPUs) and multiple networked computers to accelerate the process.

Cryptography Tools

It is often the case that we must ensure the confidentiality of an investigation and its evidence. To accomplish this, we can turn to a variety of cryptography tools that are available for multiple platforms. Perhaps the simplest approach to encrypting files is to use the compression utilities found in most operating systems, but you must ensure you provide a password. The advantage is that these applications are ubiquitous and the files are mostly usable across platforms.

If you need something a little more robust, you can try any number of available encryption tools. One of the most popular and recommended open source solutions is VeraCrypt, which is based on the now defunct TrueCrypt. This tool is free and available for Windows, OS X, and Linux systems. VeraCrypt supports multiple cryptosystems, including AES, TwoFish, and Serpent. It also supports the creation of hidden, encrypted volumes within other volumes, as shown in Figure 9-2. Finally, the tool is under constant development, with regular security updates.

Hashing Utilities

The most popular hashing algorithms for forensic analysis are MD5 and SHA-1, and they are supported by all the popular tools we discuss in this chapter. If you need a standalone hashing utility, many operating systems include these by default. Mac OS

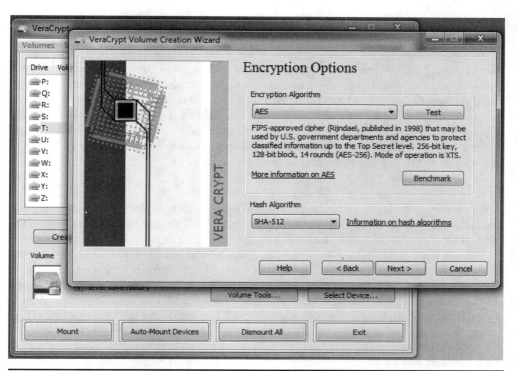

Figure 9-2 VeraCrypt creating an encrypted volume

has the md5 tool available from the command line. Linux typically has both the md5 tool as well as sha1sum. Finally, Microsoft provides the File Checksum Integrity Verifier (FCIV) tool as a free but unsupported download. FCIV is able to compute both MD5 and SHA-1 hashes.

Analysis Utilities

The most widely used commercial analysis tools are Guidance Software's EnCase and Access Data's Forensic Toolkit (FTK). These tools are not cheap, but there are also a number of free or less-expensive options, including The Sleuth Kit. We describe each of these in turn in this section.

EnCase

EnCase is probably the most widely used analysis tool among law enforcement agencies as well as some of the larger corporations. It is a bit inaccurate to describe it solely as an analysis tool because it can actually perform acquisition (both live and dead), analysis, and reporting. In terms of acquisition, the product offers the option to run agents in all your endpoints and servers that can be used for remote acquisition over the network. This means you don't need to physically seize the devices in order to acquire their data.

One of EnCase's contributions to the field was the creation of the proprietary (but widely used) EnCase Evidence File format. Files in this format typically have an .E01 extension, though this is not necessary. What made the format so impactful was its integration of compression, encryption, and metadata all within the same file. If you are developing a raw or bit-for-bit image of an evidence drive, you would end up with multiple files: the copy, the hash value, and the metadata (for example, evidence label and case number). You could very well have other files associated with the copy. Furthermore, if you wanted to save space or ensure the confidentiality of the evidence, you would have to compress and/or encrypt the files separately. EnCase's format allows all this to be incorporated into one file in an almost transparent manner.

FTK

Another very popular suite is the Forensic Toolkit, which is almost as widely used as EnCase. Users of both systems sometimes point to FTK's more intuitive user interface, but that is clearly a subjective issue. What truly sets FTK apart from other solutions is its foundational data management model. Because this tool is built on top of a data-base management system, it is able to process very large volumes of data efficiently. In the latest release, FTK boasts support for ElasticSearch, which is a very popular open source search engine designed to deal with big data sources. The data preprocessing and indexing associated with these features, however, can make the initial case upload take longer than other solutions.

The Sleuth Kit

Rounding out our analysis suites is Brian Carrier's open source The Sleuth Kit. Whereas EnCase and FTK go to great lengths to present a homogeneous user experience that hides the many tools that are working behind the scenes to support the analyst, The Sleuth Kit is more unabashedly a collection of interoperable tools, many of which use a command-line interface exclusively. However, if you would rather have a graphical user interface (GUI) comparable to the commercial solutions, you can use Autopsy with The Sleuth Kit to get the job done, as shown in Figure 9-3. Collectively, these tools do most of what EnCase and FTK do, but rather than thousands of dollars per license, there is no cost for them.

OS and Process Analysis

An operating system (OS) is a software system that manages and controls all interactions with a computer. Though there are clearly a variety of operating systems in use today, they all perform the same three basic functions:

- Manage all computer resources such as memory, CPU, and disks
- Provide a user interface
- Provide services for running applications

It is the first of these that is of particular interest to a forensic analyst, because every action that occurs on a computer system is mediated by its OS.

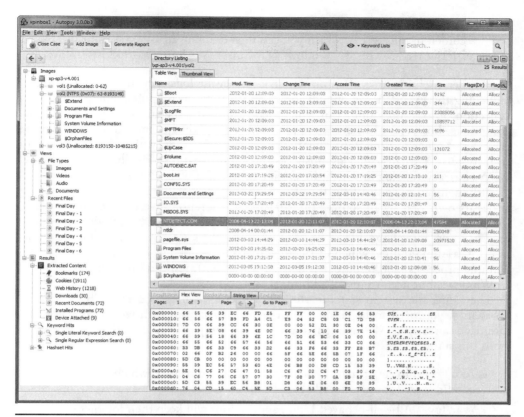

Figure 9-3   The Autopsy interface for The Sleuth Kit

If you are investigating a Microsoft Windows system, two of the most important sources of information are the registry and the event log. The registry is the principal data store where Windows stores most system-wide settings. Though all major analysis suites include viewers for this database, you can also examine it directly on any Windows computer by launching the Registry Editor application. There are literally hundreds of interesting artifacts you can find in the registry, including the following:

- **Autorun locations**   This is where programs tell Windows that they should be launched during the boot process. Malware oftentimes uses this for persistence (for example, HKLM\Software\Microsoft\Windows\CurrentVersion\Run).

- **Most Recently Used lists**   Often referred to as MRUs, this is where you'd find the most recently launched applications, recently used or modified documents, and recently changed registry keys. For example, if you wanted to see recently used Word documents, you would look in HKEY_CURRENT_USER\Software\Microsoft\Office\12.0\Common\Open Find.

- **Wireless networks** Every time a computer connects to a wireless network, this is recorded in the registry, which you can then examine an as investigator in HKLM\ SOFTWARE\Microsoft\Windows NT\CurrentVersion\NetworkList\Profile.

Another useful source of information is the event logs, which you can access by launching the Event Viewer application in any Windows computer. There is actually a collection of logs, the number of which depends on the specific system. All Windows computers, however, will have an application log in which applications report usage, errors, and other information. There is also a security log in which the OS maintains security-related events such as unsuccessful login attempts. Finally, every Windows system has a system log in which the OS records system-wide events.

Although Linux doesn't have the convenience of a centralized registry like Windows, it has its own rich set of sources of artifacts for a forensic investigator. For starters, a lot of relevant data can be found in plaintext files, which (unlike Windows) makes it easy to search for strings. Linux also typically includes a number of useful utilities such as dd, sha1sum, and ps, which can help you acquire evidence, hash it, and get a list of running processes (and resources associated with them), respectively. You can do all this in Windows, but need to install additional tools.

The Linux file system starts in the root directory, which is denoted by a slash. As an analyst, you need to be familiar with certain directories with which you should be familiar as an analyst. We highlight a few of these, but you should build up your own list from this start.

- **/etc** This is the primary system configuration directory, which contains a subdirectory for most installed applications.
- **/var/log** All well-behaved Linux applications will keep their log files in plaintext files in this directory, making it a gold mine for analysts.
- **/home/$USER** Here, $USER is a variable name that you should replace with the name of a given user. All user data and configuration data are kept here.

Note that this list is just a start. You should build up your own list from here.

Mobile Device Forensics

While there is some amount of forensic analysis that you can do on a live Windows or Linux system, mobile devices require dedicated forensic tools. The exceptions to this rule are jailbroken iPhones or iPads and rooted Android devices, because both of these expose an operating system that is very similar to Linux and includes some of the same tools and locations. To make things a bit more interesting, many phones require special cables although the migration toward USB-C in recent years is simplifying this as more devices adopt this interface.

Among the challenges involved in mobile forensics is simply getting access to the data. The mobile OS is not designed to support acquisition, which means that the forensic analyst must first get the device to load an alternate OS. This usually requires a custom bootloader, which is an almost essential feature of any mobile forensics toolkit.

Another peculiarity of mobile devices is that much of their data is stored in miniature database management systems such as SQLite. These systems require special tools to properly view their data. The advantage of them, however, is that they almost never delete data when the user asks them to. Instead, they mark the rows in the database table as deleted and keep their entire contents intact until new data overwrites them. Even then, the underlying file system may allow recovery of this deleted information. As with the bootloader, any common analysis suite will include the means to analyze this data.

Log Viewers

Every major OS provides the means to view the contents of its log files. The reason you may need a dedicated log viewer is that the built-in tools are meant for cursory examination and not for detailed analysis, particularly when the logs number in the thousands. Like most other features described so far, this functionality is oftentimes found in the forensic analysis suites. If you need a dedicated log viewer, there is no shortage of options, including many free ones.

A scenario in which a standalone log viewer would make sense is when you are trying to aggregate the various logs from multiple computers in order to develop a holistic timeline of events. You would want a tool that allows you to bring in multiple files (or live systems) and filter their contents in a variety of ways. Some tools that allow you to do this include Splunk, SolarWinds Event Log Consolidator/Manager, and Ipswitch's WhatsUp.

Building Your Forensic Kit

There is no one-size-fits-all answer for what you should put in your forensic kit. It really depends on your environment and workflow processes. Still, there are some general tool types that almost everyone should have available if their work includes forensic analyses.

Jump Bag

The jump bag is a prepackaged set of tools that is always ready to go on no notice. This is your first line of help when you are asked to drop everything you're doing and respond to an incident that may involve a forensic examination. Because you want to ensure that the bag is always ready, you'll probably want to develop a packing list that you can use to inventory the bag after each use to ensure it is ready for the next run. You'll probably want to include each of the following items in it.

Write Blockers and Drive Adapters

Hardware write blockers prevent modifications to a storage device while you acquire their contents. They come in many flavors and price points, but they all do essentially the same thing. The most important consideration is the type of interfaces they support. You should consult your asset inventory to see how many different types of disk interfaces are in use in your environment. Some tools support SCSI and ATA, but not SATA, and others may not support USB devices. As long as you have an adapter and cable for each type of storage device interface in your organization, you should be in good shape.

Cables

A good part of your jump bag will probably be devoted to cables of various types. A good rule of thumb to follow is that if you've ever needed a particular cable before, then you should probably keep it in your jump bag forever. Here are some ideas for the cables you may want to start with:

- Ethernet cables (crossover, straight-through, one-way)
- Serial cables (various flavors of USB and RS-232)
- Power cables
- A small Ethernet hub
- Antistatic wrist straps

Wiped Removable Media

You may not have a few hours to wipe a hard drive before responding to an incident, so it pays to keep a few packed. The type of interface doesn't much matter (as long as it is supported by your write blocker), but the capacity does. A good rule of thumb is to look into your asset inventory and find the largest workstation or external drive in your organization and pack at least twice that amount of storage in your bag. Servers tend to have significantly larger drives than workstations, so if that is a concern, you may have to invest in a portable RAID solution such as Forensic Computers' Forensic Data Monster. Solutions like these are portable and designed to facilitate the acquisition of evidence.

A common approach in organizations that deal with fairly frequent investigations is to set up a network-attached storage (NAS) solution specifically for forensic images. As long as you have a fast network connection, you'll be able to image any workstation or server with ease. An added advantage is that the NAS can serve as an archival mechanism for past investigations that may still be pending in court. In these cases, it is important to abide by your organization's data-retention policies.

Camera

The camera is an often-overlooked but critical item in your jump bag. It is important to photograph the crime or incident site, but pretty much any digital camera with a flash will do. A useful addition to your camera is a small ruler that you can include in shots whenever you need to capture a sense of distance or scale. Ideally, the ruler should have a matte surface to minimize glare.

Crime Scene Tape

This may sound like overkill, but having some means of notifying others in the area that they should not enter is critical to the seizure process. Crime scene (or other restricted-area-labeled) tape does the job nicely and inexpensively.

Tamper-Proof Seals

When the amount of evidence you collect, or the distance you have to transport it, requires the assistance of others (for example, drivers), you probably want to seal the evidence containers with a tamper-resistant seal. In a pinch, you can use tape and sign your name across it. However, if you can afford them, dedicated lockable containers will be best.

Documentation and Forms

Depending on your organization, many forms and other documents may only exist in digital form. Still, it is a good idea to have hard copies printed and in your jump bag because you never know whether you'll be able to access your corporate data store in the middle of an incident response. Here are some items most of us would keep in our bags.

Chain of Custody Form   Figure 9-1 showed a typical chain-of-custody form, but you should tailor it to your own organization's requirements if you don't already have one. The important aspect is to ensure there are enough copies to go with each seized piece of evidence. Ideally, your evidence transport containers have a waterproof pouch on the outside into which you can slide a form for the container (individual items in it may still need their own forms).

Incident Response Plan   It is not unusual for an incident response to start off as one thing and turn into something else. Particularly when it comes to issues that may have legal implications (for example, forensic investigations), it is a good idea to have a copy of the plan in your jump bag. This way, even if you are disconnected from your network, you will know what you are expected or required to do in any situation you encounter.

Incident Log   Every good investigator takes notes. When you're performing a complex investigation, as most digital forensics ones are, it is important to document every action you take and every hypothesis you are considering. The most important reason for this level of thoroughness is that your conclusions are only as valid as your processes are repeatable. In other words, any qualified individual with access to the same evidence you have should be able to follow your notes and get the same results that you did. Keeping a notebook and pen in your jump bag ensures you are always ready to write down what you do.

Call/Escalation List   If the conditions on the ground are not what you thought they'd be when you started your investigation, you may have to call someone to notify them of an important development or request authorization to perform some action. Though the call/escalation list should really be part of your incident response plan, it bears singling it out as an important item in your jump bag.

Chapter Review

Digital forensics investigations require a very high degree of discipline and fixed adherence to established processes. A haphazard approach to these activities can mean the difference between successful resolution of an incident, or watching a threat actor get away with criminal behavior. The challenge is in striking the right balance between quick responses to incidents that don't require this level of effort and identifying those cases that do early enough to adjust the team's approach to them. Because you might not know which events can escalate to forensic investigations, you should always be ready to perform in this manner with no notice.

The CSA+ exam will require you to know the four-step process (seizure, acquisition, analysis, reporting) and which actions you take during each. For example, you may see questions that present you with a scenario in which some part of the process has already been completed and you are asked what's the next thing you do. This may require familiarity with the way in which you would use some of the most common tools, such as the Linux dd utility. Though you will probably not see a question that requires you to issue a command with arguments, you may have to interpret the output of such a tool and perform some sort of simple analysis of what may have happened.

Questions

1. In the event of a serious incident, which task is *not* a critical step to take in controlling the crime scene?

    A. Record any interactions with digital systems.

    B. Verify roles and training for individuals participating in the investigation.

    C. Remove power from currently running systems.

    D. Carefully document who enters and leaves the scene.

2. What is the practice of controlling how evidence is handled to ensure its integrity during an investigation called?

    A. Chain of control

    B. Chain of concern

    C. Chain of command

    D. Chain of custody

3. As part of the forensic analysis process, what critical activity often includes a graphical representation of process and operating system events?

    A. Registry editing

    B. Timeline analysis

    C. Network mapping

    D. Write blocking

4. During forensic acquisition, why is a high-level format normally insufficient when preparing the destination media?

 A. High-level formatting completely wipes the drive, but may add additional artifacts.

 B. High-level formatting only erases the file data, leaving the system structure intact.

 C. High-level formatting only erases the file system structure data, leaving the file data intact.

 D. High-level formatting removes bad sectors, but leaves file data intact.

5. The practice of modifying or deleting file modification data is referred to as what?

 A. Timestomping

 B. Timestamping

 C. Timelining

 D. Timeshifting

Use the following command-line input to answer Questions 6-8:

```
dd if=/dev/sda of=/dev/sdc bs=2048 conv=noerror,sync status=progress
```

6. How many bits of data are read and written at a time?

 A. 2048

 B. 16384

 C. 256

 D. 512

7. What is the name of the destination image?

 A. sda

 B. /dev/sda

 C. sync

 D. sdc

8. What is the purpose of the command?

 A. To copy the primary partition to an image file

 B. To restore the contents of a hard drive from an image file

 C. To copy the entire contents of the hard drive to an image file

 D. To delete the entire contents of /dev/sda

Use the following scenario to answer Questions 9–12:

You are called to a scene of a high-profile incident and asked to perform forensic acquisition of digital evidence. The primary objective is a Linux server that runs several services for a small company. The former administrator is suspected of running illicit services using company resources and is refusing to provide passwords for access to the system. Additionally, there are several company-owned mobile phones that appear to be functioning sitting on the desk beside the servers.

9. What is one of the first tasks you undertake in preparing to analyze the server's hard drive?

    A. Hash all storage media and then make a copy of the hard drive.

    B. Begin analysis on the target system and perform recurring MD5 hashes.

    C. Copy the entire contents to a SAN or external storage and begin analysis.

    D. Perform analysis immediately on the server before loss of power.

10. What utility will allow you to make a bit-for-bit copy of the hard drive contents?

    A. MFT

    B. dd

    C. MD5

    D. GPU

11. What type of specialized software might you use to recover the credentials required to get system access?

    A. Forensic duplicator

    B. dd

    C. Password cracker

    D. MD5

12. You want to take the mobile phones back to your lab for further investigation. Which two tools might you use to maintain device integrity as you transport them?

    A. Faraday bag and a tamper-evident seal

    B. Write blocker and crime scene tape

    C. Thumb drive and crime scene tape

    D. Forensic toolkit and tamper-evident seal

Answers

1. **C.** Removing power should not be done unless it's to preserve life or limb, or under other exigent circumstances. In many cases, it's possible to recover evidence residing in running memory.

2. **D.** A *chain of custody* is a history that shows how evidence was collected, transported, and preserved at every stage of the investigation process.

3. **B.** Timeline analysis is the practice of arranging extracted data from a UNIX file system, the Windows registry, or a mobile device in chronological order to better understand the circumstances of a suspected incident.

4. **C.** The destination media should be free from anything that may contaminate the evidence. Completely removing the data requires overwriting each block of the destination storage medium, which may always be performed if you're using high-level formatting tools.

5. **A.** Timestomping is an advanced technique to manipulate file creation or modification data to thwart forensics techniques. It's often used by malware to make the process of timelining more difficult.

6. **B.** The **bs** argument indicates the number of bytes transferring during the process. Because there are 8 bits in a byte, you will multiply the 2048 by 8 to get 16384 bits.

7. **D.** The **of** argument indicates the *output file* of the process.

8. **C.** The source file is the entire hard drive, indicated by the argument **/dev/sda**. You should be careful to double-check the spelling of both input and output files to avoid overwriting the incorrect media.

9. **A.** You want to conduct your analysis on a copy of the evidence and not on the original, but be sure to take a cryptographic hash of the original evidence before you copy anything.

10. **B.** dd is a common utility found in most Linux-based systems. It can duplicate data across files, devices, partitions, and volumes.

11. **C.** Password crackers are specialized software designed to guess passwords and decrypt the protected resources. The software can be very resource intensive since cracking usually requires a lot of processing power or storage capacity.

12. **A.** A Faraday container will prevent the devices from communicating over radio waves by absorbing and redistributing their RF energy. You should secure the bag with a tamper-evident seal to easily identify whether its contents were interfered with.

10

Selecting the Best Course of Action

In this chapter you will learn:
- How to diagnose incidents by examining network symptoms
- How to diagnose incidents by examining host symptoms
- How to diagnose incidents by examining application symptoms

Diagnosis is not the end, but the beginning of practice.

—Martin H. Fischer

Introduction to Diagnosis

The English word *diagnosis* comes from the Greek word *diagignōskein,* which literally means "to know thoroughly." Diagnosis, then, implies the ability to see through the myriad of irrelevant facts, honing in on the relevant ones, and arriving at the true root cause of a problem. Unlike in Hollywood, real-world security incidents don't involve malware in bold red font conveniently highlighted for our benefit. Instead, our adversaries go to great lengths to hide behind the massive amount of benign activity in our systems, oftentimes leading us down blind alleys to distract us from their real methods and intentions. The CSA+ exam, like the real world, will offer you plenty of misleading choices, so it's important that you stay focused on the important symptoms and ignore the rest.

Network-Related Symptoms

We start our discussion as you will likely start hunting many of your adversaries: from the outside in. Our network sensors oftentimes give us the first indicators that something is amiss. Armed with this information, we can then interrogate hosts and the processes running on them. In the discussion that follows, we assume that you have architected your network with a variety of sensors whose outputs we will use to describe possible attack symptoms.

Bandwidth Utilization

Bandwidth, in computing, is defined as the rate at which data can be transferred through a medium, and it is usually measured in bits per second. Networks are designed to support organizational requirements at peak usage times, but they usually have excess capacity during non-peak periods. Each network will have its own pattern of utilization with fairly predictable ebbs and flows. Attackers can use these characteristics in two ways. First, patient ones can hide data exfiltration during periods of peak use by using a low-and-slow approach that can make them exceptionally difficult to detect by just looking at network traffic. Most attackers, however, will attempt to download sensitive information quickly and thus generate distinctive signals.

Figure 10-1 shows a suspicious pattern of NetFlow activity. Though one host (10.0.0.6) is clearly consuming more bandwidth than the others, this fact alone can have a multitude of benign explanations. It is apparent from the figure that the host is running a web server, which is serving other hosts in its own subnet. What makes it odd is that the traffic going to the one host in a different subnet is two orders of magnitude greater than anything else in the report. Furthermore, we must ask ourselves why a web server is connecting on a high port to a remote web server. When looking at bandwidth consumption as an indicator of compromise, you should look not only at the amount of traffic, but also at the endpoints and directionality of the connection.

Beaconing

Another way in which attackers oftentimes tip their hands is by using a common approach for maintaining contact with compromised hosts. Most firewalls are configured to be very careful about inbound connection requests but more permissive about outbound ones. The most frequently used malware command-and-control (C2) schemes have the compromised host periodically send a message or beacon out to a C2 node. *Beaconing* is a periodical outbound connection between a compromised computer and an external controller. This beaconing behavior can be detected by its two common characteristics: periodicity and destination. Though some strains of malware randomize the period of the beacons or the destination address or both, most have a predictable pattern.

Detecting beacons by simple visual examination is extremely difficult because the connections are usually brief (maybe a handful of packets in either direction) and easily get lost in the chatter of a typical network node. It is easier to do an endpoint analysis and see how regularly a given host communicates with any other hosts. To do this, you would have to sort your traffic logs first by internal source address, then by destination address, and finally by time. The typical beacon will then jump out and become apparent.

Src IP	Src Port	Dst IP	Dst Port	Protocol	Packets	Bytes/Pkt
10.0.0.3	54902	192.168.0.7	80	TCP	2491	740
10.0.0.6	55097	172.31.21.3	443	TCP	100227	1528
10.0.0.12	993	10.0.0.3	48450	TCP	2210	762
10.0.0.6	443	10.0.0.7	54122	TCP	2271	1040
10.0.0.6	443	10.0.0.3	53112	TCP	1022	810

Figure 10-1 NetFlow report showing suspicious bandwidth use

NOTE Some legitimate connections will look like beacons on your network. An example from our personal experience is certain high-end software, which periodically checks with a license server to ensure it is allowed to be used.

Irregular Peer-to-Peer Communication

Most network traffic follows the familiar client/server paradigm in which there is a (relatively) small number of well-known servers that provide services to a larger number of computers that are not typically servers themselves. Obviously, there are exceptions, such as n-tier architectures in which a front-end server communicates with back-end servers. Still, the paradigm explains the nature of most network traffic, at least within our organizational enclaves. It is a rare thing in a well-architected corporate network for two peer workstations to be communicating with each other. This sort of peer-to-peer communication is usually suspicious and can indicate a compromised host.

Sophisticated attackers will oftentimes dig deeper into your network once they compromise their initial entry point. Whether this first host they own is the workstation of a hapless employee who clicked a malicious link or an ill-configured externally facing server, it is rarely the ultimate target for the attacker. *Lateral movement* is the process by which attackers compromise additional hosts within a network after having established a foothold in one. The most common method of achieving this is by leveraging the trusted tools built into the hosts. All they need is a valid username and password to use tools such as SMB and PsExec in Windows or SSH in Linux. The required credentials can be obtained in a variety of ways, including cached/stored credentials on a compromised host, password guessing, and pass-the-hash attacks on certain Windows domains. Here is a list of things to look for:

- **Unprivileged accounts connecting to other hosts**   Unless a well-known (to you) process is being followed (for example, hosts sharing printers), any regular user connection to a peer host is likely to indicate a compromise and should be investigated.

- **Privileged accounts connecting from regular hosts**   It is possible for a system or domain administrator to be working at someone else's computer (for example, fixing a user problem) and needing to connect to another resource using privileged credentials, but this should be rare. We already described why this can be problematic in Chapter 3 when we discussed jump boxes. These connections should get your attention.

- **Repeated failed remote logins**   Many attacks will attempt lateral movement by simply guessing passwords for remote calls. Any incidences of repeated failed login attempts should be promptly investigated, particularly if they are followed by a successful login.

Detecting the irregular peer-to-peer communications described here can be extremely hard because all you would see are legitimate users using trusted tools to connect to other computers within your network. Context matters, however, and the question to ask as an analyst should be, does this user account have any legitimate reason to be connecting from this host to this other resource?

Tales from the Trenches: Package Analysis

A colleague of ours once told us about a black-box pen test he was doing on a pretty well-secured organization. After a couple of days of not getting anywhere, he decided to send a package to an employee who (as attested by her social media profile) would be away from the office for a couple of weeks. In the package was a mobile phone with an invoice to the employee for full market value (to ensure it would eventually be returned). The phone was loaded with wireless hacking tools and would connect over the cellular data network back to his workstation. Within a day, the battery was depleted but our colleague had been able to connect his rogue device to the wireless network undetected and compromise multiple workstations, all from the comfort of his office. And yes, he did get his phone back in the mail.

Rogue Devices on the Network

One of the best things you can do to build and maintain secure networks is to know what's on them. Both hardware and software asset management is the bedrock upon which the rest of your security efforts are built. If you don't know what hosts belong on your network, then you won't be able to determine when an unauthorized one connects. Unfortunately, this lack of asset awareness is the case in many organizations, which makes it easy for attackers to join their devices to target networks and compromise them.

There are two main ways in which an attacker can connect: physically through a network plug and wirelessly. Though you would think that it would be pretty easy to detect a shady character sitting in your lobby with a laptop connected to the wall, the real threat here is with employees who connect their own wireless access points to the network in order to provide their own devices with wireless access where there may have been none before. Rare as this is, it is damaging enough to require that we mention it here. The likelier scenario is for an attacker to connect wirelessly.

In either case, you need a way to tell when a new host is connected. The best approach, of course, is to deploy Network Access Control (NAC) to ensure each device is authenticated, potentially scanned, and then joined to the appropriate network. NAC solutions abound and give you fine-grained controls with which to implement your policies. They also provide you with centralized logs that can be used to detect attempted connections by rogue devices.

If you don't have NAC in your environment, your next best bet is to have all logs from your access points (APs) sent to a central store in which you can look for physical

(MAC) addresses that you haven't seen before. This process, obviously, is a lot more tedious and less effective. The easiest way for an attacker to get around this surveillance is to change the MAC address to one that is used by a legitimate user. The challenge, of course, is that this could cause problems if that user is also on the network using the same MAC address, but one could simply wait until the user is gone before attempting impersonation.

Scan Sweeps

Some attackers, particularly those more interested in volume than stealth, will use scan sweeps to map out an environment after compromising their first host in it. They may download and run a tool like nmap or they can use a custom script or even a feature of a hacking toolkit they bought on the Dark Web. Whatever their approach, the symptoms on the network are mostly the same: one host generating an abnormally large number of connection attempts (but typically no full connections) to a multitude of endpoints.

A good way to detect scan sweeps is by paying attention to ARP messages. The Address Resolution Protocol (ARP) is the means by which interfaces determine the address of the next hop toward the ultimate destination of a packet. An ARP request is simply a node broadcasting to every other node in its LAN the question, "Who is responsible for traffic to this IP address?" If the IP address belongs to another host on the same LAN, then that host responds by providing its own media access control (MAC) or physical address. At that point, the source host will send an IP packet encapsulated in a point-to-point Ethernet frame to the interface address from the responder. If, on the other hand, the IP address belongs to a different LAN, the default gateway (that is, IP router) will respond by saying it is responsible for it.

When an attacker attempts a scan sweep of a network, the scanner will generate a large number of ARP queries, as shown on Figure 10-2. In this example, most of the requests will go unanswered because there are only a handful of hosts on the network segment though the subnet mask is for 255 addresses. This behavior is almost always indicative of a scan sweep and, unless it is being done by an authorized security staff member, it should

Time	Source	Destination	Protocol	Length	Info
1.88519600	Vmware_4a:58:30	Broadcast	ARP	42	who has 192.168.192.162? Tell 192.168.192.6
1.88528900	Vmware_4a:58:30	Broadcast	ARP	42	who has 192.168.192.163? Tell 192.168.192.6
1.88540000	Vmware_4a:58:30	Broadcast	ARP	42	who has 192.168.192.164? Tell 192.168.192.6
1.88555900	Vmware_4a:58:30	Broadcast	ARP	42	who has 192.168.192.165? Tell 192.168.192.6
1.88566200	Vmware_4a:58:30	Broadcast	ARP	42	who has 192.168.192.166? Tell 192.168.192.6
1.88574400	Vmware_4a:58:30	Broadcast	ARP	42	who has 192.168.192.167? Tell 192.168.192.6
1.88583400	Vmware_4a:58:30	Broadcast	ARP	42	who has 192.168.192.168? Tell 192.168.192.6
1.88591000	Vmware_4a:58:30	Broadcast	ARP	42	who has 192.168.192.169? Tell 192.168.192.6
1.88601800	Vmware_4a:58:30	Broadcast	ARP	42	who has 192.168.192.170? Tell 192.168.192.6
1.88610000	Vmware_4a:58:30	Broadcast	ARP	42	who has 192.168.192.171? Tell 192.168.192.6
1.88618800	Vmware_4a:58:30	Broadcast	ARP	42	who has 192.168.192.172? Tell 192.168.192.6
1.88626800	Vmware_4a:58:30	Broadcast	ARP	42	who has 192.168.192.173? Tell 192.168.192.6
1.88643300	Vmware_4a:58:30	Broadcast	ARP	42	who has 192.168.192.174? Tell 192.168.192.6
1.88654100	Vmware_4a:58:30	Broadcast	ARP	42	who has 192.168.192.175? Tell 192.168.192.6
1.88663100	Vmware_4a:58:30	Broadcast	ARP	42	who has 192.168.192.176? Tell 192.168.192.6
1.88671500	Vmware_4a:58:30	Broadcast	ARP	42	who has 192.168.192.177? Tell 192.168.192.6

Figure 10-2 ARP queries associated with a scan sweep

be investigated. The catch, of course, is to ensure that you have a sensor in every subnet that is monitoring ARP messages.

Host-Related Symptoms

After noticing unusual network behaviors like the ones we discussed in the previous sections (or after getting an alert from an IDS/IPS or other sensor), your next step is to look at the suspicious host to see if there is a benign explanation for the anomalous behavior. It is important to follow the evidence and not jump to conclusions, because it is oftentimes difficult to get a clear picture of an intrusion simply by examining network traffic or behaviors.

Running Processes

Someone once said, "Malware can hide, but it has to run." When you're responding to an incident, one of your very first tasks should be to examine the running processes. Every operating system provides a tool to do this, but you must be wary of trusting these tools too much because the attacker might be using a rootkit that would hide their activities from these tools. Still, most incidents do not involve such sophisticated concealment, so running top or ps in Linux or looking at the Processes tab of the Windows Task Manager (and showing processes from all users) can be very helpful.

 EXAM TIP For many of us, we first look at the processes running on a system before we decide whether to capture its volatile memory. In the test, it is always preferable to capture memory first, and then look at running processes. We reverse the order here for pedagogical reasons.

On a typical system, the list of running processes will likely number a few dozen or so. Many of these will have names like svchost.exe and lsass.exe for Windows or kthreadd and watchdog for Linux. Unless you know what is normal, you will struggle to find suspicious processes. A solution to this challenge is to baseline the hosts in your environment and make note of the processes you normally see in a healthy system. This will allow you to rapidly filter out the (probably) good and focus on what's left. As you do this, keep in mind that attackers will commonly use names that are similar to those of benign processes, particularly if you're quickly scanning a list. Common examples include adding an *s* at the end of svchost.exe, or replacing the first letter of lsass.exe with a numeral 1. Obviously, any such change should automatically be investigated.

Another way in which processes can reveal their nefarious nature is by the resources they utilize, such as network sockets, CPU cycles, and memory. It is exceptionally rare for malware to not have a network socket of some sort at some point. Some of the less-sophisticated ones will even leave these connections up for very long periods of time. So if you have a process with a name you've never seen before and it is connected to an external host, you may want to dig a bit deeper. An easy way to see which sockets belong to which processes is to use the netstat command. Unfortunately, each operating system implements this tool in a subtly different way, so you need to use the right parameters, as shown here:

- Windows

  `netstat -ano`
- Mac OS

  `netstat -v`
- Linux

  `netstat -nap`

Another resource of interest is the processor. If a malicious process is particularly busy (for example, cracking passwords or encrypting data for exfiltration), it will be using a substantial amount of CPU cycles, which will show up on the Windows Task Manager or, if you're using Linux, with the top or ps utilities.

Memory Contents

Everything you can tell about a computer through the techniques discussed in the previous section can also be done on a copy of its volatile memory. The difference, of course, is that a volatile memory analysis tool will not lie even if the attacker used a rootkit on the original system. The reason why you probably won't go around doing full memory captures of every computer involved in an incident response is that it takes time to capture them and even longer to analyze them.

 NOTE There are tools used by threat actors that reside only in memory and have no components stored on the file system. These sophisticated tools all but require incident responders to rely on memory forensics to understand them.

You will need a special tool to dump the contents of memory to disk, and you probably don't want that dump to go to the suspected computer's hard drive. Your best bet is to have a removable hard drive in your jump bag. Ensure that the device has enough capacity for the largest amount of memory on any system you could be called to investigate, and that you wipe its contents before you use it. Finally, install on it on one of the many free applications available for memory capture. Among our favorites are Access Data's FTK Imager (which can also acquire file systems) for Windows systems and Hal Pomeranz's Linux Memory Grabber for those operating systems.

Once you have a memory image, you will need an analysis suite to understand it. The reason is that the layout and contents of memory are large, complex, and variable. They follow predictable patterns, but these are complicated enough to render manual analysis futile. Among the most popular tools for memory forensics is the open source Volatility Framework, which can analyze Windows, Linux, and Mac OS memory images and runs on any of those three platforms. Having taken an image of the memory from the suspected computer, you will be able to open it in Volatility and perform the same tasks we described in the previous section (albeit in a more trustworthy manner), plus conduct a myriad of new analyses that are beyond the scope of this book.

 EXAM TIP You do not need to understand how to perform memory forensics for the exam; you only need to know why memory dumps are valuable to incident response.

File System

A *file system* is the set of processes and data structures that an operating system uses to manage data in persistent storage devices such as hard disk drives. These systems have traditionally been (and continue to be) the focal point of incident responses due to the richness of the relevant artifacts that can be found in them. It is extremely difficult for adversaries to compromise a computer and not leave evidence of their actions on the file system.

 NOTE The word *artifact* is frequently used in forensics and, though there is no standard definition for it in this context, is generally taken to denote a digital object of interest to a forensic investigation.

Unauthorized Software

The most blatant artifact since the beginning of digital forensics is the illicit binary executable file. Once an adversary saves malware to disk, it is pretty clear that the system has been compromised. There are at least two reasons why threat actors still rely widely on this technique (as opposed to the newer memory-only or file-less malware): convenience and effectiveness. The truth is that it is oftentimes possible to move the file into its target unimpeded because many defensive systems rely on signature detection approaches that can easily be thwarted through code obfuscation. Even behavioral detection systems (that is, those that look at what the code *does*) are constantly playing catch-up to new evasion techniques developed by the attackers.

Having bypassed the antimalware systems (if any) on the target, this software will continue to do its work until you find it and stop it. This task is made orders of magnitude easier if you have a list of authorized programs that each computer is allowed to run. *Software whitelisting* is the process of ensuring that only known-good software is allowed to execute on a system. The much more common alternative is software *blacklisting,* which is when we prevent known-bad (or suspected-bad) software from running. Whitelisting is very effective at reducing the attack surface for organizations that implement it. However, it is also deeply unpopular with the rank-and-file user because any new application needs to be approved through the IT and security departments, which delays the acquisition process.

Even if you don't (or can't) implement software whitelisting, you absolutely should have an accurate list of the software that is installed in every computer. This software asset inventory is important not only to more easily detect unauthorized (and potentially harmful) software, but also for license auditability and upgrade-planning purposes.

Together with a hardware inventory, these two are the most essential steps for ensuring the security of your networks.

Unauthorized Changes

A common technique to maintain access to compromised systems is to replace system libraries, such as dynamically linked libraries (DLLs) in Windows systems, with malicious ones. These stand-ins provide all the functionality of the original, but also add whatever the attacker needs. Replacing these files requires elevated privileges, but there is a variety of ways for an adversary to accomplish this. Once the switch is made, it becomes hard to detect unless you've taken some preparatory actions.

In Windows systems, there are built-in features that are helpful in detecting unauthorized changes to files. One of these is automatic logging of access or changes to files in sensitive folders. This feature is called Object Access Auditing and can be applied globally or selectively as a group policy. Once it's in place, Windows will generate an event whenever anyone reads, modifies, creates, or deletes a file in the audited space. For example, modifying an audited file would generate an event with code 5136 (a directory service object was modified) and record the user responsible for the change as well as the time and what the change was. Linux has an equivalent audit system that provides similar features. Obviously, you want to be selective about this because you could generate thousands if not millions of alerts if you are too gratuitous about it.

Another way to detect changes to important files is to hash them and store the resulting value in a safe location. This would only be useful for files that are never supposed to change in any way at all, so you would have to be selective. Still, for most if not all of your libraries and key programs, this approach works well. You would still have to manually check the hashes over time to ensure they haven't changed, but it is a simple process to script and schedule on any system. If you need a more comprehensive solution to file integrity monitoring, there are commercial organizations such as Tripwire that offer solutions in this space.

Data Exfiltration

Apart from writing malware to your file systems and modifying files in them for malicious purposes, adversaries will also want to steal data as part of certain attacks. The data that would be valuable to others is usually predictable by the defenders. If you work in advanced research and development (R&D), your project files would probably be interesting to uninvited guests. Similarly, if you work in banking, your financial files would be lucrative targets. The point is that we can and should identify the sensitivity of our data before an incident so that we can design controls to mitigate risks to them.

A common approach to exfiltrating data is to first consolidate it in a staging location within the target network. Adversaries don't want to duplicate efforts or exfiltration streams because such duplication would also make them easier to detect. Instead, they will typically coordinate activities within a compromised network. This means that even if multiple agents are searching for sensitive files in different subnets, they will tend to copy those files at the coordination hub at which they are staged, prepared, and relayed to an external repository. Unfortunately, these internal flows will usually be difficult to detect because they may resemble legitimate functions of the organization. (A notable exception is described in the section "Irregular Peer-to-Peer Communication" earlier in this chapter.)

Detecting the flow from the staging base outward can be easier if the amount of data is large or if the adversaries are not taking their time. The exfiltration will attempt to mimic an acceptable transfer such as a web or e-mail connection, which will typically be encrypted. The important aspect of this to remember is that the connection will look legitimate, but its volume and endpoint will not. Even if a user is in the habit of uploading large files to a remote server for legitimate reasons, the pattern will be broken unless the attackers also compromise that habitually used server and use it as a relay. This case would be exceptionally rare unless you were facing a determined nation-state actor. What you should do, then, is to set automated alarms that trigger on large transfers, particularly if they are to an unusual destination. NetFlow analysis is helpful in this regard.

For a more robust solution, some commercial entities sell data loss prevention (DLP) solutions, which rely on tamper-resistant labels on files and networks that track them as they are moved within and out of the network. DLP requires data inventories and a data classification system in addition to technical controls. DLP is not explicitly covered in the CSA+ exam, but if data exfiltration is a concern for you or your organization, you should research solutions in this space.

Data Exfiltration: A Real-World Case

One of the tactics used by the threat actor alternatively known as APT28 or Fancy Bear is as effective as it is low tech. This group is known to create a fake Outlook Web Access (OWA) page that looks identical to the target organization's, has a message indicating the OWA session timed out, and prompts the users to reenter his credentials. The page is hosted on a domain that has a name very similar to the target's (for example, mail.state.qov instead of state.gov). The target is sent a spear-phishing e-mail with a link to the decoy site that seems interesting and appropriate to the target. When the link is clicked within OWA, it forwards the OWA tab to the fake timed-out page and opens the decoy site on a new tab. When the user closes or switches out of the decoy tab, he sees the (fake) OWA prompt and reenters his credentials. The fake page then forwards them to the (still valid) OWA session. At this point, the threat actor simply creates an IMAP account on some computer and uses the user's credentials to synchronize his folders and messages. This is data exfiltration made easy. Apart from the phony OWA domain name, everything else looks perfectly legitimate and is almost impossible to detect as an attack unless you are aware of this specific tactic.

Capacity Consumption

We have already seen how the various indicators of threat activity all consume one or more types of resources. Whether it is memory, CPU cycles, disk space, or network bandwidth, most attackers will create spikes in capacity consumption. Part of your job as an analyst is to proactively think about where and when these spikes would occur based on your own risk assessment or threat model, and then provide the capability to monitor resources so that you can detect the spikes. The CSA+ exam will not test you on the proactive aspect of this process, but you will be expected to know how to identify these anomalies in a scenario. You are likely to be presented an image like Figure 10-3 and be asked questions about the resources being consumed and what they may be indicative of. The figure, by the way, is of a Windows 7 system that is mostly idle and not compromised.

When faced with unexplained capacity consumption, you should refer to the steps we described for analyzing processes, memory, network connections, and file systems. The unusual utilization will be a signal, but your response depends on which specific resource is being used.

Unauthorized Privileges

Regardless of the type or purpose of the attack, the adversaries will almost certainly attempt to gain elevated privileges. Sometimes, the exploit itself will provide access to a privileged account such as *system* (in Windows) or *root* (in Linux). Some remote execution vulnerabilities, when exploited, place the adversary in a privileged context.

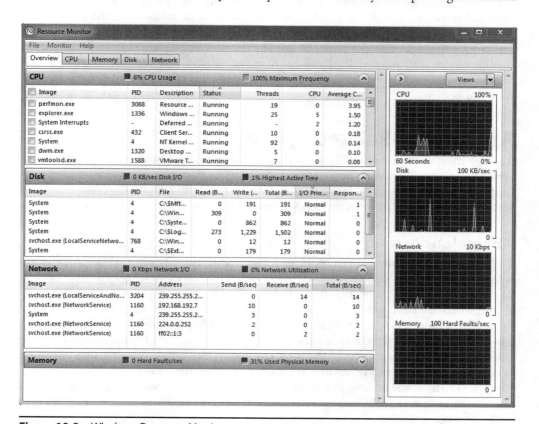

Figure 10-3 Windows Resource Monitor

More commonly, however, the attacker will have to take some action to get to that status. These actions can be detected and oftentimes leave artifacts as evidence.

Privilege escalation is the process by which a user who has limited access to a system elevates that access in order to acquire unauthorized privileges. Note that this could easily apply to an authorized user of the system gaining unauthorized privileges, just as much as it applies to a remote attacker. The means by which this escalation occurs are very system dependent, but they tend to fall into three categories: acquiring privileged credentials, exploiting software flaws, and exploiting misconfigurations. The credentials can be obtained by social engineering or password guessing, but would be anomalous in that a user would be connecting from or to computers that are not typical for that person. Detecting the exploitation of software flaws requires an awareness of the flaws and monitoring systems that are vulnerable until they can be patched. Obviously, this would not normally be detectable in the event of a zero-day exploit.

Once elevated privileges are detected, your response depends on the situation. The simplest approach would be to disable the suspected account globally and place any hosts that have an active session for that user into an isolated VLAN until you can respond. The risk there is that, if the account user is legitimate, you may have interfered with a teammate performing an important function for the company, which could have financial impacts. A more nuanced approach would be to monitor all the activities on the account in order to determine whether they are malicious or benign. This approach can reduce the risk of a false positive, but it risks allowing an attacker to remain active on the system and potentially cause more harm. Absent any other information, you should prioritize the protection of your information assets and contain the suspicious user and systems.

Application-Related Symptoms

Though most of your work will take place at the network and host levels, it is also sometimes necessary to examine application symptoms as part of an incident response. By "application," we mean user-level as opposed to system-level features or services. In other words, we are talking of software like Microsoft Office and not web or e-mail services.

Anomalous Activity

Perhaps the most common symptom of possible infections is unusual behavior in the infected application. Web browsers have long been a focus of attackers not only because of their pervasiveness, but also their complexity. In order to provide the plethora of features that we have grown used to, browsers are huge, complicated, and oftentimes vulnerable applications. Our increasing reliance on plug-ins and the ability to upload as well as download rich content only complicates matters. It is little wonder that these popular applications are some of the most commonly exploited. The first sign of trouble is usually anomalous behavior such as frozen pages, rapidly changing uniform resource locators (URL) in the address bar, or the need to restart the browser. Because web browsers are common entry points for attacks, these symptoms are likely indicative of the early stages of a compromise.

Other commonly leveraged applications are e-mail clients. Two popular tactics used by adversaries are to send e-mail messages with links to malicious sites and to send infected attachments. The first case was covered in the preceding paragraph because it is the web browser that would connect to the malicious web resource. In the second case, the application associated with the attachment will be the likely target for the exploit. For example, if the infected file is a Microsoft Word document, it will be Word that is potentially exploited. The e-mail client, as in the link case, will simply be a conduit. Typical anomalous behaviors in the targeted application include unresponsiveness (or taking a particularly long time to load), windows that flash on the screen for a fraction of a second, and pop-up windows that ask the user to confirm a given action (for example, allowing macros in an Office document).

A challenge with diagnosing anomalous behaviors in user applications is that they oftentimes mimic benign software flaws. We have all experienced applications that take way too long to load even though there is no ongoing attack. Still, the best approach may be to immediately move the host to an isolated VLAN and start observing it for outbound connection attempts until the incident response team can further assess it.

Introduction of New Accounts

Regardless of the method of infection, the attacker will almost always attempt to elevate the privileges of the exploited account or create a new one altogether. We already addressed the first case, so let's now consider what the second might look like. The new account created by the attackers will ideally be a privileged domain account. This is not always possible in the early stages of an attack, so it is not uncommon to see new local administrator accounts or regular domain accounts being added. The purpose of the attacker is twofold: to install and run tools required to establish persistence on the local host, and to provide an alternate and more normal-looking persistence mechanism in a domain account. In either case, you may want to reset the password on the account and immediately log off the user (if a session is ongoing). Next, monitor the account for attempted logins in order to ascertain the source of the attempts. Unless the account is local, it is not advisable to simply isolate the host because the attacker could then attempt a connection to almost any other computer.

Unexpected Output

Among the most common application outputs that are indicative of a compromise are pop-up messages of various kinds. Unexpected user access control (UAC) pop-ups in Windows, as shown in Figure 10-4, are almost certainly malicious if the user is engaged in routine activities and not installing new software. Similarly, certificate warnings and navigation confirmation dialogs when the user in not taking any actions are inherently suspicious.

Unexpected Outbound Communication

Perhaps the most telling and common application behavior that indicates a compromise is the unexpected outbound connection. We already spoke about why this is so common in attacks during our discussion of network symptoms. It bears repeating that it is

Figure 10-4
User access
control (UAC)
pop-up for
unsigned
software

exceptionally rare for a compromise to not involve an outbound connection attempt by the infected host. The challenge in detecting these is that it is normally not possible for a network sensor to tell whether that outbound connection to port 443 was initiated by Internet Explorer or by Notepad. The first case may be benign, but the latter is definitely suspicious. Because most malicious connections will attempt to masquerade as legitimate web or e-mail traffic, you will almost certainly need a host-based sensor or intrusion detection system (IDS) to pick up this kind of behavior. Assuming you have this capability, the best response may be to automatically block any connection attempt from an application that has not been whitelisted for network connections.

The challenge is that an increasing number of applications are relying on network connectivity, oftentimes over ports 80 or 443, for a variety of purposes. It is also likely that an application that did not used to communicate like this may start doing so as the result of a software update.

EXAM TIP   The fact that an application all of a sudden starts making unusual outbound connections, absent any other evidence, is not necessarily malicious. Look for indicators of new (authorized) installations or software updates to assess benign behavior.

Service Interruption

Services that start, stop, restart, or crash are always worthy of further investigation. For example, if a user notices that the antimalware icon in the status bar suddenly disappears, this could indicate that an attacker disabled this protection. Similarly, error messages stating that a legitimate application cannot connect to a remote resource may be the result of resource allocation issues induced by malicious software on the host. An examination of the resource manager and log files will help you determine whether or not these symptoms are indicative of malicious activities.

Memory Overflows

Another resource that is often disrupted by exploits or malware is main memory. The reason for this is that memory is an extremely complex environment, and malicious activities are prone to disrupt the delicate arrangement of elements in that space. If an attacker is off by even a byte when writing to memory, this could cause memory errors that terminate processes and display some sort of message indicating this condition to the user. This type of symptom is particularly likely if the exploit is based on stack or buffer overflow vulnerabilities. Fortunately, these messages sometimes indicate that the attack failed. Your best bet is to play it safe and take a memory dump so you can analyze the root cause of the problem.

Chapter Review

Like bloodhounds in a hunt, incident responders must follow the strongest scents in order to track their prey. The analogy is particularly apt, because you too will sometimes lose the scent and have to wander a bit before reacquiring it. Starting from the network level and working your way to the host and then individual applications, you must be prepared for ambiguous indicators, flimsy evidence, and occasional dead ends. The most important consideration in both the real world and the CSA+ exam is to look at the aggregated evidence before reaching any conclusions. As you go through this investigative process, keep in mind Occam's razor: the simplest explanation is usually the correct one.

Questions

1. The practice of permitting only known-benign software to run is referred to as what?

   A. Blacklisting

   B. Whitelisting

   C. Blackhatting

   D. Vulnerability scanning

2. Which of the following is not considered part of the lateral movement process?

   A. Internal reconnaissance

   B. Privilege escalation

   C. Exfiltration

   D. Pivoting attacks

3. What is a common technique that attackers use to establish persistence in a network?

   A. Buffer overflow

   B. Adding new user accounts

   C. Deleting all administrator accounts

   D. Registry editing

PART III

4. Which one of the following storage devices is considered to be the most volatile?

    A. Random-access memory

    B. Read-only memory

    C. Cloud storage

    D. Solid-state drive

5. Which of the following is not an area to investigate when looking for indicators of threat activity?

    A. Network speed

    B. Memory usage

    C. CPU cycles

    D. Disk space

6. What is a useful method to curb the use of rogue devices on a network?

    A. SSID

    B. FLAC

    C. WPA

    D. NAC

Use the following scenario to answer Questions 7–10:

You receive a call from the head of the R&D division because one of her engineers recently discovered images and promotional information of a product that looks remarkably like one that your company has been working on for months. When reading more about the device, it becomes clear to the R&D head that this is in fact the same product that was supposed to have been kept under wraps. She suspects that the plans have been stolen. When inspecting the traffic from the R&D workstations, you notice a few patterns in the outbound traffic. The machines all regularly contact a domain registered to a design software company, exchanging a few bytes of information at a time. However, all of the R&D machines communicate regularly to a print server on the same LAN belonging to Logistics, sending several hundred megabytes in regular intervals.

7. What is the most likely explanation for the outbound communications from all the R&D workstations to the design company?

    A. Command-and-control instructions

    B. Exfiltration of large design files

    C. License verification

    D. Streaming video

8. What device does it make sense to check next to discover the source of the leak?

    A. The DNS server

    B. The printer server belonging to Logistics

C. The mail server

D. The local backup of the R&D systems

9. Why is this device an ideal choice as a source of the leak?

    A. This device might not arouse suspicion due to its normal purpose on the network.

    B. This device has regular communications outside of the corporate network.

    C. This device can emulate many systems easily.

    D. This device normally has massive storage resources.

10. What is the term for the periodic communications observed by the R&D workstations?

    A. Fingerprinting

    B. Chatter

    C. Footprinting

    D. Beaconing

Answers

1. **B.** Whitelisting is the process of ensuring that only known-good software can execute on a system. Rather than preventing known-bad software from running, this technique only allows approved software from running in the first place.

2. **C.** Lateral movement is the process by which attackers compromise additional hosts within a network after having established a foothold in one. This is often achieved by leveraging the trust between hosts to conduct internal reconnaissance, privilege escalation, and pivoting attacks.

3. **B.** A clever way that attackers use for permanence is to add administrative accounts or groups and then work from those new accounts to conduct additional attacks.

4. **A.** Random-access memory (RAM) is the most volatile type of storage listed. RAM requires power to keep its data, and once power is removed, it loses its content very quickly.

5. **A.** Spikes in memory CPU, disk, or network usage (not necessarily network speed) might be indicative of threat activity. It's important to understand what the normal levels of usage are to more easily identify abnormal activity.

6. **D.** Network Access Control (NAC) is a method to ensure that each device is authenticated, scanned, and joined to the right network. NAC solutions often give you fine-grained controls for policy enforcement.

7. **C.** Some types of software, particularly those for high-end design, will periodically check licensing using the network connection.

8. **B.** A common approach to removing data from the network without being detected is to first consolidate it in a staging location within the target network. Noting the size of the transfers to the print server, it makes sense to check to see if it is serving as a staging location and communicating out of the network.

9. **A.** This device is a good choice because an administrator would not normally think to check it. However, because a print server normally has no reason to reach outside of the network, it should alert you to investigate further.

10. **D.** Beaconing is a periodical outbound connection between a compromised computer and an external controller. This beaconing behavior can be detected by its two common characteristics: periodicity and destination. Beaconing is not always malicious, but it warrants further exploration.

PART IV

Security Architectures

- **Chapter 11** Frameworks, Policies, Controls, and Procedures
- **Chapter 12** Identity and Access Management
- **Chapter 13** Putting in Compensating Controls
- **Chapter 14** Secure Software Development
- **Chapter 15** Tool Sets

Frameworks, Policies, Controls, and Procedures

In this chapter you will learn:
- Common information security management frameworks
- Common policies and procedures
- Considerations in choosing controls
- How to verify and validate compliance

Innovation and best practices can be sown throughout an organization—but only when they fall on fertile ground.

—Marcus Buckingham

Security Frameworks

A security program is a framework made up of many entities: logical, administrative, and physical protection mechanisms, procedures, business processes, and people, all working together to provide a level of protection for an environment. Each has an important place in the framework, and if one is missing or incomplete, the whole framework may be affected. The program should work in layers: one layer provides support for the layer above it and protection for the layer below it. Because a security program is a framework, organizations are free to plug in different types of technologies, methods, and procedures to accomplish the necessary protection level for their environment.

NIST

The National Institute for Standards and Technology (NIST) is an organization within the U.S. Department of Commerce that is charged with promoting innovation and industrial competitiveness. As part of this mission, the NIST develops and publishes standards and guidelines aimed at improving practices, including cybersecurity across a variety of sectors. Though it is certainly worth your time to familiarize yourself with these publications, you should be familiar with two in particular as a CSA+ candidate: NIST Special Publication 800-53 (Security and Privacy Controls for Federal Information Systems and Organizations) and the Cyber Security Framework (CSF).

SP 800-53

One of the standards that NIST has been responsible for developing is called Special Publication 800-53 (Security and Privacy Controls for Federal Information Systems and Organizations), currently on its fourth revision. it outlines controls that agencies need to put into place to be compliant with the Federal Information Processing Standards (FIPS). Basically, this publication provides specific guidance on how to select security controls as part of the Risk Management Framework described in SP 800-37. Table 11-1 outlines the control categories addressed in this publication.

The control categories (families) are the management, operational, and technical controls prescribed for an information system to protect the confidentiality, integrity, and availability of the system and its information. Government auditors use SP 800-53 to ensure that government agencies are compliant with government-oriented regulations. It is worth noting that, although this publication is aimed at federal government organizations, many others have voluntarily adopted it to help them better secure their systems.

 NOTE The categorization of controls can be confusing. Administrative controls can also be called management or policy controls. Technical and logical controls are similarly synonymous. Finally, physical controls are sometimes called operational, depending on the organization and the context.

Identifier	Family	Class
AC	Access Control	Technical
AT	Awareness and Training	Operational
AU	Audit and Accountability	Technical
CA	Security Assessment and Authorization	Management
CM	Configuration Management	Operational
CP	Contingency Planning	Operational
IA	Identification and Authentication	Technical
IR	Incident Response	Operational
MA	Maintenance	Operational
MP	Media Protection	Operational
PE	Physical and Environmental Protection	Operational
PL	Planning	Management
PM	Program Management	Management
PS	Personnel Security	Operational
RA	Risk Assessment	Management
SA	System and Services Acquisition	Management
SC	System and Communications Protection	Technical
SI	System and Information Integrity	Operational

Table 11-1 NIST SP 800-53 Control Categories

Cyber Security Framework

On February 12, 2013, the President of the United States signed Executive Order 13636 calling for the development of a voluntary cybersecurity framework for organizations that are part of the critical infrastructure. The goal of this construct was for it to be flexible, repeatable, and cost-effective so that it could be prioritized for better alignment with business processes and goals. A year to the day later, the NIST published the Cyber Security Framework (CSF), which was the result of a collaborative process with members of the government, industry, and academia. As of this writing, over 30 percent of U.S. organizations have adopted the CSF. That figure is expected to reach 50 percent by the year 2020. The CSF is divided into three main components:

- The **Framework Core** consists of the various activities, outcomes, and references common to all organizations. The CSF breaks these down into five functions, 22 categories, and 98 subcategories.

- The **Implementation Tiers** categorize the degree of rigor and sophistication of cybersecurity practices, which can be Partial (tier 1), Risk Informed (tier 2), Repeatable (tier 3), or Adaptive (tier 4). The goal is not to force an organization to move to a higher tier, but rather to inform its decisions so that it can do so if it makes business sense.

- The **Framework Profile** describes the state of an organization with regard to the CSF categories and subcategories. It allows decision-makers to compare the "as-is" situation to one or more "to-be" possibilities, allowing them to align cybersecurity and business priorities and processes in ways that make sense to that particular organization.

The CSF Core organizes cybersecurity activities into five higher-level functions with which you should be familiar. Everything we do can be aligned with one of these.

- **Identify**   Understand your organization's business context, resources, and risks.
- **Protect**   Develop appropriate controls to mitigate risk in ways that make sense.
- **Detect**   Discover in a timely manner anything that threatens your security.
- **Respond**   Quickly contain the effects of anything that threatens your security.
- **Recover**   Return to a secure state that enables business activities after an incident.

 EXAM TIP   You should remember the five functions of the CSF and the fact that it is voluntary and is not a one-size-fits-all solution to cybersecurity.

ISO

When the need to expand and globally standardize security standards was identified, this task was taken on by the International Organization for Standardization (ISO) and the International Electrotechnical Commission (IEC). ISO is the world's largest developer and publisher of international standards. The standards this group works on range from meteorology, food technology, and agriculture to space vehicle engineering, mining, and information technology. The IEC develops and publishes international standards for all electrical, electronic, and related technologies. These two organizations worked together to build a family of global Information Security Management System (ISMS) standards, known as the ISO/IEC 27000 series, some of which are listed here:

- ISO/IEC 27000   Overview and vocabulary
- ISO/IEC 27001   ISMS requirements
- ISO/IEC 27002   Security management
- ISO/IEC 27003   ISMS implementation
- ISO/IEC 27004   ISMS measurement
- ISO/IEC 27005   Risk management
- ISO/IEC 27006   Certification requirements
- ISO/IEC 27007   ISMS auditing
- ISO/IEC 27008   Guidance for auditors
- ISO/IEC 27031   Business continuity
- ISO/IEC 27033   Network security
- ISO/IEC 27034   Application security
- ISO/IEC 27035   Incident management
- ISO/IEC 27037   Digital evidence collection and preservation

This group of standards serves as industry best practices for the management of security controls in a holistic manner within organizations around the world. The list of standards that make up this series grows each year. Each standard has a specific focus (such as metrics, governance, or auditing). It is common for organizations to seek an ISO/IEC 27001 certification by an accredited third party. The third party assesses the organization against the ISMS requirements laid out in ISO/IEC 27001 and attests to the organization's compliance level.

COBIT

The *Control Objectives for Information and related Technology (COBIT)* is a framework and set of *control objectives* developed by ISACA (formerly the Information Systems Audit and Control Association but now known only by its acronym) and the IT Governance Institute (ITGI). It defines goals for the controls that should be used to properly manage IT and to ensure that IT maps to business needs. COBIT is broken down into four domains: Plan and Organize, Acquire and Implement, Deliver and Support, and Monitor and Evaluate. Each category drills down into subcategories. For example, the Acquire and Implement category contains the following subcategories:

- Acquire and Maintain Application Software
- Acquire and Maintain Technology Infrastructure

- Develop and Maintain Procedures
- Install and Accredit Systems
- Manage Changes

So this COBIT domain provides goals and guidance to companies that they can follow when they purchase, install, test, certify, and accredit IT products. This is very powerful because many companies use an ad hoc and informal approach when making purchases and carrying out procedures. COBIT offers a "checklist" approach to IT governance by providing a list of things that must be thought through and accomplished when carrying out different IT functions.

COBIT lays out executive summaries, management guidelines, frameworks, control objectives, an implementation toolset, performance indicators, success factors, maturity models, and audit guidelines. It lays out a complete roadmap that can be followed to accomplish each of the 34 control objectives this model deals with. Figure 11-1 illustrates how the framework connects business requirements, IT resources, and IT processes.

COBIT can bridge the gap between a high-level framework and the selection and implementation of effective procedures and controls. When you develop your security policies that are aligned with the ISO/IEC 27000 series, these are high-level documents that have statements like, "Unauthorized access should not be permitted." But who is authorized? How do we authorize individuals? How are we implementing access control to ensure that unauthorized access is not taking place? How do we know our access control components are working properly? This is really where the rubber hits the road, where words within a document (policy) come to life in real-world practical implementations. COBIT provides the objective that the real-world implementations (controls) you chose

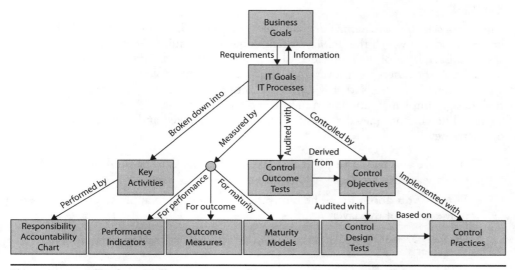

Figure 11-1 COBIT framework

to put into place need to meet. For example, COBIT outlines the following control practices for user account management:

- Using unique user IDs so that users can be held accountable for their actions
- Checking that the user has authorization from the system owner for the use of the information system or service, and the level of access granted is appropriate to the business purpose and consistent with the organizational security policy
- Implementing a procedure to require users to understand and acknowledge their access rights and the conditions of such access
- Ensuring that internal and external service providers do not provide access until authorization procedures have been completed
- Maintaining a formal record, including access levels, of all persons registered to use the service
- Conducting a timely and regular review of user IDs and access rights

An organization should make sure it is meeting at least these goals when it comes to user account management; in turn, this is what an auditor is going to go by to ensure the organization is practicing security properly. Many of today's practices for auditing security compliance are based on COBIT because they are considered industry best practices.

 NOTE Many people in the security industry mistakenly assume that COBIT is purely security focused. In reality, it deals with all aspects of information technology, security only being one component.

SABSA

The *Sherwood Applied Business Security Architecture (SABSA)*, shown in Table 11-2, is a layered model in which the first layer defines business requirements from a security perspective. Each layer of the model decreases in abstraction and increases in detail so that it builds upon the others and moves from policy to practical implementation of technology and solutions. The idea is to provide a chain of traceability through the strategic, conceptual, design, implementation, and metric and auditing levels.

The following outlines the questions that are to be asked and answered at each level of the framework:

- *What* **are you trying to do at this layer?** The assets to be protected by your security architecture
- *Why* **are you doing it?** The motivation for wanting to apply security, expressed in the terms of this layer
- *How* **are you trying to do it?** The functions needed to achieve security at this layer
- *Who* **is involved?** The people and organizational aspects of security at this layer

	Assets (What)	Motivation (Why)	Process (How)	People (Who)	Location (Where)	Time (When)
Contextual	The business	Business risk model	Business process model	Business organization and relationships	Business geography	Business time dependencies
Conceptual	Business attributes profile	Control objectives	Security strategies and architectural layering	Security entity model and trust framework	Security domain model	Security-related lifetimes and deadlines
Logical	Business information model	Security policies	Security services	Entity schema and privilege profiles	Security domain definitions and associations	Security processing cycle
Physical	Business data model	Security rules, practices, and procedures	Security mechanisms	Users, applications, and user interface	Platform and network infrastructure	Control structure execution
Component	Detailed data structures	Security standards	Security products and tools	Identities, functions, actions, and ACLs	Processes, nodes, addresses, and protocols	Security step timing and sequencing
Operational	Assurance of operation continuity	Operation risk management	Security service management and support	Application and user management and support	Security of sites, networks, and platforms	Security operations schedule

Table 11-2 SABSA Architectural Framework

- *Where* **are you doing it?** The locations where you apply your security, relevant to this layer
- *When* **are you doing it?** The time-related aspects of security relevant to this layer

SABSA is a framework and methodology for enterprise security architecture and service management. Because it is a *framework,* it provides a structure for individual architectures to be built from. Because it is also a *methodology,* it provides the processes to follow to build and maintain this architecture. SABSA provides a lifecycle model so that the architecture can be constantly monitored and improved upon over time.

TOGAF

Another enterprise architecture framework is *The Open Group Architecture Framework (TOGAF),* which has its origins in the U.S. Department of Defense. It provides an approach for designing, implementing, and governing an enterprise information architecture that can be used to develop the following architecture types:

- Business architecture
- Data architecture

- Applications architecture
- Technology architecture

This framework can be used to create individual architectures through the use of its Architecture Development Method (ADM). This method is an iterative and cyclic process that allows requirements to be continuously reviewed and the individual architectures updated as needed. These different architectures can allow a technology architect to understand the enterprise from four different views (business, data, application, and technology) so she can ensure her team develops the necessary technology to work within the environment—and all the components that make up that environment—and meet business requirements. The technology may need to span many different types of network types, interconnect with various software components, and work within different business units. As an analogy, when a new city is being constructed, people do not just start building houses here and there. Civil engineers lay out roads, bridges, waterways, and commercial and housing zoned areas. A large organization that has a distributed and heterogeneous environment that supports many different business functions can be as complex as a city. So before a programmer starts developing code, the architecture of the software needs to be developed in the context of the organization it will work within.

ITIL

The Information Technology Infrastructure Library (ITIL) is the de facto standard of best practices for IT service management. ITIL was created because of the increased dependence on information technology to meet business needs. Unfortunately, a natural divide exists between business people and IT people in most organizations because they use different terminology and have different focuses within the organization. The lack of a common language and understanding of each other's domain (business versus IT) has caused many companies to ineffectively blend their business objectives and IT functions. This improper blending usually generates confusion, miscommunication, missed deadlines, missed opportunities, increased cost in time and labor, and frustration on both the business and technical sides of the house. ITIL is a customizable framework that provides the goals, the general activities necessary to achieve these goals, and the input and output values for each process required to meet these determined goals. Although ITIL has a component that deals with security, its focus is more toward internal service level agreements (SLAs) between the IT department and the "customers" it serves. The customers are usually internal departments. The main components that make up ITIL are illustrated in Figure 11-2.

Policies and Procedures

For a company's security plan to be successful, it must start at the top level and be useful and functional at every single level within the organization. Senior management needs to define the scope of security and identify and decide what must be protected and to what extent. Management must understand the regulations, laws, and liability issues it is responsible for complying with regarding security and ensure that the company as a

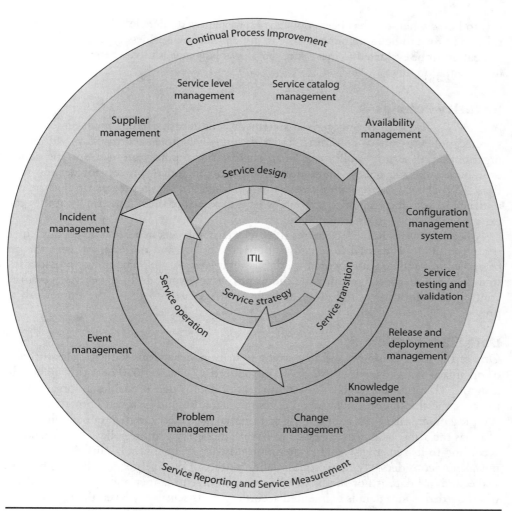

Figure 11-2 ITIL

whole fulfills its obligations. Senior management also must determine what is expected from employees and what the consequences of noncompliance will be. These decisions should be made by the individuals who will be held ultimately responsible if something goes wrong. But it is a common practice to bring in the expertise of the security officers to collaborate in ensuring that sufficient policies and controls are being implemented to achieve the goals being set and determined by senior management.

A security program contains all the pieces necessary to provide overall protection to a organization and lays out a long-term security strategy. A security program's documentation should include security policies and procedures. The more detailed the rules are, the easier it is to know when one has been violated. However, overly detailed documentation and rules can prove to be more burdensome than helpful. The business type, its culture, and its goals must be evaluated to make sure the proper language is used when writing security documentation.

Security Policies

A *security policy* is an overall general statement produced by senior management (or a selected policy board or committee) that dictates what role security plays within the organization. A security policy can be an organizational policy, an issue-specific policy, or a system-specific policy. These documents must include a process for dealing with those who choose not to comply with them. This establishes a process that others can understand and thus recognize not only what is expected of them, but also what they can expect as a response to their noncompliance.

Policies are written in broad terms to cover many subjects in a general fashion. Much more granularity is needed to actually support the policy, and this happens with the use of procedures and controls, which we discuss in a later section. The policy provides the foundation. The procedures provide the security framework, and the necessary security controls (administrative, technical, and physical) are used to fill in the framework to provide a full security program.

Data Classification

One of the most common and important security policies deals with the classification of organizational data, which is a topic introduced in Chapter 5. The rationale behind assigning classification levels to different types of data is that it enables an organization to gauge the amount of funds and other resources that should go toward protecting each. A typical organization has a lot of information that is created and maintained, but not all of it has the same value. A key reason to have a data classification policy is to organize it according to its sensitivity to loss, alteration, disclosure, or unavailability. Many people mistakenly consider only the confidentiality aspects of data protection, but we need to make sure our data is not modified in an unauthorized manner and that it is available when needed. Once data is segmented according to its sensitivity level, the organization can decide what processes and security controls are necessary to protect it.

Data Ownership

Data ownership policies are typically combined with data classification ones because it is difficult to separate the two issues. The main reason is that the data is classified by the person who "owns" it. Data ownership policies establish the roles and responsibilities of data owners within the organization. The data owner (information owner) is usually a member of management who is in charge of a specific business unit, and who is ultimately responsible for the protection and use of a specific subset of information. The data owner has due care responsibilities and thus will be held responsible for any negligent act that results in the corruption or disclosure of the data. Data owners decide the classification of the data for which they are responsible and alter classifications if business needs arise. These individuals are also responsible for ensuring that the necessary security controls are in place, defining security requirements per classification and backup requirements, approving any disclosure activities, ensuring that proper access rights are being used, and defining user-access criteria. The data owners approve access requests or may choose to delegate this function to business unit managers. Also, data owners will deal with security violations pertaining to the data they are responsible for protecting.

A key issue to address in a data ownership policy is who owns the personal data that an employee brings into an organizational information system. For example, if employees are allowed to check e-mail or social media sites from work, their personal data will traverse and be stored, albeit temporarily, on corporate information systems. Does it now belong to the company? Are there expectations of privacy? What about personal e-mail received by employees at their work accounts? These issues should be formally addressed in a data ownership policy.

Data Retention

There is no universal agreement on how long you should retain data that you own. Legal and regulatory requirements (where they exist) vary among countries and sectors. What is universal is the need to ensure your organization has and follows a documented data retention policy. Doing otherwise is flirting with disaster, particularly when dealing with pending or ongoing litigation. It is not enough, of course, to simply have a policy; you must ensure it is being followed and you must document this through regular audits.

A very straightforward and perhaps tempting approach would be to look at the lengthiest legal or regulatory retention requirement on your organization and then apply that timeframe to all your data retention. The problem with this is that it will probably make your retained data set orders of magnitude greater than it needs to be. Not only does this impose additional storage costs, but it also makes it more difficult to comply with electronic discovery (e-discovery) orders. When you receive an e-discovery order from a court, you are typically required to produce a specific amount of data (usually pretty large) within a given timeframe (usually very short). Obviously, the more data you retain, the more difficult and expensive this process will be.

A better approach is to find the specific data sets that have mandated retention requirements and handle those accordingly. Everything else has a retention period that minimally satisfies the business requirements. You probably will find that different business units within medium and large organizations will have different retention requirements. For instance, you may want to keep data from your research and development (R&D) division for a much longer period than you would keep data from the customer service division. R&D projects that are not particularly helpful today may be so at a later date, but audio recordings of customer service calls probably don't have to hang around for a few years.

Passwords

The password policy is perhaps the most visible of security policies because every user will have to deal with its effects on a daily basis. A good password policy should motivate users to manage their passwords securely, describe to them how this should be accomplished, and prescribe the consequences of failing to comply. The three main elements in most password policies relate to generation, duration, and use.

When creating passwords, users should be informed of the requirements of an acceptable one. Commonly, these standards include some or all of the following:

- Minimum length (for example, eight characters or greater)
- Requirement for specific types of characters (such as uppercase, lowercase, numbers, and special characters)
- Prohibition against reuse (for example, cannot be any of the last four passwords)
- Minimum age (to prevent flipping in order to reuse an old password)
- Maximum age (for example, 90 days)
- Prohibition against certain words (such as user's name or company name)

The policy should also cover the use of different passwords. For example, users should not use the same password for multiple systems, so that a compromise of one does not automatically lead to the compromise of all user accounts. Admittedly, this is a difficult provision to enforce, particularly when it comes to the reuse of passwords for personal and organizational use. Still, it may be worth including for educational purposes as well as to potentially mitigate some liability for the organization.

Acceptable Use

The *acceptable use policy (AUP)* specifies what the organization considers an acceptable use of the information systems that are made available to the employee. Using a workplace computer to view pornography, send hate e-mail, or hack other computers is almost always forbidden. On the other hand, many organizations allow their employees limited personal use, such as checking personal e-mail and surfing the Web during breaks. The AUP is a useful first line of defense, because it documents when each user was made aware of what is and is not acceptable use of computers (and other resources) at work. This makes it more difficult for a user to claim ignorance if he or she subsequently violates the AUP.

Account Management

A preferred technique of attackers is to become "normal" privileged users of the systems they're compromising as soon as possible. They can accomplish this in at least three ways: compromise an existing privileged account, create a new privileged account, and elevate the privileges of a regular user account. The first approach can be mitigated through the use of strong authentication (for example, strong passwords and two-factor authentication) and by having administrators only use privileged accounts for specific tasks and only from jump boxes. The second and third approaches can be mitigated by paying close attention to the creation, modification, or misuse of user accounts. These controls all fall within the scope of an account management policy.

When new employees arrive, they should follow a well-defined process that is aimed at ensuring not only that they understand their duties and responsibilities, but also that they are assigned the required company assets and that these are properly configured, protected, and accounted for. Among these assets is a user account that grants them access to the information systems and authorization to create, read, modify, execute, or delete resources (for example, files) within it. The policy should dictate the default expiration date of accounts, the password policy (unless it is a separate document), and the information to which a user should have access. This last part becomes difficult because the information needs of the users will typically vary over time.

Adding, removing, or modifying the permissions that a user has should be a carefully controlled and documented process. When is the new permission(s) effective? Why is it needed? Who authorized it? Organizations that are mature in their security processes will have a change-control process in place to address user privileges. While many auditors will focus on who has administrative privileges in the organization, there are many custom sets of permissions that approach the level of an admin account. It is important, then, to have and test the processes by which elevated privileges are issued.

Another important practice in account management is the suspension of accounts that are no longer needed. Every large organization eventually stumbles across one or more accounts that belong to users who are no longer part of the organization. In some extreme cases, these users left several months ago and had privileged accounts. The unfettered presence of these accounts on our networks gives our adversaries a powerful means to become a seemingly legitimate user, which makes our job of detecting and repulsing them that much more difficult.

The Problem with Running as Root

It is undoubtedly easier to do all our work from one user account, especially if that account has all the privileges we could ever need. The catch, as you may well know, is that when our accounts are compromised, the malicious processes will run with whatever privileges the account has. If we run as root (or admin) all the time, we can be certain that when our attackers compromise our box, they will instantly have the privileges to do whatever they need or want to do.

A better approach is to do as much of our daily work as we can using a restricted account, and elevate to a privileged account only when we must. Consider the following:

- Windows operating systems allow you to right-click any program and select **Run As...** in order to elevate your privileges. From the command prompt, you can just use the command **runas /user:<AccountName>** to accomplish the same goal.

- In Linux operating systems, you can simply type **sudo <SomeCommand>** at the command line in order to run a program as the super (or root) user. If the program is a GUI one, you need to start it from the command line using the command **gksudo** (or **kdesudo** for Kubuntu). Linux has no way to run a program with elevated privileges directly from the GUI; you must start from the command line.

- In Mac OS X, you use **sudo** from the Terminal app just like you would do from a Linux terminal. However, if you want to run a GUI app with elevated privileges, you need to use **sudo open –a <AppName>** since there is no "gksudo" or "kdesudo" command.

Procedures

Procedures are detailed, step-by-step tasks that should be performed to achieve a certain goal. The steps can apply to users, IT staff, operations staff, security members, and others who may need to carry out specific tasks. Many organizations have written procedures on how to install operating systems, configure security mechanisms, implement access control lists, set up new user accounts, assign computer privileges, audit activities, destroy material, report incidents, and much more.

Procedures spell out how the policies, standards, and guidelines will actually be implemented in an operating environment. If a policy states that all individuals who access confidential information must be properly authenticated, the supporting procedures will explain the steps for this to happen by defining the access criteria for authorization, how access-control mechanisms are implemented and configured, and how access activities are audited. If a standard states that backups should be performed, then the procedures will define the detailed steps necessary to perform the backup, the timelines of backups, the storage of backup media, and so on. Procedures should be detailed enough to be both understandable and useful to a diverse group of individuals. In the next few sections, we discuss some issues you should consider with regard to specific common procedures.

Continuous Monitoring Procedures

In Special Publication 800-137, the NIST defines information security *continuous monitoring* as "maintaining ongoing awareness of information security, vulnerabilities, and threats to support organizational risk management decisions." A continuous-monitoring procedure, therefore, would describe the process by which an organization collects and analyzes information in order to maintain awareness of threats, vulnerabilities, compliance, and the effectiveness of security controls. Obviously, this is a complex and very broadly scoped effort that requires coordination across multiple business units and tight coupling with the organization's risk management processes.

When continuous monitoring reveals actionable intelligence (for example, a new threat or vulnerability), there should be a pre-established process in place to deal with this situation. The *remediation plan* describes the steps that an organization takes whenever its security posture worsens. This plan will likely have references to multiple procedures, some of which we discuss in this chapter. For example, if the issue is a newly discovered vulnerability in an application, the remediation plan would point the security team to the patching procedure discussed later in this chapter. If, on the other hand, the change is due to an awareness that a security control is not as effective as it was thought to have been, the team would have to consider whether the control-testing procedure was effective or should be updated.

Evidence Production Procedures

When parties go to court, the manner in which evidence is introduced is almost as important as the evidence itself, which is the reason why having a well-documented (and enforced) procedure can be the difference between prevailing or losing. *Evidence production* is a legal request for documents, files, or any other tangible items that may have bearing on a legal procedure. This oftentimes happens during the early (discovery) portion of a legal action, which is why the term *evidence production* is sometimes used interchangeably with *electronic discovery,* or *e-discovery.* It is important to note, however, that e-discovery is a subset of evidence production, because the latter includes seizure (discussed in Chapter 9), which the former doesn't. Because we've discussed actions at the scene of an incident or crime already, it is worthwhile to consider e-discovery procedures here.

The discovery of electronically stored information (ESI) is called e-discovery, which is the process of producing for a court or external attorney all ESI pertinent to a legal proceeding. For example, if your company is being sued for damages resulting from a faulty product, the plaintiff's attorney could get an e-discovery order compelling you to produce all e-mail between the QA team and senior executives in which the product's faults are discussed. If your data retention policy and evidence production procedures are adequate, e-discovery should not require excessive efforts. If, on the other hand, you have been slack about retention, such an order could cripple the organization.

The Electronic Discovery Reference Model (EDRM) identifies the following eight steps, though they are not necessarily all required, nor are they performed in a linear manner:

- **Identification** of data required under the order
- **Preservation** of this data to ensure it is not accidentally or routinely destroyed while the order is being complied with
- **Collection** of the data from the various stores in which it may be housed
- **Processing** to ensure the correct format is used for both the data and its metadata
- **Review** of the data to ensure it is relevant
- **Analysis** of the data for proper context
- **Production** of the final data set to those requesting it
- **Presentation** of the data to external audiences to prove or disprove a claim

The evidence production procedure should specify how these steps are to be performed in your organization. Clearly, this should be carefully coordinated with your data retention policy to ensure you don't destroy information prematurely or have to wade through excessively large volumes of data in order to comply with court orders.

Patching Procedures

Security *patch management* is the process by which fixes to software vulnerabilities are identified, tested, applied, validated, and documented. These five functions should be codified in a formal procedure within every organization. The identification function requires having complete, accurate, and updated software inventories. Only when you know exactly what software is running on your systems can you identify the need for (and sources of) patches. Once you determine the need for a patch and acquire it from a trusted source, you have to test it in order to determine what effects it may have on your business processes. It is not unusual for security patches to break something, which requires the IT and security staff to look for these unintended effects. The organization's leaders would then have to decide whether to apply the patch anyway, implement other controls, or do nothing and assume the risk. The process by which this determination is made should be described in the standard patching procedure.

Once the decision is made to push out the patch onto production systems, this should not be done all at once. Different organizations will have procedures that prioritize patching of systems that are high risk (for example, outward-facing systems), noncritical (that is, if they break because of the patch, it won't hurt the company much), or whose work unit leaders offer to be guinea pigs for the rest of the organization. There is no universal right answer for this sequencing, but the approach should be formally documented.

After the patches are installed, they have to be documented and validated. Documentation of patching means that you update your software inventory to reflect the fact that a specific installation of the software is now patched (or not). Every unpatched system should require a formal waiver that includes how (if at all) the risk of not being patched is being mitigated. Finally, the patches should be validated to ensure they serve the intended purpose. This usually entails adding plug-ins to vulnerability scanners and perhaps even running a special scan.

Compensation Control Development Procedures

As we discussed in the preceding section, sometimes leaders will knowingly choose to take actions that leave vulnerabilities in their information systems. This usually happens either because the fix is too costly (for example, a patch would break a critical business process) or because there is no feasible way to fix the vulnerability directly (for example, an older X-ray machine at a hospital). Compensation controls are security controls that are not directly applied to a vulnerable system but that compensate for the lack of a direct control. For example, if you have a vulnerable system that is no longer supported by its vendor, you may put it in its own VLAN and create ACLs that allow it to communicate with only one other host, which has been hardened against attacks. You may also want to deploy additional sensors to monitor traffic on that VLAN and activity on the hardened host. The process by which these decisions are made and the compensation controls developed should be codified in its own separate procedure, or included in another related procedure.

Control-Testing Procedures

Security controls may fail to protect information systems against threats for a variety of reasons. If the control is improperly installed or configured, or if you chose the wrong control to begin with, then the asset will remain vulnerable. (You just won't know it.) For this reason, you should have a formal procedure that describes the steps by which your organization's security staff will verify and validate the controls they use. Verification is the process of ensuring that the control was implemented correctly. Validation ensures that the (correctly installed) control actually mitigates the intended threat.

Exception Management Procedures

There will be times when an organization will choose to violate its own policies or procedures. We already saw some of this when we introduced compensation control development earlier in this chapter. Whatever the reason for this decision, it is critical that it be made by the right people, with access to the right information, and with proper documentation. These are the essential elements of an exception management procedure.

The first step should always be to involve the right people in the conversation. The exception will typically have effects (real or potential) on multiple parts of the organization. Once these business units are identified, their leaders should designate a decision-maker who will represent their interests in the conversation. Each of these stakeholders will have specific responsibilities and authorities with regard to the exception, which will inform the process by which the decision will ultimately be made. For example, if the decision predominantly affects one unit, then that stakeholder should have a significant say on whether or not it is accepted. After the stakeholders and their roles in the process are established, the group should be presented with the full set of known facts and assumptions about the situation, the proposed exception, and its possible effects. The exception management procedure should spell out how they will reach a decision on whether or not to grant the exception to policy. It should also describe the process by which the duration of the exception is determined as well as what to do if there are irreconcilable differences during the decision-making process.

Controls

Controls are put into place to reduce the risk an organization faces, and they come in three main flavors: administrative, technical, and physical. Administrative controls are commonly referred to as "soft controls" because they are more management oriented. Examples of administrative controls are security documentation, risk management, personnel security, and training. Logical controls (also called technical controls) are software or hardware components, as in firewalls, IDS, encryption, identification, and authentication mechanisms. Finally, physical controls are items put into place to protect facility, personnel, and resources. Examples of physical controls are security guards, locks, fencing, and lighting.

Physical Controls

Physical controls are safeguards that deter, delay, prevent, detect, or respond to threats against physical property. It is important to understand certain physical controls must support and work with administrative and logical (technical) controls to provide appropriate security. Examples of physical controls include having a security guard verify individuals' identities prior to entering a facility, erecting fences around the exterior of the facility, making sure server rooms and wiring closets are locked and protected from environmental elements (humidity, heat, and cold), and allowing only certain individuals to access work areas that contain confidential information.

Logical Controls

Logical controls (sometimes called technical controls) are the software tools used to restrict subjects' access to objects. A subject can be a user or a process, whereas an object is any system resource. These controls are core components of operating systems, add-on security packages, applications, network hardware devices, protocols, encryption mechanisms, and access control matrices. They work at different layers within a network or system and need to maintain a synergistic relationship to ensure there is no unauthorized access to resources and that the resources' availability, integrity, and confidentiality are guaranteed. Technical controls protect the integrity and availability of resources by limiting the number of subjects that can access them and protecting the confidentiality of resources by preventing disclosure to unauthorized subjects.

Administrative Controls

Administrative controls are security mechanisms implemented by management primarily through policies and procedures. An example of this is personnel controls, which indicate how employees are expected to interact with security mechanisms and address noncompliance issues pertaining to these expectations. These controls indicate what security actions should be taken when an employee is hired, terminated, suspended, moved into another department, or promoted. Specific procedures must be developed for each situation, and many times the human resources and legal departments are involved with making these decisions.

Control Selection

A good way to reduce the likelihood of incidents and disasters is to ensure your security plan includes the right set of tools. These controls need to be carefully considered in the context of your own conditions in order to decide which are effective and which aren't. The first step is to understand the risks. The core concept here is that you can't ever eliminate all risks and should therefore devote your scarce resources to taking the most likely or dangerous risks and mitigating them to a point where their likelihood is acceptable to the senior leaders.

Once you are fixed on the right set of risks, you can more easily identify the controls that will appropriately mitigate them. The relationships between risks and controls is many to many, because a given risk can have multiple controls assigned to it just like a given control can be mitigating multiple risks. In fact, having multiple controls mitigating one risk, though it may be less efficient, may provide resiliency in protecting a particularly valuable asset. The selection of controls is driven by your organizational parameters and your selection criteria.

Organizationally Defined Parameters

Unsurprisingly, organizational policies play a large role in control selection and determine the values of key parameters in the process. An *organizationally defined parameter* is a variable that defines selected portions of the controls to support specific organizational requirements or objectives. In some cases, the minimum and maximum values of these parameters are dictated by laws or government regulations. Most frequently, however, these values (or range of values) correspond to the organization's risk appetite. Examples of these organizationally defined parameters are the frequency with which system backups must be conducted, the time before a data breach must be disclosed, and the maximum number of people who can have access to particularly sensitive information.

Selection Criteria

The selection of security controls should always be driven by a risk assessment. Risk to the confidentiality, integrity, or availability of information resources, combined with the organization's risk appetite, will determine the baseline security levels for each system. The baseline security level is the minimally acceptable set of protections for a given resource. Of course, there may be additional requirements that are driven by factors such as recommendations from the board or from external advisors or preferences from senior leaders. The set of security *control selection criteria* consists of the baseline security levels for each system combined with any additional requirements imposed by laws, regulations, or policies. This last source is usually captured in the organizationally defined parameters described in the previous section.

Once security controls are selected, they should be validated. This means that we compare three sets of values: the base risk exposure of the asset, the predicted risk exposure after applying the control, and the actual exposure after applying the control. A validated security control will always reduce the risk to the asset by at least the predicted amount.

Regulatory Compliance

Some organizations are subject to governmental statutes and regulations that may impose threshold requirements on securing information systems. Typically, being noncompliant with applicable regulations can lead to fines, penalties, and even criminal charges. While describing all aspects of regulatory compliance is beyond the scope of this book (and the CSA+ exam), you should be familiar with the more common laws and regulations, highlighted here:

- **Sarbanes-Oxley Act (SOX)**   This law, enacted in 2002 after the Enron and WorldCom financial crises, is intended to protect investors and the public against fraudulent and misleading activities by publicly traded companies. Its effect on information security controls is mostly in the area of integrity protections. SOX-regulated organizations have a higher bar when it comes to ensuring that digital records are not improperly altered.

- **Payment Card Industry Data Security Standard (PCI DSS)**   This industry standard applies to any organization that handles credit or debit card data. We already discussed it in Chapter 5, but it bears repeating that its main impact on security controls is focused on vulnerability scanning.

- **The Gramm-Leach-Bliley Act (GLBA)**   This 1999 law applies to financial institutions and is intended to protect consumers' personal financial information. Notably, it includes what is known as the Safeguards Rule, which requires financial institutions to maintain safeguards to protect the confidentiality and integrity of personal consumer information.

- **Federal Information Security Management Act (FISMA)**   Enacted in 2002, FISMA applies to information systems belonging to or operated by federal agencies or contractors working on their behalf. Among its key provisions are requirements on the minimum frequency of risk assessments, security awareness training, incident response, and continuity of operations.

- **Health Insurance Portability and Accountability Act (HIPAA)**   This law mostly deals with improving the healthcare system, but it has important elements that impact information security policies and procedures. Significantly, it includes the Security and Privacy Rules, which place specific requirements on protecting the confidentiality, integrity, availability, and privacy of patient data.

 EXAM TIP   You do not need to memorize all these regulations, but you do need to be aware of the general nature of regulatory requirements and their impact on the formulation of organizational policies and procedures as well as the selection of controls.

Verification and Quality Control

There is an old Russian proverb that says "trust, but verify." It is not uncommon for organizations to put significant amounts of effort into developing frameworks, policies, procedures. and controls only to discover (sometimes years later) that their security posture is not what they thought. Every implementation should be followed with verification and quality controls to ensure it was done properly. Just as importantly, there should be an ongoing periodic effort to ensure that the safeguards are still being done right and that they are still effective in the face of ever-changing threats.

Verification, in the context of information security, is the process of ensuring that policies and procedures are being followed. *Quality control* is the process of sampling our controls and ensuring they provide a certain baseline of security, which is to say they are effective against previously identified risks. As a CSA+, you should be aware of some of the main ways in which organizations conduct verification and quality control, which we highlight in the next sections.

Audits

An *audit* is a systematic inspection by an independent third party, oftentimes driven by regulatory compliance requirements. Though it is certainly possible for an organization to call in auditors to assess information security or other aspects of the business, the costs associated with this sort of activity make it prohibitive in most cases. That being said, a growing number of organizations conduct nonregulatory requirements when they want to be sure that some aspect of their security is up to a specific set of standards.

Assessments

An *assessment* is any process that gathers information and makes determinations based on it. This rather general term encompasses audits and a host of other evaluations, such as vulnerability scans and penetration tests. More important than remembering its definition is understanding the importance of continuous assessments to ensure that the security of your systems remains adequate to mitigate the risks in your environment. Among the more popular assessments are the following:

- Vulnerability assessment
- Penetration test

- Red team assessment
- Risk assessment
- Threat modeling
- Tabletop exercises

Every organization should have a formal assessment program that specifies how, when, where, why, and with whom the different aspects of its security will be evaluated. This is a key component that drives organizations toward continuous improvement and optimization. This program is also an insurance policy against the threat of obsolescence caused by an ever-changing environment.

Certification

Certification is the comprehensive technical evaluation of the security components of a system and their compliance with applicable regulations. A certification process may use safeguard evaluation, risk analysis, verification, testing, and auditing techniques to assess the appropriateness of a specific system. The goal of a certification process is to ensure that a system, product, or network satisfies all security requirements. This process is usually applied whenever a new component (for example, a server or sensor) is being introduced into an existing system, or whenever new systems are provisioned for the organization.

Some organizations have a second step called accreditation before introducing the new capability. *Accreditation* is the formal acceptance of the adequacy of a system's overall security and functionality by management. The certification information is presented to management, or the responsible body, and it is up to management to ask questions, review the reports and findings, and decide whether to accept the product and whether any corrective action needs to take place. Once satisfied with the system's overall security as presented, management makes a formal accreditation statement. By doing this, management is stating that it understands the level of protection the system will provide in its current environment and understands the security risks associated with installing and maintaining this system.

Maturity Models

The maturity of an organization with regard to cybersecurity is a measure of how introspective its security processes are. In other words, if there is no real awareness of processes and security is managed through crises, we can conclude the organization is very immature. On the other hand, if there are formal, documented processes that are periodically examined for the purpose of continuous improvement, we can conclude that the organization is very mature. There are a number of maturity models, but perhaps the most useful is the one developed by Carnegie Mellon University's Software Engineering Institute, known as the CMMI.

Capability Maturity Model Integration (CMMI) is a comprehensive, integrated set of guidelines for developing products and software. It can be used to evaluate security engineering practices and identify ways to improve them. The model describes procedures, principles, and practices that underlie process maturity. This model was developed to help software vendors improve their development processes by providing an evolutionary path from an ad hoc "fly by the seat of your pants" approach to a more disciplined and repeatable method that improves quality, reduces the lifecycle of development, provides better project management capabilities, allows for milestones to be created and met in a timely manner, and takes a more proactive approach than the less effective reactive approach. It provides best practices to allow an organization to develop standardized approaches that can be used across many different groups. The goal is to continue to review and improve upon the processes to optimize output, increase capabilities, and provide higher-quality products and services at a lower cost through the implementation of continuous improvement steps.

The five maturity levels of the CMMI model are depicted in Figure 11-3 and described in the following list.

1. **Initial**   The development process is ad hoc or even chaotic. The company does not use effective management procedures and plans. There is no assurance of consistency, and quality is unpredictable. Success is usually the result of individual heroics.

2. **Repeatable**   A formal management structure, change control, and quality assurance are in place. The company can properly repeat processes throughout each project. The company does not have formal process models defined.

3. **Defined**   Formal procedures are in place that outline and define processes carried out in each project. The organization has a way to allow for quantitative process improvement.

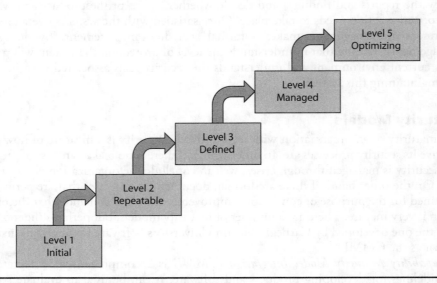

Figure 11-3   Capability Maturity Model Integration

4. **Managed**   The company has formal processes in place to collect and analyze quantitative data, and metrics are defined and fed into the process-improvement program.

5. **Optimizing**   The company has budgeted and integrated plans for continuous process improvement.

Chapter Review

This chapter is a bit longer (and perhaps drier) than others in this book, but it is packed with important information that will allow you to understand security frameworks, policies, procedures, and controls. While you will probably see a handful of specific questions on these topics in the CSA+ exam, you will definitely see their influence not only on most exam questions, but in your real-world organization. Though many of us prefer to spend our time fighting our cyber foes or improving our technical defenses, it is just as important to develop the formal documents that will ensure that the entire organization is pulling in the right direction. Without the appropriate policies and procedures in place, our efforts may very well ultimately be doomed to fail at securing our systems.

Questions

1. Which of the following is *not* a category for access controls and their implementation?

    A. Administrative

    B. Physical

    C. Virtual

    D. Logical

2. Which is the NIST publication that outlines various security controls for government agencies and information systems?

    A. Special Publication 800-53

    B. Special Publication 800-37

    C. ISO/IEC 27000

    D. ISO/IEC 27001

3. Which of the following standards, composed of five core volumes, is widely accepted for service management of information technology assets?

    A. Information Security Management System (ISMS)

    B. Cyber Security Framework (CSF)

    C. The Open Group Architecture Framework (TOGAF)

    D. Information Technology Infrastructure Library (ITIL)

4. Which of the following NIST publications describes a voluntary cybersecurity structure for organizations that are part of the critical infrastructure?

   A. Cyber Security Framework (CSF)

   B. International Organization for Standardization (ISO)

   C. Information Security Management System (ISMS)

   D. Control Objectives for Information and related Technology (COBIT)

5. The ISO/IEC 27000 series describes which of the following?

   A. Control Objectives for Information and related Technology (COBIT)

   B. Information Security Management System (ISMS)

   C. Architecture Development Method (ADM)

   D. International Electrotechnical Commission (IEC)

6. Who is responsible for ensuring that data security controls are in place, defining classification requirements, and approving disclosure?

   A. Systems administrators

   B. Chief Security Officer

   C. Data owners

   D. Chief Information Officer

7. What device is part of a formal process to improve a cybersecurity posture by developing comprehensive and repeatable security processes unique to the organization?

   A. Verification

   B. Maturity model

   C. Quality control

   D. Regulatory compliance

8. Which component of the Cyber Security Framework describes the degree of sophistication of cybersecurity practices?

   A. Framework Core

   B. Implementation Tiers

   C. NIST SP 800-53 control categories

   D. ITIL processes

9. Which are the key functions of the Framework Core of the Cyber Security Framework (CSF)?

   A. Identify, Protect, Detect, Respond, Recover

   B. Identify, Process, Detect, Respond, Recover

   C. Identify, Process, Detect, Relay, Recover

   D. Identify, Protect, Detect, Relay, Recover

10. The directives that originate from senior management and govern the role of security practices in an organization are referred to by which term?

   A. Administrative policy

   B. Technical policy

   C. Security policy

   D. Physical policy

Answers

1. **C.** Access controls are the mechanisms put into place to protect the confidentiality, integrity, and availability of systems, and are categorized as administrative, logical, or physical.

2. **A.** The NIST released Special Publication 800-53 (Security and Privacy Controls for Federal Information Systems and Organizations), which aims to establish a unified information security framework for the federal government and related organizations.

3. **D.** The Information Technology Infrastructure Library (ITIL) is the de facto standard of best practices for IT service management. It provides the goals, the general activities necessary to achieve these goals, and the input and output values for each process required to meet these determined goals in a common language.

4. **A.** The CSF focuses on aligning cybersecurity activities with business processes and including cybersecurity risks as part of the organization's risk management processes. The Framework consists of three parts: the Framework Core, the Framework Profile, and the Framework Implementation Tiers.

5. **B.** The International Organization for Standardization (ISO) and the International Electrotechnical Commission (IEC) 27000-series, also known as the "ISMS Family of Standards," provides best practice recommendations on information security management.

6. **C.** Data owners classify data and are ultimately responsible for its protection, use, and disclosure.

7. **B.** Maturity models are used to create processes that are unique to the operating environment and help improve operational performance and the security posture.

8. **B.** CSF Implementation Tiers categorize the degree of rigor and sophistication of cybersecurity practices, which can be Partial (tier 1), Risk Informed (tier 2), Repeatable (tier 3), or Adaptive (tier 4).

PART IV

9. **A.** The Framework Core consists of five functions that can provide a high-level view of an organization's management of cybersecurity risk: Identify, Protect, Detect, Respond, Recover.

10. **C.** A security policy is guidance produced by the senior management, policy board, or committee that dictates what role security plays within the organization.

CHAPTER 12

Identity and Access Management

In this chapter you will learn:

- Various parameters for context-based authentication
- Security issues and best practices for using common authentication protocols
- Security issues with various components of the network environment
- Commonly used exploits against authentication and access systems

The value of identity of course is that so often with it comes purpose.

—Richard Grant

A 2016 study from Shape Security, a Silicon Valley cybersecurity company, asserted that nearly 90 percent of the password attacks on public-facing company portals were done using automated tools to reuse login and password credentials collected from other breaches. This works because we tend to pick passwords that are easy to break, and then reuse the same weak passwords across many sites. Although the reported 2 percent success rate may not seem noteworthy, it becomes a serious concern when we consider events such as the massive 1.5 billion user breach that Yahoo recently suffered. The difficulty with dealing with this scale of attack is that these systems were never meant to provide the visibility for such volume, nor is infrastructure in place to handle the increased demand. An elegant and comparatively low-cost solution to this authentication challenge is to enable and enforce *multifactor authentication*. This technique of identity assurance requires two or more pieces of information when a user attempts to access a system. Factors fall into three categories: something you know, something you have, and something you are (or something you do). The most effective multifactor systems use factors from at least two of these categories. For example, one factor might be the traditional login and password combination, while another might be a passcode delivered via SMS to a mobile device, or perhaps a biometric feature. Despite using multiple factors for authentication, it's still a challenge to verify the identity of the person behind the screen. A complementary solution to using multiple factors is the concept of *context-based authentication*, which aims to make the authentication process more secure by seamlessly and transparently incorporating factors such as location data, time, or even typing patterns. The user is often unaware of these additional factors being validated and processed.

EXAM TIP Passwords and PINs are examples of something you know. Smart cards, hardware authentication devices, and USB dongles fall into the category of something you have. Something you are and something you do include a biometric characteristic or any other trait inherent to the user such as handwriting or speech pattern.

Security Issues Associated with Context-Based Authentication

Context-based authentication aims to provide increased security and usability by ensuring one or several parameters fall within approved limits, or match historical user data when used in combination with standard login procedures. These parameters include time, IP address, location, device, and biometrics. The goal is to give context to each login event, but doing so requires an upfront investment in infrastructure to generate the identity data required to make the system function. For each parameter that's part of the process, at least two activities need to happen. The first is the initial cataloging of user data. This might be as straightforward as collecting device information, but data such as biometric measurements are likely to add additional requirements. Depending on where your organization operates, you may have to comply with strict laws regarding the storage and transmission of biometric data, which includes fingerprints, voice recordings, iris scans, and even typing patterns.

The second activity is the comparison and validation process. As with any other type of pattern matching, the challenge here will be to reduce false positives and negatives. It's not useful to have a robust multifactor system if it prevents legitimate users from getting access to the resources they need in a timely fashion. This process also needs to be speedy enough so that it doesn't add noticeable wait time for the user. The last thing you want is users circumventing the process because it's slower than what they're used to. Although this certainly requires higher cost for setup, the benefits are increased security, flexibility, and usability over traditional methods. When attempting to take advantage of these systems, attackers will often target the individual parameters or flaws within the implementation of the verification of the multiple factors. A very common approach is to provide false information using a method called *spoofing*, which is simply any action where an unauthorized user presents seemingly legitimate but fabricated data to a system to gain access. We'll take a deeper look at the various ways attackers try to game systems and the strengths and weaknesses of various context-based authentication techniques in the following sections.

Time

The time parameter in context-based authentication is used to determine the authenticity of a user based on when the activity occurs. It's a bit of a common-sense test: does it make sense for a user to attempt login when there is no need for it, or when it is outside of business hours? This of course requires that the limits of access be defined, and that location is taken into consideration because of time zone differences. If the time limits are known, this is where an attacker might manipulate input to a system to gain access by pretending to be in a different time zone, for example. Time and location should therefore be closely tied together in preventing unauthorized access. For example, if a user has logged into the system successfully at 10 A.M. GMT from a New York location and attempts to do so again at 11:30 A.M. GMT from a San Francisco location, then you can conclude that this is a suspicious attempt.

Timing can also be brought into the authentication process with the concept of a *time window.* Some two-factor systems, such as the RSA SecurID mechanism, provide a code to the user during a login attempt, often using a hardware device called a *fob,* which uses a built-in clock along with a hard-coded secret key to provide continuously changing values. In the case of SecurID, a new code is generated and displayed every 60 seconds. With this device, a user will always have less than a minute to provide the code before it becomes invalid.

Location

Wireless location services began as a public safety mandate issued by the Federal Communications Commission (FCC) in 1996. The agency hoped to provide improved response to emergencies by using the data from cellular service providers to get very accurate location information during 911 calls. It was the commercial potential for location services, however, that motivated many companies and manufacturers to improve accuracy and speed-of-location information on mobile devices. Nowadays, nearly every mobile device is delivered with at least one application that relies on location services. Using location as a parameter for context-based authentication is a common way to prevent many illegitimate login attempts by only accepting requests from known and trusted localities. There are several methods of reporting location from devices, most of which fall into two categories: network-based location and device-based location. Network-based location info is derived from data about the network that the device resides on. By looking up the IP address, for example, you can determine the country, city, and postal code by querying the Internet registry responsible for that block of IP addresses. However, this method has some significant weaknesses because it's easy to falsify IP addresses. Furthermore, if the attacker has somehow already compromised a device on a trusted network and is using that as a jumping-off point for a larger campaign, then attempting to filter by location in this manner doesn't help much.

Modern smartphones and laptops use a combination of sensors for location functions. The Global Positing System (GPS) sensors are still the most widely used method for device location reporting. These systems rely on a constellation of satellites to pinpoint the device location anywhere on earth. With three satellites in view, a device can get positing information down to the meter, and with four it's possible to also get elevation details. Because it's not always possible to get a direct line-of-sight to GPS satellites at all time, especially in urban areas or indoors, these phones often use a feature called *assisted GPS (A-GPS)* to improve the accuracy of positing information. Like standard GPS, A-GPS calculates its location data based on the information it gets from its distance from at least three objects of known position, but instead of using the positions of orbiting satellites it relies on those of fixed cellular towers. By combining these two sources, handsets can provide reliable positioning information even in environments where it's normally difficult to get good connectivity.

An attacker has a few options when it comes to faking positional data. In defending against this, it's important to understand how location is reported from these devices. The location data is provided to the phones by sensors and is then stored on the device and presented to the authentication server as required. An attacker can either falsify GPS signal data or manipulate the location data on the device itself. The latter requires far less technical expertise and cost. In fact, apps are available for both iOS and Android that will allow a user to easily falsify mobile phone location data. These apps often work only with jailbroken or rooted devices, so one way to ensure legitimate location data is to prevent such modified devices from joining the network.

Spoofing GPS

Many legacy systems, like GPS, were invented at a time when it was computationally or financially infeasible for anyone but nation-state actors to compromise them. Over the last decade, several attacks on GPS have proven effective, repeatable, and, most importantly, affordable. No examples better highlight the ease with which we can now spoof GPS than those performed by ordinary users armed with some technical familiarity and high-quality tutorials. In 2016, the *Pokémon Go* mobile app game gained worldwide popularity at a rate never seen before. In the game, players are challenged to collect virtual creatures, called Pokémon, using their GPS-guided mobile phones. As players maneuver in the real world to locate and capture their targets, the mobile app overlays avatars of the Pokémon near real landmarks using the device camera and screen. As users travel more in the real world, they gain more opportunities to catch the Pokémon, and thus more points in the game. Some players, realizing that they could gain a significant advantage by manipulating the location data provided to the game, quickly developed various cheating methods. The most impressive of these cheats was one that required the mobile device to be placed in a Faraday box and fed false GPS information from a nearby signal generator. The mobile device, shielded from real GPS satellite signals, would interpret the fabricated signals as the legitimate source for location data and in turn pass it to the app. By adjusting the signals produced by the signal generator regularly, these clever players could simulate movement required for additional points in the game, without having to move an inch. The cheat was both inexpensive and reliable.

Frequency

Frequency and speed of login attempts can also provide an important parameter into context-based authentication. Even the most talented programmer has her limits when typing. At peak performance, humans cannot input, interpret, and iterate anywhere near the speed that a machine can. So it's obvious when machines are performing actions that humans should be doing, particularly during activities such as logging onto a system.

This is the idea behind frequency-based authentication parameters. If a system observes SSH login attempts at a rate that doesn't seem possible, it can then blacklist or throttle that address to prevent further probing. Attackers know that it's trivial for administrators to implement rate limiting using iptables or similar tools, so they may adjust their attempts to seem more "human like." Still, many hacking tools (for example, password crackers) put a premium on speed, which gives alert analysts an opportunity to detect many attacks.

Behavioral

Behavioral factors are those based on user interaction with the computer, such as typing rate and mouse movement. A major weakness in traditional password-based authentication systems is that once the session is validated, there are rarely additional attempts to verify that the same user in still in control. Should an attacker *hijack* a session, he can ride the credentials of the original user to gain unauthorized access. There are several barriers to implementing a continuous authentication solution. For example, it's likely to annoy legitimate users to have to manually authenticate regularly. The key, therefore, is to make the process unseen to the user.

The Defense Advanced Research Projects Agency calls this process "Active Authentication," where a learning system generates a "cognitive fingerprint" based on user behavior with their machines. Developing this user profile takes a bit of time, but it's an effective way to keep attackers out of your systems. As artificial intelligence algorithms become more powerful, however, developing automated ways to simulate human behavior, particularly in terms of object recognition, becomes realistic for a moderately resourced but motivated attacker. Several examples of this evolving cat-and-mouse game have been recently demonstrated by the security research community. In one example, researchers demonstrate automated methods of defeating CAPTCHA tests—the web challenges that aim to differentiate humans from machines by presenting tasks in which a person would have a distinct advantage in solving, such as image or sound recognition. Advances in replicating human behavior will have implications on any behavior-based authentication parameter.

Security Issues Associated with Identities

A *digital identity* is a distinct representation of a real-world subject within an information system. Most of us have multiple identities, such as the ones we use at work, in social media, and in personal e-mail. Each requires *authentication,* which is the process (partially described earlier) by which a subject verifies its ownership of a particular identity for the purpose of obtaining authorization to access specific objects or resources. Therein lies the problem: authenticating identities and providing appropriate authorizations require complex mechanisms that can be exploited by savvy adversaries. This challenge is compounded by workforce trends.

As more companies become increasingly decentralized and mobile, the task of identity management (IDM) emerges as a critical part of the overall IT enterprise. Cloud-enabled productivity apps give users the ability to tie in from any location and from any device, but at a cost. The requirements to maintain security and productivity without increasing cost, downtime, and burden to the user make this a challenging effort. Despite advancements in technology, there are still issues that remain in nearly every part of the trust chain, from user to application.

Personnel

People are the core of a business, but they also present the greatest threat to its security posture. Because a computer cannot positively verify a person's identity and intention, an IDM solution must collect the right information quickly enough to make an accurate decision. Modern solutions use a combination of the previously discussed parameters to deliver quick access to employees and guests, while remaining agile enough to deny access to unauthorized users. Despite the best technological controls, human error still accounts for the preponderance of incidents. People share passwords, lose devices, and fall victim to phishing e-mails regularly. If an attacker can collect all the information that makes a user unique on a network, then it's trivial for him to pass himself off as that user. User training is the primary method to address the security issues associated with your organization's members. Referred to as "securing the human" by the SANS Institute, the practice of educating users on the threats and training them to act appropriately in the network environment helps the organization manage risk. Training users on best practices for protecting their credentials and looking for the signs of compromise will improve your organization's security posture faster than many technological solutions.

Endpoints

Networks exist to reliably exchange information from node to node. Endpoints must be able to verify that they are who they say they are quickly. Endpoint authentication, also known as *device authentication,* usually relies on values derived from device hardware or operating system configuration. A common mechanism for endpoint authentication is through the key or token generated by the endpoint that is presented to the network or requested resource. Endpoints are particularly vulnerable to abuse regarding authentication because it's easy to spoof or replay endpoint data.

 NOTE The Media Access Control (MAC) address is a unique value used to identify network-connected devices at the data-link layer of the OSI network model. This value is assigned to a Network Interface Card (NIC) during the manufacturing process, but forging a device's MAC address is trivial. The ability to change this value is now a built-in part of many operating systems.

Servers

A widely used technique to authenticate servers is through the use of public key certificates defined by the X.509 standard. These digital certificates are issued to the server's owning organization by a trusted Certificate Authority (CA), which is required to take steps to verify the identity of the requesting organization. These steps often include paying a significant fee as well as providing corporate documents. The process makes it difficult for a threat actor to be issued a certificate for someone else's organization. Still, it is possible to steal someone else's certificate, as was allegedly done during the Stuxnet operation. This approach, as it is commonly implemented, only verifies the identity of one end of the connection—typically the server. Even then, it is possible for attackers to insert themselves in the chain and present fake certificates. Though this generates warnings on the clients' browsers, these messages are oftentimes dismissed by the users.

It is better to mutually authenticate servers and clients, and for this we have the Kerberos authentication protocol. Kerberos is found in nearly all operating systems in one form or another. Like the mythological creature, Kerberos has three key components that are used to challenge during a request for access: the Authentication Service (AS), the Ticket Granting Server (TGS), and the Key Distribution Center (KDC). Figure 12-1 shows the relationship between the client and components of the Kerberos exchange. When the client sends a request to authenticate, the AS will check the KDC database of existing users to verify the user's existence. If a user is successfully located, the AS will return two messages to the client—one that contains a TGS session key and another that has a Ticket Granting Ticket (TGT). The TGT message has information about the client, a timestamp, and a copy of the TGS session key. It is then encrypted with a symmetrical key, which the client does not have. The other message has some user information and another copy of the TGS session key. This message is encrypted with the user's secret key, so if the user is not in possession of this key, the client will be unable to read the TGS session key. If the client successfully decrypts the message to get the TGS session key, it can then use that key, along with the TGT, to query the TGS.

PART IV

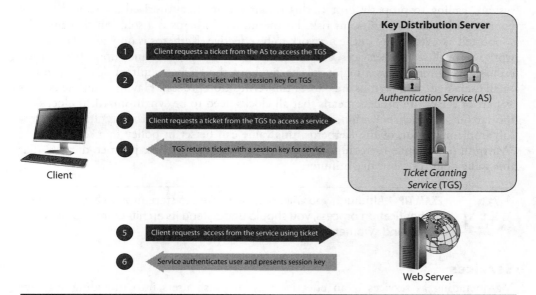

Figure 12-1 Relationship between the three "heads" of the Kerberos protocol

At this point, the message that the client sends to the TGS has two parts. The first part is the TGT, which remains encrypted with the secret key. The second part is an *authenticator*, which has the client ID and is encrypted with the TGS session key (which the TGS does not currently know). The TGS is in possession of the secret key, so it will decrypt the TGT message without a problem. It will use the copy of the TGS session key that it finds in that message to decrypt the authenticator. Now that the TGS can read both messages, it will perform a few steps, such as verify that the tickets haven't expired and that the authenticator doesn't already exist. The TGS now prepares two messages similar to how the client originally did. One message will have a service session key that is encrypted with the TGS session key, and the other will have a service ticket that contains a copy of the service session key and is encrypted with a service secret key. The client will be able to decrypt the first message using the stored TGS session key, but will not be able to decrypt the second.

The client will again prepare two messages for the service. The first will be the service ticket, which is still encrypted by the service secret key, and the second message will be an authenticator, which has client data and is encrypted by the service session key. The requested service will then use its service secret key to decrypt the service ticket, revealing the service session key, which it will use to decrypt the authenticator. Finally, if all the user and timestamps check out, the service will return its own authenticator to the client containing a service ID encrypted with the service session key. Because the client machine already has this key, it will decrypt that authenticator message and verify the service ID. From now on, until the ticket expires, the client can use the cached service ticket to continue accessing services.

Kerberos has been in use for decades, and you need to understand some key points about its usage. The KDC database is critical to the integrity of the entire Kerberos system. Failing to properly protect this resource from unauthorized access will expose your organization to significant risk. Furthermore, Kerberos is a solution that must be supported by every node in the network to be effective. Kerberos is only useful on a network where all servers, services, and clients are "Kerberos aware" and support encrypted exchanges. Timing plays a major role throughout the Kerberos authentication process. In all exchanges, timestamps are part of the verification process. Having multiple devices as part of the entire process means that all clocks need to be synchronized. If clocks are too far out of synchronization, Kerberos will not authenticate properly. In the Microsoft implementation of the Kerberos, this value can be set in policy in a setting called "Maximum tolerance for computer clock synchronization." Best practice dictates that this value doesn't exceed five minutes.

 EXAM TIP Although you will not be expected to step through a full Kerberos authentication process, you should understand its architecture and use of tickets and symmetric keys.

Services

Masquerading as services is an effective way to phish users into providing sensitive data. At the user level, it's extremely difficult to detect a fake service. However, there

```
<identity>
    <certificate encodedValue="String"/>
    <certificateReference findValue="String"
        isChainIncluded="Boolean"
        storeName="AddressBook/AuthRoot/CertificateAuthority/Disallowed/My/Root/TrustedPeople/TrustedP
        storeLocation="LocalMachine/CurrentUser"
        X509FindType= Enumeration./>
    <dns value="String"/>
    <rsa value="String"/>
    <servicePrincipalName value="String"/>
    <usePrincipalName value="String"/>
</identity>
```

Figure 12-2 Syntax of the identity element used by the Windows Communication Foundation

are solutions to ensure the authenticity of a service, depending on the network environment. To prevent abuses by rogue services, Microsoft's .NET Framework has a feature called Service Identity and Authentication. The Windows Communication Foundation (WCF) infrastructure will ensure that the identity value of the requested service matches a preset value. Figure 12-2 shows the syntax of the identity element in the WCF. When a client attempts to connect to a service using this feature, it will first perform whatever standard authentication procedure is in place. Once the service successfully authenticates to the client machine, it will then compare a stored value called the *endpoint identity* to the value that the service provides during that interaction. If these match, the client machine can then access the service. Elements of the identity value include certificate information, DNS, RSA value, service names, and user name. This is essentially a second authentication process that happens under the hood.

Roles

You may recall our discussion about role-based access control in Chapter 3. A blog user, for example, might have the username "tony" and be assigned the role of "editor." Another user called "karen" might have the role of "admin." Each user may have multiple simultaneous roles (for example, contributor, editor, and approver), and each role will allow access to certain resources. These access control levels are based on the necessary operations and tasks users need to carry out to fulfill responsibilities within an organization. This approach can be complex because an administrator must translate an organizational authorization policy into permissions when configuring access controls. As the number of objects and users grows within an environment, users are bound to be granted unnecessary access to some objects, thus violating the least-privilege rule and increasing the risk to the company.

Attackers will often attempt to determine which users have elevated permissions based on their roles. Sometimes, users with elevated roles may not be aware of these elevated privileges, which creates a security problem. Auditing roles should be a part of your assessment to ensure that users are only getting the roles necessary for their tasks.

NOTE In the majority of cases, roles are associated with identities and not authenticated directly. You can think of it as an extension of an identity, describing what kinds of activities can be performed. The relationship may be one-to-many, meaning that a single identity can have multiple roles and invoke the required privileges based on the task.

Applications

Applications are constantly the target of malicious actors looking for ways into a system. Web applications designed to be accessed by the public will restrict what a public user is able to query or execute. Attackers will often try to manipulate the input to these applications to achieve *privilege escalation*, or elevated access to the target application or operating system. A successful attack is usually the result of a software flaw or misconfiguration. We can use the principles covered in our previous discussion on vulnerability assessment in Chapters 5 and 6 to identify and deal with these vulnerabilities.

Security Issues Associated with Identity Repositories

An identity repository is any resource that stores the credentials necessary to validate a user's network access. Attackers will often target identity stores to add or change user attributes. Routinely monitoring these repositories for signs of manipulation will alert you to an attacker's presence.

Directory Services

A directory service server is essentially a central repository for storing and managing information. Administrators rely on directory services to provide management and security options at scale. For the users, directory services allow them to quickly locate network resources without having to remember addresses. Nearly any information about the network can be stored in a directory service data store. Both users and the resources they seek are assigned unique identifiers, and users can often be authenticated and authorized to enterprise services and applications based on this information. Directory services need to be scalable and able to integrate well with various other services on the network.

Active Directory

Active Directory (AD) plays a critical role in many organizations. As the directory service for Windows environments, AD allows organizations to centrally manage resources while providing network security policy. Any user, system, resource, or service in an AD environment is considered an *object,* which has *attributes* associated with it, including name and description. The goal of many attackers who target AD environments is to gain a foothold in a network, pivot across systems, and eventually gain access to the AD domain controllers. This type of access would give an attacker complete control over all the objects associated with the organization.

Two primary approaches to protecting these environments are to reduce the attack surface of the AD and to enable auditing functionality. By default, AD has several privileged account groups such as Enterprise Admins (EA), Domain Admins (DA), and Built-in Admins (BA). Using the principle of least privilege (POLP), you should only have the necessary number of administrators active on the network with just the right amount of privilege for day-to-day administration. The second technique for improving AD security is to develop a system for event log monitoring and to enable detailed object auditing. Many incidents can be discovered very early if the right levels of auditing and reporting are enabled. Using advanced features such as Object Access Auditing as part of your directory-wide security policy, you can determine when a sensitive object is accessed or changed, and report those changes as necessary. By default, this value is not enabled, but when combined with a well-designed SIEM solution, it will provide you with speed and flexibility in identifying unusual network behavior before any damage occurs.

 EXAM TIP Under no circumstances should administrative rights to an AD service be shared. Malicious individuals who obtain administrative access to AD domain controllers have total control over the network. Even non-malicious but inexperienced users with access can cause unanticipated problems should they make incorrect configuration changes.

LDAP

Underpinning most directory services in use today is the Lightweight Directory Access Protocol (LDAP). LDAP provides a cross-platform open standard for maintaining directory services on a network. Users can query the LDAP server to get responses based on specifically formatted statements. It's possible for an attacker to craft statements that trigger the LDAP server to provide additional information not normally authorized for the requester—or worse, to get the server to execute arbitrary code. Suppose that this system allows the requester to search for only a particular kind of resource—in this case, printers and storage devices. Figure 12-3 shows an example of a normal user and her request and response compared to that provided by an attacker. In the legitimate request, the user specifies a search for either storage devices or printers. Note that the attacker formats his query in such a way that when interpreted, the input values appear to be LDAP commands and are executed at a higher level than the user is normally allowed. The system provides the results for all users based on its interpretation of (**uid=***).

The key to defending against this type of attack is to validate and sanitize user input to prevent extra commands from being interpreted. You can achieve this by escaping special characters and restricting user input that contains regular expressions.

TACACS+

Terminal Access Controller Access Control System Plus (TACACS+) is an authentication, authorization, and accounting (AAA) protocol that originated with Cisco in the 1990s. As an alternative to Kerberos, TACACS+ uses a client/server approach to determine a user's access level to anything on the network. At the time of the connection attempt, the user is compared against the user database, and the policy is then applied

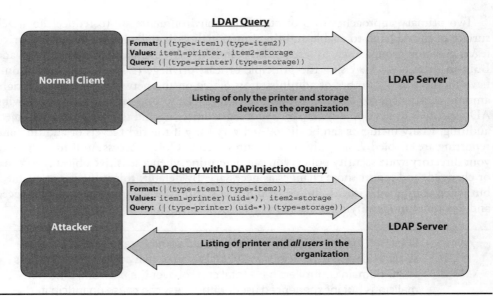

Figure 12-3   Legitimate LDAP query compared to an LDAP injection query

to that user. With TACACS+, the authentication, authorization, and accounting functions are treated as separate and independent. Though designed to be used primarily for device AAA, the protocol is often used for network AAA functions as well. Despite its strong suitability for network AAA, TACACS+ has some fundamental weaknesses in its protocol. Even though it uses TCP, it is particularly vulnerable to replay attacks because every sequence number always starts with 1. This means that an attacker doesn't have to guess where the sequence of a legitimate exchange left off because the TACACS+ system will always accept a session beginning with sequence number 1. Additionally, the session IDs are relatively short during TACACS+ exchanges, and the pool of possible IDs is small enough to be vulnerable to so-called "birthday attacks," or collisions in a cryptographic hash function.

 NOTE   Although it shares most of its name with TACACS and XTACACS, the newer TACACS+ is an entirely different protocol that is not compatible with the older authentications methods.

RADIUS

The Remote Authentication Dial-In User Service (RADIUS) is like TACACS+ in that both AAA protocols provide authentication services for administrators and users. However, whereas TACACS+ encrypts usernames and passwords during the authentication process, RADIUS only encrypts user passwords. Additionally, RADIUS uses UDP rather than

TCP, meaning that reliability may suffer depending on network state. Because UDP is a best-effort transport protocol, it's more difficult to determine when faults occur during the transaction. From a security point of view, this means that forging packets in spoofing attempts is easier because there is no confirmation of packet receipt. RADIUS also allows the use of a "shared secret" across the network; therefore, a breach of the entire network is far easier should any one weak endpoint be compromised. This, combined with the lack of complexity (or entropy) of the shared secret, means that offline attacks against the secret are more likely to succeed.

Some implementations of RADIUS are also susceptible to *buffer-overflow* attacks, which occur when too much data is forced into memory space (or buffer) and the resulting excess spills outside of dedicated memory limits and into other areas of memory. This type of attack against the RADIUS system can be used to exploit arbitrary malicious code, to leak sensitive user data, or as part of a denial-of-service attack.

Security Issues Associated with Federation and Single Sign-On

Federated identity is the concept of using a person's digital identity to gain access to various services, many times across multiple organizations. The identity is provided by a broker known as the *federated identity manager*. When verifying her identity, the user needs only to authenticate with the manager, and the application that's requesting the identity information needs to then trust it as well. Many popular platforms, such as Google, Amazon, and Twitter, take advantage of their large memberships to provide federated identity services for third-party websites, saving the user from having to create separate accounts for each site.

Using a federated identity to provide authentication is often done with Single Sign-On (SSO). In a business setting, a user might have to provide credentials for e-mail services, CRM, directory, or any other business web applications. SSO simplifies the process of logging into multiple systems across a single organization by requiring the user to only maintain a single set of credentials, and it often ties into existing LDAP databases. The primary benefits of using SSO are on both the user and administrator sides. Users only need to remember a single password or PIN, which reduces the fatigue associated with managing multiple passwords. Additionally, they'll save time from having to reenter credentials for every service desired. For the administrator, this means fewer calls about password problems. Figure 12-4 shows the flow of an SSO request using the Security Assertion Markup Language (SAML) standard, a widely used method of implementing SSO.

SAML provides access and authorization decisions using a system to exchange information between a user, the identity provider (IDP), and the service provider (SP). When a user requests access to a resource on the service provider, the SP creates a request for identity verification for IDP. The IDP will provide feedback about the user, and the SP can make its decision on an access control based on its own internal rules and the positive or negative response from the IDP. If access is granted, a token is generated in lieu of the actual credentials and passed on to the SP.

Figure 12-4 Single Sign-On flow for a user-initiated request for identity verification

Although SSO improves the user experience when accessing multiple systems, it does have a significant drawback in the potential increase in impact should the credentials be compromised. Using an SSO platform thus requires a greater focus on the protection of the user credentials. This is where including multiple factors and context-based solutions can provide strong protection against malicious activity. Furthermore, as SSO centralizes the authentication mechanism, that system becomes a critical asset and thus a target for attacks. Compromise of the SSO system, or loss of availability, means loss of access to the entire organization's suite of applications that rely on the SSO system.

Manual vs. Automatic Provisioning/Deprovisioning

Provisioning is the coordination of efforts behind creating user accounts on a service and setting the appropriate roles and access associated with them. Part of what makes SSO so desirable for administrators is the ability to create and destroy accounts for services very rapidly. Auto-provisioning is a way to create account on-the-fly as users are authenticated to a new system. Auto-provisioning means that IDP is asserting that the user should be allowed to hold an account with the SP. This clearly requires the SP to trust in the IDP's validation of users, which is further illustration of the criticality of the IDP in this process. Controlling and consolidating access privileges is not an easy task, but we must be careful to control provisioning functions to control the size of our attack surface. Orphan accounts (those without an assigned owner) and accounts with incorrect levels of access can cause confusion for administrators if not managed correctly.

Self-Service Password Reset

One of the goals for a self-sustaining network is to remove the need for administrator intervention whenever possible. Traditionally, administrators spend an inordinate amount of time dealing with problems such as password resetting. Although it might not be problematic for the administrator of a small business to have a close eye on this type of activity, it becomes challenging as the organization increases in size and complexity. Allowing users to rest their own passwords using an identity manager will allow administrators more time to focus on the rest of the network. However, by removing oversight into the reset process, you provide an opportunity for an attacker to take advantage.

Exploits

Why are authentication systems such a prime target for attackers? To answer this, we must remind ourselves that authentication is the process of validating identity and granting access to some number of resources. Once accepting this information, a system will often make subsequent decisions on the basis of the initial credentials supplied by the client. If an attacker can fool a system with false credentials or stolen credentials, he can assume the user's identity and perform whatever tasks that user is authorized to do.

Impersonation

At the heart of the challenge is identifying and communicating just the right amount of information to the authentication system to make an accurate decision. These are machines after all, and they will never truly know who we are or what our intentions might be. They can only form a decision based on the information we give them and the clues about our behavior as we provide that data. If an attacker is clever enough to fabricate enough of this user information, he is effectively the same person in the eyes of the authentication system.

Sometimes attackers will impersonate a service to harvest credentials or intercept communications. Fooling a client can be done one of several ways. First, if the server key is stolen, the attacker appears to be the server without the client possibly knowing. Additionally, if an attacker can somehow gain trust as the Certificate Authority from the client, or if the client does not check that the attacker is actually a trusted CA, then the impersonation will be successful.

Man in the Middle

Essentially, MITM attacks are impersonation attacks that face both ways: the attacker impersonates both the client to the real server and the server to the real client. Acting as a proxy or relay, the attacker will use his position in the middle of the conversation between parties to collect credentials, capture traffic, or introduce false communications. Even with an encrypted connection, it's possible to conduct an MITM attack that works similarly to an unencrypted attack. In the case of HTTPS, the client browser establishes an SSL connection with the attacker, and the attacker establishes a second SSL connection with the web server. The client may or may not see a warning about the validity of the client. In the case that a warning appears, it's very likely that the victim may ignore or click though the warning, which highlights the importance of user training. It's possible for the warning to not appear at all, which would indicate that the attacker has managed to get a certificate signed by a trusted Certificate Authority.

Session Hijack

Session hijacking is a class of attacks where an attacker takes advantage of valid session information, often by stealing and replaying it. HTTP traffic is stateless and often uses multiple TCP connections, so it uses sessions to keep track of client authentication. Session information is just a string of characters that appears in a cookie file, the URL itself, or other parts of the HTTP traffic. An attacker can get existing session information through traffic capture, MITM attack, or by predicting the session token information.

PART IV

Capturing and repeating session information is how an attacker might be able to take over, or hijack, the existing web session to impersonate a victim.

Cross-Site Scripting

Cross-site scripting (XSS) is a type of injection attack that leverages a user's browser to execute malicious code that can access sensitive information in the user's browser, such as passwords and session information. Because the malicious code resides on the site that the user accesses, it's often difficult for the user's browser to know that the code should not be trusted. XSS thus takes advantage of this inherent trust between browser and site to run the malicious code at the security level of the website. XSS comes in two forms: persistent and nonpersistent. With persistent attacks, malicious code is stored on a site, usually via message board or comment postings. When other users attempt to use the site, they unwittingly execute the code hidden in the previously posted content. Nonpersistent attacks, also referred to as *reflected* XSS, take advantage of a flaw in the server software. If an attacker notices an XSS vulnerability on a site, he can craft a special link, which when passed to and clicked on by other users, would cause the browser to visit the site and reflect the attack back onto the victim. This could cause an inadvertent leak of session details or user information to whatever server the attacker specifies. These links are often passed along through e-mail and text messages and appear to be innocuous and legitimate.

Privilege Escalation

Privilege escalation is simply any action that allows a user to perform tasks she is not normally allowed to do. This is often done by exploiting a bug, implementation flaw, or misconfiguration. Escalation can happen in a *vertical* manner, meaning that a user gains the privileges of a higher-privilege user. Alternatively, *horizontal* privilege escalation can be performed to get the access of others in the same privilege level. Attackers will use these privileges to modify files, download sensitive information, or install malicious code.

Jailbreaking and Rooting

Jailbreaking, the act of bypassing Apple iOS restrictions, uses privilege escalation to allow users to perform functions that they normally could not. Jailbreaking allows Apple mobile device users to install custom software or modified operating systems. Similarly, "rooting" an Android gives a user privileged access to the device's subsystem. Developing these kinds of exploits is a big deal because mobile device manufacturers expend enormous resources to standardize their devices. While gaining freedom to install additional apps and modify a mobile device seems like a good idea, it makes the device less secure because it's likely that the protections that could prevent malicious activity were removed to achieve the jailbreak or root in the first place.

Rootkits

Rootkits are among the most challenging types of malware because they are specially designed to maintain persistence and root-level access on a system without being detected. As with other types of malware, rootkits can be introduced by leveraging vulnerabilities to achieve privilege escalation and clandestine installation. Alternatively, they might be presented to a system as an update to BIOS or firmware. Rootkits are difficult to detect because they sometimes reside in the lower levels of operating systems, such as in device drivers and in the kernel, or even in computer hardware itself so the system cannot necessarily be trusted to report any modifications it has undergone.

Chapter Review

Recent breaches have highlighted several weaknesses in the authentication systems we use to protect privileged data. The subsequent access to personal and corporate data has resulted in damaging and expensive cybercrimes. The challenge is that attackers often use cracked or stolen user credentials to gain access—credentials that are assumed to come from a legitimate source. The reliance on just a login and password, or single-factor authentication, remains a key issue. Humans are terrible at picking and using passwords. Systems that use context-based authentication methods alongside multifactor authentication provide enhanced protection against malicious actors masquerading as legitimate users. However, as security professionals we must understand some drawbacks to using these systems as we work to make security more usable and transparent to users.

Questions

1. Which of the following would *not* be a consideration in context-based authentication?

   A. The one-time passcode used for authentication was incorrect.

   B. The login attempt occurred outside of regular working hours.

   C. The transaction was initiated from a foreign country.

   D. The commands should have been manually entered, but they were issued faster than any human could type.

2. In order to mitigate the security risks that your staff can pose to identity management, you would consider doing all the following *except* which one?

   A. Remind users never to share credentials with anyone else.

   B. Provide a demonstration of how their online identities can be stolen.

   C. Force complex passwords that must change every two months.

   D. Disable hyperlinks in e-mail messages.

3. You are investigating an incident in which a user account in the accounting department appears to have deleted a critical marketing spreadsheet in a shared folder. Each department has its own VLAN and no other files appear to have been affected. The employee owning that user account claims to not know about this. What is the likeliest explanation?

   A. A workstation in the accounting department was probably comprised.

   B. The VLANs are not properly segmented.

    C. The roles associated with the account may have been inappropriate.

    D. The file server was likely compromised.

4. Which of the following are features of the standard Kerberos authentication protocol? (Choose two.)

    A. It uses asymmetric encryption for authentication.

    B. It uses symmetric encryption for session security.

    C. It requires use of AS, KDC, and TGS.

    D. It requires use of AD, KDC, and GTS.

5. Which of the following statements is *not* true of Single Sign-On (SSO) solutions?

    A. They decrease the impact of compromised credentials.

    B. Identities are verified by a federated identity manager or identity provider (IDP).

    C. They are widely implemented using the Security Assertion Markup Language (SAML).

    D. They reduce the number of passwords users have to memorize.

6. Which of the following exploits is likely to trigger a certificate warning on the victim's web browser if HTTPS is used in the connection?

    A. Session hijacking

    B. Cross-site scripting

    C. Man-in-the-middle

    D. SQL injection

Use the following scenario and illustration to answer Questions 7–10:

You are investigating a series of potentially unrelated incidents affecting a small business. Four hosts were involved in these events and are illustrated in the simplified network diagram.

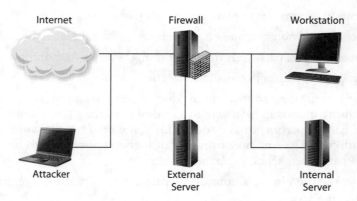

7. The internal server's logs recorded repeated login attempts to a domain administrator account from an external IP address suspected to be the attacker. These attempts were ultimately successful. The server is a domain controller implementing Kerberos. Which of the following is true?

    A. All objects and subjects in the domain are compromised.

    B. We only know that the internal server is compromised at this point.

    C. Any TGTs for the user at the workstation are now invalid.

    D. The external server will no longer be able to respond to requests from the workstation's user.

8. The workstation's user learns of the compromised server and immediately changes the domain account's password. Why will this be an ineffective response?

    A. The password would also have to be changed at the external server.

    B. Changing the password will prevent access to the external server.

    C. The password was not compromised, so it need not be changed.

    D. Changing the password will update the information on the compromised internal server, to which the attacker now has full access.

9. The external server provides virtual private network (VPN) services for remote users. While examining NetFlow data at the firewall, you notice large flows on port 443 from the workstation to a remote user that are correlated to equally large flows on port 443 from the remote user to an external web server. What is likely happening?

    A. The remote user is an attacker who compromised the VPN server, pivoted to the workstation, and is now exfiltrating data.

    B. The remote user is the victim of a cross-site scripting attack.

    C. The remote user is simply visiting the same site as the workstation's user and uploading similarly large files to it.

    D. The remote user is an attacker who compromised the VPN server and is now conducting a man-in-the-middle attack.

10. You decide to investigate the VPN server and connect to it over SSH. You use netstat to examine network connections, ps to look at running processes, and search to look for newly created suspicious files. You find nothing out of the ordinary. What can you conclude?

    A. The VPN server appears to be secure and you should allow the remote user to connect again.

    B. You should also look for new user accounts and check your log files before reaching any conclusions.

    C. You can't reach any conclusions strictly from built-in tools because a rootkit could interfere with their outputs.

    D. There must be a rootkit in play because you know the server was compromised.

PART IV

Answers

1. **A.** One-time passwords are not context sensitive, which means they wouldn't fall into this type of authentication. The other options allude to issues of time, location, and behavior, all of which can play roles in context-based authentication.

2. **C.** Complex and changing passwords may help improve security in many ways, but they will probably also increase the risk imposed by personnel to identity management because users are likely to adopt bad password practices such as writing them down or using variations of previous passwords.

3. **C.** The likeliest among the given choices is that the user account had access to the shared folder and the user inadvertently deleted the file. Given that only one file was deleted, it is unlikely that this would indicate a compromise, and even if the VLANs were incorrectly implemented, that should not have allowed that user account to delete the file.

4. **B, C.** Though some implementations of Kerberos support the optional use of asymmetric encryption, the standard does not. Furthermore, sessions are always secured using symmetric encryption. The key components of a Kerberos implementation are the Authentication Server (AS), the Key Distribution Center (KDC), the Ticket Granting Server (TGS), and the Service Servers (SS).

5. **A.** The main disadvantage of Single Sign-On (SSO) is that compromised credentials will affect multiple systems.

6. **C.** A man-in-the-middle attack involving an HTTPS connection will generate a certificate warning on the victim's browser unless the attacker has stolen the target server's private key, which is very rare. None of the other exploits will normally generate such warnings.

7. **A.** Because Kerberos centralizes secret keys and is implemented domain-wide, all secret keys should be considered compromised at this point since the attacker controls the Kerberos server.

8. **D.** The main disadvantage of Kerberos is that it centralizes all the secret keys in the Key Distribution Center (KDC). Any domain password changes and changes to the secret keys will be available to the attacker who now controls the server.

9. **D.** In a man-in-the-middle attack, traffic is commonly relayed through a malicious host to the legitimate endpoints. It is easiest to conduct this type of attack from the local network, so it makes the most sense to conclude that the attacker leveraged compromised VPN credentials and is now intercepting all of the workstation's user traffic to and from the website.

10. **C.** Rootkits will prevent system tools from accurately reporting the state of a computer. If these tools had reported evidence of compromise, you could conclude that an attack took place. However, finding no evidence is no reason to conclude that there is no compromise.

CHAPTER 13

Putting in Compensating Controls

In this chapter you will learn:

- Best practices for security analytics using automated methods
- Techniques for basic manual analysis
- Applying the concept of "defense in depth" across the network
- Processes to continually improve your security operations

Needle in a haystack's easy. Just bring a magnet.

—Keith R.A. DeCandido

Security Data Analytics

Modern corporate networks are incredibly diverse environments, with some generating gigabytes of data in just logging and event information per day. The scripting techniques and early monitoring utilities are quickly approaching the end of their utility because variety and volume of data now exceed what they were originally designed for. Managing information about your network environment requires a sound strategy and tactical tools for refining data into information, over to knowledge, and onto actionable wisdom. Figure 13-1 shows the relationship between what your tools provide at the tactical level and your goal of actionable intelligence. Data and information sources on your network are at least as numerous as the devices on the network. Log data comes from network routers and switches, firewalls, vulnerability scanners, IPS/IDS, unified threat management (UTM) systems, and mobile device management (MDM) providers. Additionally, each node may provide its own structured or unstructured data from services it provides. It's the goal of security data analytics to see through the noise of all this network data to produce an accurate picture of the network activity, from which we make decisions in the best interest of our organizations.

Data Aggregation and Correlation

The process of collecting the correct data to inform business decisions can lead to frustration, particularly if the sources are heterogeneous. After all, data ought to be

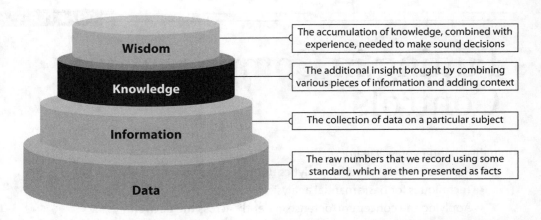

Figure 13-1 Relationship among the various levels of data, information, knowledge, and wisdom

a benefit rather than an impediment to your security team. To understand why data organization is so critical to security operations, we must remember that no single source of data is going to provide what's necessary to understand an incident. When detectives investigate a crime, for example, they take input from all manner of sources to get the most complete picture possible. The video, eyewitness accounts, and forensics that they collect all play a part in the analysis of the physical event. But before a detective can begin analysis on what happened, the clues must be collected, tagged, ordered, and displayed in a way that it useful for analysis. This practice, called *data aggregation,* will allow your team to easily compare similar data types, regardless of source. The first step in this process usually involves a *log manager* collecting and normalizing data from sources across the network. With the data consolidated and stored, it can then be displayed on a timeline for easy search and display. Figure 13-2 shows a security information and event management (SIEM) dashboard that displays the security events collected over a fixed period of time. This particular SIEM is based on Elasticsearch, Logstash, and Kibana, collectively called the ELK stack. The ELK stack is a popular solution for security analysts who need large-volume data collection, a log parsing engine, and search functions. From the total number of raw logs (over 3000 in this case), the ELK stack generates a customizable interface with sorted data and provides color-coded charts for each type.

From these charts, we can see the most commonly used protocols and most talkative clients at a glance. Unusual activity is also very easy to identify. Take a look at the "Top Destination Ports" chart shown in Figure 13-3. Given a timeframe of only a few minutes, is there any good reason why one client attempts to contact another over so many ports? Without diving deeply into the raw data, you can see that there is almost certainly scanning activity occurring here.

Many SIEM solutions offer the ability to craft *correlation* rules to derive more meaningful information from observed patterns across different sources. For example, if you observe traffic to UDP or TCP port 53 that is not directed to an approved DNS

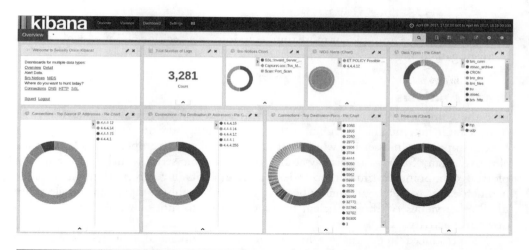

Figure 13-2 SIEM dashboard showing aggregated event data from various network sources

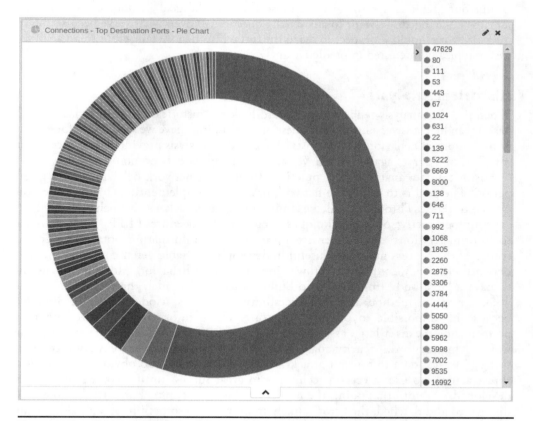

Figure 13-3 SIEM dashboard chart showing all destination ports for the traffic data collected

server, this might be evidence of a rogue DNS server present in your network. You are taking observations from two or more sources to inform a decision about which activities to investigate further.

Trend Analysis

Like the vulnerability scanners discussed in Chapter 6, many security analytics tools provide built-in trend analysis functionality. Determining how the network changes over time is important in assessing whether countermeasures and compensating controls are effective. Many SIEMs can display source data in a time-series, which is a method of plotting data points in time order. Indexing these points in a successive manner makes it much easier to detect anomalies because you can roughly compare any single point to all other values. With a sufficient baseline, it's easy to spot new events and unusual download activity.

We introduced trend analysis in Chapter 2, and discussed how trends could be internal, temporal, or spatial (among others). Back then, we were focused on its use in the context of threat management. Here, we apply it in determining the right controls within our architectures to mitigate those threats. The goal in both cases, however, remains unchanged: we want to answer the question, "Given what we've been seeing in the past, what should we expect to see in the future?" When we talk about trend analysis, we are typically interested in predictive analytics.

Historical Analysis

Whereas trend analysis tends to be forward-looking, historical analysis focuses on the past. It can help answer a number of questions, including "have we seen this before?" and "what is normal behavior for this host?" This kind of analysis provides a reference point (or a line or a curve) against which we can compare other data points.

Historical data analysis is the practice of observing network behavior over a given period. The goal is to refine the network baseline by implementing changes based on observed trends. Through detailed examination of an attacker's past behavior, analysts can gain perspective on the techniques, tactics, and procedures (TTPs) of an attacker to inform decisions about defensive measures. The information obtained over the course of the process may prove useful in developing a viable defense plan, improving network efficiency, and actively thwarting adversarial behavior. Although it's useful to have a large body from which to build a predictive model, there is one inherent weakness to this method: the unpredictability of humans. Models are not a certainty because it's impossible to predict the future. Using information gathered on past performance means a large assumption that the behavior will continue in a similar way moving forward. Security analysts therefore must consider present context when using historical data to forecast attacker behavior. A simple and obvious example is a threat actor who uses a certain technique to great success until a countermeasure is developed. Up until that point, the model was highly accurate, but with the hole now discovered and patched, the actor is likely to move on to something new, making your model less useful.

EXAM TIP   The difference between trend and historical analyses is small; most practitioners use the terms interchangeably. For purposes of the CSA+ exam, trend analysis helps predict future events, and historical analysis helps compare new observations to past ones.

Manual Review

Although it's tempting to believe that machines can do it all, at the end of the day a security team's success will be defined by how well its human analysts can piece together the story of an incident. Automated security data analytics might take care of the bulk noise, but the real money is made by the analysts. Let's look back at our previous examples of network scanning to explore how an analyst might quickly piece together what happened during a suspected incident. Figure 13-4 gives a detailed list of the discrete data points used for the previous graph. We can see that in under a second, the device located at IP address 4.4.4.12 sent numerous probes to two devices on various ports, indicative of a network scan.

Search				
			« 1... 2 3 **4** 5 6 ...10 »	
Time ⌄	source_ip	source_port	destination_ip	destination_port
▶ April 6th 2017, 17:57:33.151	4.4.4.12	47629	4.4.4.14	7002
▶ April 6th 2017, 17:57:33.151	4.4.4.12	47629	4.4.4.15	1068
▶ April 6th 2017, 17:57:33.151	4.4.4.12	47629	4.4.4.15	3784
▶ April 6th 2017, 17:57:32.973	4.4.4.12	47629	4.4.4.14	1805
▶ April 6th 2017, 17:57:32.973	4.4.4.12	47629	4.4.4.14	2875
▶ April 6th 2017, 17:57:32.973	4.4.4.12	47629	4.4.4.15	50003
▶ April 6th 2017, 17:57:32.973	4.4.4.12	47629	4.4.4.14	5800
▶ April 6th 2017, 17:57:32.973	4.4.4.12	47629	4.4.4.15	1972
▶ April 6th 2017, 17:57:32.972	4.4.4.12	47629	4.4.4.15	6881
▶ April 6th 2017, 17:57:32.972	4.4.4.12	47629	4.4.4.15	50800
▶ April 6th 2017, 17:57:32.972	4.4.4.12	47629	4.4.4.14	9535
▶ April 6th 2017, 17:57:32.972	4.4.4.12	47629	4.4.4.15	541
▶ April 6th 2017, 17:57:32.972	4.4.4.12	47629	4.4.4.15	2200
▶ April 6th 2017, 17:57:32.972	4.4.4.12	47629	4.4.4.15	40911
▶ April 6th 2017, 17:57:32.972	4.4.4.12	47629	4.4.4.15	1112
▶ April 6th 2017, 17:57:32.972	4.4.4.12	47629	4.4.4.14	2260
▶ April 6th 2017, 17:57:32.972	4.4.4.12	47629	4.4.4.15	6156

Figure 13-4   SIEM list view of all traffic originating from a single host during a network scan

PART IV

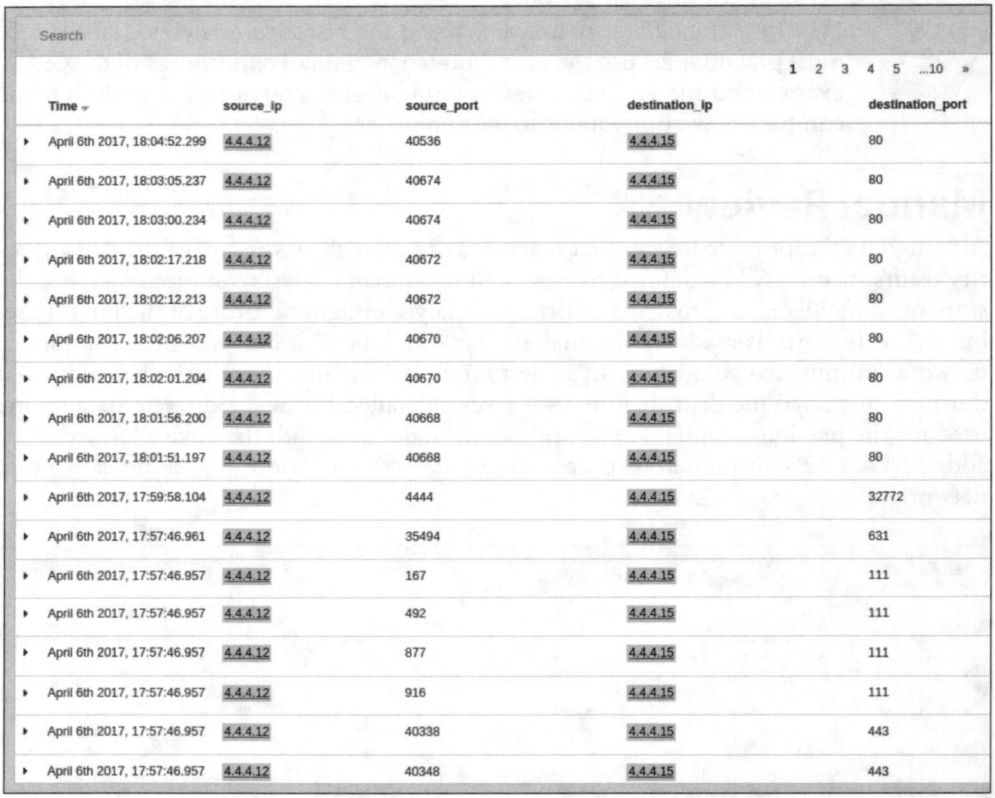

Time ⌄	source_ip	source_port	destination_ip	destination_port
April 6th 2017, 18:04:52.299	4.4.4.12	40536	4.4.4.15	80
April 6th 2017, 18:03:05.237	4.4.4.12	40674	4.4.4.15	80
April 6th 2017, 18:03:00.234	4.4.4.12	40674	4.4.4.15	80
April 6th 2017, 18:02:17.218	4.4.4.12	40672	4.4.4.15	80
April 6th 2017, 18:02:12.213	4.4.4.12	40672	4.4.4.15	80
April 6th 2017, 18:02:06.207	4.4.4.12	40670	4.4.4.15	80
April 6th 2017, 18:02:01.204	4.4.4.12	40670	4.4.4.15	80
April 6th 2017, 18:01:56.200	4.4.4.12	40668	4.4.4.15	80
April 6th 2017, 18:01:51.197	4.4.4.12	40668	4.4.4.15	80
April 6th 2017, 17:59:58.104	4.4.4.12	4444	4.4.4.15	32772
April 6th 2017, 17:57:46.961	4.4.4.12	35494	4.4.4.15	631
April 6th 2017, 17:57:46.957	4.4.4.12	167	4.4.4.15	111
April 6th 2017, 17:57:46.957	4.4.4.12	492	4.4.4.15	111
April 6th 2017, 17:57:46.957	4.4.4.12	877	4.4.4.15	111
April 6th 2017, 17:57:46.957	4.4.4.12	916	4.4.4.15	111
April 6th 2017, 17:57:46.957	4.4.4.12	40338	4.4.4.15	443
April 6th 2017, 17:57:46.957	4.4.4.12	40348	4.4.4.15	443

Figure 13-5   Listing of HTTP exchange between 4.4.4.12 and 4.4.4.15 after scan completion

In addition to source, destination, and port information, each exchange is assigned a unique identifier in this system. After the scan is complete a few minutes later, we can see that the device located at 4.4.4.12 establishes several connections over port 80 to a device with the 4.4.4.15 IP address, as shown in Figure 13-5. It's probably safe to assume that it's standard HTTP traffic, but it would be great if we were able to take a look. It's not unheard of for attackers to use well-known ports to hide their traffic.

This SIEM allows us to get more information about what happened during that time by linking directly to the packet capture of the exchange. The capture of the first exchange in that series shows a successful request of an HTML page. As we review the details in Figure 13-6, it appears to be the login page for an administrative portal.

Looking at the very next capture in Figure 13-7, we see evidence of a login bypass using SQL injection. The attacker entered **Administrator' or 1=1 #** as the username, indicated by the text in the **uname** field. When a user enters a username and password, a SQL query is created based on the input from the user. In this injection, the username is populated with a string that, when placed in the SQL query, forms an alternate

```
4.4.4.12:40668_4.4.4.15:80-6-1121361501.pcap

Sensor Name: onion-eth1
Timestamp: 2017-04-06 18:01:51
Connection ID: CLI
Src IP: 4.4.4.12 (Unknown)
Dst IP: 4.4.4.15 (Unknown)
Src Port: 40668
Dst Port: 80
OS Fingerprint: 4.4.4.12:40668 - UNKNOWN [S20:64:1:60:M1460,S,T,N,W7..:?:?] (up: 233 hrs)
OS Fingerprint: -> 4.4.4.15:80 (link: ethernet/modem)

SRC: GET / HTTP/1.1
SRC: Host: 4.4.4.15
SRC: User-Agent: Mozilla/5.0 (X11; Linux x86_64; rv:45.0) Gecko/20100101 Firefox/45.0
SRC: Accept: text/html,application/xhtml+xml,application/xml;q=0.9,*/*;q=0.8
SRC: Accept-Language: en-US,en;q=0.5
SRC: Accept-Encoding: gzip, deflate
SRC: Connection: keep-alive
SRC:
SRC:
DST: HTTP/1.1 200 OK
DST: Date: Thu, 06 Apr 2017 14:50:16 GMT
DST: Server: Apache/2.0.52 (CentOS)
DST: X-Powered-By: PHP/4.3.9
DST: Content-Length: 667
DST: Connection: close
DST: Content-Type: text/html; charset=UTF-8
DST:
DST: <html>
DST: <body>
DST: <form method="post" name="frmLogin" id="frmLogin" action="index.php">
DST: .<table width="300" border="1" align="center" cellpadding="2" cellspacing="2">
DST: ..<tr>
DST: ...<td colspan='2' align='center'>
DST: ...<b>Remote System Administration Login</b>
DST: ...</td>
DST: ..</tr>
DST: ..<tr>
DST: ...<td width="150">Username</td>
DST: ...<td><input name="uname" type="text"></td>
DST: ...</tr>
DST: ..<tr>
DST: ...<td width="150">Password</td>
DST: ...<td>
DST: ...<input name="psw" type="password">
DST: ...</td>
DST: ...</tr>
DST: ..<tr>
DST: ...<td colspan="2" align="center">
DST: ...<input type="submit" name="btnLogin" value="Login">
DST: ...</td>
```

Figure 13-6   Packet capture details of first HTTP exchange between 4.4.4.12 and 4.4.4.15

SQL statement that the server will execute. This gets interpreted by the SQL server as follows:

```
SELECT * FROM users WHERE name='Administrator' or 1=1 #'
and password='boguspassword'
```

Because the **1=1** portion will return **true**, the server doesn't bother to verify the real password and grants the user access. You can see the note "Welcome to the Basic Administrative Web Console" in the same figure, showing that the attacker has gained access.

Note that just because the attacker now has access to a protected area of the web server, this doesn't mean he has full access to the network. Nevertheless, this behavior is clearly malicious, and it's a lead that should be followed to the end. In the following subsections, we discuss how the approach to manual review we just presented using an SIEM and packet captures can be extended to other sources of information.

```
4.4.4.12:40670_4.4.4.15:80-6-159015080.pcap

Sensor Name: onion-eth1
Timestamp: 2017-04-06 18:02:06
Connection ID: CLI
Src IP: 4.4.4.12 (Unknown)
Dst IP: 4.4.4.15 (Unknown)
Src Port: 40670
Dst Port: 80
OS Fingerprint: 4.4.4.12:40670 - UNKNOWN [S20:64:1:60:M1460,S,T,N,W7:.:?:?] (up: 233 hrs)
OS Fingerprint: -> 4.4.4.15:80 (link: ethernet/modem)

SRC: POST /index.php HTTP/1.1
SRC: Host: 4.4.4.15
SRC: User-Agent: Mozilla/5.0 (X11; Linux x86_64; rv:45.0) Gecko/20100101 Firefox/45.0
SRC: Accept: text/html,application/xhtml+xml,application/xml;q=0.9,*/*;q=0.8
SRC: Accept-Language: en-US,en;q=0.5
SRC: Accept-Encoding: gzip, deflate
SRC: Referer: http://4.4.4.15/
SRC: Connection: keep-alive
SRC: Content-Type: application/x-www-form-urlencoded
SRC: Content-Length: 68
SRC:
SRC: uname=Administrator%27+or+1%3D1+%23&psw=boguspassword&btnLogin=Login
DST: HTTP/1.1 200 OK
DST: Date: Thu, 06 Apr 2017 14:50:26 GMT
DST: Server: Apache/2.0.52 (CentOS)
DST: X-Powered-By: PHP/4.3.9
DST: Content-Length: 586
DST: Connection: close
DST: Content-Type: text/html; charset=UTF-8
DST:
DST: <html>
DST: <body>
DST:
DST: <!-- Start of HTML when logged in as Administator -->
DST: .<form name="ping" action="pingit.php" method="post" target="_blank">
DST: ..<table width='600' border='1'>
DST: ..<tr valign='middle'>
DST: ...<td colspan='2' align='center'>
DST: ...<b>Welcome to the Basic Administrative Web Console<br></b>
DST: ...</td>
DST: ..</tr>
DST: ..<tr valign='middle'>
DST: ...<td align='center'>
DST: ....Ping a Machine on the Network:
DST: ...</td>
DST: ....<td align='center'>
DST: ....<input type="text" name="ip" size="30">
DST: ....<input type="submit" value="submit" name="submit">
```

Figure 13-7   Packet capture details of a second HTTP exchange between 4.4.4.12 and 4.4.4.15 showing evidence of a SQL injection

 NOTE   Software-defined networking (SDN) addresses several challenges that make correlation so difficult. Because the network is centrally controlled to optimize the performance, the SDN provider is also a perfect place to perform data collection. This reduces the need to perform collection, formatting, and normalizing tasks for each device. Rather, these tasks can be performed once across the entire network.

Firewall Log

Firewalls have served as the primary perimeter defense mechanism for networks large and small for many decades. Before the era of next-generation security appliances and advanced endpoint protection, firewall logs were often the primary source for information about malicious activity on the network. Figure 13-8 is a snippet of the logging data from the Uncomplicated Firewall (ufw), the default iptables firewall configuration tool for the Ubuntu operating system. Note the series of **block** actions against 4.4.4.12.

```
Apr  6 17:57:29 edda kernel: [375785.492469] [UFW BLOCK] IN=ens160 OUT=
MAC=00:00:00:00:2d:ff:00:0c:29:c5:00:00:00:00 SRC=4.4.4.12 DST=4.4.4.1 LEN=66 TOS=0x00
PREC=0x00 TTL=64 ID=40983 DF PROTO=UDP SPT=51096 DPT=53 LEN=46

Apr  6 17:57:33 edda kernel: [375789.493762] [UFW BLOCK] IN=ens160 OUT=
MAC=00:00:00:00:2d:ff:00:0c:29:c5:00:00:00:00 SRC=4.4.4.12 DST=4.4.4.1 LEN=66 TOS=0x00
PREC=0x00 TTL=64 ID=41751 DF PROTO=UDP SPT=51096 DPT=53 LEN=46

Apr  6 17:57:37 edda kernel: [375793.495254] [UFW BLOCK] IN=ens160 OUT=
MAC=00:00:00:00:2d:ff:00:0c:29:c5:00:00:00:00 SRC=4.4.4.12 DST=4.4.4.1 LEN=66 TOS=0x00
PREC=0x00 TTL=64 ID=41964 DF PROTO=UDP SPT=51096 DPT=53 LEN=46

Apr  6 17:57:42 edda kernel: [375798.496433] [UFW BLOCK] IN=ens160 OUT=
MAC=00:00:00:00:2d:ff:00:0c:29:c5:00:00:00:00 SRC=4.4.4.12 DST=4.4.4.1 LEN=44 TOS=0x00
PREC=0x00 TTL=37 ID=37826 PROTO=TCP SPT=50062 DPT=143 WINDOW=1024 RES=0x00 SYN URGP=0

Apr  6 17:57:42 edda kernel: [375798.496448] [UFW BLOCK] IN=ens160 OUT=
MAC=00:00:00:00:2d:ff:00:0c:29:c5:00:00:00:00 SRC=4.4.4.12 DST=4.4.4.1 LEN=44 TOS=0x00
PREC=0x00 TTL=37 ID=41141 PROTO=TCP SPT=50062 DPT=199 WINDOW=1024 RES=0x00 SYN URGP=0

Apr  6 17:57:42 edda kernel: [375798.496457] [UFW BLOCK] IN=ens160 OUT=
MAC=00:00:00:00:2d:ff:00:0c:29:c5:00:00:00:00 SRC=4.4.4.12 DST=4.4.4.1 LEN=44 TOS=0x00
PREC=0x00 TTL=48 ID=24746 PROTO=TCP SPT=50062 DPT=111 WINDOW=1024 RES=0x00 SYN URGP=0
```

Figure 13-8 Selection of entries from a Linux firewall log indicating a series of blocked traffic

We can see in each entry a listing of pertinent details about the action, including time, source IP, and port number. When we compare this data with the information provided in Figure 13-3, we can see how the visual presentation might appeal more to an analyst, particularly when dealing with very large volumes of traffic.

Syslog

Syslog is a messaging protocol developed at the University of California, Berkeley, to standardize system event reporting. Syslog has become a standard reporting system used by operating systems and includes alerts related to security, applications, and the OS. The local syslog process in UNIX and Linux environments, called syslogd, collects messages generated by the device and stores them locally on the file system. This includes embedded systems found in routers, switches, and firewalls, which use variants and derivatives of the UNIX system. There is, however, no preinstalled syslog agent in the Windows environment. Syslog is a great way to consolidate logging data from a single machine, but the log files can also be sent to a centralized server for aggregation and analysis. Figure 13-9 shows the typical structure of the syslog hierarchy.

The syslog server will gather syslog data sent over UDP port 514 (or TCP port 514, in the case that message delivery needs to be guaranteed). Analysis of aggregated syslog data is critical for security auditing because the activities that an attacker will conduct on a system are bound to be reported by the syslog utility. These clues can be used to reconstruct the scene and perform remedial actions on the system. Each syslog message includes a facility code and severity level. The facility code gives information about the originating source of the message, whereas the severity code indicates the level of severity associated with the message. Table 13-1 is a list of the severity codes as defined by RFC 5424.

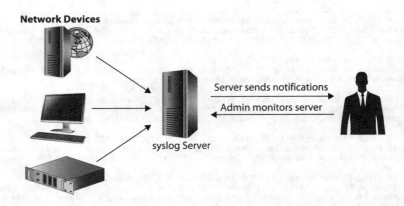

Network Devices

Server sends notifications

Admin monitors server

syslog Server

Figure 13-9   Typical hierarchy for syslog messaging

NOTE   The syslog protocol for event messaging does not specify how exactly messages should be formatted. As a result, messages from different devices may have slight variations in how they're presented to the syslog server. The protocol just provides a standardized way to get the message from client to server.

Authentication Logs

Auditing and analysis of login events is critical for a successful incident investigation. All modern operating systems have a way to log successful and unsuccessful attempts. Figure 13-10 shows the contents of the auth.log file indicating all enabled logging activity on a Linux server. Although it might be tempting to focus on the failed attempts, you should also pay attention to the successful logins, especially in relation to those failed attempts. The chance that the person logging in from 4.4.4.12 is an administrator who made a mistake the first couple of times is reasonable. However, when you combine this information with the knowledge that this device has just recently performed a suspicious network scan, the likelihood that this is an innocent mistake goes way down.

Value	Severity	Keyword	Description
0	Emergency	emerg	System is unusable.
1	Alert	alert	Action must be taken immediately.
2	Critical	crit	Critical conditions.
3	Error	err	Error conditions.
4	Warning	warning	Warning conditions.
5	Notice	notice	Normal but significant conditions.
6	Informational	info	Informational messages.
7	Debug	debug	Debug-level messages.

Table 13-1   Syslog Severity Codes, Keywords, and Descriptions

```
Apr  6 11:08:27 edda sshd[5761]: pam_unix(sshd:auth): authentication failure; logname=
uid=0 euid=0 tty=ssh ruser= rhost=4.4.4.12  user=root
Apr  6 11:08:29 edda sshd[5761]: Failed password for root from 4.4.4.12 port 52724 ssh2
Apr  6 11:08:49 edda sshd[5761]: message repeated 2 times: [ Failed password for root from
4.4.4.12 port 52724 ssh2]
Apr  6 11:08:49 edda sshd[5761]: Connection closed by 4.4.4.12 port 52724 [preauth]
Apr  6 11:08:49 edda sshd[5761]: PAM 2 more authentication failures; logname= uid=0 euid=0
tty=ssh ruser= rhost=4.4.4.12  user=root
Apr  6 11:10:48 edda sshd[5812]: Accepted password for root from 4.4.4.12 port 52793 ssh2
Apr  6 11:10:48 edda sshd[5812]: pam_unix(sshd:session): session opened for user root by
(uid=0)
Apr  6 11:10:48 edda systemd-logind[983]: New session 1079 of user root.
```

Figure 13-10   Snapshot of the auth.log entry in a Linux system

 EXAM TIP   When dealing with logs, consider the time zone difference for each device. Some might report in the time zone you operate in, some might use GMT, whereas others might be off altogether.

Event Logs

Event logs are similar to syslogs in the detail they provide about a system and connected components. Windows allows administrators to view all of a system's event logs with a utility called the *Event Viewer.* This feature makes it much easier to browse through the thousands of entries related to system activity, as shown in Figure 13-11. It's an essential tool for understanding the behavior of complex systems like Windows—and particularly important for servers, which aren't designed to always provide feedback through the user interface.

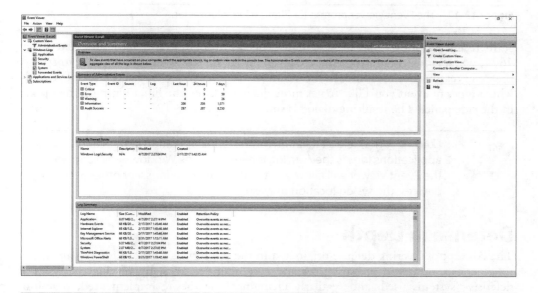

Figure 13-11   The Event Viewer main screen in Windows 10

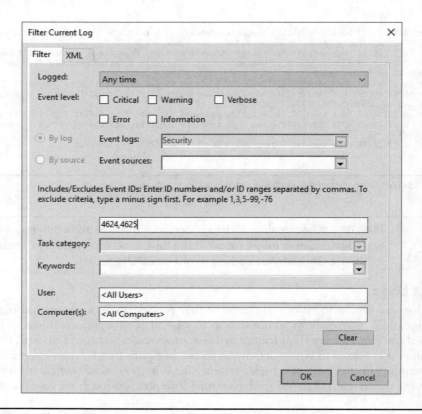

Figure 13-12 The Event Viewer prompt for filtering log information

In recent Windows operating systems, successful login events have an event ID of 4624, whereas login failure events are given an ID of 4625 with error codes to specify the exact reason for the failure. In the Windows 10 Event Viewer, you can specify exactly which types of event you'd like to get more detail on using the Filter Current Log option in the side panel. The resulting dialog is shown in Figure 13-12.

EXAM TIP The default location for the Linux operating system and applications logs is the /var/log directory. In the Windows environment, the Event Viewer will allow you to view the event logs. For other network devices, the syslog location may vary.

Defense in Depth

The concept of layering defense originated in the military as a way of forcing an enemy to expend resources in preparing for and conducting attacks. By varying the types of defensive systems used, and regularly changing how they're implemented, practitioners can make it cost-ineffective for an adversary to sustain an offensive campaign. By spreading resources across locations, a defender can ensure that if one mechanism fails,

Figure 13-13
Personnel,
processes, and
technology
provide defense
in depth

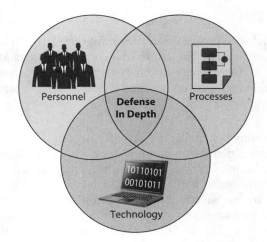

additional hurdles stand between the attacker and their goal. The same concept of varying techniques as part of a rigorous defense plan can be applied to digital systems. For example, you might place firewalls at the perimeter of your network, enable ACLs on various devices, use network segmentation, and enforce group polices. If an attacker circumvents one obstacle, he would have to employ another, different technique against the other defensive measures. Using layers of technical apparatuses alone isn't enough as it relates to information security; as Figure 13-13 depicts, we must combine processes, people, and technology to achieve the original intent of defense in depth. Defense in depth, as a multifaceted approach for physical and network defense, does suffer from one significant flaw in that it's used primarily as a tool of attrition. As a strategy, attrition warfare aims to wear an adversary down to the point of exhaustion so that they no longer possess the will to continue. However, how do we deal with an adversary with unlimited willpower? Given enough time, an enemy will likely discover methods to circumvent the security measures we place on the network. It's important, therefore, that defense in depth never be employed in a static manner: it must constantly be reevaluated, updated, and used alongside other best practices.

Counterattack

A secondary effect of good defense in depth in the physical world is that it often leaves an attacker vulnerable to counterattack since the adversary's resources are depleted. Whereas there are well-studied laws and doctrines covering this concept in physical wartime operations, the notion of counterattack in cyberspace is legally confusing. Additionally, it's challenging to determine the true scope of certain offensive operations given how interconnected the world is. How can we be certain that by responding to an attack with our own internally developed response we don't disrupt another's network, or cross international boundaries? Unfortunately, law and policy haven't fully caught up to what is technically capable—and the discussions (and arguments) continue to this day.

PART IV

Personnel

Human capital is an organization's most important asset. Despite advancements in automation, humans remain the center of a company's operation. Dealing with the human dimension in an increasingly automated world is an enormous challenge. Humans make errors, have different motivations, and learn in different ways.

Training

Employee training is a challenging task for organizations because it is sometimes viewed as a superfluous expense with no immediate outcomes. As a result, organizations will sacrifice training budgets in favor of other efforts more clearly tied to the mission. Skimping on training is, however, a critical mistake because an organization whose workers have stale skillsets are less effective and more prone to error.

We'll cover two aspects of security training in this section. The first is general security awareness training. The focus for this type of training is the typical employee with an average level of technical understanding. Training these types of users on proper network behavior and how to deal with suspicious activity will go a long way. They are, in a way, a large part of the network's defense plan. If they are well trained on what to watch for, prevention, and reporting procedures, this removes a huge burden from the security team. The second type of training is that for the security staff. Because so much of the knowledge about the domain is being created in real time, security analysts will take part in daily on-the-job training. However, it may not always be sufficient to address the variety of challenges that they are likely to encounter. If an organization is not prepared to train its analysts to face these challenges, either through in-house instruction or external training, it may quickly run into organizational and legal problems. Imagine a situation in which management doesn't fund a security team's training on the latest type of ransomware. Where does the fault lie if the company is breached and all of its data encrypted? In this case, providing training would have resulted in displacement of a portion, if not all, of the risk associated with the malware.

Dual Control

By assigning the responsibility for tasks to teams of individuals, as opposed to a single person, an organization can reduce the chances for catastrophic mistakes or fraud. *Dual control* is a practice that requires the involvement of two or more parties to complete a task. A dramatic example of this in use outside of computer security is the missile launch process of some ships and submarines. Aboard some vessels, particularly those carrying nuclear warheads, launching missiles requires the involvement of two senior military officers with special keys inserted at physically separate locations. The goal, of course, is to avoid putting the awesome power of such destructive weapons in the hands of an individual. In this case, splitting the responsibility of executing the task will assist in preventing accidental launch because two individuals must act in concert. Furthermore, because the keys must be engaged in different areas, it makes it impossible for a single person with two keys from enabling the system on his own.

An implementation of this principle in cybersecurity would be access control to a sensitive account that is protected by two-factor authentication using a password and a hardware token. Authorized users would each have a unique password only they know. To log in, however, they would have to enter their username and password and then call into an operations center for the code on a hardware token.

Separation of Duties

Another effective method to limit a user's ability to adversely affect sensitive processes is the practice of *separation of duties*. Also referred to as *segregation of duties,* this practice places the subordinate tasks for a critical function under dispersed control. This is like dual control, with the primary difference being that the parties are given completely different tasks that work together toward a greater goal. As it applies to security, separation of duties might be used to prevent any single individual from disrupting business-critical processes, accessing sensitive data, or making untested administrative changes across an organization. For example, your organization might break down the requirements to delete sensitive data into several steps: verify, execute, and approve. By giving each task to different people, you can be sure that no one person can perform the deletion task alone. Ideally, the parties involved in performing the task do not belong to the same group. By granting access to individuals who don't work in the same group, the team can reduce the likelihood of conflicts of interest or, worse, collusion. Should an attacker compromise an account and attempt to use those credentials, a separation of duties policy would prevent access because only one condition would be met for access. Separation of duties also applies generally to the reporting structure of your team. Security team auditors, for example, should not report to members of the production team. Imagine the awkward position if, as a junior analyst, you must report problems with a production system to your boss, who manages these systems.

 NOTE In smaller organizations, it may be difficult to separate duties due to the lack of available personnel. Using additional compensating controls such as periodic reviews and auditing is one way to mitigate the risks inherent in these environments.

Third Parties and Consultants

Outside consultants are called to assist because of their special knowledge in an area. In practice, they often act in much the same way as regular employees, although they may not have been subject to the same level of vetting due to time constraints. They will often be tightly integrated with existing teams for effectiveness and efficiency. Since consultants will undoubtedly be exposed to confidential or proprietary company information, an organization must weigh the risks associated with this as part of the greater compensating controls strategy. This strategy must include a nondisclosure agreement (NDA), clearly defined policies for the use of outside equipment on the company network, and a comprehensive description of responsibilities and expectation for the contractor.

Cross-Training

An organization can choose to rotate employees assigned to certain jobs to expose them to a new environment and give them additional context for their role in the organization's processes. *Cross-training* is not only a cost-effective way to provide training, but it's also a way of ensuring that backup personnel are available should primary staff be unavailable. Cross-training has obvious benefits for technical training, but there are additional benefits outside of improving skill. It also helps in team development by providing an opportunity for team members to cover for one another, and it gives each member improved visibility over another's role in the company.

Rotation of Duties

Whereas separation of duties mandates the involvement of multiple individuals with executing critical tasks, *rotation of duties* is the practice of regularly varying the assignments of an employee. This further mitigates collusion or any attempts to circumvent the protections provided by separation of duties. Job rotation is useful in minimizing the effect of dishonesty because it forces the organization to focus on the role, rather than the individual. For example, if a single employee is charged with all duties related to making purchases, then the chances that this employee gets away with unauthorized purchases or embezzlement are far higher than if the role is regularly reassigned across the organization.

Mandatory Vacation

Given the stress associated with dealing with sensitive data and processes on a day-to-day basis, it's a good idea to direct team members to take vacations for at least a week at regular intervals. This serves two purposes related to security. First, by removing an individual from a position temporarily, it allows problems that may have been concealed to become apparent. Furthermore, as workers remain in high-stress position for extended periods, the chances for burnout and complacency increase. Thus, mandatory vacations help prevent the occurrence of mistakes and make the employee more resilient to social engineering attempts. For the sake of continuity, it's good practice to align mandatory vacations with rotation of duties and cross-training.

Succession Planning

As much as companies would like to hold on to their best and brightest forever, it's a reality that people move on at some point. Planning for this departure is a necessary part of any mature organization's continuity process. In the military, succession planning is a well-understood and practiced concept. The inherent risks with service, along with the normal schedule of assignments, means that units must think in the future tense and work on achieving present-day mission success. As with our armed forces, a succession plan in your organization means an orderly transition of responsibilities to a designated person. Ideally, this person is preselected and prepared on the new role with minimal disruption, but this isn't always the case. You must also recognize the natural tension between succession planning and training. Organizations must strike a balance between taking care of current employees with training, but not so much that they neglect preparing for the future force. To prevent this, the organization and its subordinate teams ought to remain focused on the tasks necessary to achieve strategic goals. A practical step in succession planning includes the creation of a playbook, or continuity book, that can be passed on during the changeover process. This playbook should have a description and technical steps involved in team processes, and it should be written in such a way that a team member can pick it up and continue operations with minimal delay. In fact, an effective way to test out the utility of your succession plan is during a job rotation, or any of the aforementioned practices that involve taking a role from the primary employee.

Processes

Filling in the gap between employees in your organization and technology tools are the processes. This key part of the network security plan needs to be well thought out and include clear policies and procedures for all users. We covered some of these concepts in Chapter 11 when we discussed frameworks such as ISO/IEC 27000, COBIT, and ITIL, which ensure an organization follows best practices and is regularly reviewing and improving its security posture. Processes should be reviewed on a yearly basis at the very least, and need to mirror what the current trends are in technology. Moreover, these processes need to be built in such a way as to remain flexible to address evolving threats.

Continual Improvement

Even though processes are designed to be unambiguous, particularly regarding appropriate behavior on the network and consequences for policy violation, they should remain "living" things subject to improvement as necessary. It should not be surprising that our personnel and technology are changing regularly. The threats to our systems change even more quickly. This constantly changing environment requires that we continually examine our processes and look for opportunities for improvement. This managed optimization is the hallmark of mature organizations.

This process of improvement requires changes, and these must be carefully managed. Most organizations implement a change control process to ensure alterations to staffing, processes, or technology are well thought out. All changes to the security processes, whether technical, staff, or policy, should be reviewed and updated to reflect the current threat.

Change Control Process

A well-structured change management process should be put into place to aid staff members through many different types of changes to the environment. This process should be laid out in the change control policy. Although the types of changes vary, a standard list of procedures can help keep the process under control and ensure it is carried out in a predictable manner. The following steps are examples of the types of procedures that should be part of any change control policy:

1. Request for a change to take place

2. Approval of the change

3. Documentation of the change

4. Testing and certification

5. Implementation

6. Reporting the finalized change to management

Scheduled Reviews

An organization should plan recurring reviews of its security strategy to keep pace with the threats it faces and to validate whether existing security policies are useful. As with software vendors, updates should be made to policy as necessary to maintain a strong security stance and remain aligned with any new business goals. In regulated environments, these reviews are typically required in order to remain in compliance. In all organizations, they require senior management focus and are absolutely essential to prevent erosion of the security posture.

Retirement of Processes

A natural part of improvement is the retirement of a process. Whether the process is no longer relevant, a new process has been developed, or the process no longer aligns with the organization's business goals, there must be a formal mechanism to remove it. Retirement of processes is similar to the change control process described earlier. The process in question is reviewed by relevant stakeholders and company leadership, the adjustments made, and the replacement policy clearly communicated to the organization. It's critical that those involved in the day-to-day execution of tasks within the processes don't continue to use outdated versions.

Technology

Your organization's network security plan cannot exist without technology. Although it is as important as people and processes, technology operates at a totally different speed. It's best used to perform repetitive tasks for which humans are ill-suited, such as enforcing policies, monitoring traffic, alerting to violations, and preventing data from leaving the network. Technological solutions can also be used as compensating controls, minimizing risk at times of human error. But the supporting relationship between people, processes, and technology also goes the other way. As malware evolves to evade next-generation security devices, it is the people and processes supporting the technology that come together to prevent catastrophic damage to your organization.

Automated Reporting

Technology is often best applied to repetitive tasks that require a high degree of accuracy. After collection and analysis are rapidly performed using any of the security data analytics techniques described earlier in this chapter, the security devices can send notifications based on the specifications and preferences of the security team. Automated reporting features are found in most modern security products, including security appliances and security suites. You should spend some time determining exactly what you'd like to report because having constant pings from your security devices can lead to "alert fatigue."

Security Appliances

Security appliances perform functions that traditionally were spread across multiple hardware devices. Nowadays, security appliances can act as firewalls, content filters, IDSs/IPSs, and load balancers. Since these devices provide several network and security functions, potentially to replacing existing devices, their interfaces often provide seamless integration between functions with a central management console. Figure 13-14 is an example of an integrated dashboard provided by a security appliance vendor.

Figure 13-14 Sample dashboard of a security appliance

Note that it provides an overview of the organization's traffic, anomalies, usage, and additional sections for details on client and application behavior. This appliance also provides a separate area for security specific alerts and settings, as shown in Figure 13-15.

In addition to providing general information about the source, destination, and frequency associated with the event, the security appliance automatically creates a packet capture. Figure 13-16 shows the details provided using the packet capture functionality of this appliance.

An analyst can review this information and make a call to escalate or to refine the rule in the case of a false positive. Additionally, any of the data found on these screens can be sent by e-mails based on a schedule.

Security Suites

Security suites are a class of software that provide multiple security- and management-related functions. Included in most security suites are endpoint scanning and protection, mobile device management (MDM), and phishing detection. Also called *multilayered security*, security suites often rely on vast databases of threat data to deliver the most up-to-date detection and protection against network threats.

Outsourcing

Outsourcing presents several challenges that you must be familiar with as a security analyst. Because you are entrusting the security of your network to an outside party, there are several steps you should take to protect your company's network and data:

- **Access control** Access to you via the company's interface should be highly and thoroughly inspected because outside access to them might mean access to you.

Figure 13-15 Overview of the security events for the organization's network

- **Contractor vetting** Both the company and its employees should be subject to rigorous standards for vetting. After all, you are potentially entrusting the fate of your organization to them. Background checks should be conducted and verified. Every effort should be made to ensure that the company's internal processes are aligned to your own.

- **Incident handling and reporting** You should understand and agree on the best procedures for incident handling. Any legal responsibilities should be communicated clearly to the company, particularly if you operate in a regulatory environment.

Security as a Service

It seems that it was just a matter of time before security joined the trend of technology functions being offered "as a service" to businesses. Security as a Service (SECaaS) is a growing phenomenon where security companies act as a service provider for security-related services as part of a subscription model. This allows for the subscribing business to invest less in onsite security infrastructure while receiving the latest protection and security expertise.

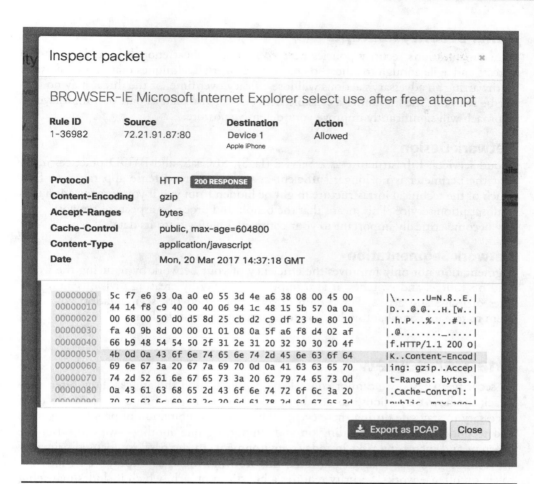

Figure 13-16 Packet inspection screen provided by the security appliance

Cryptography

Cryptographic principles underpin many security controls found on our network. Cryptographic hash functions, for example, provide a way for us to maintain integrity. They provide a virtual tamper-proof seal for our data. Similarly, digital signatures give us a way to verify the source of a message, often using a public-key infrastructure (PKI). Perhaps the most well-known principle, encryption, provides confidentiality of our data. The use of encryption might be mandatory, depending on the domain your organization operates in. Regulatory requirements such as the Health Insurance Portability and Accountability Act (HIPAA), the Payment Card Industry (PCI), and Sarbanes-Oxley (SOX) Act compel organizations to use encryption when dealing with sensitive data.

Other Security Concepts

Your organization's security policies need to be both robust enough to address known threats and agile enough to adjust to emerging dangers. Techniques that might be useful in thwarting an adversary's actions will lose efficacy over time, or the threat may no longer be relevant. Incorporating a sensible network defense plan as part of a multilayered approach will significantly improve your defensive posture.

Network Design

Cloud services, Infrastructure as a Service (IaaS), SECaaS, and BYOD practices mean that the perimeter is no longer sufficient as your primary defense apparatus. In fact, much of the technical infrastructure might be hidden from you if your organization uses a subscription service. This means that the people and processes aspects of network security become critically important to your company holding onto its data.

Network Segmentation

Segmentation not only improves the efficiency of your network by reducing the workload on routers and switches, it also improves security by creating divisions along the lines of usage and access. For certain organizations, network segmentation will allow them to remain compliant with regulations regarding sensitive data.

Chapter Review

As security analysts, we cannot control the people behind the attacks, how often they attack, or how they choose to go about it, but we can give our own team the tools necessary to stay safe during these events. Through a combination of people, processes, and technology—each depending on and supporting one another—we can offset the inherent and increasing risks in today's environment. In the past, we focused primarily on technology as the enabler. However, this works as much as a sports team focusing solely on offense works. Security requires a holistic approach, which includes managing our technology, understanding how it aligns with our business processes, and giving the people in our organization the tools to be successful. People, processes, and technology are all integral to dealing with risk.

Questions

Use the following scenario to answer Questions 1–3:

You notice a very high volume of traffic from a host in your network to an external one. You don't notice any related malware alerts, and the remote host does not show up on your threat intelligence reports as having a suspected malicious IP address. The source host is a Windows workstation belonging to an employee who was involved in an altercation with a manager last week.

1. You are not sure if this is suspicious or not. How can you best determine whether this behavior is normal?

   A. Manual review of syslog files

   B. Historical analysis

   C. Packet analysis

   D. Heuristic analysis

2. You decide to do a manual review of log files. Which of the following data sources is *least* likely to be useful?

   A. Firewall logs

   B. Security event logs

   C. Application event logs

   D. Syslog logs

3. Which of the following personnel security practices might be helpful in determining whether the employee is an insider threat?

   A. Security awareness training

   B. Separation of duties

   C. Mandatory vacation

   D. Succession planning

4. Your organization requires that new user accounts be initiated by human resources staff and activated by IT operations staff. Neither group can perform the other's role. No employee belongs to both groups, so nobody can create an account by themselves. Of which personnel security principle is this an example?

   A. Dual control

   B. Separation of duties

   C. Succession

   D. Cross-training

5. Your organization stores digital evidence under a two-lock rule in which anyone holding a key to the evidence room cannot also hold a key to an evidence locker. Each lead investigator is issued a locker with key, but they can only enter the room if the evidence custodian unlocks the door to the evidence room. Of which personnel security principle is this an example?

   A. Dual control

   B. Separation of duties

   C. Succession

   D. Cross-training

6. Your organization has a process for regularly examining assets, threats, and controls and making changes to your staffing, processes, and/or technologies in order to optimize your security posture. What kind of process is this?

   A. Succession planning

   B. Trend analysis

   C. Security as a service

   D. Continual improvement

Refer to the following illustration and scenario for Questions 7–9:

You notice an unusual amount of traffic to a backup DNS server in your DMZ. You examine the log files and see the results illustrated here. All your internal addresses are in the 10.0.0.0/8 network, while your DMZ addresses are in the 172.16.0.0/12 network. The time is now 3:20 p.m. (local) on April 6th.

```
Apr 6 15:17:02 mercury sshd[2092]: Failed password for invalid user root from
192.168.192.6 port 34443 ssh2
Apr 6 15:17:02 mercury sshd[2092]: Failed password for invalid user root from
192.168.192.6 port 34443 ssh2
Apr 6 15:17:02 mercury sshd[2092]: Failed password for invalid user root from
192.168.192.6 port 34443 ssh2
Apr 6 15:17:03 mercury sshd[2097]: Failed none for invalid user root from
192.168.192.6 port 34444 ssh2
Apr 6 15:17:05 mercury sshd[2097]: Failed password for invalid user root from
192.168.192.6 port 34444 ssh2
Apr 6 15:17:07 mercury sshd[2097]: Failed password for invalid user root from
192.168.192.6 port 34444 ssh2
Apr 6 15:17:07 mercury sshd[2097]: Failed password for invalid user root from
192.168.192.6 port 34444 ssh2
Apr 6 15:17:08 mercury sshd[2099]: Failed none for invalid user root from
192.168.192.6 port 34445 ssh2
Apr 6 15:17:12 mercury sshd[2099]: Failed password for invalid user root from
192.168.192.6 port 34445 ssh2
Apr 6 15:17:12 mercury sshd[2099]: Failed password for invalid user root from
192.168.192.6 port 34445 ssh2
Apr 6 15:17:12 mercury sshd[2099]: Failed password for invalid user root from
192.168.192.6 port 34445 ssh2
Apr 6 15:19:25 mercury sshd[2153]: Failed none for invalid user root from
192.168.192.6 port 34475 ssh2
Apr 6 15:19:29 mercury sshd[2153]: Failed password for invalid user root from
192.168.192.6 port 34475 ssh2
Apr 6 15:19:34 mercury sshd[2153]: Failed password for invalid user root from
192.168.192.6 port 34475 ssh2
Apr 6 15:19:35 mercury sshd[2153]: Session opened for user root from
192.168.192.6 port 34475 ssh2
```

7. What does the log file indicate?

   A. Use of a brute-force password cracker against an SSH service

   B. Need for additional user training on remembering passwords

   C. Manual password-guessing attack against an SSH service

   D. Pivoting from an internal host to the SSH service

8. What would be your best immediate response to this incident?

    A. Implement an ACL to block incoming traffic from 192.168.192.6.

    B. Drop the connection at the perimeter router and begin forensic analysis of the server to determine the extent of the compromise.

    C. Start full packet captures of all traffic between 192.168.192.6 and the server.

    D. Drop the connection at the perimeter router and put the server in an isolation VLAN.

9. How could you improve your security processes to prevent this attack from working in the future?

    A. Block traffic from 192.168.192.6.

    B. Improve end-user password security training.

    C. Implement automated log aggregation and reporting.

    D. Disallow external connections to SSH services.

Use the following scenario to answer Questions 10–11:

You were hired as a security consultant for a mid-sized business struggling under the increasing costs of cyber attacks. The number of security incidents resulting from phishing attacks is trending upward, which is putting an increased load on the business's understaffed security operations team. That team is no longer to keep up with both incident responses and an abundance of processes, most of which are not being followed anyway. Personnel turnover in the security shop is becoming a real problem. The CEO wants to stop or reverse the infection trend and get security costs under control.

10. What approach would you recommend to quickly reduce the rate of compromises?

    A. Trend analysis

    B. Automated reporting

    C. Security as a Service

    D. Security awareness training

11. How would you address the challenge of an overworked security team? (Choose two.)

    A. Cross-training the security staff

    B. Outsourcing security functions

    C. Retirement of processes

    D. Mandatory vacations

    E. Increasing salaries and/or bonuses

Answers

1. **B.** Historical analysis allows you to compare a new data point to previously captured ones. Syslog files and captured packets would be unlikely to tell whether the behavior is normal unless they contained evidence of compromise. Heuristic analysis could potentially be useful, but it is not as good of an answer as historical analysis.

2. **D.** Windows systems are not normally configured to use syslog. All other log files would likely be present and might provide useful information.

3. **C.** If the employee is required to go on vacation and the unusual activity ceases, then it is likely due to employee activity. Because the replacement individual would have the exact same duties, the absence of such activity by the substitute might indicate malicious or at least suspicious behavior.

4. **B.** Separation of duties is characterized by having multiple individuals perform different but complementary subtasks that, together, accomplish a sensitive task.

5. **A.** Dual control is characterized by requiring two people to perform similar tasks in order to gain access to a controlled asset.

6. **D.** Continual improvement is aimed at optimizing the organization in the face of ever-changing conditions. Trend analysis could be a source of data for this effort, but this would be an incomplete answer at best.

7. **A.** The speed at which successive attempts were made make it unlikely that this incident was the result of a manual attack or a forgetful user. There is no evidence to indicate that pivoting, which is lateral movement inside a target network once an initial breach is made, has taken place yet, given that the connection was established less than a minute ago.

8. **D.** The immediate goal of the response should be to isolate the host suspected of being compromised. Blocking future attempts and learning what the attacker is up to are both prudent steps, but should be done only after the server is isolated.

9. **D.** The only given choice that would stop this attack in the future is to prevent external connections to SSH. Remote users who need such access should be required to connect over a VPN first, which would give them an internal IP address.

10. **D.** The issue seems to be that users are more often falling for phishing attacks, which points to a need for improved personnel training more so than any other approach.

11. **B, C.** Outsourcing some of the security operations can strike a balance between the need to keep some functions in-house while freeing up time for the security team. Additionally, the organization appears to have excessive processes that are not being followed, so retiring some of those would likely lead free up some more time. Cross-training might be helpful if the workload was uneven compared to the skillsets, but there is no mention of that being the case in the scenario.

Secure Software Development

In this chapter you will learn:

- The software development lifecycle (SDLC)
- General principles for secure software development
- How to ensure the security of software
- Best practices for secure coding

Give me six hours to chop down a tree and I will
spend the first four sharpening the axe.

—Abraham Lincoln

When you're developing software, most of the effort goes into either planning and design (in good teams) or debugging and fixes (in other teams). You are very unlikely to be working as a software developer if your principal role in your organization is cybersecurity analyst. You are, however, almost certainly going to be on the receiving end of the consequences for software that is developed in an insecure manner. Quite simply, the skills, priorities, and incentives of developers are very different than those of their security teammates. It is in everyone's best interest then to bridge the gap between these communities, which is why CompTIA included the objectives we cover here in the CSA+ exam.

The Software Development Lifecycle

There are many approaches to building software, but they all follow some sort of predictable pattern called a *lifecycle*. It starts with identifying an unmet need and it ends with retiring the software, usually so that a new system can take its place. Whether you use formal or agile methodologies, you still have to identify and track the user or organizational needs; design, build, and test a solution; put that solution into a production environment; keep it running until it is no longer needed; and finally dispose of it without breaking anything else. In the sections that follow, we present the generic categories of effort within this lifecycle, though your organization may call these by other names. Along the way, we'll highlight how this all fits into the CSA+ exam.

EXAM TIP You do not need to memorize the phases of the software development lifecycle, but you do need to know how a cybersecurity analyst would contribute to the development effort at different points in it.

DevOps and DevSecOps

Historically, the software development and quality assurance teams would work together, but in isolation from the IT operations teams who would ultimately have to deal with the end product. Many problems stemmed from poor collaboration between these two during the development process. It is not rare to have the IT team berating the developers because a feature push causes the former group to have to stay late or work on a weekend or simply drop everything they were doing in order to "fix" something that the developers "broke." This friction makes a lot of sense when you consider that each team is incentivized by different outcomes. Developers want to push out finished code, usually under strict schedules. The IT staff, on the other hand, wants to keep the IT infrastructure operating effectively. A good way to solve this friction is to have both developers and operations staff (hence the term DevOps) work together throughout the software development process. *DevOps* is the practice of incorporating development, IT, and quality assurance (QA) staff into software development projects in order to align their incentives and enable frequent, efficient, and reliable releases of software products. Recently, the cybersecurity team is also being included in this multifunctional team, leading to the increasing use of the term *DevSecOps,* as illustrated here.

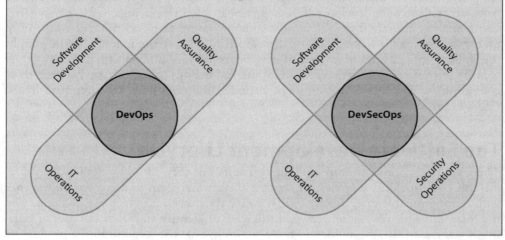

Requirements

All software development should start with the identification of the requirements that the finished product must satisfy. Even if those requirements are not explicitly listed in a formal document, they will exist somewhere before the first line of code is written.

Generally speaking, there are two types of requirements: functional requirements that describe *what* the software must do, and nonfunctional requirements that describe *how* the software must do these things, or what the software must be like. Left to their own devices, many software developers will focus their attention on the functionality and only begrudgingly (if at all) pay attention to the rest.

Functional Requirements

A *functional requirement* defines a function of a system in terms of inputs, processing, and outputs. For example, a software system may receive telemetry data from a temperature sensor, compare it to other data from that sensor, and display a graph showing how the values have changed for the day. This requirement is not encumbered with any specific constraints or limitations, which is the role of nonfunctional requirements.

Nonfunctional Requirements

A *nonfunctional requirement* defines a characteristic, constraint, or limitation of the system. Nonfunctional requirements are the main input to architectural designs for software systems. An example of a nonfunctional requirement, following the previous temperature scenario, would be that the system must be sensitive to temperature differences of one tenth of a degree Fahrenheit and greater. Nonfunctional requirements are sometimes called *quality requirements*.

Security Requirements

The class of requirements in which we are most interested is that dealing with security. A *security requirement* defines the behaviors and characteristics a system must possess in order to achieve and maintain an acceptable level of security by itself, and in its interactions with other systems. Accordingly, this class includes both functional and nonfunctional aspects of the finished product.

Development

Once all the requirements have been identified, the development team starts developing or building the software system. The first step in this phase is to design an architecture that will address the nonfunctional requirements. Recall that these are the ones that describe the characteristics of the system. On this architecture, the detailed code modules that address the features or functionality of the system are designed so that they satisfy the functional requirements. After the architecture and features are designed, software engineers start writing, integrating, and testing the code. At the end of the development phase, the system has passed all unit, integration, and system tests and is ready to be rolled out onto a production network.

Implementation

The implementation phase is usually when frictions between the development and operations teams start to become real problems unless these two groups have been integrated beforehand. The challenges in this transitory phase include ensuring that the software will run properly on the target hardware systems, that it will integrate properly with other systems (for example, Active Directory), that it won't adversely affect the performance of any other system on the network, and that it doesn't compromise the security of the overall information system. If the organization used DevOps or DevSecOps from the beginning, most of the thorny issues will have been identified and addressed by this stage, which means implementation becomes simply an issue of provisioning and final checks.

User Acceptance Testing

Every software system is built to satisfy the needs of a set of users. Accordingly, the system is not deemed acceptable (or finished) until the users or their representatives declare that all the features have been implemented in ways that are acceptable to them. Depending on the development methodology used, user acceptance testing could happen before the end of the development phase or before the end of the implementation phase. Many organizations today use agile development methodologies that stress user involvement during the development process. This means that user acceptance testing may not be a formal event but rather a continuous engagement.

Operation and Maintenance

By most estimates, operation and maintenance (O&M) of software systems represents around 75 percent of the total cost of ownership (TCO). Somewhere between 20 and 35 percent of O&M costs are related to correcting vulnerabilities and other flaws that were not discovered during development. If you multiply these two figures together, you can see that typically organizations spend between 15 and 26 percent of the TCO for a software system fixing defects. This is the main driver for spending extra time in the design, secure development, and testing of the system before it goes into O&M. By this phase, the IT operations team has ownership of the software and is trying to keep it running in support of the business, while the software developers have usually moved on to the next project and see requests for fixes as distractions from their main efforts. This should highlight, once again, the need for secure software development before it ever touches a production network.

Secure Software Development

It turns out that developing secure code is not all that difficult, but it does take a remarkable amount of time, discipline, and attention to detail. These three items translate into significant costs for the organization, which is the main reason why we tend to build insecure software: because doing it right the first time is very expensive. As you saw in our brief discussion of O&M, these high development costs pale in comparison to the even higher costs of fixing and maintaining bad code once it is placed in production. Even if there are significant schedule and costs constraints for the development team, they can still take a number of steps to build a more secure product. We divide these into two categories: those steps that we take while building the code and those that we take as we test it.

Secure Coding

Secure coding is all about reducing the number of vulnerabilities in a software product to a degree that can be mitigated by controls in the operational environment. In other words, secure code seldom has to be sent back to the programmers for fixing because any flaws can be compensated by operational controls. The truth is that there is no such thing as perfectly secure code, except for some exceptionally small and expensive systems. For most of us, this is an exercise in reducing, not eliminating, the flaws using some combination of the steps we discuss in this section.

Input Validation

If there is one universal rule to developing secure software, it is this: don't *ever* trust any input entered by a user. This is not just an issue of protecting our systems against malicious attackers; it is equally applicable to innocent user errors. The best approach to validating inputs is to perform context-sensitive whitelisting. In other words, consider what is supposed to be happening within the software system at the specific points in which the input is elicited from the user, and then allow only the values that are appropriate. For example, if you are getting a credit card number from a user, you would only allow 16 consecutive numeric characters. Anything else would be disallowed.

Perhaps one of the most well-known examples of adversarial exploitation of improper user input validation is Structured Query Language (SQL) injection (SQLi). SQL is a language developed by IBM to query information in a database management system (DBMS). Because user credentials for web applications are commonly stored in a DBMS, many web apps will use SQL to authenticate their users. A typical *insecure* SQL query to accomplish this in PHP is shown here:

```
$result = mysql_query("SELECT * FROM userdb WHERE username='$form_username'
        AND password='$form_password'");
$num_rows = mysql_num_rows($result);
if($num_rows > 0){
    $authenticated = True;
else
    $authenticated = False;
```

Absent any validation of the user inputs, the user could provide the username **attacker' or 1=1 --** and **pawned** (or anything or nothing) for the password, which would result in the following query string:

```
"SELECT * FROM userdb WHERE username='attacker' or 1=1 --'
        AND password='pawned'"
```

If the DBMS for this web app is MySQL, that system will interpret anything after two dashes as a comment, which will be ignored. This means that the value in the password field is irrelevant because it will never be evaluated by the database. The username can be anything (or empty), but because the logical condition 1=1 is always true, the query will return all the registered users. Because the number of users is greater than zero, the attacker will be authenticated.

Clearly, we need to validate inputs such as these, but should we do it on the client side or the server side. Client-side validation is often implemented through JavaScript and embedded within the code for the page containing the form. The advantage of this approach is that errors are caught at the point of entry, and the form is not submitted to the server until all values are validated. The disadvantage is that, as you will see later when we discuss interception proxies, client-side validation is easily negated using commonly available and easy-to-use tools. The preferred approach is to do client-side validation to enhance the user experience of benign users, but double-check everything on the server side to ensure protection against malicious actors.

Parameter Validation

The issue of parameter validation is akin to the issue of input validation mentioned earlier. Parameter validation is where the values being received by the application are validated to be within defined limits before they are processed. The main difference between input validation and parameter validation is whether the application was expecting a value to come from a user input or from some part of the software system as a parameter. Attacks in this area deal with manipulating values that the system would assume are beyond the user being able to configure, mainly because there isn't a mechanism provided in the interface to do so.

An illustrative example is in the use of cookies for web applications. In an effort to provide a rich end-user experience, web application designers have to employ mechanisms to keep track of the thousands of different web browsers that could be connected at any given time. The HTTP protocol by itself doesn't facilitate managing the state of a user's connection; it just connects to a server, gets whatever objects are requested in the HTML code, and then disconnects. Instead, we employ the technique of passing a cookie to the client to help the server remember things about the state of the connection. A cookie isn't a program but rather just data that is exchanged between the client and server, stored by the client, and used to track the state of the interactions between them. Because accessing and modifying a cookie is usually beyond the reach of most users, some web developers don't think about this as a serious threat when designing their systems. However, malicious actors can take advantage of cookies for attacks such as session hijacking.

Static Code Analysis

Input and parameter validation are two practices that can be verified by having someone examine the source code looking for vulnerable procedures. Static code analysis is a technique meant to help identify software defects or security policy violations and is carried out by examining the code without executing the program (hence the term *static)*. The term *static analysis* is generally reserved for automated tools that assist analysts and developers, whereas manual inspection by humans is generally referred to as *code review*. Because it is an automated process, it allows developers and security staff to quickly scan their source code for programming flaws and vulnerabilities.

Figure 14-1 shows an example of a tool called Lapse+, which was developed by the Open Web Application Security Project (OWASP) to find vulnerabilities in Java

Figure 14-1   Code analysis of a vulnerable web application (source: www.owasp.org)

applications. This tool is highlighting an instance wherein user input is directly used, without sufficient validation, to build a SQL query against a database. In this particular case, this query is verifying the user name and password. This insecure code block would allow a threat actor to conduct a SQL injection attack against this system. This actor would likely gain access by providing the string **"foo' OR 1==1 --"** if the database was on a MySQL server.

Automated static analysis like that performed by Lapse+ provides a scalable method of security code review and ensures that secure coding policies are being followed. There are numerous manifestations of static analysis tools, ranging from tools that simply consider the behavior of single statements to tools that analyze the entire source code at once. However, you should keep in mind that static code analysis cannot usually reveal logic errors or vulnerabilities (that is, behaviors that are only evident at runtime), and therefore should be used in conjunction with manual code review to ensure a more thorough evaluation.

Code Reviews

One of the best practices for quality assurance and secure coding is the code review, which is a systematic examination of the instructions that comprise a piece of software performed by someone other than the author of that code. This approach is a hallmark of mature software development processes. In fact, in many organizations, developers are not allowed to push out their software modules until someone else has signed off on them after doing code reviews. Think of this as proofreading an important document before you send it to an important person. If you try to proofread it yourself, you will probably not catch all those embarrassing typos and grammatical errors as easily as if someone else were to check it.

Code reviews go way beyond checking for typos, though that is certainly one element of it. It all starts with a set of coding standards developed by the organization that wrote the software. This could be an internal team, an outsourced developer, or a commercial vendor. Obviously, code reviews of off-the-shelf commercial software are extremely rare unless the software is open source or you happen to be a major government agency. Still, each development shop will have a style guide or documented coding standards that cover everything from how to indent the code to when and how to use existing code libraries. Therefore, a preliminary step to the code review is to ensure the author followed the team's standards. In addition to helping the maintainability of the software, this step gives the code reviewer a preview of the magnitude of work ahead; a sloppy coder will probably have a lot of other, harder-to-find defects in his code, and each of those defects is a potential security vulnerability.

Regression Testing

Software is almost never written securely on the first attempt. Organizations with mature development processes will take steps like the ones we've discussed in this chapter to detect and fix software flaws and vulnerabilities before the system is put into production. Invariably, errors will be found, leading to fixes. The catch is that fixing a vulnerability may very well inadvertently break some other function of the system or even create a new set of vulnerabilities. *Regression testing* is the formal process by which code that has been modified is tested to ensure no features and security characteristics were compromised by the modifications. Obviously, regression testing is only as effective as the standardized suite of tests that were developed for it. If the tests provide insufficient coverage, regression testing may not reveal new flaws that may have been introduced during the corrective process.

Security Testing

So far, we've focused on the practices, including testing, that would normally be performed by the software development or quality assurance team. As the project transitions from development to implementation, the IT operations and security teams typically perform additional security tests to ensure the confidentiality, integrity, and availability not only of the new software, but of the larger ecosystem once the new program is introduced. If an organization is using DevSecOps, some or most of these security tests could be performed as the software is being developed because security personnel would be part of that phase as well. Otherwise, the development team gives the software to the security team for testing, and these individuals will almost certainly find flaws that will start a back-and-forth cycle that could delay final implementation.

Web App Vulnerability Scanning

Web app vulnerability scanning is a specific form of the vulnerability scanning we discussed in Part II of this book (Chapters 5 and 6). Unlike the tests we discussed when addressing secure coding practices, web app vulnerability scans are normally external tests that are conducted from the perspective of a malicious user. Like other vulnerability scanners, these will only try to identify vulnerabilities for which they have a plug-in. Some of the most common checks are listed here:

- Outdated server components (for example, those for which patches are available)
- Misconfigured server
- Secure authentication of users
- Secure session management (for example, random session tokens)
- Information leaks (for example, revealing too much information about the server)
- Cross-site scripting (XSS) vulnerability
- Improper use of HTTPS (for example, allowing SSL)

Many commercial and open source web application vulnerability scanners are available. In Chapter 15 of this book, we address one of the most popular tools, called Nikto. Most of these scanners allow you to develop customized tests for your specific environment, so if you have some unique policies or security requirements that must be satisfied, it is worthwhile to learn how to write plug-ins or tests for your preferred scanner.

Interception Proxies

An *interception proxy* is a software tool that is inserted between two communicating endpoints for the purpose of examining, modifying, or logging messages between the two. Typically, an interception proxy will be in the same network (or even host) as one of the endpoints, which is usually the client. In the context of security testing, these proxies are most commonly used to examine the security of web apps and mobile apps, because they allow the security tester to inspect every message between the client and the server. Here is a list of security characteristics that can be tested using an interception proxy:

- **Input validation**   Although input validation can be tested through the standard user interface, it is usually easier to do formal (or scripted) tests using one environment, which makes the use of a proxy more efficient.

- **Parameter validation**   By modifying values that shouldn't be available to the user (for example, hidden form fields or cookies) or were validated on the client side, the security team can verify that server-side validation is taking place.

- **Plaintext credentials**   Although it is relatively easy to ensure that web apps use HTTPS for sending credentials, this is a lot harder when dealing with mobile apps unless you can intercept the traffic. This could also be done with a packet sniffer.

- **Session tokens**   Sessions are normally tracked through the use of a token, which is a value assigned by the server and oftentimes called a session ID. If this value is not truly random, threat actors could guess valid session IDs and use them to impersonate legitimate users. Proxies facilitate statistical analysis of session tokens to ensure they are sufficiently random.

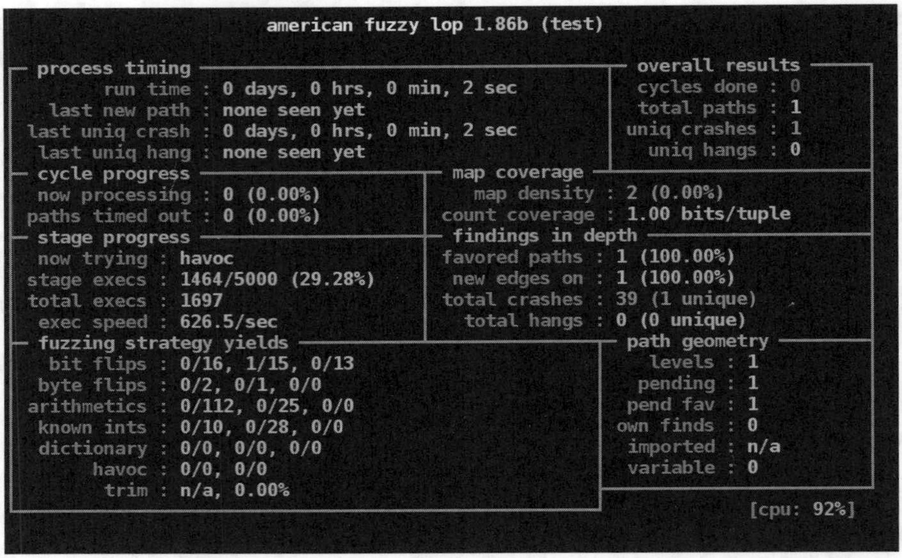

```
                        american fuzzy lop 1.86b (test)
┌─ process timing ─────────────────────┐  ┌─ overall results ──────┐
│        run time : 0 days, 0 hrs, 0 min, 2 sec │  cycles done : 0        │
│   last new path : none seen yet        │  total paths : 1        │
│ last uniq crash : 0 days, 0 hrs, 0 min, 2 sec │  uniq crashes : 1       │
│  last uniq hang : none seen yet        │   uniq hangs : 0        │
├─ cycle progress ─────────┐  ┌─ map coverage ──────────────┤
│  now processing : 0 (0.00%)       │   map density : 2 (0.00%)       │
│ paths timed out : 0 (0.00%)       │  count coverage : 1.00 bits/tuple │
├─ stage progress ─────────┤  ├─ findings in depth ──────────┤
│   now trying : havoc              │  favored paths : 1 (100.00%)    │
│  stage execs : 1464/5000 (29.28%) │  new edges on : 1 (100.00%)     │
│  total execs : 1697               │ total crashes : 39 (1 unique)   │
│  exec speed : 626.5/sec           │  total hangs : 0 (0 unique)     │
├─ fuzzing strategy yields ─────────┤  ├─ path geometry ──────────────┤
│  bit flips : 0/16, 1/15, 0/13     │     levels : 1                  │
│  byte flips : 0/2, 0/1, 0/0       │    pending : 1                  │
│ arithmetics : 0/112, 0/25, 0/0    │   pend fav : 1                  │
│  known ints : 0/10, 0/28, 0/0     │  own finds : 0                  │
│  dictionary : 0/0, 0/0, 0/0       │   imported : n/a                │
│       havoc : 0/0, 0/0            │   variable : 0                  │
│        trim : n/a, 0.00%          │                                 │
└───────────────────────────────────┘  └──────────────── [cpu: 92%] ─┘
```

Figure 14-2 A fuzzer testing an application

Fuzzing

Fuzzing is a technique used to discover flaws and vulnerabilities in software by sending large amounts of malformed, unexpected, or random data to the target program in order to trigger failures. Attackers could manipulate these errors and flaws to inject their own code into the system and compromise its security and stability. Fuzzing tools are commonly successful at identifying buffer overflows, denial of service (DoS) vulnerabilities, injection weaknesses, validation flaws, and other activities that can cause software to freeze, crash, or throw unexpected errors. Figure 14-2 shows a popular fuzzer called American Fuzzy Lop (AFL) crashing a targeted application.

Fuzzers don't always generate random inputs from scratch. Purely random generation is known to be an inefficient way to fuzz systems. Instead, they often start with an input that is pretty close to normal and then make lots of small changes to see which seem more effective at exposing a flaw. Eventually, an input will cause an interesting condition in the target, at which point the security team will need a tool that can determine where the flaw is and how it could be exploited (if at all). This observation and analysis tool is oftentimes bundled with the fuzzer, because one is pretty useless without the other.

Stress Testing

Another type of testing that also attempts to break software systems does so by creating conditions that the system would not reasonably be expected to encounter during normal conditions. *Stress testing* places extreme demands that are well beyond the planning thresholds of the software in order to determine how robust it is. The focus here is on attempting to compromise the availability of the system by creating a DoS condition.

The most common type of stress testing attempts to give the system *too much* of something (for example, simultaneous connections or data). During development, the team will build the software so that it handles a certain volume of activity or data. This volume may be specified as a nonfunctional requirement, or it may be arbitrarily determined by the team based on their experience. Typically, this value is determined by measuring or predicting the maximum load that the system is likely to be presented. In order to stress-test the system with regard to this value, the team would simply exceed it under different conditions and see what happens. The most common way to conduct these tests is by using scripts that generate thousands of simulated connections or by uploading exceptionally high volumes of data (either as many large files or fewer huge ones).

Not all stress tests are about overwhelming the software; it is also possible to underwhelm it. This type of stress testing provides the system with *too little* of something (for example, network bandwidth, CPU cycles, or memory). The idea here is to see how the system deals with a threat called *resource starvation,* in which an attacker intentionally causes the system to consume resources until none are left. A robust system would gracefully degrade its capabilities during an event like this, but wouldn't fail altogether. Insufficient-resource tests are also useful to determine the absolute minimum configuration necessary for nominal system performance.

Resource Starvation

A resource starvation attack attempts to compromise the availability of information systems by depleting the resources required for them to operate. The three most common varieties of this type of attack are listed here:

- **Network bandwidth** This variety is perhaps the best known because of distributed denial of service (DDoS) attacks that drown a target with billions of packets per second.

- **Memory** Depleting a system's memory is easy if the system has memory leaks, which are memory allocations that are not eventually reclaimed by the system. This is also possible if you can cause the program to spawn an endless number of recursive procedure calls or if there is no limit to how many items you can add to an online shopping cart.

- **CPU** CPU starvation attacks are normally harder to pull off because you need to exploit a flaw in the system that ties up the CPU for an extended period. For example, certain asymmetric cryptography procedures, such as key pair generation, are CPU intensive. If an attacker can cause the system to generate a large number of key pairs, it would eventually not be able to perform any other function.

Best Practices

Perhaps the most important principle is that of quality. *Quality* can be defined as fitness for purpose. In other words, how good something is at whatever it is meant to do. A quality car will be good for transportation. We don't have to worry about it breaking down or failing to protect its occupants in a crash or being easy for a thief to steal. When we need to go somewhere, we simply go to where we left the car and count on it taking us to wherever we need to go. Similarly, we don't have to worry about quality software crashing, corrupting our data under unforeseen circumstances, or being easy for someone to subvert. Sadly, many developers still think of functionality first (or only) when thinking about quality. When we look at things holistically, we should see that quality is the most important concept in developing secure software.

This, of course, is not a new problem. Secure software development has been a challenge for a few decades. Unsurprisingly, there is an established body of best practices to minimize the flaws and vulnerabilities in our code. You should be familiar with what some of the best-known advocates for secure coding recommend, which are introduced next.

Software Engineering Institute

The Software Engineering Institute (SEI) at Carnegie-Mellon University is a federally funded research and development center that has focused on secure software engineering for over three decades. The U.S. Department of Defense has funded the SEI since 1984 in large part due to the realization that software systems, particularly military ones, should be built securely. The contributions of the SEI extend well beyond the government, however, and it is recognized as one of the world's leading authorities on software engineering in general and secure coding in particular.

Among the products developed by the SEI is a top ten list of secure coding practices. We briefly list these items here. (Note that we have touched on most if not all of them in this book so far.)

1. Validate all inputs.
2. Don't ignore compiler warnings.
3. Architect for security.
4. Avoid unnecessary complexity.
5. Deny by default.
6. Use least privilege.
7. Don't share data you don't have to.
8. Defend in depth.
9. Strive for quality.
10. Use secure coding standards.

Another of SEI's contributions is the development of the Capability Maturity Model Integration (CMMI), which we discussed in Chapter 11. Although the CMMI is aimed at process improvement in general, there is a specific model called CMMI for Development (or CMMI-DEV) that applies to the development of services and products such as software. Moreover, a guide called Security by Design specifies four process areas for CMMI-DEV that allow organizations to improve and appraise their capabilities to develop products with adequate levels of security. This guide is intended to help organizations build security into their products early in their lifecycles to avoid the common trap of trying to bolt security onto products at the later stages of their development. The four process areas are listed here:

- **Organizational Preparedness for Secure Development** Focuses on the development and maintenance of the organizational capabilities required for secure development, such as developing the workforce and acquiring the necessary tools.

- **Security Management in Projects** Expands the organization's project management processes to include the definition, planning, and integration of security-related practices.

- **Security Requirements and Technical Solution** Establishes security requirements for the products as well as practices for the secure architecting, design, and implementation.

- **Security Verification and Validation** Builds upon the practices of verification and validation to ensure that the security requirements are met and that the product is adequately resistant to malicious attacks in its intended environment.

EXAM TIP You do not need to memorize the CMMI-DEV or Security by Design extensions to the CMMI. We discuss them so that you better understand how the CMMI applies to cybersecurity. You will be expected to understand the CMMI's five maturity levels, however, which are covered in Chapter 11.

OWASP

The Open Web Application Security Project (OWASP) is an organization that deals specifically with web security issues. Along with a long list of tools, articles, and resources that developers can follow to create secure software, it also has individual member meetings (chapters) throughout the world. The group provides development guidelines, testing procedures, and code review steps, but is probably best known for the top ten web application security risk list that it maintains. The top risks identified by this group as of the writing of this book are as follows:

A1: Injection

A2: Broken Authentication and Session Management

A3: Cross-Site Scripting (XSS)

A4: Insecure Direct Object References

A5: Security Misconfiguration

A6: Sensitive Data Exposure

A7: Missing Function Level Access Controls

A8: Cross-Site Request Forgery (CSRF)

A9: Using Components with Known Vulnerabilities

A10: Unvalidated Redirects and Forwards

This list represents the most common vulnerabilities that reside in web-based software and are exploited most often. You can find out more information pertaining to these vulnerabilities at https://www.owasp.org/index.php/Top_10_2013-Top_10.

SANS

The SANS Institute is one of the most respected organizations in the fields of information security and cybersecurity training. One of its focus areas is application security (AppSec), and it regularly makes resources available on its web page (https://software-security.sans.org/resources). SANS has extended its popular "Securing the Human" program, which focuses on user security awareness, to include a specialized thread aimed at developers. Within it, SANS lists a large number of recommendations and best practices, many of which were introduced in this chapter. Here are additional ones of which you should be aware:

- *Display generic error messages.* Overly specific error messages to the user are not helpful to legitimate users, but can be a treasure trove of information for attackers trying to compromise the system. Error data should be stored securely in the logs so it is available to the people who will actually do something good with it: the O&M team.

- *Implement account lockouts.* Although many organizations do this as a matter of habit on their domain controllers, a remarkable number of distributed applications will allow attackers to brute-force passwords unhindered. As a corollary, the mechanism by which users reset their passwords should be secure and, ideally, use two factors.

- *Limit sensitive data use.* It is oftentimes easier to provide too much information and let the users decide what they need than to carefully analyze every item of sensitive information before allowing it to show up in the system. This is particularly problematic when caching or form auto-completion is permitted in web browsers.

- *Use HTTPS everywhere.* Even when organizations go to great lengths to protect data at rest, they don't always protect it as it traverses the Internet. There really is no good reason why every organization should not be using HTTPS, particularly for web apps and mobile apps.

- *Use parameterized SQL queries.* We have already seen how easy and dangerous SQL injection attacks can be if we let user input strings be inserted directly into a SQL query. A very simple solution is to use parameterized queries in which the user inputs are prevented from being interpreted as SQL commands.

- *Automate application deployment.* Even secure software can be rendered vulnerable if it is improperly configured. The challenge is that complex systems have dozens (if not hundreds) of configuration parameters. Using automation (for example, scripts) can ensure that every deployment is done to exactly the same (hopefully secure) standard.

Center for Internet Security

The Center for Internet Security (CIS) is a nonprofit organization with the ambitious goal of enhancing the cybersecurity of private and public organizations around the world. By all accounts, it is making progress toward this goal. What sets the CIS apart is the fact that, at its very core, the center is about collaboration, as is evident in the purpose of its four core divisions. The Integrated Intelligence Center receives threat intelligence reports from public and private organizations and shares these with every other subscriber. The Multi-State Information Sharing and Analysis Center (MS-ISAC) performs a similar function, but it's focused on state, local, tribal, and territorial (SLTT) government partners and also provides some vulnerability mitigation and incident response. The third division, the Trusted Purchasing Alliance, leverages the combined purchasing power of its SLTT and nonprofit partners to obtain deals that individual organizations would not be able to negotiate. Finally, the Security Benchmarks Division produces two product streams that are the subject of the following subsections.

System Design Recommendations

The CIS uses focus groups and consensus building among its hundreds of members and partners to identify best practices for secure system designs. Of particular interest to cybersecurity analysts are the 20 CIS Controls, which are generally agreed to significantly improve an organization's security posture. Besides identifying these controls, the CIS offers specific guidance on how to implement them in any organization's information systems.

Benchmarks

Whereas the 20 CIS Controls provide global system design recommendations, the CIS Benchmarks are detailed guides to securing a specific platform (for example, Microsoft Windows 10 Enterprise or Ubuntu Linux 16.04). These benchmarks are equivalent to the Security Technical Implementation Guides (STIGs) published by government entities such as the Defense Information System Agency (DISA) to protect federal information systems. In addition to the detailed benchmarks, the CIS also provides pre-hardened images of some open source platforms.

Chapter Review

Although you may not spend much time (if at all) developing software, as a security analyst you will certainly have to deal with the consequences of any insecure coding practices. Your best bet is to be familiar with the processes and issues and be part of the solution. Simply attending the meetings, asking questions, and sharing your thoughts could be the key to avoiding a catastrophic compromise that results from programmers who didn't realize the potential consequences of their (otherwise reasonable) decisions. Ideally you are part of a cohesive DevSecOps team that consistently develops high-quality code. If you are not, maybe you can start your organization down this path.

As for the CSA+ exam, you should have an awareness of the major issues with developing secure code. You will be expected to know how a cybersecurity analyst can proactively or, if need be, reactively address vulnerabilities in custom software systems. Some of the key concepts here are the security tests you can run such as web app vulnerability scans, stress tests, and fuzzing. You may be asked about the software development lifecycle, but you don't have to be an expert in it.

Questions

1. The practice of testing user input to reduce the impact of malformed user requests is referred to as what?

   A. Input validation

   B. Static code analysis

   C. Manual inspection

   D. Stress testing

2. Which phase in the software development lifecycle often highlights friction between developers and business units due to integration and performance issues?

   A. Implementation

   B. Design

   C. Planning

   D. Maintenance

3. To reduce the amount of data that must be examined and interpreted by a web application, what method can be used to catch errors before submission?

   A. Server-side validation

   B. Proxy validation

   C. Client-side validation

   D. Stress validation

4. What key process is often used to determine the usability and suitability of newly developed software before implementation across an organization?

   A. User acceptance testing

   B. Parameter validation

   C. Regression testing

   D. Data filtering

Use the following scenario and illustration to answer Questions 5–10:

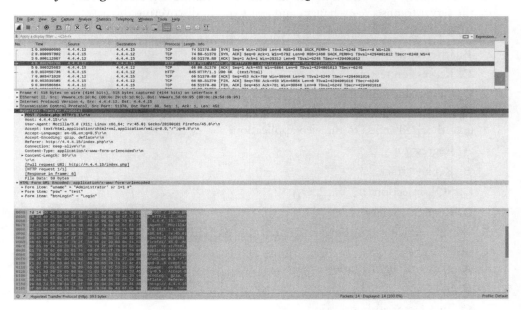

Your accounting department's administrator has reached out to your team because one of the department's analysts has discovered a discrepancy in the accounting reports. Some of the department's paper documents do not match the stored versions, leading them to believe the database has been tampered with. This database is for internal access only, and you can assume that it hasn't been accessed from outside the corporate network. The administrator tells you that the database software was written several years ago by one individual and that they haven't been able to update the system since the initial rollout. You are also provided traffic capture data by the local admin to assist with the analysis.

5. After hearing the description of how the software was developed by one person, what process do you know would have improved the software without needing to run it?

   A. Runtime analysis

   B. Just-in-time analysis

   C. Fuzzing

   D. Code review

6. What tool might you employ to monitor communication between endpoints and the server to observe exchanges and assist you in discovering the flaw?

   A. Jump box

   B. Interception proxy

   C. Regression testing

   D. Client-side validation

7. Based on the traffic-capture data, what is the most likely method used to gain unauthorized access to the web application?

   A. Regression

   B. Replay attack

   C. SQL injection

   D. Request forgery

8. What practice might have prevented this particular type attack from being successful?

   A. Network segmentation

   B. SSL

   C. Two-factor authentication

   D. Input validation

9. To prevent input from being interpreted as actual commands, what method should the developer have used?

   A. Regression testing

   B. Generic error messages

   C. Session tokens

   D. Parameterized queries

10. You have updated the server software and want to actively test it for new flaws. Which method is the *least* suitable for your requirement?

- **A.** Fuzzing
- **B.** Static code analysis
- **C.** Stress testing
- **D.** Web app vulnerability scanning

Answers

1. **A.** Input validation is an approach to protecting systems from abnormal user input by testing the data provided against appropriate values.

2. **A.** Implementation is all about seeing how the software works in its production environment. Although problems are bound to surface, the most productive organizations have mature mechanisms for feedback for improvement.

3. **C.** Client-side validation checks are those performed on data in the user browser or application before the data is sent to the server. This practice is used alongside server-side validation to improve security and to reduce the load on the server.

4. **A.** User acceptance testing is a method to determine whether a piece of software meets specifications and is suitable for the business processes.

5. **D.** Code review is the systematic examination of software by someone not involved in the initial development process. This ensures an unbiased perspective and promotes adherence to coding and security standards.

6. **B.** An interception proxy is a software tool that is inserted between two endpoints, usually on the same network, to monitor traffic and help with security testing.

7. **C.** SQL injection is a technique of manipulating input to gain control of a web application's database server. It is effective and powerful, and often facilitates data manipulation or theft.

8. **D.** Input validation is the practice of constraining and sanitizing input data. This is an effective defense against all types of injection attacks by checking the type, length, format, and range of data against known good types.

9. **D.** Using parameterized queries is a developer practice for easily differentiating between code and user-provided input.

10. **B.** All methods except for static code analysis are considered active types of assessments.

Tool Sets

In this chapter you will learn:

- The major cybersecurity tools and technologies for analysts
- When and how you might use different tools and technologies
- How to choose among similar tools and technologies

We shape our tools and thereafter our tools shape us.

—Marshall McLuhan

The purpose of this chapter is to introduce you to (or perhaps reacquaint you with) the tools with which you will need to be familiar for the CSA+ exam. We are not trying to provide a full review of each tool or even cover all the features. Instead, we give you enough information to understand the purpose of each tool and when you may want to use one over the other. For convenience, we group these tools into five categories: preventative, collective, analytical, exploitative, and forensic. If you read about a tool for the first time in this chapter, you may want to spend more time familiarizing yourself with it before you take the exam.

Each of the five tool categories may be further subdivided into classes of tools. For example, the preventative category has a class of tools called "firewalls." All tools within a class do pretty much the same thing, albeit in different ways. For each tool class, we provide an overview before comparing notable products in that class. We then provide an illustrative scenario that offers a more detailed description of each tool and how it fits in that scenario.

EXAM TIP   You do not need to know these tools in detail for the exam, but you do need to know when and how you would use the different classes of tools.

Preventative Tools

The first class of tools we'll discuss includes all those that help us prevent incidents. They allow us to create defensive perimeters around an application, host, or network. For best results, we employ these tools to create concentric perimeters that, generally speaking, provide a number of defensive layers proportional to the value of the assets they protect.

Firewalls

Firewalls are systems that restrict the flow of network data according to specific sets of rules, which in turn enforce an organization's security policies. An organizational security policy provides high-level directives on acceptable and unacceptable actions as they pertain to protecting critical assets. The firewall has a more detailed security policy that dictates, among other things, what IP addresses and ranges are allowed as well as what ports can be accessed. A firewall policy or rule set is commonly called an *access control list (ACL)*. A simple rule, such as the one shown here, could be used to allow SMTP traffic to travel from system 10.1.1.2 to system 172.16.1.1:

```
permit tcp any host 10.1.1.2 host 172.16.1.1 eq smtp
```

The parameters of this rule are the protocols (TCP and "any" version of IP), the hosts' IP addresses, and the port number (SMTP = 25). This is an example of stateless *packet filtering* because the firewall only looks at the listed parameters. A *stateful packet inspection (SPI) firewall* could use that same rule but would also keep track of the state of the connection between the endpoints. If a legitimate connection doesn't exist (that is, one that starts with a TCP three-way handshake and ends with a four-way handshake), then the packet is not allowed even if it matches this rule. If we wanted to be even more intrusive, we could use an *application-level firewall,* which also understands the protocols used by specific applications and allows only packets that "make sense" for that application.

Entire books have been written on firewalls, so we'll focus our discussion on the specific type of firewalls with which you will have to be familiar for the CSA+ exam. A *Next-Generation Firewall (NGFW)* incorporates the attributes of the previously discussed firewalls but adds a number of important improvements. Most significantly, it incorporates an intrusion prevention system (IPS) engine. This means that, in addition to ensuring that the traffic is behaving in accordance with the rules of the applicable protocols, the firewall can look for specific indicators of attack even in otherwise well-behaved traffic. NGFWs oftentimes include features that allow them to share signatures with a cloud-based aggregator so that once a new attack is detected by one, all other firewalls manufactured by that vendor become aware of the attack signature. Another characteristic of an NGFW is its ability to connect to external data sources such as Active Directory, whitelists, blacklists, and policy servers. This feature allows controls to be defined in one place and pulled by every NGFW on the network, which reduces the chances of inconsistent settings on the various firewalls that typically exist in large networks.

Tools

The NGFW market is consistently led by three companies: Check Point, Cisco, and Palo Alto Networks. There are many companies, but these three set the tone as well as command the largest shares. It is difficult to do a comprehensive comparison of their products in a few pages because they are exceptionally feature rich and are constantly evolving. Instead, Table 15-1 highlights some key features and describes when one vendor's product might be a better fit than the others.

Vendor	Platform Type	Key Features	Price	Best For...
Check Point	Hardware, software, and cloud	Integrated mobile security, endpoint protection, cloud-based sandboxing, and threat intelligence feeds	Mid to High	Balanced, mature approach between traditional SPI and NGFW, regulatory compliance
Cisco	Hardware and cloud	Behavioral IOCs and virtual firewalls	Mid	Traditional SPI firewall functionality with NGFW add-ons, TCO, heterogeneous cloud environments
Palo Alto	Hardware, software, and cloud	Endpoint protection, automatic IOC generation/sharing, threat intelligence feeds, and cloud-based malware detection	High	All-in-one state-of-the-art solution, if price is no object

Table 15-1 Comparison of Next-Generation Firewall Offerings

Scenario

You work at a large organization that just recently finished recovering from a major incident involving a sophisticated adversary. This experience resulted in the allocation of new funding for security infrastructure upgrades. A key finding in the lessons-learned report was the fact that the indicators of compromise (IOCs) associated with this threat actor were known in the threat intelligence community, of which you are not a part. As a senior analyst, you are part of the team charged with improving security. You have a significant investment in Cisco products, but want to consider the best fit regardless of brand. As you consider your hardware options, you remember that some NGFWs are able to automatically exchange IOCs with similar devices around the world. If only you'd had that capability a month ago!

Check Point   This company's claim to fame is having pioneered the stateful packet inspection (SPI) firewall. Check Point is not always "first to market" with innovative features, but when it does implement them, they tend to be very well done. Still, Check Point has a very robust research and development arm and is considered among the market leaders. Check Point also has a very good reputation when it comes to complex deployments in very large organizations as well as in some niche use cases (for example, ruggedized ICS/SCADA protection) and with regard to regulatory compliance. Because your organization is large and the upgrades could be complicated, Check Point might help you make the transition easier.

Cisco   Cisco's NGFW solutions are common in Cisco-only (or Cisco-mostly) deployments. Its solutions are marketed as Cisco ASA with FirePOWER Services, and they represent a (subscription-based) FirePOWER service on a traditional ASA firewall. When it comes to traditional firewall features and protection, Cisco leads compared to the other manufacturers. That said, its NGFW features compare well with the other two, though they tend to not be as robust or innovative. If total cost of ownership (TCO) is a principal concern, Cisco NGFWs compete very well. This is particularly relevant in the scenario because you already have a significant investment in Cisco devices.

Palo Alto   Palo Alto Networks is widely regarded as the industry leader in NGFW innovation, frequently rolling out new features ahead of its competitors. An example of this is the introduction of cloud-based malware detection into the market with its Wild-fire subscription service, which is integrated with its threat intelligence cloud. Integration is a major theme within Palo Alto's product line, which can result in faster detection and better protection, particularly against previously unknown threats. This innovation comes at a cost, however, because Palo Alto's solutions tend to be more expensive than its competitors'. If ever there was a time to jump on the Palo Alto bandwagon, this might be it since you are better resourced.

IDS and IPS

An *intrusion detection system (IDS)* is a system that captures network traffic, compares it to a set of rules or heuristics, and generates some sort of notification if there is any evidence of unauthorized activity. An *intrusion prevention system (IPS)* is simply an IDS that attempts to stop the intrusions it detects, and not simply generate alerts. It follows that an IPS is a special class of IDS that retains all the latter's features and adds responsive capabilities. Although both can be network or host based, we will focus our attention on the network version.

Tools

We already discussed two of these systems (Snort and Bro) in Chapter 2 when we looked at their IDS capabilities. We'll now circle back and explore how these systems can be used to detect and prevent intrusions. Table 15-2 provides a comparison of three IDS/IPS tools.

Scenario

You recently joined a small business as its only cybersecurity analyst. The company has a reasonable security architecture using some older Cisco routers and firewalls, but it doesn't have an IPS. You quickly realize that this a critical area for improvement, but also know that money is tight. You have written some basic Snort rules but are not really proficient with it or any other system. A scheduled meeting with the Director of IT next week might be an opportunity to propose some improvements in this area.

Bro   Bro is not really meant to be used as an IPS, but its powerful scripting language certainly allows for this. At its core, this IDS does two things: it captures all sorts of events (labeling them neither good nor bad) and then runs scripts that analyze the events looking for signatures or anomalies that might indicate a security incident. These scripts can take actions ranging from sending a warning message to changing configurations

Tool	Developer	OS/UI	Key Features	Pricing	Best For...
Bro	Vern Paxson	Linux, BSD, and Mac OS	Rule and heuristic based.	Open source	Auditing, network forensics, anomaly-based detection, and malware analysis
Snort	Martin Roesch	Linux, BSD, Mac OS, and Windows	Rule based. Rule language is very popular. Extensive rule sets.	Open source	Ease of use, multiplatform support, and finding trained operators
Sourcefire	Cisco	Adaptive Security Appliance (ASA)	Tight integration with Cisco products. Based on Snort.	Commercial	Implementing next-generation IPS and integrating with Cisco environments

Table 15-2   Comparison of IDS/IPS Tools

on systems in order to thwart a threat. What might make Bro a particularly good fit for the scenario is that it records *everything*, even as you are getting familiarized with it and building a library of scripts. This means that you would be able to run new scripts on already-acquired data to detect things that happened before you were fully up to speed. The fact that it is free also fits your limited budget.

Snort   Snort, though also an IDS, is more frequently used as an IPS than Bro. Its scripting language is not as powerful as Bro's, but it is plenty to stop any network threat for which you can develop a signature. This is a key difference between Snort and Bro, in that the latter can look for both signatures and anomalous behaviors. Unlike Bro, Snort does not automatically log everything it sees on the network, which may be attractive if you have limited means to store large amounts of event data. Like Bro, however, Snort is free and open source, which means you should be able to afford it. Because you have some Snort experience (in this scenario), you already have a leg up on deploying it in your new organization.

Sourcefire   Sourcefire started its life as the commercial version of Snort. It quickly grew in capabilities and was later expanded into a set of offerings under the Firepower line of security products. The Sourcefire company was acquired by Cisco in 2013, and the Firepower IPS was integrated into Cisco products even as it was further improved. This system is offered as a time-limited (typically annual) license in Cisco's Adaptive Security Appliance (ASA) line of products. The licensing model is one that increases with the number of hosts being supported, so a small organization like the one in the scenario would probably be able to afford it, particularly if the Cisco firewalls you already have can support Sourcefire Firepower. Unlike Bro and Snort, this IPS comes with commercial support, which could make things easier for you as you settle into your new role.

Host-Based Intrusion Prevention Systems

As the name implies, a host-based intrusion prevention system (HIPS) is an IPS that only inspects and responds to the traffic in and out of a host's network interfaces. Unlike its network-based brethren, the protection is afforded only to one device. Although this may seem like a limitation, it actually enhances the overall security posture by allowing the HIPS to become finely tuned to the traffic and pattern at one specific host. This is doubly true of an HIPS that doesn't just rely on signatures but also incorporates behavioral or heuristic approaches.

The only reason why you *wouldn't* want to have HIPSs deployed across your organization is if you don't have the resources (for example, time, money, or personnel) to properly install and maintain them. Apart from the direct costs for the licenses, it is important to note that an anomaly-based HIPS can require a significant amount of human supervision during the training period (that is, the period of time it takes the system to learn what "right" looks like). During this period, you may also have to deal with loss of productivity as the HIPS incorrectly classifies benign traffic as malicious. Some of these costs can be mitigated by ensuring your solution includes centralized management and monitoring capabilities.

Antimalware

Antimalware (sometimes called antivirus) software is designed to detect and neutralize malicious software, including viruses, worms, and Trojan horses. The vast majority of commercially available antimalware software is rule based, with new malware definition files getting downloaded from the vendor on a weekly (or shorter) basis. This software works by identifying a distinctive attribute of the malware, extracting that as its signature, and then updating all software systems with it. Antimalware identifies malware that is already known to the vendor, which means that it might not detect new malware (or "old" malware that has been modified).

At least 16 major antimalware products are on the market at the time of this writing. Although none offers 100 percent protection against malicious software, multiple independent reports put them in the range of 96 to 99.9 percent effectiveness against *known* malware, according to independent testing. This makes antimalware products some of the most cost-effective protections around. Still, it is not difficult to develop malware that is specifically designed to be invisible to any one product. This means that if a sophisticated adversary knows which antimalware product you use, it is not at all difficult to bypass it.

 NOTE The term *antivirus* is still widely used but almost certainly refers to antimalware. None of the major vendors in this market limit their work strictly to computer viruses, which are not all that common these days.

Enhanced Mitigation Experience Toolkit

The Enhanced Mitigation Experience Toolkit (EMET) is a free Microsoft product designed to enhance the protection of Windows systems against a variety of threats, particularly unknown (or zero-day) ones. Among the key features in EMET that improve the security posture are the following:

- **Data Execution Prevention (DEP)**   When a process calls a function, it causes the allocation of memory space for (executable) code and (presumably non-executable) data. Buffer overflow exploits overrun the data space and cause "data" to overwrite the memory space, allowing arbitrary code execution. DEP prevents this situation by marking the data space as non-executable and preventing data from being written to code space.

- **Address Space Layout Randomization (ASLR)**   Buffer overflows and other forms of attack require the attacker to know (or be able to guess) the location in memory of specific data (typically code). ASLR, when properly implemented, makes it infeasible (or at least very difficult) to determine the location of a specific instruction or data item.

- **Control Flow Guard (CFG)**   Return-oriented programming (ROP) is an attack technique in which the adversary hijacks the normal flow of a process and causes it to perform malicious actions. CFG mitigates the risk of ROP by creating a virtual map of the allowable flows within the program and preventing any flows that are not mapped.

It is important to note that these features are typically part of the Windows systems without EMET. However, in order to be useful, every program needs to be compiled by the developer to take advantage of them. Unfortunately, many programs are not compiled in this manner, making them vulnerable to multiple classes of attack. EMET works by compensating these shortcomings when the programs are not built to leverage these features and by allowing the user control over which features are enabled for which programs, as shown in Figure 15-1.

NOTE   Microsoft announced that EMET will reach end of life in July of 2018, arguing that these features are key parts of Windows 10.

Web Proxies

A *web proxy* is a system that intercepts and then forwards web traffic between clients and servers. Such proxies are commonly used to carry out content filtering to ensure that Internet use conforms to the organization's acceptable-use policy. They can block unacceptable web traffic, provide logs with detailed information pertaining to the sites specific users visited, monitor bandwidth-usage statistics, block restricted website usage, and screen traffic for specific keywords (such as porn, confidential, or Social Security numbers). The proxy servers can be configured to act as caching servers, which keep local

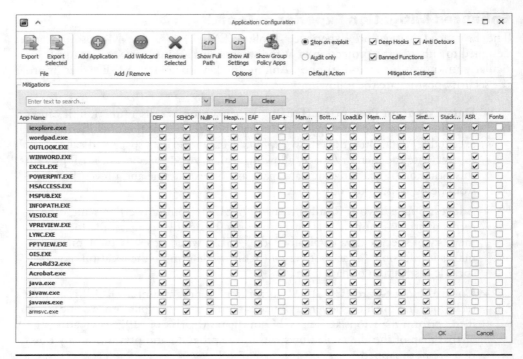

Figure 15-1 EMET mapping security features to programs

App Name	DEP	SEHOP	NullP...	Heap...	EAF	EAF+	Man...	Bott...	LoadLib	Mem...	Caller	SimE...	Stack...	ASR	Fonts
iexplore.exe	✓	✓	✓	✓	✓	✓	✓	✓	✓	✓	✓	✓	✓	✓	☐
wordpad.exe	✓	✓	✓	✓	✓	☐	✓	✓	✓	✓	✓	✓	✓	☐	☐
OUTLOOK.EXE	✓	✓	✓	✓	✓	☐	✓	✓	✓	✓	✓	✓	✓	☐	☐
WINWORD.EXE	✓	✓	✓	✓	✓	☐	✓	✓	✓	✓	✓	✓	✓	✓	☐
EXCEL.EXE	✓	✓	✓	✓	✓	☐	✓	✓	✓	✓	✓	✓	✓	✓	☐
POWERPNT.EXE	✓	✓	✓	✓	✓	☐	✓	✓	✓	✓	✓	✓	✓	✓	☐
MSACCESS.EXE	✓	✓	✓	✓	✓	☐	✓	✓	✓	✓	✓	✓	✓	☐	☐
MSPUB.EXE	✓	✓	✓	✓	✓	☐	✓	✓	✓	✓	✓	✓	✓	☐	☐
INFOPATH.EXE	✓	✓	✓	✓	✓	☐	✓	✓	✓	✓	✓	✓	✓	☐	☐
VISIO.EXE	✓	✓	✓	✓	✓	☐	✓	✓	✓	✓	✓	✓	✓	☐	☐
VPREVIEW.EXE	✓	✓	✓	✓	✓	☐	✓	✓	✓	✓	✓	✓	✓	☐	☐
LYNC.EXE	✓	✓	✓	✓	✓	☐	✓	✓	✓	✓	✓	✓	✓	☐	☐
PPTVIEW.EXE	✓	✓	✓	✓	✓	☐	✓	✓	✓	✓	✓	✓	✓	☐	☐
OIS.EXE	✓	✓	✓	✓	✓	☐	✓	✓	✓	✓	✓	✓	✓	☐	☐
AcroRd32.exe	✓	✓	✓	✓	✓	✓	✓	✓	✓	✓	✓	✓	✓	☐	☐
Acrobat.exe	✓	✓	✓	✓	✓	✓	✓	✓	✓	✓	✓	✓	✓	☐	☐
java.exe	✓	✓	✓	☐	✓	☐	✓	✓	✓	✓	✓	✓	✓	☐	☐
javaw.exe	✓	✓	✓	☐	✓	☐	✓	✓	✓	✓	✓	✓	✓	☐	☐
javaws.exe	✓	✓	✓	☐	✓	☐	✓	✓	✓	✓	✓	✓	✓	☐	☐
armsvc.exe	✓	✓	✓	✓	✓	☐	✓	✓	✓	✓	✓	✓	✓	☐	☐

copies of frequently requested resources, allowing organizations to significantly reduce their upstream bandwidth usage and costs while significantly increasing performance.

It is worth noting that although most web proxies support HTTPS traffic, doing so effectively requires additional steps. For starters, you will be examining the contents of a "conversation" that is encrypted and can therefore be reasonably expected (by the user) to be private. It is essential that your organizational policies make it clear to the users that this can happen, or else you could find yourself in legal trouble.

The next step is to ensure that all clients in your organization trust the Certificate Authority (CA) with which you will be signing the internal certificates. At issue is the fact that, when using HTTPS, a client requests from the server a certificate that is issued by a trusted CA and matches the domain of the requested resource. When a web proxy is mediating this conversation, it will present its own certificate to the client to secure the internal connection and use the server's certificate to secure the external half of the connection. If the proxy's CA is not trusted by the client, the browser will generate a certificate warning every time, which is something we really don't want our users to get used to clicking through.

EXAM TIP Web proxies are typically focused on the client, ensuring it does not access or upload disallowed content, while protecting it from downloading malicious data.

Web Application Firewalls

Whereas web proxies control what is done by and to web clients, we also need similar protections for our servers so that we have assurance that external clients won't be able to easily attack them. A *web application firewall (WAF)* is a system that mediates external traffic to a protected server. The WAF is configured for the specific web apps (or classes of web apps) that it is intended to protect. In other words, the WAF "speaks the language" of the web app so as to identify unusual or disallowed requests to it. It is able to determine which URLs, directories, and parameters are acceptable and which are suspicious. This is something that traditional firewalls cannot do.

NOTE   Requirement 6.6 of the Payment Card Industry Data Security Standard (PCI DSS) requires covered organizations either to have all web application code reviewed by a specialized organization or to deploy a WAF for any web-facing applications.

Tools

The three most popular WAFs are detailed in Table 15-3.

Scenario

Your friend is starting an online business and, having heard you just aced your CSA+ exam, approaches you for advice on how to protect his web storefront and comply with the PCI DSS requirements. The venture capitalists backing the startup expect the business to grow rapidly and have invested a significant amount of first-round funding. The web infrastructure is yet to be developed, so there are no legacy issues to consider. The one system admin who has been hired is proficient with Apache, but is somewhat familiar with Nginx.

SecureSphere   Imperva's SecureSphere is one of the market-leading WAFs. One of its distinctive features is *dynamic profiling,* which automatically learns protected applications' legitimate structure and behaviors, as well as the normal behaviors of their users.

Tool	Developer	OS/UI	Key Features	Pricing	Best For...
SecureSphere	Imperva	Appliance and cloud	Dynamic profiling and threat intelligence feeds	Commercial	Larger organizations
ModSecurity	Trustwave	BSD, Linux, and Windows	Integration with OWASP CRS and rule- and anomaly-based detection	Open source	Apache servers
NAXSI	NBS System	BSD and Linux	High performance, with a focus on whitelisting	Open source	Nginx servers and busy sites

Table 15-3   Comparison of Monitoring Tools

Taking a page from NGFWs, SecureSphere is able to exchange known threat sources and indicators of new attacks with a threat intelligence system in the cloud, which reduces the vulnerability to attacks and actors that have already been seen elsewhere. With an extensive feature set, the ability to learn normal and abnormal patterns, and a connection to threat intelligence resources, SecureSphere is arguably one of the most powerful WAFs in the market. This, however, comes with a price in the tens of thousands of dollars per appliance, which puts SecureSphere out of the reach of many smaller organizations.

Because the startup is well funded and the infrastructure is yet to be developed, this may be the right time to think long-term and make the investment in SecureSphere. Although it may be overkill in the early days of the company, it would support very rapid growth.

ModSecurity   ModSecurity is an open source toolkit for web application monitoring, logging, and control. It was originally developed as an Apache server module (hence the "Mod" part of the name), but has since been adapted to work with Microsoft Internet Information Server (IIS) as well as Nginx (though there are some issues and limitations). ModSecurity is able to leverage the Open Web Application Security Project (OWASP) Core Rule Set (CRS), which is a set of detection rules for the most common web application attacks. The CRS is specifically developed by OWASP for ModSecurity, though it also works with compatible WAFs. In addition to this traditional rule-based detection, ModSecurity is also able to aggregate multiple (less-critical) rule matches so that, collectively, they trigger a higher-level alert. This anomaly-based approach is meant to catch adversaries who go for small, incremental attacks that would otherwise not show up on an analyst's screen.

Because the system admin in the scenario is proficient with Apache, ModSecurity would provide a very low-cost solution that would not require specialized hardware, licenses, or additional hires. Apache with ModSecurity, however, may not be the best choice among the three systems we discuss in terms of performance for a rapidly growing business.

NAXSI   NAXSI stands for *Nginx Anti XSS and SQL Injection*, and XSS stands for *cross-site scripting*. As a related aside, Nginx is an open source web server developed specifically to outperform Apache in high-use environments. It follows that NAXSI also focuses on performance and does so by zeroing in on a relatively small rule set that reportedly identifies the features of 99 percent of known web application attacks. By taking some fairly draconian measures with these rules, NAXSI implements a "deny by default" policy. It is then up to the system administrator to create whitelists that will allow legitimate traffic through, while letting NAXSI drop everything else. Obviously, tuning a NAXSI implementation is critical, but this is facilitated by a semi-supervised self-learning feature that this WAF can use to automatically generate whitelists.

The system admin in the scenario would probably have a lot of learning to do in order to get a NAXSI solution up and running. Still, if funds are limited and performance during a rapid growth phase is important, this may be the best fit. It would probably be a bit more expensive than the Apache ModSecurity option, but it may also be able to better support a large customer base in the future.

Collective Tools

Even if our preventative tools are very effective at blocking the vast majority of the threats against our systems, we would still need to keep an eye on them (and the system at large) to ensure they were still effective in an ever-changing threat environment. In reality, our tools and other controls will fail more often than we'd like to admit. This underscores the importance of collecting information for point or historical analyses. Collective tools run the gamut from very focused command-line tools like the perennial ping to exceptionally complex security information and event management (SIEM) solutions.

Security Information and Event Management

Security information and event management (SIEM) systems are at least as much analytical as they are collective tools. All tools in this category perform four basic functions: collect, store, analyze, and report. Most of the collected information comes from various systems' logs, which are exported and sent to the SIEM system. The SIEM will then typically normalize the format of the data from these disparate sources so that they can be compared with each other. It then stores everything in a system that is optimized for quick retrieval, which is needed to analyze vast amounts of information. Whether the analysis is the result of a simple user query or the end product of sophisticated processes of correlation, SIEMs also have to produce a variety of reports for different purposes that range from internal lessons learned to regulatory compliance.

Tools

There are dozens of players in the SIEM marketplace, but for the purposes of the CSA+ exam, we focus on only six. These are highlighted in Table 15-4 and further described in the context of the scenario presented next.

Scenario

After a couple of (fairly) small security incidents, your mid-sized firm is ready to make an investment in more robust event management capabilities. As the senior cybersecurity analyst on staff, you are assigned the task of identifying and acquiring the best solution. You are not given a blank check but still have a reasonable amount of funds, so you don't have to go for a free solution. The timing is critical, since your forecasts call for significant growth in the next 18 months involving both new hires and a couple of small acquisitions. You do a lot of government work, so you don't have a big cloud presence (choosing to keep the data on premises instead), but this clientele also makes you a likely target for advanced persistent threats.

Unified Security Management Platform   The AlienVault Unified Security Management (USM) system is a proprietary extension of the Open Source Security Information Manager (OSSIM), which we discuss later. In addition to the OSSIM capabilities, USM includes data analytics and visualizations, log management, phone and e-mail support, documentation, a knowledgebase, and a full day of training. AlienVault also offers a subscription threat intelligence service in addition to the crowd-sourced Threat Exchange, which supports OSSIM and USM. All this is available as a virtual or

Tool	Developer	OS/UI	Key Features	License	Best For...
Unified Security Management Platform	AlienVault	Hardware or virtual appliance	Integration of SIEM, discovery, vulnerability assessment, and intrusion detection into one platform	Commercial	Big needs on tight budgets, AWS and Azure integration, and low cost
ArcSight	HP Enterprise	Hardware or virtual appliance	Third-party integration, high degree of customization, and event correlation	Commercial	Midsized or larger organizations needing full incident investigation support
Kiwi Syslog	SolarWinds	Windows	Centralized monitoring/ storing of syslog, Windows events, and SNMP traps	Commercial	System event and SNMP monitoring and compliance
OSSIM	AlienVault	Virtual appliance	Integration of SIEM, discovery, vulnerability assessment, and intrusion detection into one platform	Open source	Big needs but no budget
QRadar	IBM	Hardware or virtual appliance, IaaS	Correlation of NetFlow and log events	Commercial	Scalability and availability
Security Intelligence Platform	Splunk	Hardware or virtual appliance, SaaS	Machine learning as well as diverse log file searching and analysis	Commercial	Diverse data sources and sophisticated analysis

Table 15-4 Comparison of SIEM Offerings

hardware appliance either on premises or tightly integrated into Amazon Web Services (AWS), with well-regarded customer service.

Because the scenario specifies that you don't have much in the way of SIEM capabilities, a product like USM would allow you to pack a lot of punch for a fairly small amount of money. The threat intelligence service subscription could also help mitigate the threat from APTs, particularly with the sophisticated analysis and reporting features in this product.

ArcSight With three distinct but related platforms, ArcSight has something for medium- to large-sized organizations. Among its distinctive features is the maturity of its correlation and analytics engine. Multiple optional modules for specialized feature sets such as user behavior analytics (UBA) and DNS malware analytics provide additional functionality only for those who want it. One of the features that differentiates ArcSight from other SIEMs (as of this writing) is an open architecture that facilitates its integration with most other security solutions. This is evident in the way it can either do its own data analytics or interface with other systems such as Hadoop and Kafka to feed third-party big data platforms.

ArcSight is one of the most respected platforms on the market, so you couldn't go wrong in selecting it in this scenario. The optional modules would provide you a nice growth path, even though the base product provides a robust set of features. Additionally, if your organization grows to the point of being able to leverage big data analytics, ArcSight would integrate very well with the most common solutions in that space.

Kiwi Syslog   Kiwi Syslog is a tool developed by SolarWinds to monitor, archive, and alert on syslog events. Technically, it is not a SIEM, though it does share some basic features with this class of tools (for example, prioritizing and alerting on messages). Kiwi is really meant to help monitor performance and for regulatory compliance issues, but these can also help identify compromises, which is the reason CompTIA lumped it in with the SIEMs. Realistically, though, Kiwi would be insufficient as a standalone SIEM.

There is nothing in the scenario that specifically calls out Kiwi Syslog as a good solution. Still, if your main challenge were the integration of log files from both Linux and Windows systems, this could be part of the solution.

OSSIM   The Open Source Security Information Manager (OSSIM) is an integrated collection of components rather than a monolithic product. OSSIM was started in 2003, and five years later became the basis for the commercial product AlienVault, described previously. It includes the Open Vulnerability Assessment System (OpenVAS) for vulnerability assessment, Suricata for network-based intrusion detection, OSSEC for host-based intrusion detection, as well as file integrity monitoring and more. The multitude of open source tools are coherently integrated into a unified web-based interface with wizards to walk you through common setups, as shown in Figure 15-2. OSSIM is distributed as an ISO that can be installed on a virtual or physical host. These hosts can participate in the Open Threat Exchange, which is a crowd-sourced IP reputation service that allows OSSIM systems to share information about known or suspected malicious addresses.

You already saw how AlienVault's USM would be a good fit for the scenario. If your budget was limited, or if you preferred to invest in workforce development in addition to platform acquisition, then OSSIM could be a good fit. The money you save by choosing this free platform could be invested in training for your staff, which could give you a better fit, depending on the specific requirements.

QRadar   IBM's QRadar stands out from other SIEMs in its ability to integrate Net-Flows, packet captures, and event logs in support of incident response. Rather than only tracking events (which could become incidents), this system tracks "offenses," which are correlated events that are more likely to be indicative of a security compromise. Analysts examining an offense can then see all the network and log data supporting it, all the

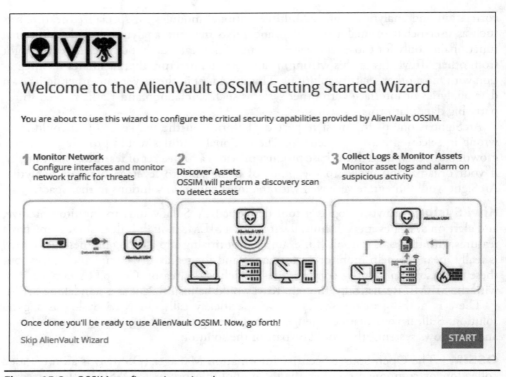

Figure 15-2   OSSIM configuration wizard

affected hosts, and all relevant vulnerabilities. Another distinctive feature of QRadar is its ability to automatically start acquiring forensic data and/or start an event ticket.

QRadar would be a good fit in the scenario if you needed tight integration between your SIEM and your response processes. In particular, if your responses typically involve network captures or NetFlow data that had to be correlated with event logs, then this would likely be your best choice provided you could afford it. Because the scenario doesn't spell out this requirement, you would have to dig a bit deeper before making the decision.

Security Intelligence Platform   Splunk is probably the best-known name in the SIEM market. Its Security Intelligence Platform (SIP) comprises two products: Splunk Enterprise and Splunk Enterprise Security. The former provides event and log collection, indexing, and analysis, whereas the latter has the traditional SIEM features that make that data actionable. Splunk started off as a log file analysis engine that grew up into a SIEM, which explains why it shines in the first role but faces stiff competition in the second role. In fact, if you are looking for advanced event correlation, other platforms may provide better products and require less effort. Like ArcSight, SIP is also able to provide user behavior analysis (UBA), which is very useful for advanced threat monitoring.

There is nothing in the scenario that makes SIP stand out as an obvious choice, so it would boil down to the best cost for the basic capabilities you need. Splunk is very competitive with other solutions, so you would have to specify your requirements and get quotes from multiple vendors. You could then compare the features and costs and choose the right platform based on those criteria.

Network Scanning

Network scanning is the interrogation of a set of hosts for specific information. A horizontal network scan, for instance, sends messages to a set of host addresses asking the question, "Are you there?" Its goal is to determine which addresses correspond to active (responding) systems. A vertical scan, on the other hand, sends messages to a set of protocol/port combinations (for example, UDP 53 or TCP 25) asking the same question, with the goal of determining which ports are listening for client connection attempts. It is also possible to combine both horizontal and vertical scans, as shown in Figure 15-3. The point of a network scan of any flavor is to find out who is listening (and responding) on a network. This is useful in finding systems that are not behaving as they ought to.

Consider the case in which a software development team sets up a test web server to ensure the web app on which the team members are working is functioning properly.

Figure 15-3 Nmap performing both horizontal and vertical scans

There is no malice, but not knowing that this server is running (and how) could seriously compromise the integrity of the defenses. On the other hand, we can sometimes find evidence that a host has been compromised and is now running a malicious service. Though these situations should be rare in a well-managed network, scanning is one of the quintessential skills of any security professional because it is one of very few ways to really know and map what is on our networks.

Nmap

Nmap is a tool that is synonymous with network scanning. The name is shorthand for "network mapper," which is an apt description of what it does. Nmap works by sending specially crafted messages to the target hosts and then examining the responses. This not only can tell which are active on the network and which of their ports are listening, but it can also help us determine the operating system, hostname, and even patch level of some systems. Though it is a command-line interface (CLI) tool, a number of front ends provide a graphical user interface (GUI), including Zenmap (Windows), NmapFE (Linux), and XNmap (Mac OS).

Packet Capture

The original commercial tool for capturing packets was the Network General Sniffer developed in the late 1980s, which forever changed the way we observe and analyze our networks by allowing us to capture real-time data. We introduced packet capture in Chapters 1 and 2, but we return to the topic here to address when and how you might want to use the various tools available. Apart from their usefulness for troubleshooting and incident response, sniffers are commonly used for logging and auditing purposes. Some organizations with particularly sensitive data (for example, financial and military) perform full packet captures of *all* traffic in some of their networks. We will not get into this big data analytics use case and will instead focus on more common uses for network packet captures (see Table 15-5).

Tools

Tool	Developer	OS/UI	Key Features	License	Best For...
Wireshark	The Wireshark Team	BSD, Linux, Mac OS, and Windows	GUI or CLI as well as powerful capture and display filters	Open source	Graphical analysis
tcpdump	tcpdump.org	BSD, Linux, and Mac OS	Standard in many OS distributions and offers powerful capture filters	Open source	Impromptu captures on non-Windows hosts
Aircrack-ng	Thomas d'Otreppe de Bouvette	BSD, Linux, Mac OS, and Windows	Cracks WEP keys as well as dictionary attacks on WPA/WPA2-PSK keys	Open source	Wireless network analysis

Table 15-5 Comparison of Packet Capture Offerings

Scenario

You are investigating suspicious NetFlow data involving your Domain Name System (DNS) server. Neither your firewalls nor your SIEM are set up to capture full packets, which you think will be needed in order to get to the bottom of this. By connecting to the switch port analyzer (SPAN) port on the right switch and capturing only port 53 traffic to/from your DNS server, you estimate that the amount of packets will not be too large for manual analysis. You do, however, want to save the packet captures for future reference, analysis, or evidentiary use.

Wireshark Wireshark is probably the most widely used, GUI-based packet analyzer. Despite the many advantages of using its graphical front end, it is important to note that it includes a CLI capability called TShark, which is useful when you can't get to a GUI (for example, when connecting over SSH) or when you want to script a packet capture. Whether you capture the traffic through the GUI or CLI, you can save it and view it on GUI later. You can similarly view captures from other tools (such as tcpdump) provided they were saved in the packet capture (PCAP) file format. Figure 15-4 shows a typical capture, whereas Figure 15-5 shows how you can drill into a specific packet to get a detailed view that includes the payload.

Because the scenario is not specific as to the interface you'd be using, this ability to do deep analysis of the packets on a graphical front end would make Wireshark a good choice. The scenario is also generic concerning the platform you'd be using to capture

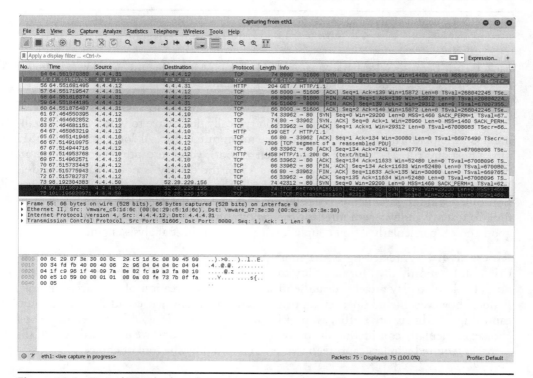

Figure 15-4 Typical Wireshark packet capture

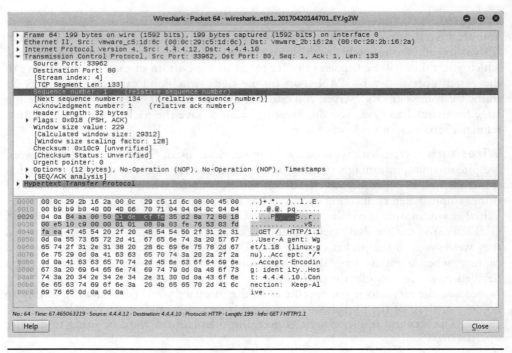

Figure 15-5 Wireshark showing packet details

packets, but because Wireshark runs on BSD, Linux, Mac OS, and Windows, it would be a feasible choice regardless of the operating system.

Tcpdump Tcpdump is a CLI tool that comes standard in many distributions of BSD, Linux, and Mac OS, which means you typically don't have to worry about installing it on the platform from which you'd like to capture traffic. As long as you can SSH into a host and run as a privileged user (such as root), you can capture packets on most non-Windows systems. As shown on Figure 15-6, the display is not as easy to read as Wireshark's, but the information captured can be the same. There is also a Windows version called windump, which is typically not installed by default. Unless you were planning to use a Windows computer for the capture in the scenario, tcpdump would be a good choice, particularly if you couple it with a more robust analysis engine.

Aircrack-ng Aircrack-ng is the most popular open source wireless network security tool. It's mostly used for its ability to audit the security of WLANs through attacks on WPA keys, replay attacks, deauthentication, and the creation of fake access points. It does, however, include packet capture functionality. Also, it could be coerced into capturing wired network traffic, as specified in the scenario. It would not be a very good choice, particularly considering the power of the other two tools we discussed here. If the scenario required wireless capture, however, this would be the tool of choice.

Figure 15-6 Typical tcpdump packet capture

Command-line Utilities

This section is a catch-all for some of the myriad CLI tools that every cybersecurity analyst must know how to use. They are all very narrowly focused, but absolutely essential under the right situations. If you are unfamiliar with any of these, you really should spend some time working with them not just for the CSA+ exam, but more importantly in order to do your job well.

Netstat   The netstat utility provides a wealth of information on the status of network connections and listening sockets. This is probably the most common use of this tool. It can also show interface statistics. Both of these features are shown in Figure 15-7. It can also provide protocol statistics such as for IP and ICMP, as you can see in Figure 15-8. Netstat is part of the default installation of almost every Linux, Mac OS, and Windows system, though some specific options are slightly different in Windows.

Ping   The ping utility simply sends four (Windows) or continuous (other OS's) Internet Control Message Protocol (ICMP) echo requests to whichever host you indicate. If the target host is configured to respond to these, it will send back an ICMP echo reply message for each message received. Ping will compare the time at which it sent the request with the time at which it received the response and then provide a total (round-trip) time for the exchange. These round-trip times can provide indicators of latency and jitter to/from that target.

Traceroute   The traceroute utility (for BSD, Linux, and Mac OS) and its Windows sibling tracert take advantage of the time to live (TTL) field in an IP packet on which an ICMP echo request is transmitted. Traceroute works by incrementing the TTL (starting with 1) in a sequence of messages to the same host. The way IP works, a receiving host will first decrement the TTL of an arriving packet. If that new value is greater than

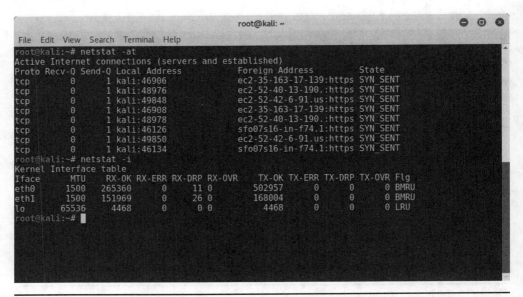

Figure 15-7 Netstat showing TCP connections, listening ports, and interface statistics

zero, the host will process the packet normally. Otherwise, it will send an ICMP "time exceeded" message to the source address. By incrementing the TTL, traceroute forces each consecutive host between the source and the ultimate destination to reveal its IP address. It is worth noting that IP packets are not guaranteed to follow the same route every time, so traceroute can return inconsistent results.

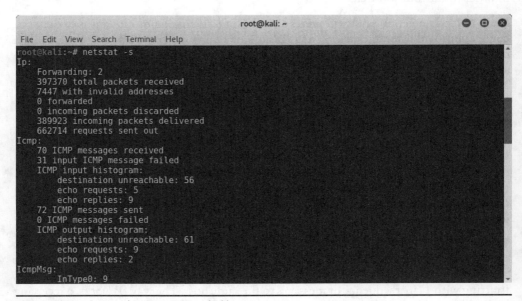

Figure 15-8 Protocol statistics provided by netstat

Ifconfig   One of the basic parameters we oftentimes need is the IP address of whichever host we are examining. The ifconfig utility (for BSD, Linux, and Mac OS) and ipconfig command (Windows) provide that information together with other IP parameters such as netmask, default gateway, and MAC address. The major difference between the two is that ifconfig allows you to configure the interfaces rather than just seeing what their parameters are. Still, most of the time we don't reconfigure interfaces during cybersecurity analysis or incident response, so they serve the same purpose in the context of the CSA+ exam.

Nslookup   The name server lookup, or nslookup, utility can be thought of as the user interface of the DNS. It allows us to resolve the IP address corresponding to a fully qualified domain name (FQDN) of a host. Depending on the situation, it is also possible to do the inverse (that is, resolve the IP address of an FQDN). The tool allows for the specification of a DNS server to be used, or it can use the system default. Lastly, it is possible to fully interrogate the target server and obtain other record data, such as MX (e-mail) and CNAME (canonical name).

OpenSSL   OpenSSL is an open source software library that allows software systems to communicate securely. Despite its name, it includes both Secure Sockets Layer (SSL) and Transport Layer Security (TLS) functionality. This library includes a command-line interface that provides the following functionality.

- Generate and validate certificates.
- Generate, sign, and verify MD5 and SHA hashes.
- Encrypt and decrypt data.
- Establish secure connections to remote servers.

Sysinternals Suite

One of the notable differences between Windows and BSD/Unix-like systems is that the former seems to have been built from the ground up thinking of the end user, whereas the latter systems appear to have been built with the superuser in mind. For many years, Windows system administrators were at a disadvantage when it came to built-in tools—that is, until the folks at Sysinternals (now owned by Microsoft) came to the rescue with multiple powerful tools for superusers. The suite includes 69 tools, but here are some of the most useful for a cybersecurity analyst:

- **Process Explorer**   Provides an abundance of information about all processes, including how much memory and CPU they use, who/what started, the origin, and even the VirusTotal score

- **Autoruns**   Allows you to quickly determine which programs are configured to start up automatically when the system is started or users log on, as well as to disable autoruns

- **Process Monitor**   Provides detailed information on the specific resources that a process owns or is using, including registry keys, DLLs, files, and other processes

Analytical Tools

The next class of tools is focused on comparing observations with reference information in order to analyze the performance of a system. Although it could be argued that SIEMs and other tools belong in this class, CompTIA tried to classify tools by their principal set of features. As tools develop, the lines frequently blur, making this effort much more difficult. You should not be too concerned about the name of the class to which a tool is assigned, but rather about the situations under which that tool would best be used.

Vulnerability Scanning

Knowing what your network looks like from the adversary's point of view is the first step in defense. Vulnerability scanning provides insight into what your network looks like and identifies weaknesses of these systems. Modern vulnerability scanners can identify software flaws and misconfigurations as well as suggest countermeasures or compensating controls. To demonstrate the features of some of the more popular vulnerability scanning tools, we'll consider a few scenarios and explore what each of these tools provides to solve our challenge. Note that while many of these tools are free for personal use, some require licenses for enterprise or business use.

Tools

The tools we discuss in this section range from cloud-based solutions for large enterprise networks to open source utilities for web app scanning. Table 15-6 provides a comparison of these tools.

Scenario

Your organization has experienced significant growth over the past few months and has recently hired its first chief information security officer (CISO). As she prepares suggestions for changes to the organization's information security policy, she wants to provide the rest of the leadership with a snapshot of the organization's network assets, including public-facing servers, endpoints, and data stores. She's interested in providing a short report for the company leadership, but wants a detailed follow-up plan for herself with technical details about each vulnerability and a plan for remediation. She notifies you that she wants this assessment conducted at least every two weeks, and would like the results automatically delivered to her inbox.

QualysGuard QualysGuard is a product of the California-based security company Qualys, an early player in the vulnerability management market. The company currently provides several cloud-based vulnerability assessment and management products through a Software as a Service (SaaS) model. For internal scans, a local virtual machine conducts the assessment and reports to the Qualys server. Figure 15-9 is a sample dashboard that shows various options under the vulnerability management module.

All network discovery, mapping, asset prioritization, scheduling, vulnerability assessment reporting, and remediation tracking tasks can be accessed via the web-based UI. The platform can generate detailed reports using several templates. Included in the default installation is a template called "Executive Report," which provides just the type

Tool	Developer	OS/UI	Type	Pricing	Best For...
QualysGuard	Qualys	Browser based	Cloud-based vulnerability scanning and management	Paid	Continuous monitoring of large networks
Nessus	Tenable	Browser based	Vulnerability scanner and manager	Paid	Continuous monitoring of large enterprises
OpenVAS	Greenbone Networks	Browser based	Vulnerability scanner and manager	Free	Continuous monitoring of large enterprises
Nexpose	Rapid7	Browser based	Vulnerability scanner and manager	Free Paid	Vulnerability identification and exploitation
Nikto	CIRT.net	Command line	Web server scanner	Free	Identifying web server flaws and misconfigurations
Microsoft Baseline Security Analyzer	Microsoft	Windows	Endpoint and server scanner	Free	Identifying missing security updates and misconfigurations in Windows environments

Table 15-6 Comparison of Vulnerability Scanning Tools

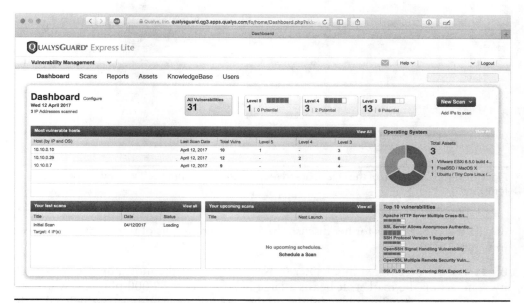

Figure 15-9 The QualysGuard dashboard for managing its cloud-based vulnerability assessment and management tasks

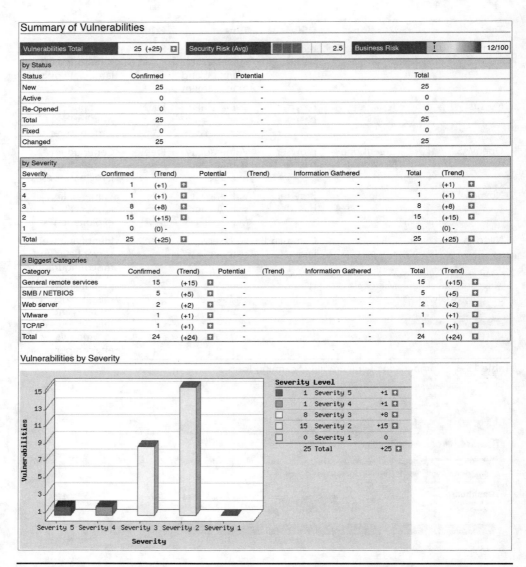

Figure 15-10 A portion of the QualysGuard report generated from the "Executive Report" template

of data the CISO needs for her discussion. A portion of results of this report can be seen in Figure 15-10.

Nessus   As we covered in Chapter 6, Nessus is one of the most popular vulnerability scanners on the market. It boasts a large library of over 80,000 plug-ins, which the platform uses to scan for vulnerabilities on the network on an ad-hoc or scheduled basis. Like QualysGuard, Nessus provides an easy way to configure assessments and view the

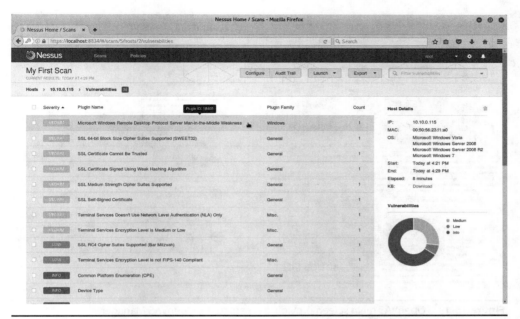

Figure 15-11 Listing of discovered vulnerabilities in the Nessus web interface

results through your favorite web browser. When Nessus discovers a vulnerability, it assigns a severity level to it in the scan results, as shown in Figure 15-11.

Technical details for each vulnerability, the method used in identifying it, and any database references can be found here. Nessus is particularly strong at assessing compliance using its library of "compliance checks." These compliance checks, or any other type of scan, can be scheduled to occur as desired, fulfilling the CISO's desire to automatically conduct periodic scans. As for reports, Nessus offers several export options, as shown in Figure 15-12.

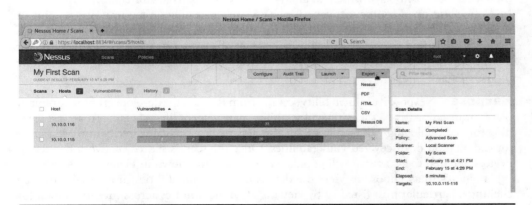

Figure 15-12 Nessus export options for report generation after vulnerability scan

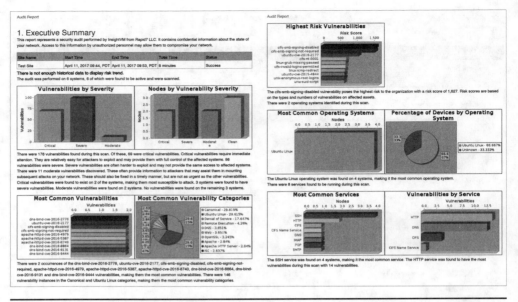

Figure 15-13 OpenVAS main screen providing access to the OpenVAS Manager

Nessus can generate reports that only list vulnerabilities with an associated exploit alongside suggested remediation steps. For an audience such as company leaders, explaining in plain language the concrete steps that may be taken to improve organizational security is key. Nessus provides these suggestions for individual hosts as well as for the network at large.

OpenVAS　OpenVAS, a fork of the initial Nessus project, is a widely used vulnerability scanner whose major benefit is its cost. OpenVAS uses a similar structure as Nessus to conduct its scans: the OpenVAS Manager is used to configure and access the OpenVAS Scanner, which schedules and runs the vulnerability scans. Figure 15-13 is an example of the OpenVAS dashboard, which an analyst accesses to manage vulnerability scans.

As free and open source software, OpenVAS relies heavily on community support in maintaining its library of nearly 50,000 network vulnerability tests (NVTs). Although the software is free, it doesn't offer the same level of support its paid alternatives do. For a large enterprise network, the price of on-demand customer support might justify the increased cost.

Nexpose　Nexpose is a vulnerability scanner from Rapid7, the developers of Metasploit. It places more emphasis on the entire vulnerability management lifecycle rather than just scanning for and cataloging vulnerabilities. It's also designed to integrate directly into Metasploit for exploitation of discovered vulnerabilities. Once the scan is started, network-connected devices, referred to as "assets," will populate the dashboard, shown in Figure 15-14.

An analyst may choose to view the details of the vulnerabilities discovered either by clicking a particular host listed or by viewing all vulnerabilities across the site to look for trends. Figure 15-15 shows the site-wide vulnerability charts, breaking all discoveries down by CVSS score.

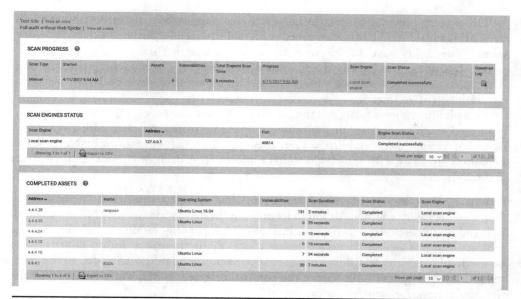

Figure 15-14 Nexpose Scan Progress screen

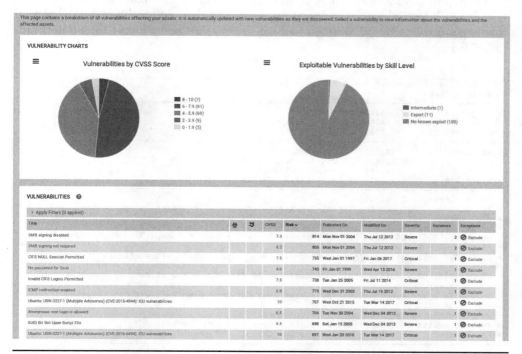

Figure 15-15 Nexpose discovered vulnerability overview and details screen

This system provides context to rate each vulnerability by how exploitable it might be. This is important because not every vulnerability has an associated exploit, nor does every vulnerability have a risk. For example, a resource that has no value cannot have a risk, so it doesn't necessarily make sense to devote energy to hardening that resource. This point must be considered when conducting risk assessments, especially in resource-constrained environments.

This platform allows for any of the previous screens to be exported, or a report may be generated. Each report contains a summary of the network, complete with an overview of both devices and vulnerabilities. The "Executive Summary" generated by Nexpose can be tailored to share with leadership to help inform their decisions about security policy and resourcing.

Nikto   Nikto, as you may remember from Chapter 6, is a command-line-based web server vulnerability scanner. Although its utility is limited to web servers, Nikto's strength is its speed in assessing the software vulnerabilities and configuration. As a command-line tool, it's also not as user friendly as other tools. Nikto requires at least a target host to be specified, with any additional options, such as nonstandard ports, added in the command line. In Figure 15-16, we see the command issued to perform a scan against the web team's new site, which operates on port 3780.

Nikto allows reports to be saved in a variety of ways, including HTML. An example of the HTML files can be found in Figure 15-17.

This report includes a summary of the command issued, information about the servers tested, and hyperlinks to the relevant resources and their vulnerability data. Although this is good for technical teams to act on, it may not be as useful for nontechnical decision-makers.

```
root@kali:~# nikto -host 4.4.4.28 -port 3780
- Nikto v2.1.6
---------------------------------------------------------------------
+ Target IP:          4.4.4.28
+ Target Hostname:    4.4.4.28
+ Target Port:        3780
---------------------------------------------------------------------
+ SSL Info:        Subject:  /CN=CompanyX/O=bl
                   Ciphers:  ECDHE-RSA-AES256-GCM-SHA384
                   Issuer:   /CN=CompanyX/O=bl
+ Start Time:        2017-04-10 12:14:28 (GMT-7)
---------------------------------------------------------------------
+ Server: Product Information
+ The site uses SSL and the Strict-Transport-Security HTTP header is not defined.
+ Root page / redirects to: https://4.4.4.28:3780/login.jsp
+ No CGI Directories found (use '-C all' to force check all possible dirs)
+ Hostname '4.4.4.28' does not match certificate's names: CompanyX
+ Allowed HTTP Methods: GET, HEAD, POST, PUT, DELETE, OPTIONS
+ OSVDB-397: HTTP method ('Allow' Header): 'PUT' method could allow clients to save files
on the web server.
+ OSVDB-5646: HTTP method ('Allow' Header): 'DELETE' may allow clients to remove files on
the web server.
+ OSVDB-67: /_vti_bin/shtml.dll/_vti_rpc: The anonymous FrontPage user is revealed through
a crafted POST.
+ /login.html: Admin login page/section found.
+ 7499 requests: 0 error(s) and 7 item(s) reported on remote host
+ End Time:          2017-04-10 12:20:26 (GMT-7) (358 seconds)
---------------------------------------------------------------------
+ 1 host(s) tested
```

Figure 15-16   Nikto command-line output for a test against a web server located at IP 4.4.4.28

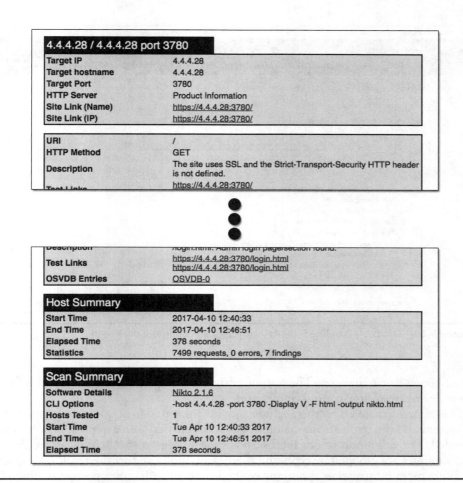

Figure 15-17 Nikto HTML output from a test against a web server located at IP 4.4.4.28

Microsoft Baseline Security Analyzer Microsoft provides a tool called the Baseline Security Analyzer to quickly identify missing security patches or software misconfigurations in Windows operating systems. Designed for use with Windows Vista, Windows XP, Windows 7, Windows 8, Windows Server 2003, Windows Server 2008, and Windows Server 2012, Baseline Security Analyzer is available as a small download directly from Microsoft. This tool is only useful for assessing Windows endpoints and servers, so if the organization is running anything else, this tool won't work on those platforms. Figure 15-18 shows the various options for starting a scan with this tool. You can scan for vulnerabilities related to passwords, server and database misconfigurations,

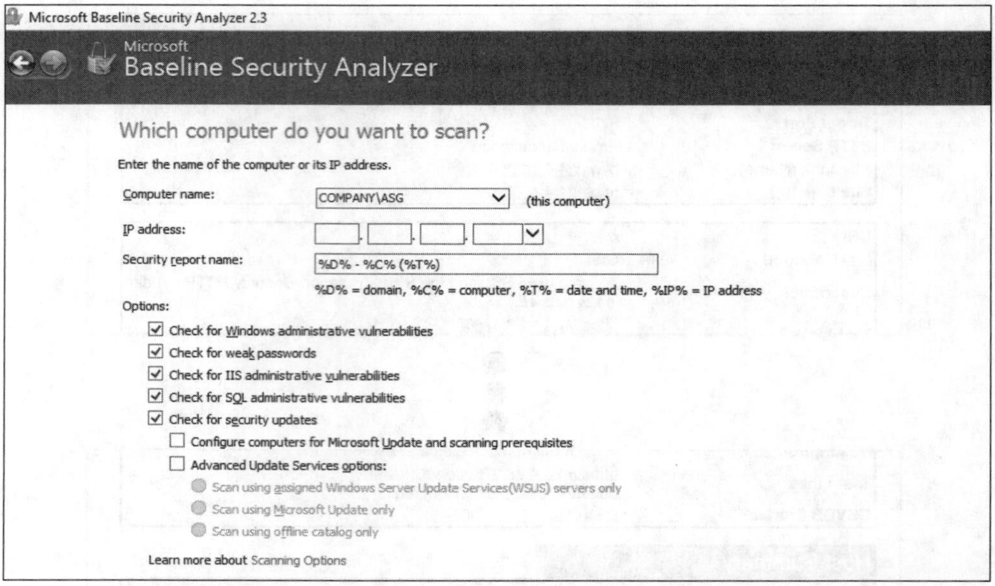

Figure 15-18 Microsoft Baseline Security Analyzer scan configuration screen

and missing security updates. The output of the resulting report can also be modified to suit your organization's naming conventions.

The reports generated by the analyzer provide information about what was tested on the system and the results from each test. For some entries, a link to possible solutions is provided. The full report of our local scan is show in Figure 15-19. You can see that the vulnerabilities are grouped by type, and there is an option to sort the result by impact.

To get more information about any of the issues, you click the appropriate link. The description is written in nontechnical language and often provides a note about the potential impact of the vulnerability.

Monitoring Tools

Network monitoring is a critical task toward understanding what's happening on the network. Whether through direct inspection of packet captures, watching for surges in traffic, or examining for unusual connections, monitoring give us the visibility on our network required to thwart attackers and improve usability.

Tools

In this section, we focus on software-based tools that gather network data to generate statistics and charts about the network. Table 15-7 provides a comparison of these monitoring tools.

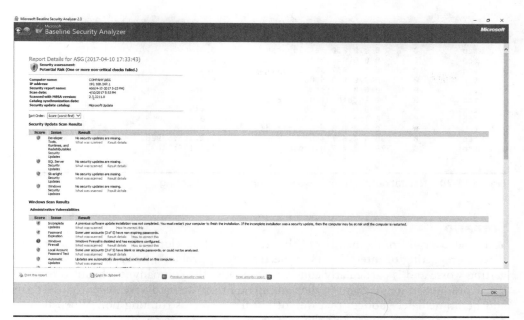

Figure 15-19　Microsoft Baseline Security Analyzer report detailing the completed scan

Tool	Developer	OS/UI	Type	Pricing	Best For...
MRTG	Tobi Oetiker	Windows, Linux, Mac, and Novell Netware	Network graphing	Free	Simple graphs
Nagios	Nagios	Browser based	Infrastructure monitoring and analytics	Free or Paid	Monitoring host resources, services, and network infrastructures
Orion	SolarWinds	Windows and Linux	Monitoring platform	Paid	Continuous monitoring of large enterprise networks
Cacti	The Cacti Group, Inc.	Browser based	Network graphing	Free	Detailed graphs
Netflow Analyzer	ManageEngine	Windows and Linux	Traffic monitoring and analytics	Paid	Gaining real-time visibility on traffic in large networks

Table 15-7　Comparison of Monitoring Tools

```
Active Internet connections (servers and established)
Proto Recv-Q Send-Q Local Address              Foreign Address        State
tcp       0      0 0.0.0.0:netbios-ssn          0.0.0.0:*              LISTEN
tcp       0      0 0.0.0.0:http                 0.0.0.0:*              LISTEN
tcp       0      0 4.4.4.7:50001                0.0.0.0:*              LISTEN
tcp       0      0 0.0.0.0:50002                0.0.0.0:*              LISTEN
tcp       0      0 0.0.0.0:ssh                  0.0.0.0:*              LISTEN
tcp       0      0 localhost:postgresql         0.0.0.0:*              LISTEN
tcp       0      0 0.0.0.0:https                0.0.0.0:*              LISTEN
tcp       0      0 localhost:4700               0.0.0.0:*              LISTEN
tcp       0      0 0.0.0.0:microsoft-ds         0.0.0.0:*              LISTEN
tcp       0     36 4.4.4.7:ssh                  10.10.1.165:53979      ESTABLISHED
tcp       0    379 4.4.4.7:microsoft-ds         10.10.1.165:54033      ESTABLISHED
```

Figure 15-20   Netstat output from fileserver during troubleshooting

Scenario

You receive a call from a member of the research and development group in your organization reporting of intermittent connectivity. The problem, he explains, seems to be getting worse and is particularly concerning because the company is scheduled to make a new product announcement in the coming months. You send a tech over to investigate and he immediately notices that one of the file servers is running hot. When he uses netstat on the server, he receives the output shown on Figure 15-20.

You notice a connection made from a foreign address that doesn't belong to the R&D subnet. You want to get more information about the types of connections made with this server and the total bandwidth consumed as part of your investigation and troubleshooting.

MRTG   The Multi Router Traffic Grapher (MRTG) is a cross-platform, network measuring tool that relies on Simple Network Management Protocol (SNMP) exchanges to produce graphs and statistics. Developed to be lightweight, the tool is written in Perl and offered as free software under the GNU General Public License. A sample graph is shown in Figure 15-21 of network traffic over several weeks.

MRTG is very fast and capable of storing traffic logs for years without appreciable increase in log storage requirements. Although the HTML output is convenient, it lacks the polished interface and correlation features offered by other network monitoring solutions.

Nagios   Nagios is a very popular monitoring and alerting platform that comes in two flavors: Nagios Core and Nagios XI. While both solutions provide monitoring and

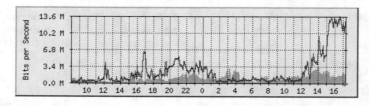

Figure 15-21   MRTG output graph of network traffic

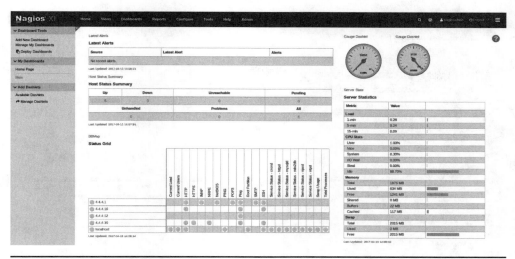

Figure 15-22 Nagios XI dashboard view of the network status

analytics capabilities for network infrastructure, Nagios Core is offered as an open source and no-cost solution. Nagios XI, on the other hand, requires an annual standard or enterprise license. Aside from the cost, the primary differences between the two options are in the reporting and interface options. Nagios XI allows for advanced configuration of the dashboards, graphs, and reports. Figure 15-22 is an example of a dashboard that provides quick access to network assets.

Details on each device are hyperlinked directly from the dashboard, so all historical information about the server in question is just a click away. Each host details screen, as shown in Figure 15-23, can be configured in the same manner as the dashboard to show the graphs and screens most relevant to your security team's needs.

Orion SolarWinds is a provider of several IT and network monitoring tools. The company began in 1999 as a developer of network performance monitoring software and has expanded to flow analysis, virtualization management, and server monitoring, each with advanced reporting options. Its main platform, Orion, provides the foundation for the entire SolarWinds suite of products. Performing protocol analysis to determine what kind of data is moving from nodes, for example, can be performed by the NetFlow Traffic Analyzer tool, which rides on the Orion framework.

Cacti Cacti is a free front end for the RRDTool, a network logging and graphing tool based on MRTG. Like MRTG, Cacti's strength is its speed in ingesting and visualizing logging data. Due to its low resource requirements, Cacti is a popular choice for web administrators who want to create quick graphs and statistics. Figure 15-24 is a display provided by the developers to highlight the precise control over graph timespans using the web interface.

Figure 15-23 Nagios XI host status details

NetFlow Analyzer ManageEngine's NetFlow Analyzer is an analysis tool for network traffic that relies on NetFlow data to give administrators a complete view of their network. In addition to performing basic bandwidth monitoring and service identification, NetFlow Analyzer also provides traffic-shaping features, which might be useful to identify and curb bandwidth abuse. Additionally, NetFlow Analyzer provides some network forensics and security-specific capabilities through an add-in module. In our scenario, you could use NetFlow Analyzer to quickly identify the server in question and whether other devices are exhibiting the same type of behavior.

Interception Proxy

For the propose of analysis, interception proxies provide extraordinary insight into user behavior because they sit in between the user and the requested resource. As an intermediary device, an interception proxy can be used in several ways to collect, modify, or block certain types of data.

Tools

Interception proxies are extremely flexible tools, capable of acting as proxies, scanners, fuzzers, and web crawlers. Table 15-8 details three of the more popular interception proxies in use today.

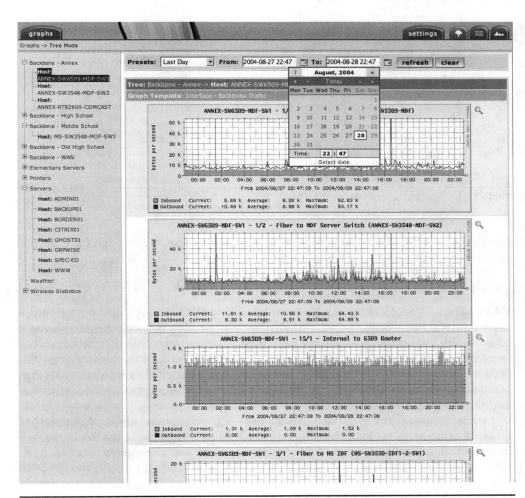

Figure 15-24 Cacti web interface showing the custom controls over timespans

Scenario

Your accounting team recently set up a new internal website to assist managers with their budgets. The website will provide managers with a snapshot of their current spending and feedback to help them plan future operations. The members of the accounting team are concerned about exposure of sensitive team financial data, so they've asked your help with letting them know what, if any, data might be visible to others and ways to correct it.

Burp Suite   Burp Suite is an integration web application testing platform. Often used to map and analyze a web application's vulnerabilities, Burp allows seamless use of automated and manual functions when finding and exploiting vulnerabilities. In proxy mode,

Tool	Developer	OS/UI	Type	Pricing	Best For...
Burp Suite	PortSwigger	Linux, Mac, and Windows	Web application testing	Free or Paid	Analysts who require feature-rich toolset for custom security testing
ZAP	OWASP	Linux, Mac, and Windows	Web application testing	Free	Web developers, penetration testers, and network and security engineers
Vega	Subgraph	Linux, Mac, and Windows	Web application testing	Free	Security analysts seeking automation and API availability

Table 15-8   Comparison of Interception Proxy Tools

Burp will allow the user to manually inspect every request passing through from the user to the server. The option to forward or drop the request is shown in Figure 15-25.

Although Burp is designed for a human to be in the decision loop, it does offer a point-and-click web-scanning feature in the paid version that might be useful for this scenario.

ZAP   The OWASP Zed Attack Proxy (ZAP) is one of OWASP's flagship projects due to its powerful features and popularity. ZAP uses its position between the user's browser and the web application to intercept and inspect user requests, modify the contents if required, and then forward them to a web server. This is exactly the same process that occurs during a man-in-the-middle attack. ZAP is also designed to be used by security practitioners at all levels. Figure 15-26 shows the results of an attack conducted with nothing more than a target specified.

In this example, ZAP rapidly fabricates a list of GET request using known directories and files to test the site. These locations should not be publically viewable, so the results here will inform an administrator of misconfigurations in the server and unexpected data exposure.

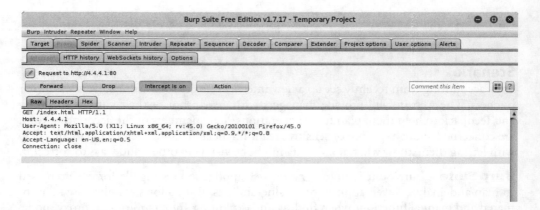

Figure 15-25   Burp Suite intercept screen and options in proxy mode

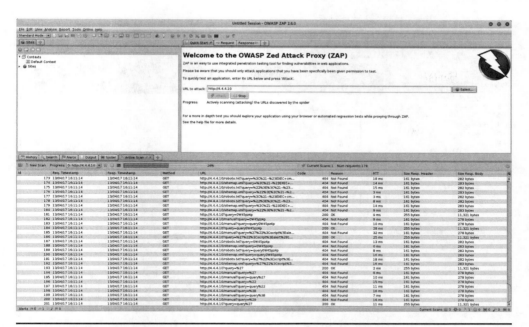

Figure 15-26 ZAP screen showing progress in active scanning attack

Vega Vega is another cross-platform interception proxy written in Java. It provides automated scanning, injection discovery, and cross-site scripting vulnerability discovery through its user interface or via an API. Usage is similar to ZAP in that a user can launch a quick attack by identifying a target. As with ZAP, the list of results will include a short description of the discovery, why it's important, and how best to remediate. An example of the information provided is shown in Figure 15-27.

Exploitative Tools

Not all vulnerabilities have exploits, but these software flaws open up the opportunity for clever programmers to bend the rules to gain unauthorized entry. *Exploit code* is code designed to take advantage of a software vulnerability to gain control over a system, access data, or prevent legitimate access to services through denial of service.

Exploitation Frameworks

Exploitation frameworks aim to provide security teams with the tools necessary to replicate attacks and validate vulnerabilities in order to prioritize security resources. Some of the more popular frameworks offer a range of penetration-testing options by providing easy access to well-known vulnerabilities, exploits, and security tools in an intuitive manner. Table 15-9 details two such frameworks: Metasploit and Nexpose.

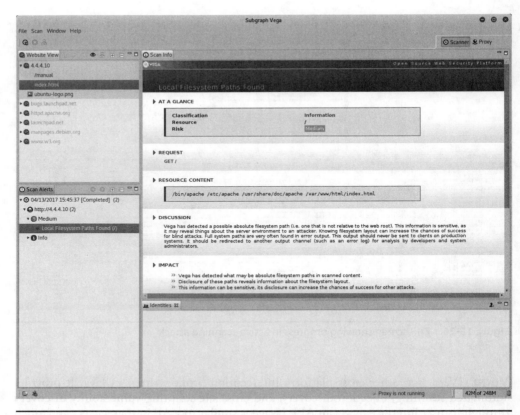

Figure 15-27 Vega reporting a possible vulnerability in an Apache web service

Tools

Tool	Developer	OS/UI	Type	Pricing	Best For...
Metasploit	Rapid7	Linux, Mac, and Windows	Exploitation framework	Free or Paid	Penetration testers and network security engineers
Nexpose	Rapid7	Browser based	Vulnerability scanner and manager	Free or Paid	Vulnerability identification and exploitation

Table 15-9 Comparison of Exploitation Frameworks

Scenario

After reading the vulnerability report you prepared a few weeks ago, your organization's CISO has a much better sense of the assets on the network and their associated vulnerabilities. She presented your findings to company leadership, which then provided feedback and additional requests for information. She calls you back into the office to discuss the next step. She believes that the best thing to do is to identify the most serious vulnerabilities and apply either the appropriate patches or compensating controls. Before beginning this process, however, you want to make sure the vulnerabilities actually exist and are actually able to be exploited.

Metasploit   Like many popular security tools, the Metasploit Framework began as an open source project and was later acquired and expanded to include paid options for commercial use. Initially developed under the larger Metasploit Project to develop and execute exploits against remote targets, the framework provides an easy way for security professionals to assess system vulnerabilities and determine exploitability. Although the Metasploit Framework itself is still free, Rapid7 offers several interfaces and professional options with a paid license. Every version ships with hundreds of exploits and payloads, referred to collectively as *modules,* which contain the relevant code and reference data. Figure 15-28 is a screenshot of the Metasploit command-line interface.

Figure 15-28   Metasploit welcome screen

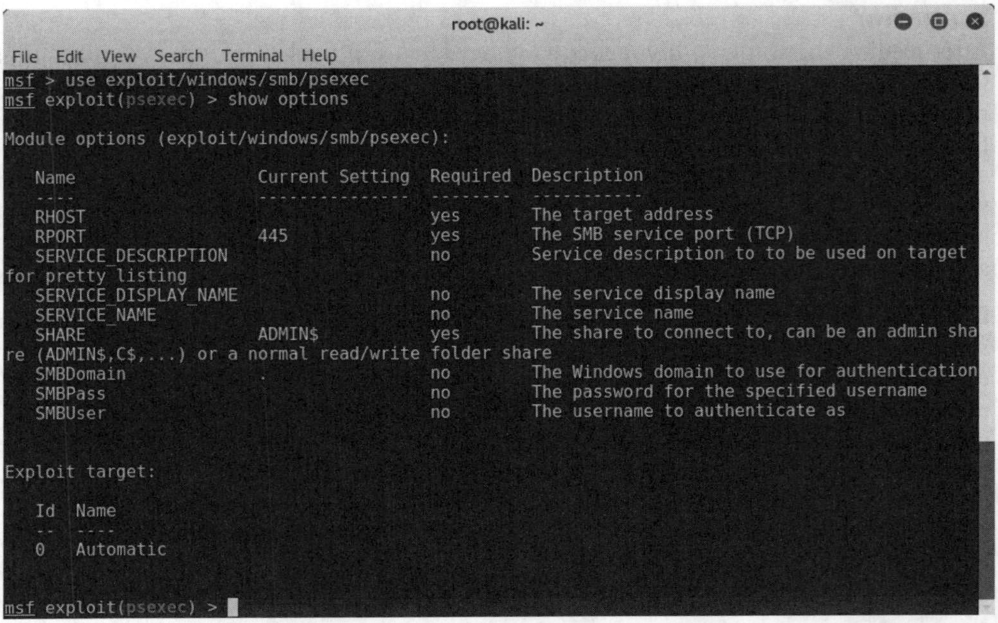

```
                              root@kali: ~                            ⊖ ▢ ✕
 File  Edit  View  Search  Terminal  Help
msf > use exploit/windows/smb/psexec
msf exploit(psexec) > show options

Module options (exploit/windows/smb/psexec):

   Name                  Current Setting  Required  Description
   ----                  ---------------  --------  -----------
   RHOST                                  yes       The target address
   RPORT                 445              yes       The SMB service port (TCP)
   SERVICE_DESCRIPTION                    no        Service description to to be used on target
for pretty listing
   SERVICE_DISPLAY_NAME                   no        The service display name
   SERVICE_NAME                           no        The service name
   SHARE                 ADMIN$           yes       The share to connect to, can be an admin sha
re (ADMIN$,C$,...) or a normal read/write folder share
   SMBDomain             .                no        The Windows domain to use for authentication
   SMBPass                                no        The password for the specified username
   SMBUser                                no        The username to authenticate as


Exploit target:

   Id  Name
   --  ----
   0   Automatic


msf exploit(psexec) >
```

Figure 15-29   Exploit selection command and options available for the module

Metasploit's main strength is the versatility it provides by way of its modular design. Exploits can be combined with payloads to take advantage of flaws and execute code in a single effort. Figure 15-29 shows an example in which a user selects the PSExec Exploit for use against a Windows operating system, along with the various options presented for its usage.

Nexpose   At its core, Nexpose is a vulnerability discovery and management tool. Because it integrates extremely well with Metasploit, it's a natural choice for security analysts wanting to pivot quickly from analysis to exploitation without leaving the interface. Using one of the commercial options of Metasploit, called Metasploit Pro, it's possible to connect to the Nexpose scan engine directly. Figure 15-30 shows a listing of vulnerabilities found during a routine scan, along with an indication of whether an exploit exists for that vulnerability. The Metasploit integration into Nexpose is useful in determining and prioritizing exploitable vulnerabilities on the network, while also reducing the burden of managing reports across the two systems.

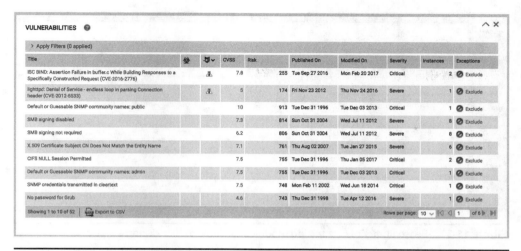

Figure 15-30 Nexpose vulnerabilities listing sorted by known exploits

Fuzzers

Software fuzzing is a technique used to discover software flaws by inputting random data into software to force instability or crashes. The resulting errors can often be traced back to the root cause by the fuzzing software for remediation and patching. Fuzzing is useful because programmers cannot always predict how their software will react given unexpected or malformed input. See Table 15-10 for a comparison of some fuzzers.

Tools

Tool	Developer	OS/UI	Type	Pricing	Best For...
Untidy	PortSwigger	Linux, Mac, and Windows	XML fuzzer	Free	Discovering vulnerabilities in web clients and servers
Peach Fuzzer	OWASP	Browser based	Automated fuzzing platform	Free or Paid	Fuzzing binaries, embedded systems, and IoT devices
Microsoft SDL fuzzers	Microsoft	Windows	Regex and file fuzzer	Free	Basic file and regular expression fuzzing capabilities

Table 15-10 Comparison of Fuzzers

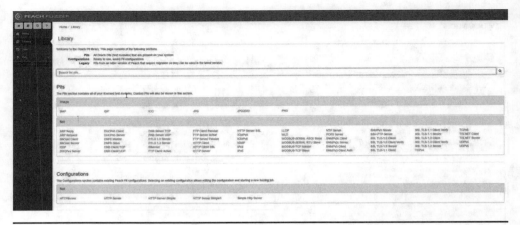

Figure 15-31   Peach library of fuzz testing modules available for use during a test

Scenario

Your human resources team recently developed a public-facing online feedback submission system and reached out to your team for suggestions on how to test it before going live. Because the app relies heavily on user input, the developers have taken steps to ensure that user input is sanitized before being executed and stored. However, they want an extra bit of assurance and want to fuzz-test the application, including URLs, forms, and any user-generated content.

Untidy   Untidy is a popular Extensible Markup Language (XML) fuzzer. Used to test web application clients and servers, untidy takes valid XML and modifies it before inputting it into the application. The untidy fuzzer is now part of the Peach Fuzzer project.

Peach Fuzzer   The Peach Fuzzer is a powerful fuzzing suite that's capable of testing a wide range of targets. Peach uses XML-based modules, called *pits,* to provide all the information needed to run the fuzz. These modules are configurable based on the testing needs. Before conducting a fuzz test, the user must specify the type of test, the target, and any monitoring settings desired. Figure 15-31 is a short listing of the pits available for image file and network protocol fuzzing.

Microsoft SDL Fuzzers   As part of its Security Development Lifecycle (SDL) toolset, Microsoft released two types of standalone fuzzers designed to be used in the verification phase of the SDL: the Minifuzz file fuzzer and the Regex Fuzzer. However, Microsoft has dropped support and no longer provides these applications for download. Figure 15-32 shows the setup screen for the SDL Regex Fuzzer.

Forensic Tools

Forensics in the real world is all about the application of the scientific method to investigate the circumstances of a crime. It relies heavily on the collection, preservation, and analysis of evidence such as fingerprints, DNA, and other artifacts to build the best

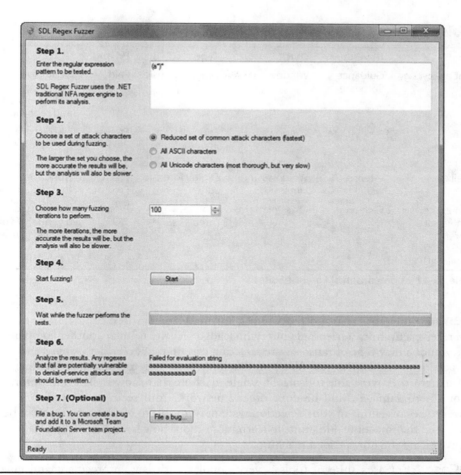

Figure 15-32   Setup screen for the Microsoft Security Development Lifecycle (SDL) Regex Fuzzer

picture possible of what happened. Digital forensics, as a branch of forensic science, relies on the same principles of discovery to build a timeline of what happened on our systems during a suspected attack.

Forensic Suites

Reconstructing what happened after the fact is inherently a difficult task, but we have many tools at our disposal to assist with this process. Forensic suites include a range of tools to uncover data thought to be lost, or data that might be lost easily, such as in the case of volatile memory. Because documentation is an important part of forensics, particularly in criminal investigations, some suites automatically document the evidence analysis progression. Table 15-11 details some of the most popular forensic suites available today.

Tools

Tool	Developer	OS/UI	Type	Pricing	Best For...
EnCase	Guidance Software	Windows	Digital forensic suite	Paid	Digital forensics collection as well as analysis and reporting
FTK	AccessData	Windows	Forensic imaging suite	Free or Paid	File discovery and volume replication
Helix	e-fense	Windows and Linux	Digital forensic suite	Free or Paid	Nondestructive forensic analysis
Cellebrite Universal Forensic Extraction Device (UFED)	Cellebrite	Cross-platform	Mobile forensic suite	Paid	Data extraction and analysis of mobile devices

Table 15-11   Comparison of Forensic Suites

Scenario

You receive a tip from a friend of yours who leads a security team at another company. He tells you of a new type of ransomware affecting certain types of older systems and shares the pertinent details with you. You pass this information on to your team members and, fortunately, they were able to isolate a single machine that showed signs of compromise before more damage could be done on the network. Your security chief is concerned, however, because none of your detection systems were able to identify the malware before it infected that machine. He wants to learn more about how it happened, so he sends you to investigate the quarantined machine.

EnCase   EnCase's suite of tools is very popular with law enforcement and government for forensics missions because of its easy-to-use GUI and chain-of-custody features. The EnCase suite include tools for forensic acquisition, analysis, and report generation. EnCase's Evidence File format is among the most common types of forensic imaging formats, due in part to its high portability. The imaged volume's data, metadata, and hashes are all included in a single file.

FTK   AccessData's Forensic Toolkit, or FTK, is a popular choice for investigators needing to create forensic images of hard drives. FTK is a favorite for forensics analysis because of its built-in logging features, making the process of documentation easier for investigators looking to preserve details of the analysis itself. One of the more popular tools included in the FTK suite is the FTK Imager, a data preview and volume imaging tool.

Helix   Helix3 Pro is the latest multiplatform forensic suite offered by e-fense. Based on the open source Knoppix live boot utility, Helix allows analysts to fully image all internal devices, including physical memory and hard disks. The program also includes utilities for mobile device analysis, offering the same nondestructive imaging features.

Cellebrite   Cellebrite is a company that developed data transfer solutions for mobile carriers and has since moved into the mobile forensics market. Its flagship product, the Universal Forensic Extraction Device (UFED), is a handheld hardware device primarily marketed to law enforcement and military communities. With the UFED, a user can extract encrypted, deleted, or hidden data from select mobile phones. Cellebrite also provides evidence preservation using techniques such as write blocking during the data extraction procedure.

Hashing

Hashing is a common technique used to verify the integrity of files by creating a small unique value of fixed size, regardless of the size of the original file. Much like placing tamper-evident tape before sending out a shipment, a hash value aims to make it obvious if the contents of a file are changed. Hashing functions rely on the concept that no two files should have the same message digest, also referred to as *fingerprints*.

Tools

There are really only two cryptographic hashing algorithms in widespread use today: MD5 and the various flavors of SHA. Of these, MD5 and SHA-1 are known to be vulnerable to attacks. Still, they remain (for now) popular. The two tools with which you need to be familiar as a cybersecurity analyst are md5sum and shasum (see Table 15-12).

Scenario

One of your junior database analysts recently completed a rollout of new database software. Every night, he backs up the entire database to an offsite location and wants to know if there is a quick way to verify the integrity of the backup files. Ideally, he wants to perform the computation immediately after completing the backup and to do so directly from the command line.

md5sum   Included with nearly every variant of Linux is the md5sum program, a simple utility that computes the 128-bit MD5 hash for a file specified. Although an MD5 is more reliable than a simple cyclic redundancy check (CDC) for verifying file integrity, its usage is no longer recommended because researchers have discovered methods to modify file content without resulting in a change to the MD5 hash. Taking a look at Figure 15-33, we can see that the md5sum utility is invoked from the command line, with the file location specified immediately after the command. The resulting output is the 128-bit MD5 fingerprint of the file.

Tool	Developer	OS/UI	Type	Pricing	Best For...
md5sum	Ulrich Drepper, Scott Miller, and David Madore	Linux, Mac, and Windows	MD5 message digest	Free	Generating MD5 message digests
shasum	Mark Shelor	Linux, Mac, and Windows	SHA message digest	Free	Generating SHA message digests

Table 15-12   Comparison of Hashing Tools

```
                              root@kali: ~/hash                        ─  □  ✕
 File  Edit  View  Search  Terminal  Help
root@kali:~/hash# ls -la
total 16
drwxr-xr-x  2 root root 4096 Apr 20 15:36 .
drwxr-xr-x 35 root root 4096 Apr 20 15:34 ..
-rw-r--r--  1 root root    6 Apr 20 15:34 a.txt
-rw-r--r--  1 root root    6 Apr 20 15:36 b.txt
root@kali:~/hash# more a.txt
aaaaa
root@kali:~/hash# more b.txt
aabaa
root@kali:~/hash# md5sum a.txt
4c850c5b3b2756e67a91bad8e046ddac  a.txt
root@kali:~/hash# md5sum b.txt
c971d4c90b90223534cab45404870c15  b.txt
root@kali:~/hash#
```

Figure 15-33   The md5sum utility in the command line

shasum   The shasum utility was created as a quick way to generate SHA hashes from files. Like md5sum, the utility calculates message digests directly from the command line and inputs them to the standard output. Figure 15-34 shows two files, a.txt and b.txt, and their associated hashes as the output of each command. Using no options, the program will calculate the 160-bit SHA-1 message digest. Using the **-a** option, we can specify a different algorithm altogether.

NOTE   In early 2017, a team of Google security researchers announced that they had successfully demonstrated a practical attack on the SHA-1 algorithm by generating two different PDF files with the same hash. The collision attack, dubbed "SHAttered," showed that with enough computation power, an attacker could compromise the algorithm that underpins many digital signatures, digital certificates, and file integrity verification processes.

Password Cracking

A common target for attackers is the operating system password file. In Windows, the Security Accounts Manager (SAM) file is the database of user passwords. In modern Linux environments, the user information is stored in the /etc/passwd file, and the password hashes are stored in the /etc/shadow file. As you can imagine, these files are protected by the system using various cryptographic methods. However, it's still possible to break into these files given the right tools.

Figure 15-34 The shasum utility in the command line

Tools

The two most popular password-cracking tools among security professionals are John the Ripper, and Cain and Abel. Though their feature sets are very similar, there are subtle differences with which you may want to become acquainted (see Table 15-13).

John the Ripper   John the Ripper is an open source password-cracking tool, initially developed for UNIX, that now has variations for many other operating systems. Figure 15-35 shows options for usage with the command-line tool. John runs attacks with wordlists, which reference a precompiled list of possible passwords, or by brute force, which tries many possible combinations in the character space. Additionally, John supports auto-detection of password hash types, the protective measure used by operation systems to prevent unauthorized viewing of the password file. The commercial version of John expands on the already impressive selection of hashes supported.

Tool	Developer	OS/UI	Type	Pricing	Best For...
John the Ripper	Alexander Peslyak	Linux, Mac, and Windows	Password recovery tool	Free or Paid	Custom password cracking
Cain and Abel	Massimiliano Montoro	Windows	Password recovery tool	Free	Dictionary, brute force, and cryptanalysis attacks

Table 15-13 Comparison of Password Crackers

```
                                    root@kali: ~                              ⊖ ⊙ ⊗
 File  Edit  View  Search  Terminal  Help
root@kali:~# john
John the Ripper password cracker, version 1.8.0.6-jumbo-1-bleeding [linux-x86-64-avx]
Copyright (c) 1996-2015 by Solar Designer and others
Homepage: http://www.openwall.com/john/

Usage: john [OPTIONS] [PASSWORD-FILES]
--single[=SECTION]          "single crack" mode
--wordlist[=FILE] --stdin   wordlist mode, read words from FILE or stdin
                  --pipe    like --stdin, but bulk reads, and allows rules
--loopback[=FILE]           like --wordlist, but fetch words from a .pot file
--dupe-suppression          suppress all dupes in wordlist (and force preload)
--prince[=FILE]             PRINCE mode, read words from FILE
--encoding=NAME             input encoding (eg. UTF-8, ISO-8859-1). See also
                            doc/ENCODING and --list=hidden-options.
--rules[=SECTION]           enable word mangling rules for wordlist modes
--incremental[=MODE]        "incremental" mode [using section MODE]
--mask=MASK                 mask mode using MASK
--markov[=OPTIONS]          "Markov" mode (see doc/MARKOV)
--external=MODE             external mode or word filter
--stdout[=LENGTH]           just output candidate passwords [cut at LENGTH]
--restore[=NAME]            restore an interrupted session [called NAME]
--session=NAME              give a new session the NAME
--status[=NAME]             print status of a session [called NAME]
--make-charset=FILE         make a charset file. It will be overwritten
--show[=LEFT]               show cracked passwords [if =LEFT, then uncracked]
--test[=TIME]               run tests and benchmarks for TIME seconds each
--users=[-]LOGIN|UID[,..]   [do not] load this (these) user(s) only
--groups=[-]GID[,..]        load users [not] of this (these) group(s) only
--shells=[-]SHELL[,..]      load users with[out] this (these) shell(s) only
--salts=[-]COUNT[:MAX]      load salts with[out] COUNT [to MAX] hashes
--save-memory=LEVEL         enable memory saving, at LEVEL 1..3
--node=MIN[-MAX]/TOTAL      this node's number range out of TOTAL count
--fork=N                    fork N processes
--pot=NAME                  pot file to use
--list=WHAT                 list capabilities, see --list=help or doc/OPTIONS
--format=NAME               force hash of type NAME. The supported formats can
                            be seen with --list=formats and --list=subformats
root@kali:~#
```

Figure 15-35   The John the Ripper utility in the command line

Cain and Abel   Cain and Abel is a Windows password-cracking tool that can operate on sniffed network traffic or locally acquired password hashes. Note that Cain isn't
officially supported for operating systems newer than Windows Vista, and its use with
those modern systems might require workarounds. Like John, Cain supports wordlist
and brute-force attacks, but can also use rainbow tables to speed up its analysis. Normally, a password-cracking tool using a wordlist will take the given plaintext, compute
the hash, and perform a search for that hash in the password file. Rainbow tables are
pre-computed lists of hashes that the program will use to perform a reverse lookup of the
possible password. In the case of the rainbow table, only the hash needs to be searched
for, so this speeds up the cracking process significantly. The tradeoff is that rainbow
tables can be extremely large in size.

 NOTE   Password-cracking software has been used successfully for many
years, but the trend of increasingly affordable hardware has ushered in the
age of hardware-accelerated password cracking. Using "rigs," composed of
several graphics processing units (GPUs), a user can brute-force passwords
orders of magnitude faster than traditional CPU-only methods.

Imaging

Imaging tools copy data from a source regardless of the file system that resides on the volume. This means that a hard drive running the Mac OS, Windows, or Linux can be copied in the same way using the same utility. Imaging tools usually allow for the entire contents of the drive to be duplicated to a single file in a remote destination. Unlike a regular file copy, forensic imaging also includes the file system's slack and free space, where the remnants of deleted files may reside.

dd

Using the dd utility is just about the easiest way to make a bit-for-bit copy of a hard drive. You can find the program in nearly every Linux distribution as well as in the Mac OS. Its primary purpose is to copy or convert files, and accordingly there are several options for block sizes and image conversion during the imaging process that might assist in follow-on analysis. The following command will perform a bit-for-bit copy of hard drive "hda" to a file called case123.img using the options to set the block size to 4096 bytes and fill the rest of the block with null symbols should it encounter an error:

```
dd if=/dev/hda of=case123.img bs=4k conv=noerror,sync
```

Chapter Review

Despite being the longest chapter in this book, this could've been a lot lengthier. As a CSA+, you really ought to be familiar with every tool we described here. Ideally, you would be proficient with each. Our goal was not to provide you with the depth of knowledge we feel you should possess on them, but rather to give a high-level survey of these essential tools of the trade. We hope that you will use this as a springboard for your own self-study into any products with which you are not familiar. Though the exam will require only a general familiarity with these, your real-world performance will likely be enhanced by a deeper knowledge of the tools of the trade.

Questions

1. You are concerned about your ability to block zero-day exploits before they enter your network. Which of the following tools would best allow you to do this?

   A. Wireshark

   B. Imperva's SecureSphere

   C. Metasploit

   D. Palo Alto Networks NGFW

2. What class of tools is best able to receive information from a variety of platforms, aggregate it into a data store, generate alerts, and allow users to query the data?

   A. Interception proxy

   B. SIEM

   C. Fuzzer

   D. HIPS

3. Which of the following is an example of a vulnerability scanner?

   A. Bro

   B. NAXSI

   C. OpenVAS

   D. Helix

4. To what class of tools does Metasploit belong?

   A. Vulnerability scanners

   B. Interception proxies

   C. Password crackers

   D. Exploitation frameworks

Use the following scenario to answer Questions 5–7:

Your company's internal development team just developed a new web application for deployment onto the public-facing web server. You are trying to ensure that it conforms to best security practices and does not introduce any vulnerabilities into your systems.

5. Which would be the best tool to use if you want to ensure that the web application is not transmitting passwords in cleartext?

   A. Nikto

   B. FTK

   C. Burp Suite

   D. Aircrack-ng

6. Having tested the web application against all the input values you can think of, you decide to try random data to see if you can force instability or crashes. Which is the best tool for this purpose?

   A. Untidy

   B. Cellebrite

   C. Cain and Abel

   D. Qualys

7. You discover a vulnerability that causes the application to crash whenever it receives a password of length 256 or greater. This is the only flaw you find, and you are under immense pressure to get the app online. The development team will need a week to fix the issue. Assuming you are already using it, which of the following security tools might allow you to mitigate the risk and allow the app to go online by tomorrow?

    A. AlienVault

    B. Sourcefire

    C. Nessus

    D. Metasploit

Use the following scenario to answer Questions 8–10:

You are an analyst at a large organization and are tracking a fairly sophisticated adversary who appears to have compromised some hosts on your network. This actor's tactics, techniques, and procedures (TTPs), gleaned from a threat intelligence feed, include consolidating files on an internal, compromised host, compressing them onto one file, encrypting them, and then sending them to an external server. The internal aggregator runs a server on TCP port 1337.

8. Using which of the following tools might you best determine if any of your internal hosts are listening on port 1337?

    A. Snort

    B. Wireshark

    C. nmap

    D. netstat

9. You find a host running an illicit server on port 1337 and move it to an isolated virtual local area network (VLAN) to prevent further data loss. The next step is to find any other compromised hosts that might be trying to communicate with the rogue server. You quickly provision a new Linux host with the same hostname and IP address and then start a web server on port 1337. Which tool might let you track compromised hosts trying to connect to that socket?

    A. tcpdump

    B. ifconfig

    C. nslookup

    D. SHAsum

10. You want to make a forensic image of the isolated server's hard drive and then ensure the integrity of all the copied data. Which combination of tools is best suited for these tasks? (Choose two.)

    A. mv

    B. cp

    C. md5sum

    D. dd

    E. shasum

Answers

1. **D.** Next-Generation Firewalls (NGFWs), such as those made by Palo Alto Networks, can connect to threat intelligence feeds to quickly identify new attacks and share those with others with similar firewalls. They also have the ability to run applications in a sandbox to determine whether they are benign or malicious before allowing them into the network.

2. **B.** Security information and event management (SIEM) systems are designed to collect, store, analyze, and report security information and events.

3. **C.** OpenVAS (in addition to Qualys, Nessus, Nexpose, Nikto, and Microsoft Baseline Security Analyzer) is a vulnerability scanner with which you should be familiar.

4. **D.** Metasploit is the most widely used open source exploitation framework.

5. **C.** Burp Suite is an integrated web application testing platform often used to map and analyze a web application's vulnerabilities. It is able to intercept web traffic and allow analysts to examine each request and response.

6. **A.** The class of tools that tests applications by bombarding them with random values is called fuzzing tools. Untidy, Peach Fuzzer, and Microsoft's Regex Fuzzer are all examples covered in this chapter.

7. **B.** Sourcefire is an intrusion prevention system that can be configured to block traffic to your web server containing the problematic password values. None of the other tools listed is an IPS or could reasonably be expected to perform the task at hand.

8. **C.** Though any of the options listed might work in certain specific conditions, nmap is the best answer because you can use it to quickly and remotely check all hosts on your network. Snort and Wireshark would only be able to identify the server(s) if they captured traffic to/from it. Netstat would require you to remotely log into all hosts and see if port 1337 was listening, which is a very time-consuming way to check a large network.

9. **A.** Tcpdump can be configured to capture only traffic destined for a given port on the local host, which would over time collect the source IP addresses of any other compromised hosts. Furthermore, tcpdump can capture packets and save them to a remote shared file, which would allow you to monitor it for changes instead of manually checking time and again.

10. **D, E.** The dd utility is often used to make a bit-for-bit forensic copy of secondary storage devices such as hard disk drives. The cp (copy) command or mv (move) command could conceivably be used to copy or move specific files, respectively, but certainly neither would be able to make a forensic duplicate of a disk or file system. In order to ensure the integrity of the data, you could use either md5sum or shasum, but the latter is preferred, particularly if you use SHA-256 or better.

PART V

Appendixes and Glossary

- **Appendix A**   Objectives Map
- **Appendix B**   About the CD-ROM
- **Glossary**

Objectives Map

	Topic (Domain, Objective, Sub-objectives)	Chapter Number	Page Number
1.0	**Threat Management**		
1.1	**Given a scenario, apply environmental reconnaissance techniques using appropriate tools and processes.**		
	Procedures/common tasks	1	4
	Topology discovery	1	10
	OS fingerprinting	1	10
	Service discovery	1	10
	Packet capture	1	11
	Log review	1	18
	Router/firewall ACLs review	1	18
	E-mail harvesting	1	8
	Social media profiling	1	8
	Social engineering	1	8
	DNS harvesting	1	6
	Phishing	1	8
	Variables	1	12
	Wireless vs. wired	1	12
	Virtual vs. physical	1	15
	Internal vs. external	1	12
	On-premises vs. cloud	1	17
	Tools	1	18
	Nmap	1	19
	Host scanning	1	9
	Network mapping	1	10

Topic (Domain, Objective, Sub-objectives)	Chapter Number	Page Number
Netstat	1	21
Packet analyzer	1	22
IDS/IPS	1	22
HIDS/NIDS	1	22
Firewall rule-based and logs	1	18
Syslog	1	18
Vulnerability scanner	1	20
1.2 **Given a scenario, analyze the results of a network reconnaissance.**		
Point-in-time data analysis	2	32
Packet analysis	2	32
Protocol analysis	2	33
Traffic analysis	2	34
NetFlow analysis	2	34
Wireless analysis	2	36
Data correlation and analytics	2	36
Anomaly analysis	2	38
Trend analysis	2	38
Availability analysis	2	39
Heuristic analysis	2	40
Behavioral analysis	2	38
Data output	2	27
Firewall logs	2	28
Packet captures	2	29
Nmap scan results	2	31
Event logs	2	31
Syslogs	2	31
IDS report	2	28
Tools	2	40
SIEM	2	40
Packet analyzer	2	42
IDS	2	43
Resource monitoring tool	2	45
NetFlow analyzer	2	45

Topic (Domain, Objective, Sub-objectives)	Chapter Number	Page Number
1.3 **Given a network-based threat, implement or recommend the appropriate response and countermeasure.**		
Network segmentation	3	52
System isolation	3	52
Jump box	3	53
Honeypot	3	54
Endpoint security	3	56
Group policies	3	58
ACLs	3	54
Sinkhole	3	56
Hardening	3	58
Mandatory access control (MAC)	3	59
Compensating controls	3	60
Blocking unused ports/services	3	60
Patching	3	61
Network Access Control (NAC)	3	61
Time-based	3	62
Rule-based	3	62
Role-based	3	62
Location-based	3	63
1.4 **Explain the purpose of practices used to secure a corporate environment.**		
Penetration testing	4	69
Rules of engagement	4	70
Timing	4	71
Scope	4	71
Authorization	4	72
Exploitation	4	72
Communication	4	72
Reporting	4	73
Reverse engineering	4	73
Isolation/sandboxing	4	80
Hardware	4	73
Source authenticity of hardware	4	73
Trusted foundry	4	74

Topic (Domain, Objective, Sub-objectives)	Chapter Number	Page Number
OEM documentation	4	75
Software/malware	4	76
Fingerprinting/hashing	4	77
Decomposition	4	77
Training and exercises	4	80
Red team	4	82
Blue team	4	82
White team	4	83
Risk evaluation	4	83
Technical Control review	4	86
Operational Control review	4	87
Technical impact and likelihood	4	84
High	4	84
Medium	4	84
Low	4	84
2.0 Vulnerability Management		
2.1 Given a scenario, implement an information security vulnerability management process.		
Identification of requirements	5	95
Regulatory environments	5	95
Corporate policy	5	97
Data classification	5	97
Asset inventory	5	98
Critical	5	99
Noncritical	5	99
Establish scanning frequency	5	106
Risk appetite	5	107
Regulatory requirements	5	107
Technical constraints	5	107
Workflow	5	108
Configure tools to perform scans according to specification	5	108
Determine scanning criteria	5	108
Sensitivity levels	5	108
Vulnerability feed	5	109
Scope	5	110
Credentialed vs. non-credentialed	5	110

Topic (Domain, Objective, Sub-objectives)	Chapter Number	Page Number
Types of data	5	111
Server-based vs. agent-based	5	110
Tool updates/plug-ins	5	111
SCAP	5	112
Permissions and access	5	113
Execute scanning	6	120
Generate reports	6	128
Automated vs. manual distribution	6	128
Remediation	6	128
Prioritizing	6	129
Criticality	6	129
Difficulty of implementation	6	130
Communication/change control	6	130
Sandboxing/testing	6	131
Inhibitors to remediation	6	131
MOUs	6	131
SLAs	6	132
Organizational governance	6	132
Business process interruption	6	132
Degrading functionality	6	132
Ongoing scanning and continuous monitoring	6	132
2.2 Given a scenario, analyze the output resulting from a vulnerability scan.		
Analyze reports from a vulnerability scan	6	133
Review and interpret scan results	6	133
Identify false positives	6	134
Identify exceptions	6	134
Prioritize response actions	6	134
Validate results and correlate other data points	6	134
Compare to best practices or compliance	6	136
Reconcile results	6	136
Review related logs and/or other data sources	6	137
Determine trends	6	137
2.3 Compare and contrast common vulnerabilities found in the following targets within an organization.		
Servers	5	100
Endpoints	5	100

Topic (Domain, Objective, Sub-objectives)	Chapter Number	Page Number
Network infrastructure	5	100
Network appliances	5	100
Virtual infrastructure	5	101
Virtual hosts	5	101
Virtual networks	5	102
Management interface	5	102
Mobile devices	5	102
Interconnected networks	5	103
Virtual private networks (VPNs)	5	103
Industrial control systems (ICSs)	5	104
SCADA devices	5	105
3.0 Cyber Incident Response		
3.1 Given a scenario, distinguish threat data or behavior to determine the impact of an incident.		
Threat classification	8	167
Known threats vs. unknown threats	8	167
Zero day	8	168
Advanced persistent threat	8	169
Factors contributing to incident severity and prioritization	8	170
Scope of impact	8	170
Downtime	8	171
Recovery time	8	172
Data integrity	8	173
Economic	8	173
System process criticality	8	174
Types of data	8	174
Personally Identifiable Information (PII)	8	174
Personal health information (PHI)	8	176
Payment card Information	8	176
Intellectual property	8	177
Corporate confidential	8	178
Accounting data	8	178
Mergers and acquisitions	8	178
3.2 Given a scenario, prepare a toolkit and use appropriate forensics tools during an investigation.		
Forensic kit	9	195
Digital forensic workstation	9	191

Topic (Domain, Objective, Sub-objectives)	Chapter Number	Page Number
Write blockers	9	195
Cables	9	196
Drive adapters	9	195
Wiped removable media	9	196
Cameras	9	196
Crime tape	9	196
Tamper-proof seals	9	196
Documentation/forms	9	197
Chain-of-custody form	9	197
Incident response plan	9	197
Incident form	9	197
Call list/escalation list	9	197
Forensic investigation suite	9	189
Imaging utilities	9	189
Analysis utilities	9	191
Chain of custody	9	186
Hashing utilities	9	190
OS and process analysis	9	192
Mobile device forensics	9	194
Password crackers	9	190
Cryptography tools	9	190
Log viewers	9	195
3.3 Explain the importance of communication during the incident response process.		
Stakeholders	7	149
HR	7	149
Legal	7	149
Marketing	7	150
Management	7	150
Purpose of communication processes	7	161
Limit communication to trusted parties	7	162
Disclosure based on regulatory/legislative requirements	7	162
Prevent inadvertent release of Information	7	162
Secure method of communication	7	162
Role-based responsibilities	7	145
Technical	7	146

PART V

	Topic (Domain, Objective, Sub-objectives)	Chapter Number	Page Number
	Management	7	148
	Law enforcement	7	148
	Retain Incident response provider	7	147
3.4	**Given a scenario, analyze common symptoms to select the best course of action to support incident response.**		
	Common network-related symptoms	10	203
	Bandwidth consumption	10	204
	Beaconing	10	204
	Irregular peer-to-peer communication	10	205
	Rogue devices on the network	10	206
	Scan sweeps	10	207
	Unusual traffic spikes	10	212
	Common host-related symptoms	10	208
	Processor consumption	10	208
	Memory consumption	10	209
	Drive capacity consumption	10	210
	Unauthorized software	10	210
	Malicious processes	10	208
	Unauthorized changes	10	211
	Unauthorized privileges	10	213
	Data exfiltration	10	211
	Common application-related symptoms	10	214
	Anomalous activity	10	214
	Introduction of new accounts	10	215
	Unexpected output	10	215
	Unexpected outbound communication	10	215
	Service interruption	10	216
	Memory overflows	10	216
3.5	**Summarize the incident recovery and post-incident response process.**		
	Containment techniques	7	151
	Segmentation	7	152
	Isolation	7	152
	Removal	7	153
	Reverse engineering	7	154

Topic (Domain, Objective, Sub-objectives)	Chapter Number	Page Number
Eradication techniques	7	156
Sanitization	7	156
Reconstruction/reimage	7	157
Secure disposal	7	157
Validation	7	158
Patching	7	158
Permissions	7	158
Scanning	7	159
Verify logging/communication to security monitoring	7	159
Corrective actions	7	160
Lessons learned report	7	160
Change control process	7	160
Update incident response plan	7	161
Incident summary report	7	161
4.0 Security Architecture and Tool Sets		
4.1 Explain the relationship between frameworks, common policies, controls, and procedures.		
Regulatory compliance	11	241
Frameworks	11	223
NIST	11	223
ISO	11	225
COBIT	11	226
SABSA	11	228
TOGAF	11	229
ITIL	11	230
Policies	11	232
Password policy	11	233
Acceptable use policy	11	234
Data ownership policy	11	232
Data retention policy	11	233
Account management policy	11	234
Data classification policy	11	232
Controls	11	239
Control selection based on criteria	11	240

PART V

Topic (Domain, Objective, Sub-objectives)	Chapter Number	Page Number
Organizationally defined parameters	11	240
Physical controls	11	239
Logical controls	11	239
Administrative controls	11	240
Procedures	11	236
Continuous monitoring	11	236
Evidence production	11	236
Patching	11	237
Compensating control development	11	238
Control testing procedures	11	238
Manage exceptions	11	238
Remediation plans	11	236
Verifications and quality control	11	242
Audits	11	242
Evaluations	11	242
Assessments	11	242
Maturity model	11	243
Certification	11	243
4.2 Given a scenario, use data to recommend remediation of security issues related to identity and access management.		
Security issues associated with context-based authentication	12	250
Time	12	250
Location	12	251
Frequency	12	252
Behavioral	12	253
Security issues associated with identities	12	253
Personnel	12	254
Endpoints	12	254
Servers	12	254
Services	12	256
Roles	12	257
Applications	12	258
Security issues associated with identity repositories	12	258
Directory services	12	258

Topic (Domain, Objective, Sub-objectives)	Chapter Number	Page Number
TACACS+	12	259
RADIUS	12	260
Security issues associated with federation and Single Sign-On	12	261
Manual vs. automatic provisioning/deprovisioning	12	262
Self-service password reset	12	262
Exploits	12	263
Impersonation	12	263
Man-in-the-middle	12	263
Session hijack	12	263
Cross-site scripting	12	264
Privilege escalation	12	264
Rootkit	12	264
4.3 **Given a scenario, review security architecture and make recommendations to implement compensating controls.**		
Security data analytics	13	269
Data aggregation and correlation	13	269
Trend analysis	13	272
Historical analysis	13	272
Manual review	13	273
Firewall log	13	276
Syslogs	13	277
Authentication logs	13	278
Event logs	13	279
Defense in depth	13	280
Personnel	13	282
Training	13	282
Dual control	13	282
Separation of duties	13	283
Third party/consultants	13	283
Cross-training	13	283
Mandatory vacation	13	284
Succession planning	13	284
Processes	13	285
Continual improvement	13	285

Topic (Domain, Objective, Sub-objectives)	Chapter Number	Page Number
Scheduled reviews	13	286
Retirement of processes	13	286
Technologies	13	286
Automated reporting	13	286
Security appliances	13	286
Security suites	13	287
Outsourcing	13	287
Security as a Service	13	288
Cryptography	13	289
Other security concepts	13	289
Network design	13	290
Network segmentation	13	290
4.4 **Given a scenario, use application security best practices while participating in the software development lifecycle (SDLC).**		
Best practices during software development	14	295
Security requirements definition	14	297
Security testing phases	14	302
Static code analysis	14	300
Web app vulnerability scanning	14	302
Fuzzing	14	304
Use interception proxy to crawl application	14	303
Manual peer reviews	14	301
User acceptance testing	14	298
Stress test application	14	304
Security regression testing	14	302
Input validation	14	299
Secure coding best practices	14	306
OWASP	14	307
SANS	14	308
Center for Internet security	14	309
System design recommendations	14	309
Benchmarks	14	309
4.5 **Compare and contrast the general purpose and reasons for using various cybersecurity tools and technologies.**		
(The intent of this objective is *not* to test specific vendor feature sets.)		

Topic (Domain, Objective, Sub-objectives)	Chapter Number	Page Number
Preventative	15	315
IPS	15	318
Sourcefire	15	319
Snort	15	319
Bro	15	318
HIPS	15	320
Firewall	15	316
Cisco	15	317
Palo Alto	15	318
Check Point	15	317
Antivirus	15	320
Antimalware	15	320
EMET	15	321
Web proxy	15	321
Web application firewall (WAF)	15	323
ModSecurity	15	324
NAXSI	15	324
Imperva	15	323
Collective	15	325
SIEM	15	325
ArcSight	15	326
QRadar	15	327
Splunk	15	328
AlienVault	15	325
OSSIM	15	327
Kiwi Syslog	15	327
Network scanning	15	329
Nmap	15	330
Vulnerability scanning	15	336
Qualys	15	336
Nessus	15	338
OpenVAS	15	340
Nexpose	15	340
Nikto	15	342
Microsoft Baseline Security Analyzer	15	343

PART V

Topic (Domain, Objective, Sub-objectives)	Chapter Number	Page Number
Packet capture	15	330
Wireshark	15	331
tcpdump	15	332
Network General	15	330
Aircrack-ng	15	332
Command-line/IP utilities	15	333
netstat	15	333
ping	15	333
tracert/traceroute	15	333
ipconfig/ifconfig	15	335
nslookup/dig	15	335
Sysinternals	15	335
OpenSSL	15	335
IDS/HIDS	15	318
Bro	15	318
Analytical	15	336
Vulnerability scanning	15	336
Qualys	15	336
Nessus	15	338
OpenVAS	15	340
Nexpose	15	340
Nikto	15	342
Microsoft Baseline Security Analyzer	15	343
Monitoring tools	15	344
MRTG	15	346
Nagios	15	346
SolarWinds	15	347
Cacti	15	347
NetFlow Analyzer	15	348
Interception proxy	15	348
Burp Suite	15	349
Zap	15	350
Vega	15	351

Topic (Domain, Objective, Sub-objectives)	Chapter Number	Page Number
Exploit	15	351
Interception proxy	15	348
Burp Suite	15	349
Zap	15	350
Vega	15	351
Exploit framework	15	351
Metasploit	15	353
Nexpose	15	354
Fuzzers	15	355
Untidy	15	356
Peach Fuzzer	15	356
Microsoft SDL File/Regex Fuzzer	15	356
Forensics	15	356
Forensic suites	15	357
EnCase	15	358
FTK	15	358
Helix	15	358
Sysinternals	15	335
Cellebrite	15	359
Hashing	15	359
MD5sum	15	359
SHAsum	15	360
Password cracking	15	360
John the Ripper	15	361
Cain & Abel	15	362
Imaging	15	363
DD	15	363

About the CD-ROM

The CD-ROM included with this book comes complete with Total Tester customizable practice exam software with more than 150 practice exam questions, a sample quiz of performance-based questions, and a secured PDF copy of the book for studying on the go.

System Requirements

The software requires Windows Vista or higher and 30MB of hard disk space for full installation, in addition to a current or prior major release of Chrome, Firefox, Internet Explorer, or Safari. To run, the screen resolution must be set to 1024 × 768 or higher. The secured PDF requires Adobe Acrobat, Adobe Reader, or Adobe Digital Editions to view.

Installing and Running Total Tester Premium Practice Exam Software

From the main screen you may install the Total Tester by clicking the Total Tester Practice Exams button. This will begin the installation process and place an icon on your desktop and in your Start menu. To run Total Tester, navigate to Start | (All) Programs | Total Seminars, or double-click the icon on your desktop.

To uninstall the Total Tester software, go to Start | Control Panel | Programs And Features, and then select the Total Tester program. Select Remove, and Windows will completely uninstall the software.

Total Tester Premium Practice Exam Software

Total Tester provides you with a simulation of the CompTIA CSA+ exam. Exams can be taken in Practice Mode, Exam Mode, or Custom Mode. Practice Mode provides an assistance window with hints, references to the book, explanations of the correct and incorrect answers, and the option to check your answer as you take the test. Exam Mode provides a simulation of the actual exam. The number of questions, the types of questions, and the time allowed are intended to be an accurate representation of the exam environment. Custom Mode allows you to create custom exams from selected domains or chapters, and you can further customize the number of questions and time allowed.

To take a test, launch the program and select CSA+ AIO from the Installed Question Packs list. You can then select Practice Mode, Exam Mode, or Custom Mode. All exams provide an overall grade and a grade broken down by domain.

Pre-assessment Test

In addition to the sample CompTIA CSA+ exam questions, the Total Tester also includes a CSA+ Pre-assessment test option to help you assess your understanding of the topics before reading the book. To launch the Assessment test, click CSA+ Assessment from the Installed Question Packs list. The CSA+ Assessment test includes 15 questions and runs in Exam Mode. When you complete the test you can review the questions with answers and detailed explanations by clicking See Detailed Results.

Performance-Based Questions

In addition to the multiple-choice practice exam questions featured in the Total Tester Premium Practice Exam Software, simulated performance-based questions are also included on the CD-ROM to allow you to practice with these question types. You can access the performance-based questions by clicking the Performance-Based Questions button on the CD-ROM's main launch page.

Performance-based questions are mostly graphical in nature and require the test taker to understand the concepts of the question from a practical and graphical aspect. You may need to point to the correct component within a graphic, arrange a sequence of steps into the correct order, match a set of terms with the correct definitions, or type a response. It is not as easy to memorize answers for these types of questions, and they in turn make passing the exam more difficult.

Secured Book PDF

The entire contents of the book are provided in secured PDF format on the CD-ROM. This file is viewable on your computer and many portable devices.

- **To view the PDF on a computer**, Adobe Acrobat, Adobe Reader, or Adobe Digital Editions is required. A link to Adobe's website, where you can download and install Adobe Reader, has been included on the CD-ROM.

 NOTE For more information on Adobe Reader and to check for the most recent version of the software, visit Adobe's website at www.adobe.com and search for the free Adobe Reader or look for Adobe Reader on the product page. Adobe Digital Editions can also be downloaded from the Adobe website.

- **To view the book PDF on a portable device**, copy the PDF file to your computer from the CD-ROM and then copy the file to your portable device using a USB or other connection. Adobe offers a mobile version of Adobe Reader, the Adobe Reader mobile app, which currently supports iOS and Android. For customers using Adobe Digital Editions and an iPad, you may have to download and install a separate reader program on your device. The Adobe website has a list of recommended applications, and McGraw-Hill Education recommends the Bluefire Reader.

Technical Support

For questions regarding the Total Tester software or operation of the CD-ROM, visit **www.totalsem.com** or e-mail **support@totalsem.com**.

For questions regarding the secured book PDF, visit **http://mhp.softwareassist.com** or e-mail **techsolutions@mhedu.com**.

For questions regarding book content, e-mail **hep_customer-service@mheducation .com**. For customers outside the United States, e-mail **international_cs@mheducation.com**.

Access control list (ACL)   A list of rules that control the manner in which a resource may be accessed.

Accreditation   The formal acceptance of the adequacy of a system's overall security and functionality by management.

Administrative control   Security mechanisms implemented by management primarily through policies and procedures; also known as a management or policy control.

Advanced persistent threat (APT)   The name given to any number of stealthy and continuous computer-hacking efforts, often coordinated and executed by an organization or government with significant resources over a longer period of time.

Anomaly analysis   Any technique focused on measuring the deviation of some observation from some baseline and determining whether that deviation is statistically significant.

Assessment   A process that gathers information and makes determinations based on it.

Audit   A systematic inspection by an independent third party, oftentimes driven by regulatory compliance requirements.

Beaconing   A periodical outbound connection between a compromised computer and an external controller.

Black hole   A device that is configured to receive any and all packets with a specific source or destination address and not respond to them at all.

Blue team   The group of participants who are the focus of a training event or exercise; they are usually involved with the defense of the organization's infrastructure.

Certification   The comprehensive technical evaluation of the security components of a system and their compliance with applicable regulations.

Chain of custody   A history that shows how evidence was collected, transported, and preserved at every stage of the investigation process.

Cloud computing   The use of shared, remote computing devices for the purpose of providing improved efficiencies, performance, reliability, scalability, and security.

Compensating control A security control that satisfies the requirements of some other control when implementing the latter is not possible or desirable.

Containment Actions that attempt to deny the threat agent the ability or means to cause further damage.

Control Objectives for Information and Related Technologies (COBIT) A framework and set of control objectives developed by ISACA and the IT Governance Institute that defines goals for the controls that should be used to properly manage IT and to ensure that IT maps to business needs.

Cross-site scripting (XSS) A vulnerability in a web application that allows malicious users to execute arbitrary client-side scripts.

DNS sinkhole A technique that responds to DNS queries for malicious domains with IP addresses that do not correspond to the adversaries' intended hosts, thus preventing malware from communicating effectively.

Dual control A practice that requires involvement of two or more parties to complete a task.

E-mail harvesting The process of acquiring e-mail addresses, oftentimes for the purpose of compromising the targets' information systems.

Evaluation An event that compares observations with specific values or criteria and reports the difference, if any, between them.

Event Any occurrence that can be observed, verified, and documented.

False positive A report that states that a given condition is present when in fact it is not.

Firewall A device that permits the flow of authorized data through it while preventing unauthorized flows.

Forensic acquisition The process of extracting the digital contents from seized evidence so that they may be analyzed.

Fuzzing A technique used to discover flaws and vulnerabilities in software by sending large amounts of malformed, unexpected, or random data to the target program in order to trigger failures.

Hardening The process of securing information systems by reducing their vulnerabilities and functionality.

Hashing function A one-way function that takes a variable-length sequence of data such as a file and produces a fixed-length result called a "hash value"; sometimes referred to as a digital fingerprint.

Heuristic A "rule of thumb" or any other experience-based, imperfect approach to problem solving.

Heuristic analysis The application of heuristics to find threats in practical, if imperfect, ways.

Honeynet A network of devices that is created for the sole purpose of luring an attacker into trying to compromise it.

Host-based intrusion detection system (HIDS) An IDS that is focused on the behavior of a specific host and packets on its network interfaces.

Incident One or more related events that compromise the organization's security posture.

Incident response The process of negating the effects of an incident on an information system.

Industrial control system (ICS) A cyber-physical system that allows specialized software to control the physical behaviors of some system.

Information Technology Infrastructure Library (ITIL) A customizable framework that provides the goals of internal IT services, the general activities necessary to achieve these goals, and the input and output values for each process required to meet these determined goals.

Input validation An approach to protect systems from abnormal user input by testing the data provided against appropriate values.

Interception proxy A relay system between a client and a server that allows all messages to be examined before being forwarded to their destinations.

International Organization for Standardization (ISO) An independent, nongovernmental international organization that is the world's largest developer and publisher of international standards.

Intrusion detection system (IDS) A system that identifies violations of security policies and generates alerts.

Intrusion prevention system (IPS) A form of IDS that is able to stop any detected violations.

Isolation A state in which a part of an information system, such as a compromised host, is prevented from communicating with the rest of the system.

Jump box A computer that serves as a jumping-off point for external users to access protected parts of a network.

Logical control A software or hardware tool used to restrict access to objects; also known as a technical control.

Man-in-the-middle attack An attack in which an adversary intercepts communications between two endpoints in order to obtain illicit access to message contents and potentially alter them.

PART V

Mandatory access control (MAC)   A policy in which access controls are always enforced on all objects and subjects.

National Institute for Standards and Technology (NIST)   An organization within the U.S. Department of Commerce that is charged with promoting innovation and industrial competitiveness.

NetFlow   A Cisco proprietary protocol for the collection and distribution of IP traffic statistics.

Netstat   A popular command-line interface tool that provides information on the status of network connections and listening sockets.

Network segmentation   The practice of separating various parts of the network into subordinate zones in order to thwart adversaries' efforts, improve traffic management, and prevent spillover of sensitive data.

Network-based intrusion detection system (NIDS)   An IDS that is focused on the packets traversing a network.

Nmap   A popular open source tool that allows the mapping of network hosts and the ports on which they are listening.

Open Web Application Security Project (OWASP)   An organization that promotes web security and provides development guidelines, testing procedures, and code review steps.

Operational control   Safeguard that deters, delays, prevents, detects, or responds to threats against physical property; also known as a physical control.

Packet analyzer   A tool that captures network traffic, performs some form of analysis on it, and reports the results; also known as a network or packet sniffer.

Patch management   The process by which fixes to software vulnerabilities are identified, tested, applied, validated, and documented.

Patching   The application of a fix to a software defect.

Payment Card Industry Data Security Standard (PCI DSS)   A global standard for protecting stored, processed, or transmitted payment card information.

Penetration test   The process of simulating attacks on a network and its systems at the request of the owner or senior management for the purpose of measuring an organization's level of resistance to those attacks and to uncover any exploitable weaknesses within the environment.

Personal health information (PHI)   Information that relates to an individual's past, present, or future physical or mental health condition.

Personally identifiable information (PII)   Information, such as social security number or biometric profile, that can be used to distinguish an individual's identity.

Phishing   The use of fraudulent e-mail messages to induce the recipient to provide sensitive information or take actions that could compromise their information systems; a form of social engineering.

Physical control   Safeguard that deters, delays, prevents, detects or responds to threats against physical property; sometimes called an operational control.

Public Key Infrastructure (PKI)   A framework of programs, procedures, communication protocols, and public key cryptography that enables a diverse group of individuals to communicate securely.

Red team   A group that acts as adversaries during a security assessment or exercise.

Regression testing   The formal process by which code that has been modified is tested to ensure no features and security characteristics were compromised by the modifications.

Regulatory environment   An environment in which the way an organization exists or operates is controlled by laws, rules, or regulations put in place by a formal body.

Remediation   The application of security controls to a known vulnerability in order to reduce its risk to an acceptable level.

Remote Authentication Dial-In User Service (RADIUS)   An authentication, authorization, and accounting (AAA) remote access protocol.

Reverse engineering   The process of deconstructing something in order to discover its features and constituents.

Risk   The possibility of damage to or loss of any information system asset, as well as the ramifications should this occur.

Risk appetite   The amount of risk that senior executives are willing to assume.

Rootkit   A typically malicious software application that interferes with the normal reporting of an operating system, often by hiding specific resources such as files, processes, and network connections.

Sandbox   A type of control that isolates processes from the operating system to prevent security violations.

Sanitization   The process by which access to data on a given medium is made infeasible for a given level of effort.

Security information and event management (SIEM)   A software product that collects, aggregates, analyzes, reports, and stores security information.

Security policy   An overall general statement produced by senior management (or a selected policy board or committee) that dictates what role security plays within the organization or that dictates mandatory requirements for a given aspect of security.

PART V

Separation of duties   A practice that divides critical functions into subordinate tasks and ensures no one person can perform all these tasks, which prevents any single individual from disrupting business-critical processes or making untested administrative changes across an organization.

Sherwood Applied Business Security Architecture (SABSA)   A layered security architecture model in which the higher layers define policies and the lower layers progressively lead to practical implementation, thus providing a chain of traceability.

Social engineering   The manipulation of people in order to get them to take actions that they otherwise wouldn't have and that typically involve a violation of a security policy or procedure.

Social media profiling   The process of obtaining and analyzing information about specific individuals from social media for the purpose of creating profiles that may include identifying information, preferences, and vulnerabilities.

Spear phishing   Phishing attempts directed at a specific individual or group.

Static code analysis   A technique that is meant to help identify software defects or security policy violations and is carried out by examining the code without executing the program.

Stress test   A test that places extreme demands that are well beyond the planning thresholds of the software in order to determine how robust it is.

Supervisory Control and Data Acquisition (SCADA)   A system for remotely monitoring and controlling physical systems such as power and manufacturing plants over large geographic regions.

syslog   A popular protocol used to communicate event messages.

Technical control   A software or hardware tool used to restrict access to objects; also known as a logical control.

Terminal Access Controller Access Control System (TACACS)   An authentication, authorization, and accounting (AAA) remote access protocol.

The Open Group Architecture Framework (TOGAF)   A framework that provides an approach to design, implement, and govern an enterprise information architecture at four levels: business, data, applications and technology.

Trend analysis   The study of patterns over time in order to determine how, when, and why they change.

Trusted foundry   An organization capable of developing prototype or production-grade microelectronics in a manner that ensures the integrity of its products.

Virtual private network   A system that connects two or more devices that are physically part of separate networks and allows them to exchange data as if they were connected to the same local area network.

Vulnerability   A flaw in an information system that can enable an adversary to compromise the security of that system.

Whaling   Spear phishing aimed at high-profile targets such as executives.

White team   The group of people who plan, document, assess, or moderate a training exercise.

Write blocker   A device that prevents modifications to a storage device while its contents are being acquired.

Zero day   A vulnerability or exploit that is unknown to the broader community of software developers and security professionals.

INDEX

A

A-GPS (assisted GPS), 251–252

AAA (authentication, authorization, and accounting) protocol, 259–261

AAR (after action review), lessons-learned, 160

acceptable use policy (AUP), 234

access control. *See also* controls
    common exploits against, 263–265
    when outsourcing, 287

access control lists. *See* ACLs (access control lists)

accounting data, corporate, 178

accounts
    detecting application incidents, 215
    lockouts, best practice, 308
    management policy, 234–235

accreditation, verification/quality control via, 243

ACLs (access control lists)
    compensating controls using, 60
    in defense against reconnaissance, 17
    in discretionary access control, 59
    in DNS zone transfers, 7
    file system ACLs, 55
    as firewall policies/rule sets, 316
    in mandatory access control, 59
    network ACLs, 55
    order of rules in, 55
    responding to network threats, 54–56
    in role-based access control, 60
    system isolation via, 52
    vulnerability scans examining, 113

Acquire and Implement domain, COBIT, 226–227

acquisition, forensic
    overview of, 187–188
    tools, 189–191

Active Authentication, 253

active reconnaissance, 9–12

active taps, packet capture, 12–13

AD (Active Directory), 58, 258–259

ad hoc (mesh) mode, wireless analysis, 38

Adaptive Security Appliance (ASA), Cisco, 317–320

Address Resolution Protocol (ARP)
    poisoning, 13–14
    scan sweeps, 207–208

Address Space Layout Randomization (ASLR), EMET, 321

ADM (Architecture Development Method), TOGAF, 230

administrative accounts, permissions after incident, 158–159

administrative (soft) controls, 239, 240

advanced persistent threats (APTs)
    Operation Aurora breach, 178
    threat classification, 169–170

after action review (AAR), lessons-learned report, 160

agent-based vulnerability scanners, 111

aggregation, 35, 269–272

air gaps, system isolation, 52

aircrack-ng wireless network tool, 332

alerts, vulnerability, 109

analysis, digital forensic
    Encase performing, 191
    overview of, 188–189
    utilities for, 191–192

analytical tools. *See* monitoring tools; vulnerability scanning

anomaly-based detection
    application-related symptoms, 214–215
    overview of, 38

antimalware (or antivirus) tools, 320

antivirus (antimalware) tools, 320

app stores, mobile device vulnerability, 102

application-layer firewalls, 17

application-related symptoms, diagnosing
    anomalous activity, 214–215
    introduction of new accounts, 215
    memory overflows, 216–217
    service interruption, 216
    unexpected outbound communication, 215–216
    unexpected output, 215

applications
    automating deployment of, 309
    identity security issues, 258
    network segmentation of, 53
    SANS Institute best practices, 308–309
APT28 (or Fancy Bear) threat actor, 212
APTs (advanced persistent threats)
    Operation Aurora breach, 178
    threat classification, 169–170
Architecture Development Method (ADM),
    TOGAF, 230
architectures, security. *See* frameworks,
    policies, controls, and procedures
ArcSight collective tool, 326–327
ARIN (American Registry for Internet
    Numbers), 6
ARP (Address Resolution Protocol)
    poisoning, 13–14
    scan sweeps, 207–208
artifacts, forensic investigations, 210
artificial intelligence algorithms, 253
AS (Authentication Service), Kerberos, 255
ASA (Adaptive Security Appliance) products,
    Cisco, 317–320
ASLR (Address Space Layout Randomization),
    EMET, 321
assembler, 155
assembly language, 79, 155
assessments, verification/quality control,
    242–243
asset inventory, 98–99
asset reporting format, SCAP, 113
assisted GPS (A-GPS), 251–252
attributes, Active Directory, 258
audits
    configuring Nessus scanner, 124
    improving AD security, 259
    ISO/IEC 27001 certification, 96
    with packet sniffers, 330
    verification/quality control via, 242
AUP (acceptable use policy), 234
authentication
    account management policy, 234
    Active Authentication, 253
    context-based, 250–253
    federation/SSO issues, 261–262
    identity security issues, 253–258
    logs, 278–279
    multifactor, 249
    verifying ownership of particular
        identity, 253
    wireless, 38

authentication exploits
    cross-site scripting, 264
    impersonation, 263
    man in the middle, 263
    overview of, 263–265
    privilege escalation, 264
    rootkits, 264–265
    session hijack, 263–264
Authentication Service (AS), Kerberos, 255
authorization
    account management policy, 234–235
    MAC requiring explicit, 59
    penetration test, 72
automated reporting
    in most security products, 286
    vulnerability scanning, 128
Autopsy interface, Sleuth Kit, 192–193
autorun
    forensic analysis with Registry Editor, 193
    Sysinternals suite, 335
availability, correlation analysis, 39–40
AWS (Amazon Web Services), USM, 326

B

bandwidth utilization, network incident
    detection, 204
Baseline Security Analyzer, 343–344
baselines
    anomaly analysis, 38
    behavioral analysis, 38
    historical data analysis, 272–273
beaconing, network incident detection,
    204–205
behavior
    context-based authentication factors, 253
    correlation analysis, 38
    endpoint security based on detection of, 57
Benchmarks, CIS, 309
best practices, secure software development,
    306–309
big data, correlation analysis, 37
binary code, reverse engineering, 154–155
birthday attacks, on TACACS+, 260
black-box (zero knowledge) pen tests, 70
black holes, 56
black markets, zero day exploits, 168
blacklisting, software, 210–211
blocking unused ports/services, hardening,
    60–61
blue team, training exercises, 82–83
branches, TTX exercises, 81

bring your own device. *See* BYOD (bring your own device)

Bro (or Bro-IDS), 44, 318–319

browsers, anomalous activity in, 214

buffer overflows, 261, 303

bug bounty programs, zero day exploits, 168

Burp Suite interception proxy, 349–350

business process interruptions, remediation, 132

BYOD (bring your own device)
   Network Access Control for, 62–63
   unmanaged patching in, 158
   vulnerabilities, 100

C

CAB (change advisory board), 131

cables, building forensic kit, 196

cached pages, Google, 5

Cacti, monitoring with, 347

Cain and Abel password recovery tool, 362

call/escalation list, forensic kit, 197

camera, forensic kit, 196

Capability Maturity Model Integration (CMMI) model, 243–245, 307

capacity, 107–108, 212–213

CAs (Certificate Authorities)
   connect to encrypted site via decrypting proxy, 33
   digital certificates, 254
   impersonation as, 263
   web proxies and, 322

CCB (change control board), incident response, 160–161

Center for Internet Security (CIS), 98

CERT (Computer Emergency Readiness Team)
   preparing for zero day, 169
   protection for known attacks, 159
   sharing indicators of incidents with, 153

Certificate Authorities. *See* CAs (Certificate Authorities)

certificates, security issues of identities, 254–256

certification, verification/quality control, 243

CFG (Control Flow Guard), EMET, 321

chain of custody, forensics, 186–187, 197

change advisory board (CAB), 131

change control
   corrective action after incident, 160–161
   forensic acquisition of evidence, 187
   process of, 285
   remediating network vulnerabilities, 130–131

change control board (CCB), incident response, 160–161

changes, detecting unauthorized, 211

Check Point NFGW firewalls, 317

chips, reversing hardware, 75

CIS (Center for Internet Security), 98

Cisco
   NFGW firewalls, 317–318
   Sourcefire IPS, 319–320

classification levels
   data, 97–98
   mandatory access control, 59
   policies for data, 232
   scanning criteria for sensitivity levels, 108–109
   threat, 167–170

clearance level, mandatory access control, 59

client devices, wireless analysis, 38

cloud computing, 17–18, 57–58

CMMI (Capability Maturity Model Integration) model, 243–245, 307

CMMI-DEV (CMMI for Development), 307

COBIT (Control Objectives for Information and related Technology), 226–228

code reviews, 300–302

coding, secure
   best practices, 306–309
   code reviews, 301–302
   input validation, 299–300
   parameter validation, 300
   regression testing, 302
   in software development, 298–299
   static code analysis, 300–301

cognitive fingerprint, Active Authentication, 253

collective tools
   command-line utilities, 333–335
   network scanning, 329–330
   packet capture, 330–333
   security information and event management (SIEM), 325–329

command-line utilities
   ifconfig, 335
   netstat, 333
   nslookup, 335
   OpenSSL, 335
   ping, 333
   sysinternals suite, 335
   traceroute, 333–334

Common Vulnerabilities and Exposures (CVE), 113, 135

Common Vulnerability Scoring System
(CVSS), 113, 129, 130
communications
detect application incidents by unexpected
outbound, 215–216
formal procedures for, 130
incident diagnosis by irregular peer-to-peer,
205–206
incident response process, 150, 161–163
penetration testing, 72–73
compensating controls
in BYOD environment, 158
defense in depth. *See* defense in depth
defined, 238
hardening network via, 60
manual. *See* manual data analysis
review Q & A, 290–294
security data analytics, 269–273
compiler, 79, 155
compliance checks, Nessus, 122–124, 339
Computer Emergency Readiness Team.
See CERT (Computer Emergency
Readiness Team)
computer languages, generations of, 79
confidential classification level, 98
configuration, as common endpoint
vulnerability, 100
consultants, clearly defined policies/NDAs
for, 283
containers, 16, 17
containment
incident response process, 151–152
isolation, 152–153
removal, 153–154
reverse engineering, 154–155
segmentation, 152
context-based authentication
behavioral parameter, 253
defined, 249
frequency parameter, 252–253
location parameter, 251–252
security issues, 250
time parameter, 250–251
continual process improvement, 285
continuity books (playbooks), succession
planning, 284–285
continuous monitoring, 132–133, 236
contractors
key role in incident response, 147–148
vetting when outsourcing, 287

control categories, NIST SP 800-53, 224
Control Objectives for Information and
related Technology (COBIT), 226–228
controls
administrative, 240
compensating. *See* compensating controls
logical, 239–240
overview of, 239
physical, 239
regulatory compliance, 241–242
review Q & A, 245–248
selecting, 240–241
testing procedures, 238
verification and quality, 242–245
cookies, parameter validation and, 300
copying forensic evidence, 188, 189–190
corporate confidential information, 178
corporate network security
penetration testing, 69–73
reverse engineering. *See* reverse engineering
review Q & A, 88–91
risk evaluation, 83–87
training and exercises, 80–83
vulnerability management, 97
corrective action, incident response, 160–161
correlation analysis
anomaly analysis, 38
approach to, 36–37
availability analysis, 39–40
behavioral analysis, 38
data aggregation and, 269–272
defined, 31
heuristics, 40
knowledge of statistics in, 37
trend analysis, 38–39
counterattacks, defense in depth, 281
counterfeit products, 73–75
CPU
detecting running processes, 209
starvation, 305
credentials
federation/SSO security issues, 262
test plaintext via interception proxy, 303
vulnerability scans, 110
crime scene
controlling digital/physical, 184–185
evidence. *See* evidence
tape, in forensic kit, 196
critical assets, inventory of, 99
Critical Security Controls (CSC), CIS, 98

criticality
- as impact of future event, 174
- prioritization of vulnerabilities, 129–130
- of system processes/incident severity, 174

cross-site scripting (XSS), injection attack, 264

cross-training personnel, 283–284

cryptography
- digital forensic tools, 190–191
- security control tools, 289

CSF (Cyber Security Framework), NIST, 225

Cuckoo Sandbox tool, 80

customers, post-incident communications to, 162

CVE (Common Vulnerabilities and Exposures), 113, 135

CVSS (Common Vulnerability Scoring System), 113, 129, 130

Cyber Security Framework (CSF), NIST, 225

D

DAC (discretionary access control), 59, 60

data
- accessing in mobile forensics, 194–195
- aggregation/correlation of, 269–272
- best practice to limit sensitive, 308
- classification of, 97–98, 232
- detecting host incidents, 211–212
- integrity, incident severity/ prioritization, 173
- ownership policy, 232–233
- relationship among levels of, 270
- retention policy, 233

Data Execution Prevention (DEP), EMET, 321–322

data loss prevention (DLP), 62–63, 212

data sources
- analyze reconnaissance results, 27–31
- validate vulnerability scan results, 137

data, types of
- configuring scanning for, 111
- corporate confidential information, 178
- incident severity/prioritization and, 174
- intellectual property, 177–178
- payment card information, 176–177
- personal health information, 176
- personally identifiable information, 174–175

Datagram Transport Layer Security (DTLS), VPNs, 103

DBMS (database management systems), forensic analysis, 187

dd forensic duplicator tool, 189–190, 363

DDoS (distributed denial of service) attacks, 39, 305

decomposition, reversing software/malware, 77–80

deep inspection, Wireshark, 42–43

defense in depth
- concept of, 280–281
- counterattack, 281
- other security concepts, 290
- personnel, 282–285
- processes, 285–289

Defense Information Systems Agency (DISA), 136

Defined level, CMMI model, 244

degaussing, 157

Deliver and Support domain, COBIT, 226

denial of service (DoS) vulnerabilities, 303–305

DEP (Data Execution Prevention), EMET, 321–322

Department of Defense. See DoD (Department of Defense)

deployment, automate application, 309

deprovisioning, manual vs. automatic, 262

destination media, forensic acquisition, 187

detect and block, endpoint security, 57

detection function, CSF Core, 225

development phase, software development lifecycle, 297

device-based location, context-based authentication, 251

device (endpoint) authentication, 254

device hardening
- blocking unused ports/services, 60–61
- compensating controls, 60
- DAC, 59
- overview of, 58–59
- patching, 61
- RBAC, 60

DevOps and DevSecOps, 296

digital certificates, 254–256

digital forensics
- acquisition phase, 187–188
- analysis phase, 188–189
- defined, 183
- investigation suite. See forensic investigation suite
- overview of, 183
- reporting phase, 189
- seizure phase, 184–187

digital identity, defined, 253

digital signatures, 289

directory services, 58, 258–259
DISA (Defense Information Systems
    Agency), 136
disassembler, 155
disassembly tools, digital forensic
    evidence, 185
discretionary access control (DAC), 59, 60
DLLs (dynamically linked libraries),
    unauthorized file changes, 211
DLP (data loss prevention), 62–63, 212
DNS (Domain Name System)
    harvesting, 6
    malware analytics with ArcSight tool, 327
    open source intelligence gathered via, 6–8
    poisoning or spoofing, 7
    sinkholes, 56
    Wireshark deep inspection of, 42–43
    zone transfers, 7
documentation
    after incident response, 158, 160–161
    crime scene, 184, 185
    data retention policy, 233
    forensic analysis, 189
    forensic kit, 197
    patch management, 237–238
    removal process during incident
        response, 154
    security program, 231–232
DoD (Department of Defense)
    advanced persistent threat, 169
    Hack the Pentagon challenge, 168
    handling documents containing PII,
        174–175
    Software Engineering Institute funded by,
        306–307
    STIG benchmark requirements, 136
    TOGAF framework originating in,
        229–230
Domain Name System. See DNS
    (Domain Name System)
DoS (denial of service) vulnerabilities,
    303–305
double-blind penetration testing, 73
downtime, prioritizing response team efforts,
    171–172
drive adapters, in forensic kit, 195
DTLS (Datagram Transport Layer Security),
    VPNs, 103
dual control, 282–283
duplicators, forensic, 189–190

dynamic code analysis, reverse engineering, 154
dynamic (ephemeral) ports, 60
dynamically linked libraries (DLLs),
    unauthorized file changes, 211

E

e-discovery, evidence production, 237
e-mail
    detecting anomalous activity in clients, 215
    harvesting from job sites, 8
economic scope of incident, 173–174
EDRM (Electronic Discovery Reference
    Model), evidence, 237
ElasticSearch, Forensic Toolkit, 192
Elasticsearch-Logstash-Kibana. See ELK
    (Elasticsearch-Logstash-Kibana) stack
electronically stored information (ESI), 237
ELF (Executable and Linkable Format),
    Linux, 79
ELK (Elasticsearch-Logstash-Kibana) stack
    correlation analysis via, 37
    features of, 41–42
    security data analytics, 270–271
EMET (Enhanced Mitigation Experience
    Toolkit), 321–322
Encase forensic suite, 358
EnCase tool, 189, 191–192
encryption
    in forensic cryptography, 190
    as logical control to restrict access, 240
    man-in-the-middle attacks on, 14
    packet capture where there is no, 11
    providing data confidentiality, 289
    sanitization via, 156
    secure disposal of devices/media via, 157
    technical control review of, 86
    using HTTPS proxies to address threat
        actors, 33
    wireless network, 15
end-user devices, endpoint vulnerabilities, 100
endpoints
    authentication, 254
    Baseline Security Analyzer assessing, 343
    identity, 257
    responding to network threats, 56–58
    vulnerabilities of, 100
ephemeric (dynamic) ports, 60
eradication, incident response, 156–157
ESI (electronically stored information), 237
Etherape tool, 34–35

event logs
    analysis of, 279–280
    analyzing results of reconnaissance, 31
    forensic analysis, 193–194
    monitoring AD security, 259
Event Viewer
    in forensic analysis, 194
    overview of, 279–280
events
    incidents vs., 150–151
    reporting with syslog, 277–278
    tracking with Bro, 44
evidence
    chain of custody, 186
    incident response tools. *See* incident
      response toolkit
    preserving, 152
    production procedure, 236–237
exception management, 238–239
exceptions, vulnerability scan reports, 134
Executable and Linkable Format (ELF),
  Linux, 79
Executive Summary, Nexpose, 342
exfiltration of data, host incident detection,
  211–212
exploitation frameworks
    comparing, 352
    Metasploit, 353–354
    Nexpose, 354–355
exploitation, penetration test process, 70, 72
exploits, authentication/access, 263–265
export options, Nessus, 339
Extensible Markup Language (XML), 356–357
external communications, incident response,
  162–163

F

facility codes, syslog, 277
Fair Disclosure regulation, SEC, 178
false positives
    in traffic analysis, 34
    in vulnerability scan report, 134
Fancy Bear (APT28) threat actor, 212
Faraday bags
    mobile device forensics, 187
    spoofing GPS, 252
FCIV (File Checksum Integrity Verifier)
  tool, 191
Federal Information Security Management
  Act (FISMA), 241

federated identity manager, 261
federation, issues with SSO and, 261–262
File Checksum Integrity Verifier (FCIV)
  tool, 191
file system
    ACLs, 55
    host incident detection, 210–212
filters, packet analysis, 32–33, 42–43
fingerprinting, reversing software/malware, 77
FIPS (Federal Information Processing
  Standards), 224
FirePOWER, Cisco ASA firewalls, 317
firewalls
    analyzing logs, 28
    application-layer, 17
    as defense against reconnaissance, 17
    logs, 276–277
    misconfigured rules for, 99
    Next-Generation Firewall tools,
      316–318
    Next-Generation Firewalls, 29, 40
    web application, 323–324
firmware, reversing hardware, 75–76
FISMA (Federal Information Security
  Management Act), 241
Forensic Data Monster, 196
forensic duplicators, 189–190
forensic investigation suite
    acquisition utilities, 189–190
    analysis utilities, 191–192
    hashing utilities, 190–191
    log viewers, 195
    mobile devices, 194–195
    OS and process analysis, 192–194
forensic investigations
    Bro in, 44
    build own forensic kit, 195–197
    data aggregation in, 270
    jump box logs in, 53
    Netflow in, 35
    phases of digital, 183–189
    removing hosts, 153
    review Q & A, 197–201
forensic kit, building your, 195–197
forensic tools
    forensic suites, 357–359
    hashing, 359–360
    imaging, 363
    overview of, 356–357
    password cracking, 360–362

formats
   EnCase Evidence File, 192
   Nessus vulnerability scanner, 128
   system log, 31
Fort Knox security, 51
Forwarders, Splunk tool, 41
FQDN (fully qualified domain name),
   nslookup, 335
frames, in switched environment, 13
Framework Core, Cyber Security
   Framework, 225
Framework Profile, Cyber Security
   Framework, 225
frameworks, policies, controls, and procedures
   controls. See controls
   frameworks. See security frameworks
   review Q & A, 245–248
   security policies, 232–235
   security policies and procedures overview,
      230–232
   security procedures, 236–239
frequency parameter, context-based
   authentication, 252–253
frozen pages, anomalous activity in, 214
FTK (Forensic Toolkit), 189, 192, 358
FTK Imager tool, forensic duplicator, 190,
   209–210
full knowledge (white-box) pen testing, 70
fully qualified domain name (FQDN),
   nslookup, 335
functional requirements, SDLC, 297
fuzzing tools, 304, 355–356

G

generations, computer language, 79
generic error messages, best practice, 308
Get Out of Jail Free Card, pen testing, 72
Ghost Fleet (Singer and Cole), 74
Gigabit speed lines, taps on, 12
GLBA (The Gramm-Leach-Bliley Act), 241
gold masters, rebuilding compromised
   hosts, 157
Google
   Bouncer technology, 102
   open source intelligence from searches
      on, 4–5
   Operation Aurora breach, 178
GPS (Global Positioning System) sensors,
   251–252

gray-box (partial knowledge) pen testing, 70
group policies, 58
groups
   bias, in risk evaluation, 86
   file system ACL, 55
   in RBAC level vs. DAC, 60

H

hardening network. See device hardening
hardware
   inventory with nmap, 31
   network function virtualization, 16
   reverse engineering, 73–76
   write blockers, 187, 195
hashing
   cryptographic functions, 289
   detecting unauthorized file changes, 211
   as original evidence in forensics, 188
   reversing software/malware, 77
   tools, 359–360
   utilities for forensic analysis, 190–191
HBSSs (host-based security systems), 113
header captures, 10, 29–30
header, Snort, 44
Helix forensic suite, 358
heuristic analysis, 40, 168
HIDSs (host-based IDSs), 43–44
HIPAA (Health Insurance Portability and
   Accountability Act)
   encrypting sensitive data, 289
   patient data protection, 242
   protection of PII, 176
   vulnerability management, 97
HIPS (host-based IDS), 320
historical analysis, threats, 272–273
HMI (Human-Machine Interaction)
   controllers, 104
honeynets/honeypots, 54
horizontal network scanning, 329
horizontal privilege escalation, 264
host-based IDSs (HIDSs), 43–44
host-based security systems (HBSSs), 113
host option, Nikto Web Scanner, 126
host-related symptoms, diagnosing
   file system, 210–212
   memory contents, 209–210
   running processes, 208–209
   unauthorized privileges, 213–214
   unexplained capacity consumption, 212–213

hosts
  containment during incident response,
    150–155
  scanning, 9–10
  vulnerabilities of virtual, 101
HR (human resources), incident response
  role, 149
HTTP, session hijacking attacks, 263–264
HTTPS proxies, 33, 322
HTTPS traffic, 263, 308
hubs, packet capture on wired networks, 13
Human-Machine Interaction (HMI)
  controllers, 104
human resources (HR), incident response
  role, 149
hypervisors
  benefits, 15–16
  vulnerabilities in virtual hosts, 101
  vulnerabilities in virtual networks, 102

I

IaaS (Infrastructure as a Service), cloud, 17
ICANN (Internet Corporation for Assigned
  Names and Numbers), 6–8
ICMP (Internet Control Message Protocol)
  analyzing header captures, 30
  echo requests, ping utility, 333
  protocol analysis of, 33
  Wireshark deep inspection of, 42–43
ICS (industrial control system) vulnerabilities,
  104–106
identification function
  CSF Core, 225
  security patch management, 237
identity and access management
  cloud computing issues, 17
  context-based authentication issues,
    250–253
  exploits, 263–265
  federation and SSO issues, 261–262
  identity repository issues, 258–261
  identity security issues, 253–258
  overview of, 249–250
  review Q & A, 265–268
identity management (IDM), 253–254
identity repositories, security issues with,
  258–261
IDM (identity management), 253–254
IDPs (identity providers), 261–262

IDSs (intrusion detection systems)
  analyzing reconnaissance results, 28–29
  configuring access for scanners, 113
  detecting unexpected outbound
    communication, 216
  incorporating IOCs into, 159
  preventative tools for, 318–320
  reconnaissance via, 22
  tools of the trade, 43–44
IEC (International Electrotechnical
  Commission), 225–226
ifconfig utility, 335
imaging tools, 363
impact and likelihood, risk evaluation,
  84–86
impersonation attacks, 263
implementation, difficulties in
  remediation, 130
implementation phase, SDLC, 297–298
Implementation Tiers, Cyber Security
  Framework, 225
improvement, continual process, 285
incident log, forensic toolkit, 197
incident response process
  communication, 161–163
  containment, 151–155
  corrective actions, 160–161
  defined, 151
  eradication, 156–157
  key roles, 145–149
  procedures when outsourcing, 287
  review Q & A, 163–166
  stakeholders, 149–150
  techniques, overview, 150–151
  validation, 158–159
incident response toolkit
  build your own forensic kit, 195–197
  digital forensics. *See* digital forensics
  forensic investigation suite, 189–195
  review Q & A, 197–201
incident severity/prioritization
  data integrity, 173
  downtime, 171–172
  economic factors, 173–174
  ransomware and, 173
  recovery time, 172
  scope of impact, 170–171
  system process criticality, 174
  types of data, 174–178

incidents, determine impact
  incident severity and prioritization,
    170–174
  review Q & A, 178–182
  threat classification, 167–170
  types of data, 174–178
incidents, diagnosing
  application-related symptoms, 214–217
  host-related symptoms. *See* host-related
    symptoms, diagnosing
  introduction to, 203
  network-related symptoms. *See* network-
    related symptoms, diagnosing
  review Q & A, 217–220
Indexers, Splunk tool, 41
industrial control systems (ICSs),
  vulnerabilities, 104–106
Information Security Management System
  (ISMS), 96, 226
Information Sharing and Analysis Center
  (ISAC), 153, 159
Information Technology Infrastructure
  Library (ITIL), 230–231
Infrastructure as a Service (IaaS), cloud, 17
infrastructure mode, wireless analysis, 36
inhibitors, remediation, 131–132
initialization vectors (IVs), wireless
  networks, 14
input validation, 299–300, 303
insider trading, 178
Integrated Intelligence Center, CIS, 309
intellectual property, 177
interception proxies, 303–304, 348–351
internal communications, incident
  response, 162
internal trends, 39
International Electrotechnical Commission
  (IEC), 225–226
International Organization for Standardization
  (ISO), 225–226
Internet Control Message Protocol. *See* ICMP
  (Internet Control Message Protocol)
Internet Corporation for Assigned Names and
  Numbers (ICANN), 6–8
Internet registries
  Domain Name System, 6–8
  open source intelligence from, 5–6
  regional, 6
intrusion detection systems. *See* IDSs
  (intrusion detection systems)

IOCs (indicators of compromise)
  in network monitoring plan, 159
  via isolation during incident response, 153
IP (Internet Protocol) addresses
  ARP poisoning via, 14
  capturing packets via, 10–11
  how ARP works, 13
  ifconfig utility providing, 335
  IPv4 and IPv6, 11–12, 30
  resolving with nslookup utility, 335
IPSs (intrusion prevention systems)
  configuring access for scanners, 113
  host-based IDS, 320
  incorporating IOCs into, 159
  preventative tools for, 318–320
  reconnaissance via, 22, 28–29
  tools of the trade for, 43–44
ISAC (Information Sharing and Analysis
  Center), 153, 159
ISMS (Information Security Management
  System), 96, 226
ISO/IEC 27000 series, 96, 226
ISO (International Organization for
  Standardization), 225–226
isolation
  containment of incident, 152–153
  corporate network security, 80
  reverse engineering, 77–80
issue-specific (functional) policy,
  corporations, 97
ITIL (Information Technology Infrastructure
  Library), 230–231

J

jailbreaking, 264
John the Ripper password recovery tool, 361
jump bag, forensic kits, 195–197
jump boxes (jump servers), 53

K

KDC (Key Distribution Server),
  Kerberos, 255
Kerberos authentication protocol, 255–256,
  259–260
Kibana, ELK tool component, 41–42
kill chain, penetration tests, 70
Kiwi Syslog collective tool, 327
known vs. unknown threats, classification,
  167–168

L

L2TP (Layer 2 Tunneling Protocol), VPNs, 103
labels, digital forensic evidence, 185
Lapse+, automatic static analysis, 300–301
laptops, location functions, 251
lateral movement, 70, 205–206
law enforcement, incident response role, 148–149
LDAP (Lightweight Directory Access Protocol), 259–261
legal counsel
    evidence production procedures, 236–237
    role of stakeholder in incident response, 149
lessons-learned report, incident response, 160
LFXs (live-fire exercises), cybersecurity training, 81–82
link layer, network segmentation at, 53
live-fire exercises (LFXs), cybersecurity training, 81–82
live forensics, devices, 186
locally developed analytics, correlation analysis, 37
location based NAC, 63
location parameter, context-based authentication, 251–252
location services, public safety, 251
log manager, data aggregation/correlation, 270–271
log viewers, forensic analysis, 195
logical (technical) controls, 239–240
login events, authentication logs, 278–279
logs
    analyzing firewall, 28
    analyzing IDS/IPS, 28–29
    analyzing system, 31
    authentication, 278–279
    consolidating with syslog, 277–278
    defending against reconnaissance, 17
    event. See event logs
    firewall, 276–277
    forensic analysis of event via, 194
    incident, 197
    MRTG measuring, 346
    as sources of data across network, 269–270
    syslog. See syslog
    time zone differences in analysis of, 279
    validating vulnerability scan results, 137
Logstash, ELK tool component, 41–42

M

MAC (mandatory access control), hardening network, 59
MAC (Media Access Control) address
    ARP poisoning via, 14
    detecting rogue devices, 207
    switched networks and, 13
machine language, 79, 154
malware
    detection using heuristics, 40
    endpoint vulnerabilities, 100
    reverse engineering, 76–80, 154–155
man-in-the-middle (MITM) attacks, 14, 263
Managed level, CMMI model, 245
managed mode (infrastructure mode), wireless analysis in, 36
managed mode, wireless analysis, 36
management
    role in incident response, 148
    as stakeholders in incident response, 150
mandatory access control (MAC), hardening network, 59
mandatory vacations, 284
manual data analysis
    authentication logs, 278–279
    as code reviews, 300
    event logs, 279–280
    firewall logs, 276–277
    overview of, 273–276
    syslogs, 277–278
marketing team, incident response role, 150
master mode, wireless analysis, 38
maturity models, verification/quality control, 243–244
maximum tolerable downtime (MTD), 171–172
MD5 hashing algorithm, forensic analysis, 190–191, 359
Media Access Control. See MAC (Media Access Control) address
memorandum of understanding (MOU), and remediation, 131
memory forensics
    detecting host incidents, 209–210
    detecting memory overflows, 216–217
    digital crime scenes, 184–185
Memory Grabber, 209
memory starvation, 305
mergers and acquisitions, corporate data, 178
mesh (ad hoc) mode, wireless analysis, 38

metadata, vulnerability management, 97–98
methodology, SABSA, 229
micro-segmentation, 52
Microsoft Baseline Security Analyzer, 343–344
Microsoft Exchange Server, forensic analysis of, 187
Microsoft SDL fuzzers, 356
MITM (man-in-the-middle) attacks, 14, 263
mobile devices
    forensic analysis of, 187
    forensic analysis utilities, 194–195
    vulnerabilities of, 102–103
ModSecurity, web application firewall, 324
Monitor and Evaluate domain, COBIT, 226
monitor mode, wireless analysis, 14, 38
monitoring
    ongoing scanning/continuous, 132–133
    updating plan after incident, 159
monitoring tools
    Burp Suite, 349–350
    Cacti, 347
    comparison of tools, 345
    Interception Proxy, 348–349
    Multi Router Traffic Grapher, 346
    Nagios, 346–347
    Netflow Analyzer, 348
    Orion, 347
    Vega, 351
    ZAP, 350
MOU (memorandum of understanding), and remediation, 131
MRTG (Multi Router Traffic Grapher), 346
MRUs (most recently used lists), forensics, 193
MS-ISAC (Multi-State Information Sharing and Analysis Center), CIS, 309
MTD (maximum tolerable downtime), 171–172
multifactor authentication, 249
multilayered security, suites, 287

N

NAC (Network Access Control)
    in BYOD environment, 158
    detecting rogue devices, 206
    mitigating infrastructure vulnerabilities, 100
    mitigating VPN vulnerabilities, 103–104
    responding to threats, 61–63
Nagios, monitoring with, 346–348
NAS (network-attached storage), forensic images, 196

National Institute of Standards and Technologies. See NIST (National Institute of Standards and Technologies)
NAXSI (Nginx Anti XSS and SQL Injection), web application firewall, 324
NDAs (non-disclosure agreements), third parties/consultants, 283
Nessus Attack Scripting Language (NASL), 112, 124
Nessus vulnerability scanner
    analyze reports, 133
    defined, 20–21
    OpenVAS vs., 125
    overview of, 120–124
    prioritization of vulnerabilities, 129
    reconcile results, 136–137
    report formats, 128
    vulnerability scanning, 338–340
NetFlow analysis, reconnaissance data, 34–35
Netflow Analyzer, 348
netstat (network statistics) command-line tool, 21, 333
Network Access Control. See NAC (Network Access Control)
network ACLs, 55
network analyzers, 10
network-attached storage (NAS), forensic images, 196
network bandwidth starvation, 305
network-based IDSs (NIDSs), 43–44
network-based location, context-based authentication, 251
network behavior anomaly analysis, 38
network design, 289
network function virtualization (NFV), 16
Network General Sniffer, packet capture tool, 330
network infrastructure vulnerabilities, 100–101
network intrusion prevention system (NIPS), 43–44
network mapping, 10
network-related symptoms, diagnosing
    bandwidth utilization, 204
    beaconing, 204–205
    irregular peer-to-peer communication, 205–206
    rogue devices on network, 206–207
    scan sweeps, 207–208

network scanning tools, 329–330
network segmentation
    containment of incident via, 152
    jump boxes facilitating, 53
    micro-segmentation, 52
    as security concept, 52, 289
    system isolation, 52
network statistics (netstat) command-line
    tool, 21, 333
network vulnerability tests (NVTs),
    OpenVAS, 125–126, 340
Nexpose vulnerability scanner, 340–342
NFV (network function virtualization), 16
NGFWs (Next-Generation Firewalls)
    companies marketing, 316–318
    defined, 29
    malware detection capabilities of, 40
    overview of, 316
Nginx Anti XSS and SQL Injection (NAXSI),
    web application firewall, 324
NIDSs (network-based IDSs), 43–44
Nikto web server vulnerability scanner
    overview of, 126–127, 342–343
    reconnaissance via, 19–20
NIPS (network intrusion prevention system),
    43–44
NIST (National Institute of Standards and
    Technologies)
    Cyber Security Framework, 225
    National Vulnerability Database, 109
    SCAP, 112–113
    security framework, 223
    SP 800-53, 224
nmap
    analyzing scan results, 31
    network mapping via, 10, 330
    reconnaissance via, 19
non-disclosure agreements (NDAs), 283
noncredentialed vulnerability scans, 110
noncritical assets, inventory of, 99
nonfunctional (quality) requirements,
    SDLC, 297
nonpersistent XSS, 264
NRO (Number Resource Organization),
    regional Internet registries, 6
nslookup utility, 335
NVD (National Vulnerability Database),
    109, 135
NVTs (network vulnerability tests),
    OpenVAS, 125–126, 340

O

O&M (operation and maintenance),
    software systems, 298
Object Access Auditing, Active Directory, 259
objects, Active Directory, 258
OEM (original equipment manufacturer)
    documentation, reverse engineering, 75
open source intelligence. *See* OSINT
    (open source intelligence)
Open Web Application Security Project.
    See OWASP (Open Web Application
    Security Project)
OpenSSL, 131, 335
OpenVAS (Open Vulnerability
    Assessment System)
    overview of, 125–126, 340
    prioritization of vulnerabilities, 129–130
    reconcile results, 136–137
    vulnerability detail screenshot, 129
operation and maintenance (O&M),
    software systems, 298
Operation Aurora breach, 178
operational control review, risk, 87
operational technology (OT) network,
    industrial control vulnerabilities, 104
optimizing level, CMMI model, 245
options, Snort, 44
orchestration, network function, 16
organizational governance, inhibiting
    remediation, 132
organizationally defined parameters,
    controls, 240
original equipment manufacturer (OEM)
    documentation, reverse engineering, 75
Orion, monitoring with, 347
OS (operating system)
    fingerprinting and port scanning, 10
    forensic analysis utilities, 192–194
OSINT (open source intelligence)
    for active reconnaissance, 9–12
    Google, 4–5
    Internet registries, 5–8
    job sites, 8
    passive reconnaissance via, 4
    in real world, 9
    social media, 8
OSSIM (Open Source Security Information
    Manager), 325–326, 327
OSVDB (Open Source Vulnerability Database),
    20, 135

OT (operational technology) network, industrial control vulnerabilities, 104
outbound communication, detecting unexpected, 215–216
Outlook Web Access (OWA) page, data exfiltration case, 212
output, detecting unexpected, 215–216
outsourcing protection, 287–288
overwriting data, 156, 157
OWA (Outlook Web Access) page, data exfiltration case, 212
OWASP (Open Web Application Security Project)
    best practices, 307–308
    Lapse+ tool, 300–301
    ZAP vulnerability scanner, 20
ownership
    file system ACLs, 55
    operation/maintenance and total cost of, 298
    policy for data, 232–233

P

PaaS (Platform as a Service), cloud, 17
packaging, digital forensic evidence, 185
packet analysis, 32–34
packet analyzers
    overview of, 42–43
    reversing hardware, 77
    Snort, 43–44
packet capture
    active reconnaissance via, 10–11
    analyzing reconnaissance results, 29–30
    point-in-time analysis of data, 32–33
    tools, 330–333
    on wired networks, 12–14
packet sniffers, 10
Palo Alto Networks, NFGW firewalls, 317–318
Pan and Organize domain, COBIT, 226
parameter validation
    secure coding, 300
    testing using interception proxy, 303
parameterized SQL queries, best practice, 308
partial knowledge (gray-box) pen testing, 70
passive optical taps, packet capture, 12
passive reconnaissance
    OSINT. *See* OSINT (open source intelligence)
    on wireless networks, 14

passive taps, packet capture, 12
Password Kit Forensic tool, 190
passwords
    account management policy, 235
    cracking tools, 190, 360–363
    industrial control system vulnerabilities, 104
    as mobile device vulnerability, 102
    in multifactor authentication, 249
    policy for, 233–234
    self-service resets, 262
    weak, 99
    weakness of authentication based on, 253
patches
    Baseline Security Analyzer identifying missing, 343
    as endpoint vulnerability, 100
    hardening network via, 61
    as industrial control system vulnerability, 104
    missing, 99
    as mobile device vulnerability, 100
    procedures, 237–238
    remediating network vulnerabilities, 128
    validation in incident response, 158
    as VPN vulnerability, 103–104
    vulnerabilities introduced by, 131
pattern-of-life (POL) traffic, live-fire cybersecurity, 82
PCI DSS (Payment Card Industry Data Security Standard)
    compensating controls, 60
    goals/requirements for merchants, 176–177
    vulnerability management requirements, 96–97
PCI DSS (Payment Card Industry Digital Security Standard)
    for credit/debit card data, 241
    requiring encryption for sensitive data, 289
PE (Portable Executable) format, Windows, 79
Peach Fuzzer, 356–357
peer-to-peer communication, detecting network incidents, 205–206
penetration testing
    authorization, 72
    communication, 72–73
    exploitation, 72
    overview of, 69–70
    reporting, 73
    rules of engagement, 70–73
    scope, 71
    timing, 71

permissions
account management policy, 234–235
discretionary access control, 59
mandatory access control, 59
role-based access control, 60
validating after incident response, 158
vulnerability scanning tool, 113
persistent XSS, 264
personal data, ownership policy for, 233
personally identifiable information (PII),
protection of, 174–175
personnel
creating defense in depth via, 282–285
identity security issues, 254
penetration tests for, 70
PHI (personal health information), protection
of, 176
phishing e-mails, 8
photographing crime scene, 196
physical destruction, sanitization via, 157
physical security
penetration tests for, 70
physical controls for, 239
safeguarding original forensic evidence, 188
vulnerabilities of SCADA, 106
PII (personally identifiable information),
174–175
ping utility, 333
plaintext credentials, interception proxy test
for, 303
Platform as a Service (PaaS), cloud, 17
playbooks (continuity books), succession
planning, 284–285
PLCs (programmable logic controllers),
industrial controls, 104
plug-ins
Nessus, 120–122, 124
vulnerability scanner, 112
point-in-time analysis
of data from reconnaissance, 32
NetFlow analysis, 34–35
packet analysis, 32–33
protocol analysis, 33–34
traffic analysis, 34
wireless analysis, 36
Pokémon Go mobile game, spoofing GPS, 252
POL (pattern-of-life) traffic, live-fire
cybersecurity, 82
policies, security
acceptable use policy, 234
account management, 234–235

BYOD patching, 158
corporate, 97
data classification, 232
data ownership, 232–233
data retention policy, 233
firewall. See ACLs (access control lists)
operational control review in risk
evaluation, 87
overview of, 230–232
passwords, 233–234
review Q & A, 245–248
scheduled reviews of, 286
using third parties and consultants, 283
POLP (principle of least privilege),
AD, 259
Portable Executable (PE) format,
Windows, 79
ports
blocking unused, 60–61
mirroring, 14
scanning, 10
server vulnerabilities, 100
preventative tools
antimalware, 320
Enhanced Mitigation Experience
Toolkit, 321
firewalls, 316–318
HIPS, 320
IDS and IPS, 318–320
web application firewalls, 323–324
web proxies, 321–322
prioritization
incident severity and. See incident
severity/prioritization
of response actions in vulnerability scan
report, 134
of vulnerabilities, 129–130
Privacy Act of 1974, PII, 174–175
privacy, data ownership policy and, 233
private data classification level, 98
privilege escalation
authentication exploit, 264
detecting introduction of new
accounts, 215
detecting unauthorized privileges, 214
identity security issues, 258
privileges
detecting host incidents via unauthorized,
213–214
documenting incidents from excessive, 158
improving AD security, 259

probability, risk analysis, 174
procedures
    compensation controls, 238
    continuous monitoring, 236
    control-testing, 238
    evidence production, 236–237
    exception management, 238–239
    review Q & A, 245–248
    security patch management, 237–238
    understanding, 236
Process Explorer, Sysinternals suite, 335
Process Monitor, Sysinternals suite, 335
processes
    automated reporting, 286
    continual improvement of, 285
    criticality of system, 174
    cryptography, 289
    defense in depth and, 285
    detecting host incidents in, 208–209
    forensic analysis utilities for, 192–194
    outsourcing, 287–288
    retirement of, 286
    scheduled reviews of, 286
    security appliances, 286–287, 289
    security suites, 287
    technology, 286
programmable logic controllers (PLCs),
  industrial controls, 104
promiscuous mode
    capturing wireless network traffic, 14
    network analyzers monitoring traffic in, 10
proprietary (corporate confidential)
  information, 178
proprietary (sensitive) data classification
  level, 98
protection function, CSF Core, 225
protocol analysis, reconnaissance data, 33–34
provisioning, manual vs. automatic, 262
public data classification level, 98
public key certificates, server
  authentication, 254

Q

QRadar tool, 327–328
qualitative analysis, risk, 84–86
quality control, 242–245
quality (nonfunctional) requirements,
  SDLC, 297
Qualysguard vulnerability scanner, 336–338
quantitative analysis, risk, 84–86

R

R&D (research and development), data
  retention policy, 233
radio frequency (RF) connections, wireless, 14
RADIUS (Remote Authentication Dial-In
  User Service), 260
RAID (redundant array of inexpensive disks),
  forensic analysis of, 187
ransomware, 172
RBAC (role-based access control), 60, 61–63
read-only memory (ROM), reversing
  hardware, 75–76
reconcile, vulnerability scanner results, 136–137
reconnaissance, analyzing
    correlation analysis, 36–40
    data sources, 27–31
    overview of, 27
    point-in-time analysis, 32–36
    review Q & A, 46–50
    tools of the trade, 40–45
reconnaissance techniques
    active reconnaissance, 9–12
    cloud computing, 17–18
    defending against, 18
    open source intelligence, 4–9
    overview of, 3–4
    penetration test process, 70
    review Q & A, 23–26
    tools of the trade, 18–22
    virtualization technologies, 15–17
    wired network considerations, 12–14
    wireless network considerations, 14–15
reconstruction, incident response, 157
recovery function, CSF Core, 225
recovery time, incident severity/
  prioritization, 172
recovery time objective (RTO), 171–172
red team, cybersecurity training exercises, 82
redundant array of inexpensive disks (RAID),
  forensic analysis of, 187
reflected XSS, 264
regional Internet registries (RIRs), 6
registered ports, 60
Registry Editor, forensic analysis, 193–194
registry, forensic analysis, 193–194
regression testing, secure coding and, 302
regulatory requirements
    compliance, 241–242
    encryption for sensitive data, 289
    external communications after incident, 162

frequency of vulnerability scans, 107
legal counsel for cyber incident, 150
rules for handling PII, 174–175
vulnerability management, 95–97
remediation of network vulnerabilities
communication/change control, 130–131
inhibitors to, 131–132
overview of, 128
plan for continuous monitoring
procedures, 236
prioritizing, 129–130
sandboxing/testing, 131
REMnux tool, 80
Remote Authentication Dial-In User Service
(RADIUS), security issues, 260
remote terminal units (RTUs), industrial
controls, 104
removal tools
containment of incident, 153–154
digital forensic evidence, 185
Repeatable level, CMMI model, 244
replay attacks, TACACS+ vulnerability, 260
reports
automated in most security products, 286
Baseline Security Analyzer, 344–345
digital forensic, 189
digital forensic, with Encase tool, 191
lessons-learned, incident response, 160
Nikto vulnerability scanner, 342–343
penetration testing, 73
summary, incident response, 161
reports, vulnerability scanner
compare to best practices or compliance, 136
generating, 128
penetration test, 70
reconcile results, 136–137
review and interpret results, 133–134
validate results, 134–135
requirements
regulatory. *See* regulatory requirements
software development lifecycle, 296–297
research and development (R&D), data
retention policy, 233
resets, self-service password, 262
resource starvation, 305
response function, CSF Core, 225
response techniques, incident response, 150–151
restoration
after removal process in incident
response, 154
of data to host in reconstruction
process, 157

retention policy, data, 233
retirement, process, 286
reverse engineering
containment of incident via, 154–155
in corporate network security, 73
defined, 154
hardware, 73–76
isolation/sandboxing, 80
software/malware, 76–80
RF (radio frequency) connections, wireless
networks, 14
Rich Site Summary (RSS) feeds, National
Vulnerability Database, 109
RIRs (regional Internet registries), 6
risk appetite, 107, 240
risk evaluation
avoiding group biases, 86
corporate network, 83–84
impact and likelihood, 84–86
most common vulnerabilities, 307–308
operational control review, 87
technical control review, 86
third parties and consultants, 283
ROE (rules of engagement), MOU, 131
rogue devices on network, detecting, 206–207
role-based access control (RBAC), 60, 61–63
role-based NAC, 62–63
roles
identity security issues, 257–258
incident response process, 145–149
role-based access control, 60
ROM (read-only memory), reversing
hardware, 75–76
root directory, forensics in Linux, 194
rooting exploits, 264
rootkit authentication exploits, 264–265
rotation of duties, personnel, 284
RSS (Rich Site Summary) feeds, National
Vulnerability Database, 109
RTO (recovery time objective), 171–172
RTUs (remote terminal units), industrial
controls, 104
rule based NAC, 62
rules
ACL, 55
misconfigured firewall, 99
penetration testing, 70–73
security data analytics via correlation,
270–272
rules of engagement (ROE), MOU, 131
running processes, detecting host incidents,
208–209

S

SaaS (Software as a Service), cloud, 17
SABSA (Sherwood Applied Business Security
    Architecture), 228–229
safeguards, original forensic evidence, 188
Safeguards Rule, Gramm-Leach-Bliley Act, 241
SAM (Security Accounts Manager) file,
    Windows, 360
SAML (Security Assertion Markup
    Language), 261
sandboxing
    endpoint security via, 57
    remediation of network vulnerabilities, 131
    reverse engineering via, 80, 154
sanitization, incident response, 156–157
SANS Institute, best practices, 308–309
SANS Internet Storm Center, 169
Sarbanes-Oxley Act (SOX), 241, 289
SCADA (Supervisory Control and Data
    Acquisition) devices, 105–106
scan sweeps, for network incidents, 207–208
scanning. *See also* vulnerability scanning
    criteria, 108–111
    defending against reconnaissance, 17
    with Nessus vulnerability scanner, 20–21
    network mapping, 10
    with nmap, 20, 330
    overview of, 9–10
    port, 10
    tools for network, 329–330
    with web application vulnerability scanner,
        10–11
    with ZAP vulnerability scanner, 20
SCAP (Security Content Automation
    Protocol), 112–113, 136
scheduled process reviews, 286
scientific method, correlation analysis, 37
scope
    define scanning, 110
    of impact, incident severity/prioritization,
        170–171
    penetration testing, 71
    of security, 230–231
SDL fuzzers, Microsoft, 356–357
SDN (software-defined networking), 16, 276
Search Heads, Splunk tool, 41
search operators, Google, 4–5
SECaaS (Security as a Service), 287
secure coding. *See* coding, secure
secure disposal, incident response, 157

Secure Socket Layer. *See* SSL
    (Secure Socket Layer)
SecureSphere web application firewall,
    323–324
SecurID two-factor systems, 251
Securing the Human program, SANS
    Institute, 254, 307–308
security
    appliances, 286–287, 289
    architectures. *See* frameworks, policies,
        controls, and procedures
    cloud computing, 17
    labels, mandatory access control, 59
    software development lifecycle, 297
    suites, processes, 287
    virtualization technology, 16–17
Security Accounts Manager (SAM) file,
    Windows, 360
Security as a Service (SECaaS), 287
Security Assertion Markup Language
    (SAML), 261
Security Benchmarks Division, CIS, 309
Security by Design guide, CMMI-DEV, 307
Security Content Automation Protocol
    (SCAP), 112–113, 136
security data analytics
    data aggregation/correlation, 269–272
    historical analysis, 272–273
    manual. *See* manual data analysis
    overview of, 279
    trend analysis, 272
security frameworks
    COBIT, 226–228
    ISO, 225–226
    ITIL, 230
    NIST, 223–225
    overview of, 223
    review Q & A, 245–248
    SABSA, 228–229
    TOGAF, 229–230
security information and event management.
    See SIEM (security information and event
    management)
Security Intelligence Platform (SIP).
    See Splunk tool
Security Technical Implementation Guides
    (STIGs), 136, 309
security testing
    fuzzing, 304
    interception proxies, 303–304
    overview of, 302

resource starvation attacks, 305
stress testing, 304–305
web app vulnerability scanning, 302–303
segmentation. *See* network segmentation
segregation (separation) of duties, 283
SEI (Software Engineering Institute) best
practices, 306–307
seizure, digital forensic, 184–187
selection criteria, security controls, 241
sensitive data, limit use of, 308
sensitive (proprietary) data classification
level, 98
sensitivity levels, scanning criteria, 108–109
separation (segregation) of duties, 283
sequels, TTX cybersecurity exercises, 81
server-based vulnerability scanners, 110–111
servers
assessing with Baseline Security
Analyzer, 343
forensic analysis of, 186–187
identity security issues, 254–255
vulnerabilities of, 100
service discovery, port scanners, 10
Service Identity and Authentication,
.NET, 257
service level agreements (SLAs), 132, 230–231
service provider (SP), SAML, 261–262
services
blocking unused, 60–61
common server vulnerabilities, 100
identity security issues, 256–257
investigating interruption of, 216
Security as a Service, 287
session hijacking attacks, authentication
exploit, 263–264
session ID, TACACS+ vulnerability, 260
session tokens, testing with interception
proxy, 303
severity codes, syslog, 277–278
SHA-1 hashing algorithm, forensic analysis,
190–191
sha1sum command, dd forensic duplicator, 190
shared secrets, RADIUS, 261
shashum hashing tool, 360
Sherwood Applied Business Security
Architecture (SABSA), 228–229
SIEM (security information and event
management)
automated data analysis, 270–272
collective tools, 325–329
correlation analysis, 37

defending against reconnaissance, 17
improving AD security, 259
manual data analysis, 273–276
as quintessential tool for cybersecurity
analyst, 40–42
trend analysis, 272
signals, reversing hardware with, 77
signature-based detection, 57, 167–168
Simple Network Management Protocol
(SNMP), MRTG and, 346
Single Sign-On (SSO), security issues,
261–262
SIP (Security Intelligence Platform).
See Splunk tool
SLAs (service level agreements), 132, 230–231
Sleuth Kit, forensic analysis, 192–193
smartphones, location functions, 251
SNMP (Simple Network Management
Protocol), MRTG and, 346
Snort tool IDS, 43–44, 319
social engineering, 8
social media profiling, 8
software
CMMI maturity model for developing,
243–245
detecting unauthorized, 210–211
forensic acquisition of, 187
reverse engineering, 76–80
using nmap to inventory, 31
whitelisting/blacklisting unauthorized,
210–211
Software as a Service (SaaS), cloud, 17
software-defined networking (SDN), 16, 276
software development
best practices, 306–309
Center for Internet Security, 309
lifecycle, 295–298
overview of, 295
review Q & A, 310–313
secure coding, 299–302
security testing, 302–305
Software Engineering Institute (SEI) best
practices, 306–307
source authenticity, reverse engineering
hardware, 73–74
source code, decomposition in reversing
software/malware, 77–80
Sourcefire IPS, 319
SOX (Sarbanes-Oxley Act), 241, 289
SP (service provider), SAML, 261–262
SP (Special Publication) 800-53, NIST, 224

spatial trends, trend analysis, 39
Special Publication (SP) 800-53, NIST, 224
SPI (stateful packet inspection) firewalls, 316, 317
Splunk tool
    correlation analysis via, 37
    features of, 41
    overview of, 328–329
spoofing GPS, 252
SQLi (Structured Query Language) injection attacks, 299–300
SSL (Secure Socket Layer)
    man in the middle attacks, 263
    OpenSSL, 335
    proxies, 33
SSO (Single Sign-On), security issues, 261–262
staging base, detecting exfiltration, 211–212
stakeholders, 149–150, 162–163
stateful packet inspection (SPI) firewalls, 316, 317
stateless packet filtering, 316
static code analysis, 154, 300–301
statistics, security analytics, 37
STIGs (Security Technical Implementation Guides), 136, 309
stress testing, 304–305
Structured Query Language (SQLi) injection attacks, 299–300
succession planning, personnel, 284–285
summary report, incident response plan, 161
Supervisory Control and Data Acquisition (SCADA) devices, 105–106
Suricata tool, 44
sweeps, network mapping, 10
switches
    packet capture on wired networks, 13
    port mirroring, 14
Sysinternals suite, 335
syslog
    analysis of, 277–278
    Kiwi Syslog tool, 327
    and reconnaissance, 18, 31
syslogd, Unix and Linux, 277
system isolation, 52
system libraries, unauthorized file changes, 211
system process criticality, incident severity/prioritization, 174
system-specific policy, corporate security, 97

T

tabletop exercises (TTXs), training, 81, 82
TACACS+ (Terminal Access Controller Access Control System Plus), 259–261
tactics, techniques, and procedures. See TTPs (tactics, techniques, and procedures) of adversaries
tamper-proof seals, forensic kits, 196–197
taps, packet capture, 10–13
Target stores vulnerability, 103
TCO (total cost of ownership), 298
tcpdump, 21, 332
technical constraints, vulnerability scans, 107–108
technical (logical) controls, 86, 239–240
technical staff role, incident respons, 146–147
technology, preventing catastrophic damage, 286
temporal trends, trend analysis, 39
Terminal Access Controller Access Control System Plus (TACACS+), 259–261
testing
    control-testing, 238
    patches, 131, 237–238
    penetration. See penetration testing
    secure coding and regression, 302
    security, 302–306
    user acceptance software, 298
TGS (Ticket Granting Server), Kerberos, 255–256
TGT (Ticket Granting Ticket) , Kerberos, 255–256
Open Group Architecture Framework (TOGAF), 229–230
third parties, NDAs/clearly defined policies for, 283
Threat Exchange, Unified Security Management, 325
threat intelligence value, 153
threat management
    analyzing reconnaissance. See reconnaissance, analyzing
    reconnaissance. See reconnaissance techniques
threats, responding to network-based
    ACLs, 54–56
    device hardening, 58–61
    endpoint security, 56–58
    group policies, 58
    honeypots and honeynets, 54

Network Access Control, 61–63
network segmentation, 52–53
overview of, 51
review Q & A, 64–68
time-based NAC, 62
time parameter, context-based authentication, 250–251
time to live (TTL) field
analyzing header captures, 30
traceroute utility, 333–334
time window, authentication process, 251
time zone differences, log analysis, 279
timelines, as forensic analysis tool, 188–189
timestamps, forensic analysis and, 189
timestomping, 189
timing considerations
Kerberos, 256
penetration tests, 71
Titan Rain, advanced persistent threat, 169
TLS (Transport Layer Security), 103, 335
TOGAF (The Open Group Architecture Framework), 229–230
tool sets
analytical tools. See analytical tools
collective tools. See collective tools
exploitative tools, 351–356
forensic tools. See forensic tools
overview of, 315
preventative tools. See preventative tools
review Q & A, 363–367
tools
analyzing results of reconnaissance, 40–45
correlation analysis via, 36–40
incident response. See incident response toolkit
reconnaissance techniques, 18–22
vulnerability scanner configuration, 108–111
vulnerability scanner updates and plug-ins, 111–114
topology discovery, network mapping, 10
total cost of ownership (TCO), operation/maintenance, 298
traceroute feature, nmap, 10
traceroute utility, 333–334
tracert utility, 333–334
traffic analysis
capturing with Netflow, 34–35
packet analysis as, 32–33
of reconnaissance data, 34–35

training
corporate network security, 80–83
cross-training personnel, 283–284
personnel in security awareness, 282
personnel in security issues, 254
security analysts, 282
Transport Layer Security (TLS), 103, 335
trend analysis
in correlation analysis, 38–39
predicting future events via, 272
vulnerability scan reports, 137–138
TrueCrypt tool, 190
trust, endpoint security and, 58
Trusted Foundry Program, DoD, 75
Trusted Purchasing Alliance, CIS, 309
TShark, 10, 22
TTL (time to live) field
analyzing header captures, 30
traceroute utility, 333–334
TTPs (tactics, techniques, and procedures) of adversaries
advanced persistent threat campaigns, 169–170
as focus of cybersecurity exercises, 81
forecasting via historical data analysis, 272–273
learning with honeypots/honeynets, 53
pen testing aligned with, 69
removal of hosts for threat intelligence value, 153
TTXs (tabletop exercises), cybersecurity training, 81, 82
Type 1 (bare-metal) hypervisors, 15–16
Type 2 hypervisors, 15–16

U

UAC (user access control), unexpected pop-ups, 215–216
UBA (user behavior analysis), 327, 328
UFED (Universal Forensic Extraction Device), Cellebrite, 359
ufw (Uncomplicated Firewall) tool, Linux, 276–277
unauthorized changes, host incidents, 211
unauthorized software, host incidents, 210
unexpected output, application incidents, 215–216
Unified Security Management (USM) tool, 325–326
unknown vs. known threats, 167–168

Untidy XML fuzzer, 356
updates
    Baseline Security Analyzer identifying
        missing, 344
    endpoint vulnerability, 100
    implementing response plan, 161
    industrial control system vulnerabilities, 104
    missing, 99
    mobile device vulnerability, 100
    patching in incident response, 158
    VPN vulnerability, 103–104
    vulnerability scanning tool, 111–114
URL (uniform resource locator), anomalous
    activity in, 214
U.S. Bullion Depository, Fort Knox, 51
usability vs. security
    hardening network and, 59
    Network Access Control and, 62
user acceptance software testing, 298
user behavior analysis (UBA)
    ArcSight tool, 327
    Splunk tool, 328
user training, 254
USM (Unified Security Management) tool,
    325–326

V

validation
    control-testing procedures, 238
    fuzzing tools identifying flaws in, 303
    incident response process, 158–159
    secure coding with input, 299–300
    secure coding with parameter, 300
    security patch management, 237–238
    of selected security controls, 241
Vega interception proxy, 351–352
VeraCrypt tool, 190–191
verification
    forensic acquisition, 188
    and quality control, 242–245
vertical network scan, 329
vertical privilege escalation, 264
virtual hosts, vulnerabilities, 101
virtual infrastructure, vulnerabilities, 101–102
virtual local area networks. See VLANs (virtual
    local area networks)
virtual networks, vulnerabilities, 102
virtualization technologies
    containers, 16
    honeynets, 54

hypervisors, 15–16
network function, 16
overview of, 15
security, 16–17
software-defined networking, 16
VirusTotal.com, 34, 76–78
VLANs (virtual local area networks), 53,
    152–153
VM (virtual machine) vulnerabilities, 101
VPN (virtual private network) vulnerabilities,
    103–104
vulnerabilities, common
    endpoints, 100
    industrial control systems, 104–105
    interconnected networks, 103
    mobile devices, 102–103
    network infrastructure, 100–101
    overview of, 99
    SCADA devices, 105–106
    servers, 100
    virtual infrastructure, 101–102
    virtual private networks, 103–104
vulnerability feeds, scanning criteria, 109
vulnerability management processes
    asset inventory, 98–99
    common vulnerabilities, 99–106
    corporate security policy, 97
    data classification, 97–98
    frequency of vulnerability scans, 106–108
    permissions and access, 113
    regulatory environments, 95–97
    review Q & A, 114–118
    scanning criteria, 108–111
    tool updates and plug-ins, 111–113
vulnerability scanners
    Microsoft Baseline Security Analyzer,
        343–344
    Nessus, 338–340
    Nexpose, 340–342
    Nikto, 342–343
    OpenVAS, 340
    Qualysguard, 336–338
    tool updates and plug-ins, 111–113
    web app, 302–303
    ZAP, 20
vulnerability scanning
    analyze reports, 133–134
    continuous monitoring/ongoing, 132–133
    execute scanning, 120
    frequency of, 106–108

generate reports, 128

Nessus, 20–21, 120–124

Nikto Web Scanner, 126–127

OpenVAS, 125–126

overview of, 119–120

remediation, 128–132

review Q & A, 138–142

server-based vs. agent-based, 110–111

validate results/correlate other data points, 134–138

validation of systems after incident, 159

W

WAPs (wireless access points), 36, 100–101

war dialing, 9–10

web application firewalls, 323–324

web application vulnerability scanner, 10–11, 302–303

web proxies, 321–322

well-known ports, TCP and UDP, 60

WEP (Wired Equivalent Privacy) vulnerability, 100

white-box (full knowledge) pen testing, 70

white team, cybersecurity training exercises, 83

whitelisting, software, 210–211, 299

WHOIS tool, used by attackers, 7–8

Wi-Fi Protected Access 2 (WPA2), 100

Wildfire subscription service, Palo Alto Networks, 317

Windows Event Logs. *See* event logs

wiped removable media, forensic kits, 196

wired networks

ARP poisoning, 13–14

hubs, 13

mirroring, 14

reconnaissance of, 12

switches, 13

taps, 12–13

wireless networks

analysis, 36

forensic analysis with Registry Editor, 194

reconnaissance considerations, 14–15

Wireshark packet analyzer

capturing wireless network traffic, 14

network protocol analyzer, 10

overview of, 331–332

reconnaissance via, 22

understanding, 42–43

WLAN (wireless local area network) analysis, 36

workflow, frequency of vulnerability scans, 108

WPA2 (Wi-Fi Protected Access 2), 100

X

XML (Extensible Markup Language), 356–357

XSS (cross-site scripting), injection attack, 264

Y

Yahoo user breach, 249

Z

ZAP (Zed Attack Proxy), 20, 350

zero day exploits

Operation Aurora breach, 178

patching in incident response, 158

preparation for, 169

threat classification, 168

zero knowledge (black-box) pen testing, 70

zero-trust environment, 58

LICENSE AGREEMENT